Kate Figes is the author of four works of non-fiction and two novels. She is a journalist and Books Editor for *You* magazine. She lives in London, and is married with two children.

Visit www.katefiges.co.uk

COUPLES
THE TRUTH

KATE FIGES

virago

VIRAGO

First published in Great Britain in 2010 by Virago Press
Reprinted 2010

A CIP catalogue record for this book
is available from the British Library.

ISBN 978-1-84408-467-8

Typeset in Plantin by M Rules
Printed and bound in Great Britain by
Clays Ltd, St Ives plc

Papers used by Virago are natural, renewable and
recyclable products sourced from well-managed forests and certified
in accordance with the rules of the Forest Stewardship Council.

Mixed Sources
Product group from well-managed
forests and other controlled sources
www.fsc.org Cert no. SGS-COC-004081
© 1996 Forest Stewardship Council
FSC

Virago Press
An imprint of
Little, Brown Book Group
100 Victoria Embankment
London EC4Y 0DY

An Hachette UK Company
www.hachette.co.uk

www.virago.co.uk

For Christoph, of course

ACKNOWLEDGEMENTS

All books are in some respects journeys for writers, as they can never quite know at the beginning where their research will take them. I am deeply grateful to a number of experts for some helpful and fascinating conversations. Penny Mansfield at One Plus One was the first to point out that we needed a book that draws together sociological, psychological and feminist thought to assess how far we have come. Susanna Abse and Andrew Balfour at the Tavistock Centre for Couple Relationships have been very generous, with patient explanations of basic psychology and the loan of numerous useful books. Peter Bell at Relate, Sally Openshaw of the British Association of Sexual and Relationship Therapists and Terry Prendergast of Marriage Care have helped a great deal, as has Cecilia D'Felice with some heartfelt insight into the complexities of relationship. Kim Beatson was particularly helpful with divorce law. Pam Fawcett has been a relationship counsellor for over fifty years and I am grateful to her for help in placing today's difficulties within a wider historical context.

I couldn't have written this book without the honesty of the many wonderful people who were happy to be interviewed. I have changed their names and disguised their circumstances as much as possible, so I hope that even you will not recognise yourselves. I have spent what must amount to months over the past three years in the library at One Plus One. Laura Dimmock and Fiona Glenn have been incredibly helpful with resources and cups of tea. Louisa Michel took on some of the transcribing of interviews when I felt overwhelmed trying to write with one eye, while the other watched the tapes piling up.

The idea for this book was first mooted many years ago by my agent Felicity Rubinstein, and I am so grateful to her for refusing to let that idea go. You want tenacity in an agent. Lennie Goodings at Virago has been a thorough and sensitive editor. I have known and admired her for the best part of three decades. I now feel honoured to be able to call her not just my editor but also my friend. My heartfelt thanks also go to Rowan Cope and the rest of the team at Little, Brown for their efforts.

On a personal level I would like to thank Annie and Wilf Weeks for Moat House, and David and Sally Hopson for Number 85. My love to my husband Christoph and our two wonderful daughters, Eleanor and Grace, goes without saying. Thank you all.

CONTENTS

1

OTHER PEOPLE'S MARRIAGES

'Apart from a war, what could be more interesting than a marriage?' writes Hilary Mantel in her introduction to Elizabeth Jenkins's novel of the 1950s *The Tortoise and the Hare*. 'A love affair, though it is one of the central concerns of fiction, is a self-limiting tactical skirmish, but a marriage is a long campaign, a grand game of strategy involving setbacks, bluffs and regroupings – a campaign pursued, sometimes, until the parties have forgotten the value of the territory they are fighting over, or have abandoned their first objectives in favour of secret ones.' A committed relationship forms the central narrative of our lives. It is the structure to which we cling for stability, love, a sense of purpose. It is one of the most basic of all human needs, yet most marriages are opaque. Few understand what really goes on in other people's relationships behind that 'glass shade' E. M. Forster refers to in *Howards End*, which 'cuts off married couples from the world'.

Most people seem happy to discuss every aspect of their love lives with their closest friends until they 'settle down' with someone, at which point their loyalty of confidence usually switches to their partner. Much of the magic of marriage or committed relationship lies in that unique pairing, and in the secrets only the two of you share. Yet such is the need to preserve the semblance of contentment that to admit disappointment or unhappiness with the relationship could be construed as failure. We cannot help but be fascinated by the private lives of others. We need to know how people live in lifelong love, how they make their relationships work, and what really goes on behind those walls of secrecy. We want to know in order to understand our own relationship, particularly now that so many established givens, the ground rules of marriage, have vanished. When we lack that window into the domestic lives of others, we have no way of knowing how relationships change through the course of life, whether we are experiencing the normal dips associated with the vicissitudes of marriage or signs of a deeper malaise. The silence surrounding a long-term relationship can be so great that often the first people hear of a couple's distress is when they announce they are separating. 'My sister rang me up to tell me she had had enough and that they were divorcing,' says Anna. 'I thought, Whoa, hang on a minute, can't we just meet up and have a cup of coffee to talk about this? Because that was the first time she had even mentioned the fact that there were problems.'

With so much mystery surrounding each marital 'bubble', we are even more susceptible to modern cultural prescriptions of how love and marriage should be. The pretty lies of romantic, passionate love surround us. 'True' love is presumed to be a perfect fit of soul mates. All our physical, sexual, intellectual, spiritual and emotional needs are supposed to be fulfilled by that one person, which is inevitably a recipe for disappointment, although few dare admit to anyone else in which particular area their True Love fails. Love is meant to be rosy, happy, which means you can't talk about the times when you are not. Love should be enough to see us through life's adversities; it means never having to say you're sorry; it means knowing instinctively what is best for the other – three of the most deceitful statements about relationships ever advocated. Real love, as every lifelong couple I met told me, is something which grows with time once the blinkers of romantic love have fallen, for it is what you learn about each other through the conflicts that spell the beginning of a true partnership rather than the end of it. Real sex is compromised by the explicit, semi-pornographic imagery that surrounds us, which portrays 'good' sex one-dimensionally as vigorously athletic, constant, always orgasmic. That imagery is never far away from our imagination as we expose our less-than-perfect bodies to each other. Sex is seen as something which has to be 'kept alive', cranked up like an ageing starter motor with toys or top tips for variety, which easily seduces couples into feeling as if they are lesser human beings, or deserving of greater sexual novelty elsewhere once they have become used to each other's bodies. Few couples can sustain the eroticism of their first sexual encounters long term, but what is not talked about is how in a good relationship sex can get better *because* of that familiarity through the years, once you accept that it changes and stop trying to recapture that earlier passion.

There is a timeless quality to certain aspects of love. There has always been passion, jealousy, loyalty, betrayal, irritation and hate. But there are new pressures on relationships, wider cultural ideals as to how we should live 'the good life', which complicate our ability to commit to love. Individual ambition, self-fulfilment and the new ethos that one can and should have everything that life has to offer sit uneasily with a relationship where compromise, caring and togetherness are essential. There is cynicism about the possibility of maintaining a lifelong relationship, a sense of mistrust, a feeling that 'If I don't look after me, then who will?' Commitment to one person today feels like a dangerous act of self-sacrifice, and people are easily confused about where the boundaries between 'me' and 'us' lie. We have new phrases for whole cohorts of people such as 'commitment-phobes' or 'thirtysomething single women', indicating that while we crave the safety and warmth of a loving relationship, we see marriage and lifelong relationship as a trap, the antithesis to freedom of spirit and the achievement of self-determined goals. In our throwaway culture people, it is presumed, can be exchanged as easily as

clothes once they hit their first difficulties in a relationship, with
the justification that they are 'unhappy', that someone else might
love them more, understand them better or make them feel sexually more alive. What is missing from the modern cultural
emphasis on rampant individualism is the deep need for shared
lives, for strong links to each other in order to be happy. A good
intimate relationship brings about self-discovery rather than self-
sacrifice. Unless we look after those closest to us we are destined
to be unlooked-after and alone.

Committed relationship has also been compromised by aspects
of social change. Increasingly couples expect to live within an
equable, companionable partnership, but these new aspirations
haven't been matched by sufficient change within the wider social
and economic structure in terms of equal pay and opportunity,
greater work–life balance and the right kind of support for working parents. Couples are arguing their way, often ferociously,
towards a more democratic fairness, compromised by the
assumptions they have grown up with about how men and
women should be as 'husbands' and 'wives'. Resentments flourish as they grapple with the logistics of earning a living and
maintaining a career as well as being at home for their children.
And how can we believe wholeheartedly in the possibility of a
loving, supportive partnership which can stand the test of time
when we face a daily barrage of talk about the family 'in crisis',
with rising rates of divorce, remarriage and single-parent families?
We want to believe in the power of love to see us through life, but
it is harder than ever to trust that it will last.

This is not a handbook. There are no simplistic 'Mars' and
'Venus' generalisations or universal recipes for success, for relationships are too complicated, individual and important for easy
answers. This book tries to move beyond the stereotypical
assumptions of how a relationship should be, and beyond the
manipulative political debates about how marriage is stronger
than cohabitation and needs to be revived. I want to take us
beyond the outdated feminist understanding of marriage as an

institution which symbolises the ownership and exploitation of women, to the real partnerships being forged by people today. Marriage as an institution may be dying, with the numbers of those cohabiting soon to exceed those who marry, but our need for relationship, commitment and love hasn't changed. In fact it could be argued that we need the constancy of close companionship now more than ever, as the world changes with unprecedented speed and uncertainty. It is the quality of relationship which matters, not its status. We need to expand the definition of marriage so that it embraces the many ways in which people support and commit to each other, for good relationship has never been more important for our health, sense of identity, purpose and fulfilment.

There are those who are resolutely single, but the majority thrive within the comfort and stability of a good, loving partnership. 'One Sunday on your own is fantastic. You don't have to wash or cook or engage with anybody,' says Hilary, who has been with her husband for twenty-five years, 'but fifty-two Sundays on your own would be awful.' We cannot live life to the full entirely on our own. We are defined as individuals not just by what we do, but by how we love and are loved, and it is a central tenet of this book that it is only through good relationships, and the growing sense of self-awareness that springs from the conflicts and differences between us, that we are allowed to be our best and true selves. But how do we make a relationship thrive when it is under attack from the many new pressures? Often all we lack are sufficient insight and the tools. Answers lie in a greater understanding of the ways in which love is compromised by heightened expectations and by social and historical change. They are found in a wider grasp of psychological processes, and how our own insecurities and disappointments feed division and discontent. Answers lie in rejecting the patriarchal notions of marriage as ownership and the straitjacket of gender roles, and creating new bonds, a new deal based on mutual respect, fairness, autonomy and kindness. But the most reassuring answers of all come to us in the knowledge that our experiences are normal, common to all, that we are not freaks or failures because we are able to peer through the 'glass shade', that bubble of privacy into other people's marriages.

That is what this book will try to do. There are perhaps as many 'truths' as there are couples. I have focused on the West, and inevitably seen only a fraction of the entire kaleidoscope through the lens of my own experience and that of those I have listened to. It has been a great privilege to have been welcomed into the confidence of 120 men and women from differing social classes and random areas of Britain. Their stories form the bedrock of this book. With the protection of anonymity, they have been as honest as they could about the highs and lows of their love life, given that few of us ever fully understand the emotional dynamics and mystery of intimacy. Many used me as an unpaid therapist, keen to talk about their difficulties. Others welcomed the opportunity to reflect upon the most important relationship of their lives, to sit back and think about what each gives to the other and why it works, or fails to. We are all so busy juggling diverse demands from career, children, family and friends, and conforming to presumed notions of how a couple should be, that nurturing those essential emotional bonds between us tends to fall to the bottom of the heap. 'We talk about the everyday practical stuff, and we have conversations about politics and art. But we don't really talk about our relationship or the dynamics of getting on unless we're having a really bad time,' says Megan. 'In which case I usually say, "Let's try to be nice to each other and draw a line under this," but we won't analyse what went wrong. It's a kind of unspoken understanding that the bond is strong enough and that maybe analysing things would break that magic.' Every person I interviewed offered a unique insight into the workings of their relationship, for which I am profoundly grateful.

The past thirty years has seen something of a boom in academic research on the nature of relationships, with longitudinal studies on lifelong couples bringing greater insight into the psychological processes of intimacy. As with my two previous works of non-fiction – *Life After Birth* and *The Terrible Teens* – I have trawled through these findings for the general reader. I was surprised to find that, just like the next person, I too have been seduced by the myths about relationship and the nature of family breakdown. Some aspects of life in love are, however, timeless. A wealth of literature from Plato and Homer to the present day illuminates the fact that so many of our difficulties with intimacy are age-old. These rich resources, together with the testimonies of the wonderful people I have met should offer enough support, reassurance and insight to make every reader's relationship work a little better, just as they have done for mine.

This is not a book about my own marriage, but inevitably it has been influenced by twenty years of a contented relationship. I believe wholeheartedly in the importance of commitment but it wasn't always that way. I was a child of divorce at the age of five in 1962, a time when we knew little about how to minimise the impact of family breakdown on the very young. My parents made a great many mistakes out of ignorance. I never trusted that relationships could stand the test of time because my parents' hadn't. I didn't want children in my early twenties because I couldn't contemplate putting them through what I presumed would be the same ordeal. My marriage, a companionable partnership with a warm and loving man, has provided the emotional backbone to my life. It has had its downs as well as ups, just like all lifelong relationships. However, I can say with complete confidence that an intimate, committed relationship holds the power to heal old hurts, provided we are prepared to take complete responsibility for its welfare. With that love, I feel more comfortable in my own skin, more able to go out into the world and work, more able to give both to him and to our children. I knew my marriage was sound but I never stopped to question why it worked, never thought it necessary to acknowledge how well we were doing in managing to stay together against difficult odds, until I began to research and to meet the people whose stories you will find in these pages.

*

When I use the word 'marriage', I mean it to encompass every type of committed relationship. I have included as many different types of long-term relationship as possible: traditional marriages where men earn the money and women look after the home, dual-earner couples where sometimes women earn more, as well as couples who are as committed to each other cohabiting as they would be married. I have met men and women who have spent the best part of their adult lives in gay and lesbian partnerships, couples with children and those without. I have met people who have married outside their faith, and have diluted a great many of the racial and religious stereotypes within their family of origin because they now have someone of another faith or race in their midst. I have met others who have had to sacrifice romantic hopes of choice and an equal loving partnership for an arranged marriage, to keep the support and love of their families. I have met younger couples full of the promise of hope, and others who have been together for more than forty years, who have forged a shared history of memories. I have met men and women who have lived through the agonising and protracted pain of a divorce before finding greater contentment in a second relationship, and others who have preferred to stay single or to live apart from their new partner.

Each and every person has displayed a level of commitment, tenacity and resilience in the face of difficulty, which to my complete surprise has contradicted the received wisdom that these days people shy at the first hurdle and separate too easily. People continue to place great hope in love and commitment. Some found exactly what they needed from a lifelong relationship after years of unhappiness. Sandra attempted suicide after her first major relationship broke up. She had grown up with an alcoholic mother and a violent, abusive father: 'My childhood was very volatile, so I am very needy. My need for love, attention and approval stems from not having had that from my parents.' But then Jane walked into her life, accepted her, soothed her emotional damage and they have been living together ever since. Roy spent ten years in a complicated sexual relationship with a married couple who had children. The experience was so draining it left him feeling bruised and wary of getting involved with anyone again. Then he met Juan on holiday in Spain, and over the next twenty years their relationship flourished between two countries until he retired and they were finally able to live together.

Sam lost both his parents when he was in his late teens, and found it hard to trust women because his mother had lied to him about the fact that she was dying. He also grew up with a fairly traditional picture of his future marriage in mind until he met Diana, an older woman with strong feminist principles and a single mother to two children. He soon discovered he liked being with someone who was capable, who knew how to put up a tent when they went camping and who earned her own living. 'We're mates, we're really good friends, and that was it for me. I know people say that friends can't be lovers but I realised when I met Diana that I had been searching for that my whole life. I want someone I can go through life with as a partner. That's the bottom line because in my experience it's easy to have good times with anyone, but to deal with the day-to-day shit and all the bad things, you need someone you can rely on and trust, someone you can get on with, a companion.'

Most value monogamy as the basis of a lifelong relationship, but that is by no means the only way. A small but seemingly growing number of couples accept that complete fidelity might be difficult if a relationship is to last the best part of half a century. Robin and Hilary came to Britain from Australia as students and stayed. They have three teenage children, were happily married and sexually monogamous until it became clear that Hilary was deeply attracted to a young lodger who had moved into their house. Robin told her to go for it. 'Our relationship is so intertwined, I didn't feel I had anything to lose, or that our relationship was in trouble. When you get into familiar sex that passion is gone – you don't tear each other's clothes off or shag in a car after a party on the way home, and you can't reconstruct that. I just thought, God, she is going to enjoy this so much, and it's not going to diminish me at all.' Since that sexual episode, Hilary has had other no-strings-attached sexual encounters, and they have found that in some ways it has invigorated their marriage. 'She loves it. She is so alive, she loves the intrigue and this is her bit of drama,' Robin told me. 'It's just like a different hobby, like going to a book group!' Sales of novels to men would soar if reading groups were *that* much fun.

The idea that couples need privacy behind the walls of the nuclear family is a modern one. It creates the presumption that all couples are similar. We keep quiet about the rows, the disappointments, the hostility, and pretend to conform to conventional notions of how couples should be without really knowing what that means any more. Yet I encountered many contented, successful relationships whose arrangements went against the received marital wisdom. These unique, bespoke partnerships evolved with time, honesty and trust but were rarely if ever explained to those outside their bubble, even to families, in case they should think their marriage was in trouble or be adversely judged. 'You can't say to people that actually my having all this no-strings-attached sex has made our marriage better. That's a mental leap too far, to think that we might have been getting off on what the other was doing,' says Hilary, who I have to say glowed with enviable happiness. The obvious, standard model of coupledom is not always the way.

Some find they are happier living as a couple apart. Lucy was married to a man throughout her twenties whom she still sees and is deeply fond of. Then she hit thirty. 'I realised that I was just ticking the boxes, marrying because I was bored and getting off on the deception with a series of affairs.' She is now in her forties, a successful businesswoman who lives apart from her new partner she refers to as her soul mate, and with whom she has an open sexual relationship. 'We spend most weekends together, and I love being a stepmother to his two kids but I couldn't live with him because he is so untidy and so strong that he would engulf me.

One day when we need to look after each other then maybe we will live together, but there's no need to now.' Lucy supports her boyfriend because she can afford to, but finds that her family and her friends are disapproving. 'They don't trust the fact that I know what I am doing, and anyway what's money for? I'm having a great time, we spend the money together and I love the fact that I can help his children when I have none of my own. People talk about the need for equality but that's a false quest. What matters is mutuality. I earn the money and he doesn't. But he gives in so many other ways, and there's a symbiosis between us which works because we both give enough to make it feel mutually beneficial.'

I met many contented people who cherished the support, intimacy and their unique shared history as a couple. They accepted that their relationship could never be perfect. But equally I met others who seemed swamped by a loneliness worse than being alone, an emotional emptiness at the heart of their relationship, a longing for a greater closeness in love. Trapped behind the façade of a happy, stable marriage, they shored up their disappointments and their low sense of self with game-playing, jostling for power, for small victories over the day-to-day. It was as if they were being sucked deeper into a downward spiral of resentment, unable to see either a way out or how they themselves contributed to the problem. Blame for past crimes was heaped firmly at the feet of one person, usually over sex or money, and with each veiled and vitriolic attack the walls of defence grew higher and the chances of a resolution less likely. In each case their differences were about a lot more than spending too much money, failing to meet their domestic responsibilities, infidelity or sexual difficulties. Their problems were being fed by a deep rage at the way their dreams of happiness and togetherness had been dashed on the floor of unrealistic expectations.

Women in particular simmered with repressed rage at having to determine every aspect of family life and then do more than their fair share. Some felt their identity as independent working women was diminished under the weight of domesticity or the shadow of *his* success. Others lived with the drip-drip humiliation of emotional and physical abuse from men who had suffered deep childhood neglect, unaware of the havoc that their experiences when young can have on an adult relationship. Gender stereotypes and assumptions about roles pervade adult intimacy, and consequently form a resonant theme throughout this book. Women are seen as the nurturers of relationship but are still far too nice. In spite of feminism's victories, too many women settle for less. I was deeply touched by the number of people I met who compromised their own happiness in order to stick by their partner through extreme physical and mental illness, alcoholism and drug abuse, unemployment or dire financial circumstances out of a sense of duty and commitment to their shared history, to their children, or to the embers of hope that they would be able to revive a loving, equable relationship again one day.

Surprising numbers confessed to secrets they hadn't told anyone else before. Some were innocent and charming. One woman always gave herself the two fluffiest pillows when she made their bed each morning, unaware that her husband had his own secret – he lit a cigarette every day on his way home from work, a mark of recalcitrant defiance because she had been the one to make him give up. Katrina, a successful businesswoman and mother, happily married to an equally successful man, has a secret bank account into which she puts £200 a month so that she can buy the little luxuries she adores and he disapproves of without feeling guilty – expensive make-up, strawberries out of season, designer clothes for their child. Diana has kept one of the first flowers Sam ever gave her, dried and pressed, to remind herself how much she deserves him after years of struggling alone with two children, but has never told him so. Others were simply secrets kept out of manners – husbands never letting on that they found their wives' excessive weight unattractive in case it should cause offence, or wives relishing the electricity of a text flirtation, knowing full well that it would never go anywhere.

Just occasionally people confessed to dark secrets of which they felt deeply ashamed – the woman who had stayed married for over forty years but had wished on more than one occasion that her husband was dead; several undisclosed, ancient affairs that bubbled to the surface – secrets which are best left buried, secrets which help to preserve the line of distinction between yourself as an individual and your life together as a couple. 'The damage that would have occurred if he had found out,' one woman told me, who had been married for more than thirty years and who had a brief affair during a low point in their marriage. 'But then I wonder sometimes whether he suspected and turned a blind eye, that he knew it would be all right so long as I didn't confess, that it was something transient that would pass. I think too, sometimes, about how I would feel if it had been him. If I suspected something I would do an awful lot to ignore it in the hope that it too would pass.'

'We're taught everything about the body and about agriculture in Madagascar and about the square root of pi,' laments Johan in Ingmar Bergman's *Scenes from a Marriage*, 'but it doesn't dawn on anyone that we must first learn about ourselves and our own feelings.' Without knowledge about the way relationships change through the course of life it is all too easy to assume that they are the natural consequence of true love, that they just happen, held together by some outside force – fate, or luck – when good loving can flourish only when we take responsibility for it ourselves. It is easy to swallow the platitudes of 'For better, for worse', and cross our fingers and hope with all our hearts that this could be 'The One' with whom we might live happily ever after. But few of us have any idea how to make a lifelong relationship work. 'I think people have no idea what they're getting into,' says Robin, who has been married for twenty-five years. 'We had to go and see a Catholic priest before we got married and had lessons. He told us things like, "This is for life, there is no divorce," and that was fine because those were the rules and it was sobering. If people had to talk to somebody about divorce, the implications and what it means before they got married, for someone to explain the fundamentals, that would be good. It's like having a baby. They tell you about the breathing and the pelvic floor exercises but what use is that to anyone when you don't know how to hold the thing, or clean it?'

Terry Prendergast of the charity Marriage Care agrees. 'We do not teach people enough about how relationships are built and then sustained. If we wanted to change things from relationship disease to relationship health, we could do it in much the same way as the Heart Foundation has changed our attitude to heart disease, with advertising and promotion. We know statistically that it takes people on average six years to do something about a relationship problem. It takes that long to acknowledge that you have difficulties because that's frightening for lots of people. You have made this huge decision, probably the biggest of your life, and now it's going pear-shaped.'

Whether we are married or cohabiting, gay or straight, remarried or living as a couple apart, the quality of our intimate relationship is fundamental to our long-term health and happiness. You couldn't devise a more comprehensive and mutually advantageous state of being. No other relationship fulfils so many of our emotional, psychological, social, spiritual and sexual needs in one neat package. We all need to feel a sense of belonging, a connection to someone who accepts us in our entirety, with weaknesses and small madnesses as well as strengths; someone who challenges and cherishes us enough to blunt the existential truth that we are all alone in this world. With that sense of safety we are more able to go out into that world and succeed. 'If you feel loved you are naturally more confident, and it means you get work into some kind of perspective,' says Sue. 'I know that I have someone to go home to that I love.' A good lifelong relationship brings joy, close friendship and a sense of humour to the humdrum of daily life, sharing the smallest pleasures from the crossword to a bar of chocolate. It offers unparalleled opportunities to heal some of the hurts of childhood. It helps to buffer life's stresses and adversities, for with two heads and differing perspectives, support and solutions can more easily be found. It makes good economic sense, for with two incomes sharing the same bed and the same teabags, the costs of home are substantially lower. It enlarges our interests and opportunities through extended networks of family and social connections. It is still the best forum for raising capable and contented children, for it is love which brings out the best of what it is to be human.

Love grows with time into something far more nourishing and essential than the promise of romance. All of the research evidence suggests that this emotional lifeline is key to our well-being. A large number of studies conducted over the past twenty-five years suggests that those who are happy in their marriage or lifelong relationship have better physical and mental health than those who are unhappily married or separated. The link between poverty, ill health and a shorter life expectancy is conclusive, but some research indicates that a supportive, committed relationship is even more important than social status to our long-term well-being.[1] In a supportive relationship, each encourages healthier behaviour in the other, cares for them when they are ill and helps to reduce stress and stress-related illnesses. Each has a stronger immune system, with more white blood cells and more effective natural killer cells.[2] The longer partners are married, the longer they can expect to live. One study of the British Household Panel Survey in 1991 found that married men were predicted to be 7.2 per cent less likely to die in the subsequent decade than their unmarried counterparts, while the figure for married women was 4.2 per cent.[3] Marriage and committed lifelong relationship is so important that people who are separated, divorced or widowed are substantially more likely than married people to develop mental health problems, and the British Household Panel Survey found that their risk of death increased by 10 per cent in the subsequent eight years.[4] Happily married parents of severely disabled children report less depression and more positive family relations than their maritally distressed counterparts. People in happier relationships cope better with the stress of unexpected unemployment than those who lack that support.[5] One American researcher estimates that economic recession was responsible for up to half of the increase in single-parent families between the 1960s and the 1980s.[6] Yet in another study of unemployed factory workers in the US, those with good, close relations with wives and near relatives had fewer physical and psychological problems than those who lacked that social support.[7] The key word here is 'happy', for there is also strong research evidence to suggest that those who are unhappily married suffer from poorer mental and physical health than their separated or divorced counterparts.[8] Distress in marriage is associated with a suppressed immune system, which means people are on average 35 per cent more likely to become ill.[9] They are more likely to drown their unhappiness with drink, drugs and smoking, and violence is more frequent in distressed relationships. If people are exposed to a great deal of negative conflict filled with contempt and unhappiness, existing health problems such as raised blood pressure and heart disease can get worse, and they lack the essential buffer of support against external stress which a good relationship can provide.[10]

The anchor of a good, stable relationship has never been more important for keeping our disappointments and conceits with life in check. 'When I was super-stressed out because the traders had misused the software and lost the company a lot of money, David teased me about being overly self-important. He walked round the house talking about how global capitalism would fall apart without me, which just put everything into perspective,' says Katrina. We have no choice but to accept that the future is unpredictable, with few jobs for life any more and a faster pace of change. Shift happens, but with that sense of constancy from someone who you trust will stay by your side, the impact of such instability is less threatening. With fewer community structures around to root us, and fewer friends and family close by, we rely on our relationship for emotional and moral support more than ever before. Among the chaotic, noisy demands of the modern world there is, as the philosopher Mary Midgley writes in *Beast and Man*, a 'deep human need for a continuous central life that lasts through genuine, but passing, changes of mood. The need to be able to rely on other people is not some shameful sort of weakness; it is an aspect of the need to be true to oneself.' One central relationship, which expands and changes with our needs, which grows as we do, is one of the most important contributors to human health and happiness. With the uncertainties of the great geopolitical shifts of the twenty-first century such as climate change, global financial upheaval, the increasing number of people over sixty and the prospect of diminishing state guarantees over provision for our general health or our later years, understanding how to strengthen that relationship could be the best investment policy of our lives.

There is no doubt that we are living through a period of profound change and disorientation as to how to sustain the most important relationship to human happiness, with rates of divorce rising, rates of marriage falling and unprecedented levels of cynicism. External forces, which previously kept marriages together, such as religion and the stigma surrounding divorce, have grown weaker. The new emphasis on marriage and relationship as the sole provider of all our emotional, physical and recreational needs means that many relationships are close to snapping under an intolerable weight of expectation. Everyone has rough patches. Do not believe the façade, the pretence of perfect happiness that so many couples present. It is those rough patches that force couples to establish how they can preserve a sense of self and individual autonomy; how they can respect and trust each other's difference and build togetherness around the things which unite rather than divide them. But there is also a sense in which modern cynicism about relationship is unnecessarily gloomy. We have never been better placed to build the happier, contented love life of our dreams, and we are all doing much better than we give ourselves credit for. We are living at the most exciting and revolutionary point in the history of relationship. We have high levels of choice, reliable contraception, sexual understanding and empowerment for women. It matters less whether you are gay or straight, black or white, older or younger than your partner or from which faith or country you originate. We can road-test relationships, we can talk about them, and with such a long life expectancy, we can even have two or three meaningful committed relationships at different stages of our lives. That person who lights your fire when you are your most youthful may not be able to have, or want, children. Your aspirations and needs could be so different at midlife that your paths diverge to the point where relationship isn't possible any more. When two people manage to ride life's changes and circumstances together, they can fathom great riches and contentment, as many of the couples in this book will reveal. But should such fortune and skill fail, no-fault divorce means that we no longer need to be trapped in miserable marriages in perpetuity. We have greater equality between the sexes and similarity of roles between men and women than ever before, and we can provide better role models of relationship and equality for our children.

The key to making relationships work lies with us. With all these new freedoms and the luxury of choice comes new responsibility to take charge of the welfare of the most significant relationship of our lives. We now have far greater understanding about the psychological processes which affect good relationships. Therapy is more acceptable. 'It was thought odd twenty-five years ago to go to counselling. There was this attitude that there must be something wrong with you. Men are also more willing now to address what's wrong in their relationship,' says Pam Fawcett, who has been a relationship counsellor for fifty years. Counselling can help people find a way out of their difficulties. However, according to research conducted by the relationship organisation One Plus One, just 15 per cent make it to that stage together, by which time it is often too late. The paucity of research on the effectiveness of marital therapy concludes that it helps to prevent breakdown in less than half of all couples.[11] Therapists are not magicians. They simply attempt to hold up a mirror to our behaviour so that we can find a way back to togetherness. If we can learn how to do that for ourselves from the very beginning, if we talk at regular intervals about the issues that cause divisions such as money, how we will live or bring up our children, our attitudes to sex and infidelity, we can forge a partnership that is strong enough to withstand adversity. It is up to us to seize the knowledge garnered over the past few decades about what makes relationships happier and sturdier, rather than leaving it to fate, or luck, or the romantic deceit that love is enough to see us through. We think of divorce as an unfortunate event, a car crash which, touch wood, will not happen to us, rather than the end result of a slow process of relationship breakdown over which we have a large amount of control. Divorce produces misery, shame, the hurt of betrayal and a huge sense of personal failure. While many divorces could be avoided with the skills of relationship-building, I met others who spent far too long extricating themselves from bad marriages which seemed always doomed to fail. There is nothing inherently virtuous any more in people sticking together because of the principle of 'Till death do us part' when they would be happier alone or with someone else. People make mistakes, and should be allowed a second chance. By accepting that fact and taking control over the way we break relationships as well as make them, we are more able to protect those who have no part in our battles – our children.

Feminism gets blamed for many of society's ills, but most particularly for the presumed demise in relations between men and women. The overwhelming evidence, though, points to the opposite: men and women are happier together because of it. The more we share in the way of similar experiences and responsibilities, the more able we are to understand one another. With greater equality there is less resentment. A growing body of research evidence suggests that those with a more equal relationship, where the decision-making is shared and each feels able to influence the other, are happier together.[12] There are still great disparities between 'his' and 'her' versions, which resound through this book. Domestic violence and sexism are still rampant, but the principle of fairness and respect for each other's integrity is clearly a sound one. There is no going back to the traditional breadwinner model now that women are educated and expect to work. What that means is that each couple has to negotiate their way towards a sense of fairness and mutuality which works for them. Men and women have to take charge of their domestic lives and fashion a fairer division of labour, which means they have to talk to each other constructively and honestly to arrive at a new deal. In the most successful relationships there is enough space between their togetherness for each to breathe. They operate in the world independently and as a couple with 'That best kind of equality, similarity of powers and capacities with reciprocal superiority in them', as imagined by the nineteenth-century philosopher John Stuart Mill, 'so that each can enjoy the luxury of looking up to the other, and can have alternately the pleasure of leading and of being led in the path of development.' They accept that each has needs, some of which cannot be met by the relationship.

Women want men in their lives – they don't see them as the enemy. In September 2007 the *Observer* newspaper asked a panel of outspoken young feminist women about their opinions of feminism. They unanimously agreed that men were lovable, likeable and an essential 'part of the solution' to finding greater balance and contentment in life. It takes a courageous, trailblazing effort of tolerance and forgiveness when people are torn in so many different directions, when work and family both demand to be put first, when recession and economic hardship increase conflict and disruption in relationships. It requires high levels of self-confidence and awareness, trust, good listening skills, an ability to postpone gratification and a sense of humour to stand a chance of riding through such storms together. But it is worth it. The happiest couples were open about the fact that there have been times when it has been incredibly difficult, times when they hated each other, when circumstances were so adverse that they considered separating, when it took a gargantuan leap of faith and imagination to trust that they could find their way through their difficulties to a better place. But through their triumph over these personal difficulties they created a unique and special bond, stronger than anything a dwindling, institutional template of marriage could offer.

No book on love can give you all the answers. While there are many similarities in the lives of couples, each of us has a unique experience. A good lifelong relationship is an exhilarating adventure, an emotional roller coaster, as far from the stereotypical notions of marriage as bourgeois routine and mediocrity as the moon is from the stars. We may crave certainty because so many other aspects of life feel so unstable, but a good relationship cannot be controlled or boxed into a corner, for that will only render it more fragile. Lifelong love has to be built on the surprise and chance nature of life. We can never be sure how things will change, or how we will alter through circumstance and the unique chemistry between us. While it is hard to imagine, when you are young, how you can possibly commit for a lifetime to someone you hardly know, once you have had children and navigated the uncertainties and vulnerabilities of ageing or illness, the need for a caring, constant presence from another human being through life is thrown into stark relief. While it may seem at times as if a partnership is inexorably doomed, sometimes all it takes is one of you to shift aspect in subtle but conscious ways. 'My marriage was on its knees at one point,' a man who had been married for thirty-two years told me, 'and I knew we would have to separate. But before we did I decided on a last-ditch experiment where I tried to give everything to the relationship that I wanted from it. In less than a fortnight things were beginning to improve because my wife was mirroring that kindness back to me. It's a truism, but we can only change things by changing how we behave, not by changing other people.' They are still together.

'Marriage is one long conversation chequered by disputes,' the

author Robert Louis Stevenson once wrote. Some might interpret
their own marriage rather differently, as one long dispute chequered by conversation. My overriding ambition in this book is to
reveal the wonder and adventure of that most essential, formative
partnership in spite of the inevitable wrestling. There is every
reason to be optimistic about the state of modern love. People
want to find ways to a greater contentment, Shakespeare's 'marriage of true minds', because we know instinctively how
important a good relationship is for us, body and soul. 'The disputes are valueless; they but ingrain the difference; the heroic
heart of woman prompting her at once to nail her colours to the
mast,' continues Stevenson. 'But in the intervals, almost unconsciously, and with no desire to shine, the whole material of life is
turned over and over, ideas are struck out and shared, the two
persons more and more adapt their notions one to suit the other,
and in process of time, without sound of trumpet, they conduct
each other into new worlds of thought.'

2

FROM ROMANCE TO REALITY

At the heart of romantic love is the notion that we each have a soul mate somewhere in the world who matches our every need and desire, epitomised by the last lines of *Jane Eyre* when she says, 'I am my husband's life as fully as he is mine. No woman was ever nearer to her mate than I am: ever more absolutely bone of his bone and flesh of his flesh.' We hope that somewhere out there is our other half, that perfect fit, 'The One', who will make life complete, understand our needs without words and match our temperament without argument. The truth is perhaps closer to the words of that most romantic and tragic fictional heroine Anna Karenina: 'If it is true that there are as many minds as there are heads, then there are as many kinds of love as there are hearts.' We grow up writing ourselves into fairy-tale romances, imagining who that person might be who will inject our lives with such magnetism. Then, as each lover passes through our lives, we wonder, 'Is this it?' 'When my first marriage went wrong I started to question my own judgement. Had this really been the girl of my dreams, those dreams you start having at the age of six?' says Marcus, who is now in his sixties. His second, happier marriage ended suddenly after twenty years when his wife died. 'Now I know that it is a lottery, even with my second wife, who was just this amazing, dynamic woman whom I loved very much. There are loads of people out there you could form a lasting partnership with, all over the world.'

All of the research evidence suggests that we choose those with whom we 'fall in love'. We screen out unsuitable partners by assessing their assets in terms of appearance, financial status and background, and are often attracted to those who are like us in looks, values or interests or who seem to provide something we feel we lack. Choosing who to love is connected to the sort of person we would like to be, and often says a great deal more about us than it does about the beloved. For some that person must be successful in a field they have ambitions in so that they too might succeed; others like to put themselves in the stronger position and rescue the weak or the meek. Often, we fall in love with someone who resembles a parental figure, giving us the opportunity either to right or to confirm the wrongs of our childhood. Only we don't see that at the time – neither of us. Falling in love can be brought on by loss or separation, being away from home or at times of fear or stress because when adrenalin or natural opioids have been triggered, people are already chemically primed to find others in a similarly aroused state more attractive.[1] Sometimes just knowing that someone likes us is enough to make us like them. Then of course there is the baby-making imperative. We fall in lust, irresistibly drawn by a sexual chemistry which keeps us bonking away for just long enough to reproduce and for another, deeper intimacy and commitment to grow so that both parents are more likely to stay around to look after the baby. Passionate love when you first meet someone is exhilarating. Endorphins flood the body. You can't get enough of each other and feel ill, like a drug addict going through withdrawal, when you are apart. Great surges of dopamine and oxytocin switch off judgemental thinking and negative emotions, and help us bond together like glue.[2,3] We idealise the other, fall in love with what we see, a beautiful face or the allure of confidence which masks something much more vulnerable inside, until the lights come on, about eighteen months to three years later.[4] Often the character traits we find most infuriating and impossible to live with at the end of an affair are the same characteristics we once found so attractive. Real love grows when the real person emerges from the smoke and mirrors of romance, once weaknesses have been accepted and compromises have been made. When that isn't possible, the love affair can be dismissed as either an infatuation or wrong from the beginning. It wasn't the 'real thing'.

'In virtually every case of the hundreds with whom I have worked in couple therapy and in couple groups,' writes the psychologist Ayala Malach Pines in her book *Falling in Love*, 'if the relationship was based on romantic love, it was possible to find a connection between the traits that attracted the couple to each other and the traits that later became the focus of their problems.' The man who was once so persistent, attentive and loving becomes jealous, possessive and overly demanding; the woman who seemed to have such energy and capability is then blamed for taking over his life. Many of those I met in more volatile and unhappier relationships had the sort of sudden, passionate beginning full of mystery, or the need to triumph over some adversity to be together, that is reminiscent of romantic fiction. 'I can remember exactly what that first summer was like,' says Lydia, who is separated from the father of her two children. 'It's Paul Weller, it's hot summer days, I can still smell it. He is very good-looking, he had lots of money because he was working abroad and not paying income tax, so I think that had a lot to do with why we got together. He kept going away, and that's quite exciting. You start feeding this whole thing of how much you miss him. If he had been here working in a normal job it would probably have fizzled out quite quickly.'

Jan is also separated from her husband, the father of her children. Soon after they met, he invited her on holiday to Jamaica. 'It was just so intense and romantic, and that's where I fell in love. It was so different to everything I had felt before. He proposed and I said yes. Matthew has this amazing sense of adventure, of places to go and see, so when you are on holiday with him it's fantastic. It's the day-to-day that he is pretty crap at.' Both Jan and Lydia fell in love with men who oozed a sense of confidence and charm, which disguised a deeper emotional turmoil and made their relationships difficult. Both married quickly, largely because of the pressure of expectation from family and friends. 'It was this inexorable path,' says Lydia. 'My two best friends were married with kids, and there was this notion that we would all do it together and our husbands would all get on with each other. I knew Paul adored me, plus I was desperate to have a baby.'

Often we fall in love with so much more than that person; with something they have that we lack. Sarah got married at the age of seventeen. 'I fell in love with his family as much as with him. They were so lovely, and my family were never really close. When we split up the thought that I was going to lose them upset me more than anything.' Molly fell in love at university with a handsome and wealthy man who to this day still gives her the physical shivers if she meets him. 'He lived in a world I wanted to live in, with lots of brothers and sisters and a massive tumbledown house in the country that we used to go to for the weekend. But I was always trying to be what he wanted me to be, and he totally zapped my confidence.' Research seems to confirm that fast and passionate start-ups, where people are inseparable and then married within months, often lead to short-lived or difficult relationships. Ted Huston at the University of Arizona has found that those couples who trod more carefully and took up to two years to make a commitment were more likely to be together thirteen years later. Of those I met with the most enduring relationships, many knew from the start that there was something about this person that was different from all of their previous lovers, but few of them felt confident about labelling that as 'love'.

Like Robin and Hilary, who met as students in Australia and had an on-off sexual relationship, with both of them seeing other people. When Hilary went to France as an au pair, 'I just thought how jealous and upset I would be if she got in touch and said, "Actually I have met someone else,"' says Robin. 'That got me thinking about what that might mean. I don't think you ever know as a positive thing that you *have* to marry a particular person. Often it's the done thing, or it seems appropriate, but for me it was just that I thought I might lose her.'

Megan met Charlie ten years ago when she was thirty, and felt she had finally found someone who was her equal. 'I'd been out with so many people who only seemed interested in getting married, and I couldn't understand why you would want to start a relationship wondering whether this was the person you might marry. But Charlie wasn't like that, and every time I thought it wasn't going anywhere he would do something really thoughtful, or reveal another lovely side to his personality and I would fall in love with him all over again. He is bright and opinionated, and I liked being with someone who for once didn't expect me to take the lead on everything.' Admiring someone's strength came up again and again. Philip and Juliet met at university, had a strong relationship which was sometimes off as well as on until eventually they married when they were both twenty-nine. 'We joke that I chose her because of her strengths. She is a big, strong, physical, tough woman and she can cope, and in the end that must have been a factor because of the genetic thing of having children. She's a professional woman, and I really admire that because that's not easy with three children. It means I am never disappointed in her.'

Sam too was surprised by how much he was attracted by Diana's strengths and capabilities. 'We went camping the year before I proposed. I love camping and the outdoor life, but Diana had two kids and all three of them hated the idea of camping, so I thought, This has got to be a good experience otherwise they are never going to want to do it again. So I got lots of good gear, got them kitted out and I was thinking that just like with all my other relationships it will be me doing everything. I really don't like the "fluffy bunny" type of girlfriend who holds up a pole and says,

"What do I do with this?" But Diana just mucked in. We were a good team and we had a fantastic summer, it was very balanced and I thought, I quite like this . . .'

Most people slide into a lifelong relationship because nothing adverse drives them apart, or because of pregnancy, or reaching thirty and thinking it's time to grow up. More often than not it's because a woman's biological clock has started ticking and she feels it's time to force the issue. Kate was pragmatic when it came to settling for Rory. 'I don't remember being starry-eyed, and there was no game-playing with him. It was all just so easy. I remember ringing him after just three or four days of trying to be cool and saying, "What are you doing tonight?" which I would never have done with any of the other people I'd gazed into the eyes of.' When Kate reached thirty she brought up the subject of their future together. 'I remember lying on the bed in a hotel in Paris and saying, "I don't want to find out after a few years that you're not interested in having children because I am," which was kind of forthright compared to how I had been before.' They have been married for fifteen years and have three children. Molly also honed in on the man she married. They had known each other at school, 'So when my mother told me he was single I sent him an email and we went out for a drink. I just thought he was a terribly nice chap, the sort of man my mother would like me to marry, and why had I never noticed how attractive he is? I think I had decided before I even saw him again, and just loved every bit of him. He just felt absolutely right. It was totally the right time after three years of unsuccessful dating and a string of sordid one-night stands with inappropriate men. I thought, there is so much security and warmth and safety with this person.'

Perhaps it takes the wisdom that comes with experience to be able to reject the strength of romantic pressure that we should be able to live happily ever after with our soul mate. 'I am ridiculously emotionally naive,' says Peggy, who is on her own in her late fifties after two failed marriages. 'I am Doris Day, Judy Garland – any one of those songs I could sing to you word-perfect. That is what I grew up looking for, and my second husband had a great line in gushing emotion. I never thought anyone could say those things as a means to an end. I thought it was a rule that you only said them if you meant it.' Ursula fell madly in love in her mid-twenties, 'I felt that if a battery has a positive and a negative side then is this the person who is that other charge for me? I did feel like it was this exciting fairy tale, and we got married very quickly.' But seventeen years and two children later they went through an acrimonious divorce which left her disillusioned, drained and very alone. 'It's a complete rocking of everything that you are. I really thought that whatever conflicts you have with some-one, if you love them you can work things out. I even told the kids that, and I feel terrible about that because now I know it's not true but I had never watched a divorce close up, so how would I know? You can't resolve every conflict, just arrive at some truth which you can agree on.' She has met someone else with whom she is having a happier time, but he is careful to keep any romantic expectations in check. 'I remember we had this amazing, honest conversation when we first met where he said, "At our age do you really want to believe that you have met someone who will love you for ever and die for you if needs be?" They're fun things to say, and it was great to have had that experience for a while when I was younger, but they are huge overstatements and it is much better to judge the actions of a person day-to-day. We have a great time, he is great with my kids, but whether it is what we will both need in twenty years' time, who knows?'

Sarah married at seventeen, and after three children and a divorce is now happily living with someone else. 'I do love him, but I don't believe in that soppy vision of love that people have any more. It's a load of old tosh. I think you love people for dif-ferent reasons. When I first met him I couldn't put him down, but now I just want to talk to him all the time. We don't have a telly, so when he comes in from work we sit down with a glass of wine and talk, sometimes for a couple of hours, and you just offload all your stuff from the day. I suppose he is like my best friend.' Madeline also found that the fairy-tale notions she had grown up with evaporated once she had been through a painful and protracted divorce. 'This idea that marriage is like *Cinderella*, that you live happily ever after, is embedded in our culture. It's in our magazines and in our songs that it's just bliss for ever. But it's not as simple as that. There is so much more.'

People have always fallen madly in love but the idea that one should find love, happiness and constant companionship throughout a lifelong marriage has been with us for less than a hundred years. For centuries love was considered a dangerous and disruptive force to be guarded against. Prior to the rise of romanticism and the romantic novel – the first form of literature to reach a mass audience – marriage was essentially an important mechanism for economic and political gain for the rich, a way of strengthening business and raising capital, safeguarding property and inheritance rights. It was much too important a decision to be left to individual couples. Love grew afterwards, if you were lucky. But even then the ideal was of a kind and good-tempered spouse who didn't pry too deeply, not the soul-baring intimacy expected of loving couples today. 'The intent of matrimony is not for man and his wife to always be taken up with each other, but jointly to discharge the duties of civil society, to govern their families with prudence and educate their children with discretion,' stated *The Lady's Magazine* in 1774.[5] The very idea that love alone constituted enough of a foundation for making or breaking a marriage was unthinkable before the romantic revolution and other equally new ideals, such as individualism and the notion of free choice, privacy away from public scrutiny for family life to flourish and a new need to be true to the emotion of love for its own sake. Any other potentially more sensible motive for marriage, which was once paramount, such as money or social status, is now seen to be mercenary or calculating. 'The romantic revolution which began late in the eighteenth century, sweeping across vast reaches of class and territory in the nineteenth to become, in the twentieth, the unassailable norm of courtship behaviour, thus carried two components,' writes Edward Shorter in his seminal social history *The Making of the Modern Family*. 'A new relationship of the couple to each other; and a new relationship for them, as a unit, to the surrounding social order.'

'For most of history it was inconceivable that people would choose their mates on the basis of something as fragile and irrational as love,' writes the American historian Stephanie Coontz in her book *Marriage, A History*, 'and then focus all their sexual, intimate and altruistic desires on the resulting marriage.' Companionship, good conversation, sexual fulfilment and male fidelity were not qualities which either men or women presumed to expect. The idea that a love affair could blossom into a lifelong, all-consuming, exclusive relationship, and that those lovers could then find privacy within their own home, was not a possibility for everyone until the massive expansion of public housing in the post-Second World War years fostered a new idealism around the nuclear family. It is astonishing how strong a hold those few short years during the 1950s still have on our understanding of what a good marriage should be. Prior to that time, many couples were rarely alone together. The rich had servants listening in; the poor lived in crowded conditions often with other families, and all husbands and wives were expected to lead separate and very different lives. Many of those without means never married at all until the period between 1850 and 1960, which the historian John Gillis has called 'The Era of Mandatory Marriage'. During this period, finding a partner was more important to one's status in society than who one married, particularly for women, who were now stigmatised as single women, 'old maids' left 'on the shelf'. Up until the end of the nineteenth century, many more people cohabited in common-law unions than those who were married in the eyes of the State or the Church, just as they are beginning to do today. We will never know the exact figures, but historians agree that for the majority, with neither property nor inheritance rights to protect, marriage meant a range of woolly commitments from 'handfast-ing' in front of witnesses to a man making a private promise to take a woman as his wife.

'Marriage' was a private contract between two individuals enforced by a community sense of what was right, but it could easily be broken and often was. Lord Hardwicke's Marriage Act of 1753 defined marriage, in an attempt to reduce the numbers of heirs and heiresses who had claims placed on their inheritance after being seduced, as well as to reverse the rising numbers of single mothers impoverished because of absconding or bigamous fathers. Banns had to be published and the service solemnised in church or certified by obtaining an official licence, and parental consent had to be obtained for those under the age of twenty-one. Children of marriages which did not meet these criteria could not inherit property. But the numbers of common-law unions and clandestine marriages continued to rise for much of the eighteenth and early nineteenth centuries, as ordinary people tried to avoid exorbitant church fees with a clergyman reading from the Book of Common Prayer.[6]

We imagine that the institution of State- or Church-controlled marriage has been with us since time began, and that intimate relationships are consequently in a state of chaos because of its slow demise. The reality, though, is that family and local networks of friends and neighbours, as well as the two people involved, have had a lot more influence over the nature of the couple relas-tionship, while the State has tried to legislate for how we live in love and has largely failed. Romance dominates our culture, yet we know instinctively that it is precarious. Couples who have rarely set foot inside a church want their vows sanctified there in the hope that, as they sacrifice themselves to this new religion of romance, they might live happily ever after. We hope with all our hearts that it will work, 'When the truth which people seem to overlook in this matter is that the marriage ceremony is quite use-less as a magic spell for changing in an instant the nature of the relations of two human beings to one another,' writes George

Bernard Shaw in his preface to *Getting Married*. 'When two people are under the influence of the most violent, most insane, most delusive and most transient of passions, they are required to swear that they will remain in that excited, abnormal and exhausting condition continuously until death do them part.'

Anyone with an ounce of experience in love – and who doesn't have that before they get married these days? – knows deep down that romantic love cannot last. 'When you fall in love for the first time it is so all-consuming, and you think you are going to be with them for ever,' says Jackie, who has had three major relationships and is now in her late fifties. 'But then the next time you fall in love you are a bit more cautious because you know that it doesn't last for ever in that fairy-tale way. You have lost that innocence, and it isn't possible to experience that again, like any first time.' We love a wedding because we all want to believe in the power of romance to see us through life, particularly when we are unhappy. The good in us looks at that couple and hopes they have the tenacity and the resilience to make it. The bad in us smirks at their idealism and whispers conspiratorially to others who are equally well married, 'How long do we give them?' Weddings are good box office. We can emote, weep with joy for the couple and for ourselves, for what might have been. 'I remember crying at my brother's wedding the year before I married Paul,' says Lydia. 'We had been together far longer than my brother had been with his bride. I remember looking at this tableau of these two young people, clearly head over heels in love with each other, and knowing that I would never feel that way about Paul, that we were already past that.'

Romance and consumerism became happy bedfellows, enforcing myths about lifelong love in marriage through the latter half of the twentieth century with advertisers using the ecstatic high of passion and the promise of love to sell a wide range of products. Romance increasingly became defined by what you consumed – red roses on Valentine's day – once a community festival – and diamond engagement rings, a tradition invented by the De Beers company with the slogan, 'A diamond is for ever'. Weddings are now big business. The Big Day has assumed a new romantic significance of commitment, and has never been more popular or so expensive. The average cost of a wedding is now approximately £25,000,[7] a phenomenal increase on the austere 1950s figure of just £600 in today's terms.[8] The bridal industry, estimated to be worth about £5 billion in 2005, finds more and more ways to milk the romantic dream with designer clothes, opulent flowers, receptions in hotels and castles and honeymoons in exotic places. Some feel moved to be even more extravagant with personalised love hearts, chocolate fountains, ice sculptures and souvenirs for all the guests. A far cry from the weddings of just over a hundred years ago when only the very rich could afford a honeymoon, a reception in a hotel or to be married in white, a fashion established by Queen Victoria. During the nineteenth century a woman of modest means got married in her 'best' dress, which often made her indistinguishable from the rest of the wedding party. The couple walked to church with their friends and then went back to the bride's house for a wedding breakfast of sandwiches and a slice of cake. Then they went straight back to work.[9] In the early 1900s, honeymoons were considered to be an opportunity for couples to practise and refine their conjugal roles rather than the romantic indulgence it is considered to be today.[10]

As the significance of marital connections and the family for society declined through the latter half of the twentieth century, marriage and weddings became more significant for individuals and their 'life story' together rather than for the community as a whole. The ostentatious wedding says more about ourselves, perhaps, in this age of celebrity and aspiration, than it does about the commitments a couple makes in public by marrying. We are allowed to be a princess, the star of our own show for one day and transcend the more mundane aspects of daily life. Consequently it has never been more popular, with some 85 per cent of all American brides opting for a formal wedding.[11] It is not just about how much is spent. New emotional demands are being

placed on family and friends. Stag and hen nights have snow-
balled from a night out to a long weekend away, with a stark
choice for those close enough to be invited – cough up your own
money on a holiday you might prefer to take with someone else,
or send a message that you are not entirely devoted. I read of a
wedding which managed to take that well-matched pair, romance
and consumerism, to its most logical conclusion – sponsorship.
They got 'friends' to donate most of the day's outgoings – mar-
quee, flowers, food – in return for advertising in a brochure on
every table. Another second marriage tested family relations to the
limit. Their closest friends and family, including the children,
were invited on holiday for two weeks in the Caribbean, but each
had to pay £2,000 for the privilege. One couple were so hard up
they came clean about the fact that it was a choice between spending their money on this holiday or essential renovations to their
house, which led to huge rifts.

The decision to have a lavish wedding is now rarely questioned.
Instead, large-scale consumption is justified – foolishly perhaps,
given the divorce statistics – with 'You only do this once.' We
know on one level that this is romantic fantasy, yet we too have
been seduced by the marketing. We know that placing all our
hopes in lifelong love is risky, but if the day is perfect we might
just be able to beat the odds by laying the best seeds supersti-
tiously for the future. If we spend enough and shout loud enough
about our love for each other, then maybe it will last. If we buy
into a myth of what constitutes a traditional wedding, and step
into roles which we believe have existed for centuries, then maybe
we can return to some of those certainties of the past, when marriage really did last until the silver wedding anniversary, or so we
think. We beat ourselves up for lacking commitment, for being
bad at love when relationships in the past were as disrupted by
poverty, migration and death as contemporary family life is disrupted by divorce. The average marriage in north-west Europe
did not last much longer than it does today, for people married
late and died young. Less than half the children who reached

adulthood did so while both their parents were alive: compare that with the one in four under sixteens who grow up with divorced parents today.[12]

It was only in the Victorian era that legalised marriage and a new sexual morality within it began to take hold. Marriages probably lasted longest during this period than at any other time because declining mortality rates had not yet been offset by rising divorce rates. It was only during the economic boom of the1950s, after decades of hardship and the Second World War, that growing numbers of people could afford to live the marital dream that they saw advertised as essential on their new TV sets and in magazines. You got married because you had to; there was something wrong with you if you didn't, and millions of men and women found themselves miserably trapped in their new homes behind the façade of marital bliss. The new science of marriage guidance emerged to help people attain that elusive happiness, and 'couples turned not just to popular culture and the mass media but also to marriage experts and advice columnists for help', writes Stephanie Coontz in *Marriage, A History*. 'If the advice didn't work, they blamed their own inadequacy.' Love and marriage not only went together like a horse and carriage, as the popular song of that time went, it was considered to be *the* gateway to the good life.

We no longer have to marry to have sex, to get away from the family home or have children, but it has absorbed a new ritual significance as couples leave one world behind and enter a new one of greater commitment. Sexual fidelity has acquired a sanctimonious moral importance as the glue cementing relationships together, now that we know that lifelong love or marriage cannot be trusted. For centuries people turned a blind eye to extramarital sexual relations in men, but now that women can just as easily partake of adultery's pleasures, it's one strike and you're out. Several surveys have shown that extramarital sexual relationships are less approved of now in the West than they were in earlier decades.[13] The more sexually explicit our culture becomes, the more faith people place in the oasis of calm that monogamy can offer. There must, it is assumed, be something wrong with a marriage if one of you has an affair.

Elizabeth forgave her husband's infidelity when he was unemployed and at a very low ebb. 'I didn't tell anyone because, if truth be told, I was slightly ashamed of my reaction in that I should have stood up to him like other women would have done and chucked him out the door.' Changing advice from agony aunts from the 1970s onwards counselled women against forgiving an affair.[14] It was now considered an unacceptable betrayal. A loving marriage was expected to provide for every emotional and sexual need. It was marriage as an institution which could cement that relationship, rather than the more constructive work of good communication and negotiation. With one failed marriage each behind them, Iris and Gerry decided to live together. Two years after discovering the earth-shattering news that Gerry had been having an affair with someone at work, Iris tricked him into getting married on his birthday. She told him they were going to the register office to attend the wedding of two friends, when actually he was attending his own. 'One of the reasons he gave for having the affair was that I didn't want to get married,' said Iris. 'I didn't particularly want to get married because once you have been married and it's failed, you know that it isn't going to give you any more security. So I married him because I still thought we could make it; I thought, you can't just give up, and this way I will prove that I am committed.'

It is so easy to drift into cohabitation that marriage has assumed super-relationship status in both social and legal terms. Marriage rates may be falling but surveys in Europe and the US show that the overwhelming majority of young people still believe in marriage and its importance as a lifelong commitment.[15, 16] It is raised romantic expectations which compromise that ideal, with 94 per cent of one nationally representative sample of American twenty to twenty-nine-year-olds saying that when they married they wanted their spouse to be their soul mate.[17] I surveyed schoolchildren in ten secondary schools in Britain between the ages of eleven and eighteen during 2007. Almost every young person said that they believed marriage should be for life and that they had a soul mate somewhere, someone who would be perfect for them. Many said they wanted partners who would respect them, who they could trust, but the idea that love can still save you, lift you out of the boredom and mediocrity of life seemed stronger than ever. People seem to demand more of marriage, as it has grown more precarious as an institution, and testing a relationship by living together before one commits is sensibly seen as a good way to avoid divorce. But many others cannot afford to marry. Research from both sides of the Atlantic shows that marriage rates are lowest among the poorest. For those on low incomes, marriage carries all sorts of hidden costs over and above those of the wedding. When men have low job or earning prospects, women are naturally more careful. Two incomes may be better than one, but if a man isn't working, a woman's income might just stretch to cover the basic needs of her children but it cannot possibly meet his needs as well. Professor Sara McLanahan of Princeton University conducted a major longitudinal study of unmarried parents, *Fragile Families*, in twenty American cities. 'For many of these couples nothing is worse than a divorce; they'd rather not marry at all than marry and fail. The surprise is these couples don't think marriage is unimportant. They want to get all their ducks in a row before they get married so they don't get divorced and those ducks are: his infidelity, low-income economic problems, financial and emotional relationship difficulties.'[18]

Many of those who marry feel that it is different to living together, that it allows each to relax, trust and invest more in the relationship, which helps to deepen love. But that is largely to do with the fact that the institution of marriage is still an external, public and legally binding statement of commitment. Jack and Rachel married in the 1960s in a very conservative area of Sussex because it just wasn't acceptable to live together. 'I did feel different when we signed the papers, which I hadn't expected. I suppose it's the force of law behind it because one does to a certain extent respect the law.' Some marry for religious reasons. 'With a Christian upbringing I was always going to marry someone,' says Philip. 'All my siblings married, and I guess we expect our children to get married because we go to church.' Others married because that was the only way they could openly be together. Sureena's family are Muslim and her mother arranged for a series of potential suitors to file through their living room. She rejected them all because she was already in love with Spike, a Christian, who eventually converted to the Muslim faith so that they could marry. Sureena would have preferred them to live together. 'I felt that marriage was something that was done to us and it was important to keep my family happy, but I also saw marriage as ownership by men, that whole patriarchal thing. It was far too idealistic to say that you could commit to someone. It was like signing away your whole life. I never liked that fairy-tale stuff anyway, I never believed in it. Now that we have kids and we've been together for thirteen years I don't see it that way at all. I am happy to say I love this person and I am committed to him completely.'

Tom and Carol got married in 1984. 'I never saw getting married as compromising for me as a woman,' says Carol. 'I saw it as gaining something, social recognition in the deepest practical sense – I'm married, now let's get on with stuff, rather than having people question your status. I was aware that being married would make things a non-issue, particularly with our family, plus if I turn up at his bedside after a horrendous crash, they can't tell me as his wife to wait outside.' Jaya and Charu have been living together for the best part of twenty-five years and have welcomed the public statement that comes with a civil partnership because it means they can be more honest as lesbians. 'We used to have to hide it when we were on holiday, for example, and say that we were just friends,' says Jaya. 'We didn't have the confidence, or feel safe, or know how to respond. But that's different now. Recently we went to buy a computer and we wanted to set up an account with both of our names on it and the salesman said, "It's usually for just one person or a couple," and I said, "We are a couple. We're not married yet but we hope to soon." The poor man went very red and then apologised.'

Many live together to test the resilience of their relationship. Approximately 60 per cent of those who cohabit go on to marry that partner.[19] But that doesn't necessarily mean that their relationship fathoms new depths of commitment. Those who hope that marriage per se will salvage a relationship which is already on the rocks, rather than taking the harder route of an honest dialogue about their hopes and desires, are destined to divorce sooner rather than later. Marriage as an institution is dying, and many simply opt for it to simplify matters once they have children or shared property or pensions to protect. 'I couldn't be more committed than I am to Charlie. I feel married to him, but there are practical issues now,' says Megan. 'We own this house together but if one of us died there would be a big inheritance-tax bill. We keep thinking that we ought to make a will because we have a child, but then if we get married you have to start the whole process again, so actually it would probably be easier just to get married.' Frank and Anna met at university and have brought up their two children together. 'When they introduced civil partnerships and not parity for people living together with children I thought, that's it,' says Anna. 'So we went to the register office at the first available slot with two of our oldest friends as witnesses. The woman marrying us said, "Do you want to say anything to each other?" We looked at each other and said, "No." Then she said, "Do you have the rings?" We said "No." Then she said, "Do you want some music?" We said "No," but I also wanted to say, "Just get on with it, we're on a parking meter." Then when it was over she said, "Do you want to kiss now?" We looked at each other, laughed and said, "*No!*"' All of the romantic associations of a wedding had evaporated after the realities of decades of a shared life. 'In fact,' adds Frank, 'someone at work heard that I had got married and thought I had split up with Anna and married someone else! It was that silly.'

There is nothing wrong with romantic love. It is delicious, energising. It is the irrational and impossible demands that we now make of it that have confused the nature of long-term relationships. We are asking for trouble if we expect romantic love to be enough to sustain us through profound differences of opinion and ambition, through argument, having children, job difficulties, unemployment, illness and bereavement. Romantic love complicates our choice of partner because we believe in the need for compatibility, when it is often the incompatibilities, the differences between us, which make life more interesting. Romance complicates sex because we slide easily into the presumption that our passion for each other must have died once our sex life becomes more routine. It complicates the inevitable conflicts between us because we assume that couples who truly love each other won't fight. It frustrates family life because we presume that the reproduction of our merged genes will be emblematic of our unique love for each other, when few things divide couples more than the hard work of looking after small children. Raised romantic expectations exacerbate the pain of divorce – the shame of failure, the hurt and humiliation of betrayal. Perhaps most importantly of all, romanticised relationships make the loss of divorce worse for our children. Children have always lived with loss, with parents dying young, with work and apprenticeships as adolescents far from home. What is new to our age is the loss of their hopes and dreams for their own future relationships as they learn to trust love less.

As the childbearing and economic imperatives for marriage have diminished, the romantic script has gathered momentum, offering people a sense of magic in an increasingly rational and depersonalised world. The more we lack a sense of set place or a given role that we can step into, the more couples have grown to rely on each other for that sense of identity and support. Close-knit social ties have loosened, trust and belief in both

Church and State have diminished, augmenting the importance of marriage and the family as anchors of personal stability and a means of self-fulfilment. 'The loneliness of life in the cities, the long commutes, the absence of meaningful contact with people in so many jobs, the anonymity of suburban life and the distances that separate close friends and family have all sharpened our emotional hungers,' writes Judith Wallerstein, the American psychologist, in her book *The Good Marriage*. Romanticism flourishes in this vacuum. Research shows that romantic love has become more important in societies where the social structures and attachments are less clear.[20] We only have to look at the boom in anything associated with Jane Austen, since Colin Firth emerged from a lake in that shirt in the BBC's production of *Pride and Prejudice* barely a decade ago, to know how far romance has swamped reality. Austen's novels have always been popular classics. But we now revel in the romanticism of her storytelling more than ever before and forget, conveniently, that she was writing about a time when a woman *had* to get married. She had no other choice in life. Austen's novels are principally concerned with women making rational, good choices in marriage, where there is mutual recognition as well as attraction rather than mere ephemeral manipulations of 'true love'. We overlook the sage words of Mary Crawford in *Mansfield Park* when she says, 'There is not one in a hundred of either sex who is not taken in when they marry. Look where I will, I see that it is so, and I feel that it *must* be so, when I consider that it is, of all transactions, the one in which people expect most from others and are least honest about themselves.'

We have been seduced by the fairy tale that we should be able to find everything we need from just one person, that romantic love is the only love worth having, that it should always be happy, instinctive, emotionally intense, sexually fulfilling and last for ever. 'I had insane expectations and I blew away my teens and early twenties waiting for Prince Charming when I should have been out there having as much fun as possible, and I regret that.' Oliver met Jerome when he was in his early thirties and they have been together for ten years. 'Jerome feels much the same way. We watch programmes like *Skins* and have this bittersweet feeling of missing out. Yet in terms of our love I feel as if it has been a kind of fairy tale for both of us because we found each other so late. I have an amazing relationship now, but the truth is I haven't had that for life. I don't believe we do mate for life, and for the first fifteen years of my life I didn't have it. I paid my dues in advance.'

Romantic expectations mask the boundaries and limits of love, which are conditional in adult relationships and therefore in need of constant review. Romantic love excuses us from behaving morally – 'I couldn't help myself' – and from taking responsibility for our actions or for the welfare of our relationship because it is this 'other' force, which, it is presumed, takes over. Often couples fail to discuss some of the most basic foundations of their partnership before they commit to each other. I was struck during interviews by the number of people who had never talked about obvious areas of contention such as where they wanted to live, their dreams and ambitions, what constituted infidelity, whether or not they wanted children and who would look after them. Romance allows people to end relationships and marriages with the words 'I don't love you any more' when that is rarely the truth; what they mean is, 'I don't want to be with you any more,' or, 'I have found someone else.' Love doesn't evaporate overnight, it forges roots and grows thicker with time. 'Romantic love is not omnipotent – and those who believe it is are too immature to be ready for it,' writes Nathaniel Branden in *The Psychology of Romantic Love*. 'Given the multitude of psychological problems that many people bring to a relationship – given their doubts, their fears, their insecurities, their weak and uncertain self-esteem – given the fact that most have never learned that a love relationship, like every other value in life requires consciousness, courage, knowledge and wisdom to be sustained – it is not astonishing that most relationships end disappointingly.'

Evidence that we now place too much faith in the power of love alone can be found in some studies which indicate that overall levels of marital quality have declined, in spite of easier divorce laws removing the most miserable marriages from the mix. Nearly half of all marriages might end in divorce, but another quarter are experienced as 'distressed'.[21] One study of the General Social Survey in the US found that the numbers of people who reported that their marriages were very happy declined gradually between 1973 and 1988, and two other American studies have found similar declines through the 1980s.[22] A study in Finland found that people were less satisfied with their sex lives at the end of the 1990s than other couples who had been together for a similar length of time were at the beginning of the 1990s. The researchers concluded that it wasn't the quality of sex which had deteriorated; their expectations had risen.[23] Raised romanticised expectations of a loving relationship undermine every aspect of togetherness in insidious ways, with the drip-drip of disillusion a constant soundtrack. Half of all divorces take place within less than seven years of the marriage, brought on more often by disappointment rather than 'irretrievable breakdown'. Sometimes love isn't enough, but we're told that it should be. When the honeymoon days wane and compromises have to be made, when the real person full of failings and irritations emerges through the mist and sparkle of romantic promise, when difficulty or adversity strikes, people are more likely to question whether they should stay, for there is no room for the bad in the romantic dream. 'I wish I'd known what I know now, which is that lots of women feel slightly cut adrift after they get married,' writes Kathryn Flett in *The Heart-Shaped Bullet*. 'Nobody wants to know that your honeymoon period is anything other than what they believe it must be and, of course, neither do you.'

'I know that I am missing out on something that has been written about by all of the great poets and writers, and sung about by all the great balladeers, and painted and expressed in countless different ways,' writes Isabel Rose. 'I'm missing out on love. I don't even know what it is.' We have no clear definition of what love is any more other than the romantic model, and few cultural reference points as to how that love changes and deepens over time. Couples can fall out, not because they don't love each other, but because they have very different ideas as to how that love should be expressed. 'I was used to being with very effusive guys,' says Olive. 'But Jerome isn't like that. I'd say he looked great and he'd say thank you, and then I'd wait for the boomerang but it wasn't coming back. I felt he wasn't appreciating me, he wasn't showing his love.' The balance of power in a relationship is also often confused by arbitrary notions of who loves the other the most, when it is perhaps the one who has the most to lose who has least in the terms of confidence or interests outside the relationship, who needs the other the most. 'I don't know if the love is equal or not,' says Diana, who is older than Sam and has lived through the end of a previous relationship with the father of her two children. 'I think he probably loves me more, but maybe I am measuring something different in that I know I can survive on my own. If he walked out or, God forbid, died I'd be OK on my own. He is not emotionally that strong, but that doesn't mean I love him less.'

The accepted idiom of love and romance is demonstrative, gushing, seductive and very female. Women are good at talking about how they feel; they are expected to be caring and kind and feel great disappointment when men are unable to express how much they care for them in similar ways. Men tend to like to show their love in more practical, less prosaic ways by bringing home the bacon, changing the light bulbs or having sex. 'He doesn't compliment me. We enjoy each other's company and laugh at the same things but it would be nice to be really noticed occasionally,' says Elizabeth. 'If I say, "Do you love me?" he just groans and says, "Of course I do," but he wouldn't just turn round spontaneously and say so. I think he is quite cut off emotionally.' Like many women I met, Elizabeth feels a residual resentment at the fact that she has compromised a great deal more than her husband for the sake of their marriage. 'He must make compromises, but I am not sure I can put my finger on what they are. I work full time too but he considers that he earns the crust and doesn't see what I do as being particularly serious work. I do all the domestic stuff, and I do occasionally say, "You could say, 'That's a nice dinner,'" but no . . . I think I bring a level of convenience, which has become a bit of a joke in our house. When we were discussing the mortgage, once, in a businesslike way because we weren't married at that point, he said, "If I die there is this policy and that," and I said, "What happens if I die?" and he said, "It will be a little inconvenient!" When we had our son I remember lying there in the hospital and saying to him, "It's going to be a little bit more inconvenient now," and even though it's a joke, and I am sure he must appreciate me, it would be really nice to hear him say so.'

We look to romance to rescue us when we feel ourselves disappearing, subsumed by domesticity and the invisibility of marriage. Beatrice fell passionately in love with the man she eventually married when she was twenty, years before she was ready to settle down. 'He completely swept me off my feet. I couldn't not think about him, and I still get palpitations thinking about that time. It was like a fairy tale, I was nursing and the caretaker, he was working and the provider of security in a very traditional way.' That was twenty-five years ago. Since then they have had two children and have had to downsize considerably by moving to the country after her husband was made redundant. He had a breakdown, became severely depressed, unable to communicate properly or express any affection and he began to drink heavily. Beatrice found herself coping with two small children in a new place, without the support of family, friends or neighbours, on her own. 'It was a difficult time because our unspoken contract was that we would be there for each other, and then to find my partner absent like that . . . I then started thinking, I've got a duty to look after him, in sickness and in health, but I didn't agree to this. But then if I am not going to be there for him at a really difficult time, what am I offering?' Her husband has now found work and the depression has eased a little but their marriage isn't as happy as it once was. She needs him to acknowledge that he is depressed and seek help for it; to acknowledge his part in their difficulties. But most important of all, she needs him to show her that he loves her. 'I want him to come back, to be how he was, but he doesn't understand when I say that. I have to accept things as they are, and that's the bit I am not sure about. I can, but I am not sure I want to. I've been putting my needs last for ten years. I could change my expectations of the marriage and get my needs met in other ways, but the bit I can't meet elsewhere is that feeling of being loved and cherished by a man. I just want to be hugged and have some lovely person look into my eyes; it's that romantic stuff that's missing. That's about feeling loved and special, that feeling of wonder between two people which I can't replace with my girl-friends. I know they love me and would do whatever I asked, but there is something specific about having one person who is completely tuned into you, and I don't have that at the moment.'

Small things such as never buying flowers or coming home with the wrong sort become hugely significant, symptomatic of those deeper, unspoken romantic disappointments. We know the relationship is basically sound. We know that marriage and commitment is about compromise. We try to focus on all the good things, but load all our disappointment with life on to the other. If he could only be a little bit more demonstrative, affectionate, confiding, appreciative, generous or just richer, then maybe our love would be stronger and our dreams would come true. Kate and Rory went through a difficult few years financially. 'We're both quite bad at talking to each other and being nice to each other, but he never does simple things to be nice to me. The number of times I have said to him, "Why don't you just buy me a bunch of flowers?" and he then says, "Well, then you'll just get cross at me for spending money," which is a fair point, but you can get a bunch of tulips for three quid. Instead of doing that he comes back with a pot plant, when he knows I kill pot plants. He thinks, I can't do anything right, whereas I think, You haven't actually thought about this because you know I love flowers and I don't like pot plants. They just don't get it how those little things matter.'

The great value of romance lies in the small, simple gestures of daily courtesy, rather than in grand, ostentatious acts normally associated with traditional relationships, where the rich man rescues a woman and seduces her with expensive jewellery and regular bouquets. In your dreams, honey. It's that cup of tea you didn't ask for but really need; that film you forgot you mentioned wanting to see months ago that he has picked up for the weekend on the way home; that sharing of the daily minutiae of home life that build a loving partnership. 'It's an equal partnership and I don't feel subservient in any way but you have to have romance, it shows caring and consideration,' says Philippa, who has been married for twenty-six years. 'Sometimes he'll get home first and not only have cooked dinner but there's a candle and a rose there, too.' The big romantic gestures tend to happen during the earlier passionate, seductive stage. 'He did lots of romantic things at the beginning, which made me feel that I was really important to him and fall for him in a big way. I went to bed one night and found that he had scattered rose petals all over it. I hadn't ever met a man like that before, and was just bowled over by it,' says Megan. She and her partner have been together for many years and have a young son, so they are both knackered and the arguments have increased. 'I was in awe of him when I first met him, but over time we have stopped putting each other on a pedestal. We have got to know each other better, and now that we've got Tom to think about as well, we have had to face things and battle through adjusting our relationship to cope with the change. But he will still do little thoughtful things, like he will make a really nice meal if he knows I'm having a difficult time at work, or get a cheesy video out, which he won't enjoy but knows that I will.'

The smallest kindnesses can go a long way. It is noticing when the other could do with a compliment, an affectionate brush of the cheek, a glass of wine. We may live with each other, but if we were sharing our home with a friend would we forget the tiniest courtesies, the smallest civilities, which make living with anyone more bearable? Women are primed to provide and notice the needs of others, particularly as mothers, but when they feel nourished in a similar way by their own partners they are inclined to give more. As Robin points out, it doesn't take much for the smallest conscious gestures to become habitual. 'From as early as I can remember I have always loved women, and it is so funny to see the ineptitude of most men. Remember their name and use it occasionally, that scores points. Compliment them, notice when they have had a haircut, what does it cost? Just say nice things and then they love you. It is common courtesy, but most English men in my experience don't get it. If a woman comes into a room for a meeting I stand up. I just do. These are the things that allow boys to get on with girls.'

Accepting that our partner cannot ever be perfect is crucial to a life of togetherness. Much unhappiness and disagreement is fed by a residual resentment that our partner cannot satisfy our every need. We cannot be everything to our partner, either. 'Sam is a great romantic. He sees the world through tinted glasses and I do not,' says Diana. When I talked to Sam he could remember their wedding day in detail as a great day. They had a top table at the reception where Diana's family sat, but both of Sam's parents had died, so for him the day was a stark reminder of the family he had lost. 'It was very much about new beginnings for me, and I got very emotional and said in my speech that life is about friends and partnerships and how I had met my best friend.' Sam was also proud of the fact that he had proposed by the sea under a full solar eclipse of the sun because he felt it was 'textbook romantic'. But for Diana their wedding was more stressful: 'A blur, I don't like being on display and I don't think about all that because those big gestures are not important to me. It's always about the little things. I remember that he sent me some flowers after our first date – I have still got one of them – and while it was lovely to have all that romantic stuff at the beginning, to tell you the truth when he proposed under the eclipse I did think, "Hang on, I want to watch this, I am never going to see this again. Couldn't you just wait five minutes?" Which is an awful thing to think, isn't it? I've never said that to anyone. But I am very loving, I adore him. I just think all that romantic stuff got knocked out of me when Gary left me.' Diana is realistic about the fact that you cannot expect to get everything from one person. 'It's probably eighty per cent perfect, which is pretty damn good and as good as it gets, I reckon. He is a wonderful, kind and caring man and he makes me feel loved in a way that I have never known before, but there are gaps. I think there are gaps in every relationship, although people pretend that there aren't and that's what we row about. Those gaps threaten him because he thinks he ought to be able to give me everything I need but that's not how life works. He says things like, "I can't give you what you want intellectually," and finds it really hurtful that I don't have conversations with him about politics or culture. He tries, but then I disagree with him and he gets really upset, so I just don't go there. If I had been younger then those gaps in intellect might have been a problem for me, but we enjoy each other's company, I feel safe and happy with him, he feeds me physically and emotionally, I still think he is drop-dead gorgeous but I can't lie when he asks and say, "Yes you give me everything I need." Why does it matter when I can go anywhere for a conversation but only to him for this love that we have, which matters so much more?'

When you have been with someone for years, squirmed inwardly at their more disgusting bathroom habits and heard the same story over and over again around the dinner table, it does feel a little silly trying to revive romanticism. The romantic mini-break on an island in the Pacific beneath a canopy of stars could be heaven if your relationship is sound and you simply want to be together. But if you see that break as a cure-all for the deeper rifts between you which have never been properly addressed, then those rifts may well widen when you run out of anything new to say to each other and the sex is just as routine as it has always been. Better just to extend a simple gesture of affection, and then another, and then another. On such foundations a deeper love can flourish. 'Last year I was on this mission trying to be closer as a couple, and I remember holding his hand in the street and him looking at me as if I was completely mad,' says Kate. 'I told him I was just trying to be nice and he said, "Oh, that's OK then."' You can't go back to the electric passion of early romance, but you can wallow in a deeper, broader love that comes from respect, intimate conversation, looking out for one another and the more lasting romance of an equal partnership where each is affirmed by the other. With time that early doubt about a relationship 'not going anywhere' evaporates with commitment. You are already there.

'We were never hand-holdingly crazy about each other,' says Juliet. 'But now after three children and all these years together I feel more like that about him than I have ever felt, and he is more loving towards me than he has ever been. I think it takes men a while to shed their young, free and single self-image through the early stages of a relationship, and then they get to need you more.' Her husband Philip recognises that there is a maturity that comes with age and realistic expectations. 'Lots of people I know, and particularly men, have this idea that the grass is greener some-where else, or they don't like living in London and long to live in the country, or they want to run their own business. I don't have fantasies of other, possibly better lives.'

Love is: 'Admiration, respect, a desire to be with one another, and none of those things have changed in forty-five years,' says Tim. 'I still love Rose, and some of our best times are those we spend alone. When you really love someone you can trust them with any thought.' Love is acceptance. 'He has such qualities, I trust him one hundred per cent, he has dignity, he cares about a lot of things that matter and even though he can be weird and quirky and sometimes he drives me nuts, these are the things that make him interesting and make up the whole man I love,' says Sue. Love is sharing a history together, where lives become so entwined that imagining life without that person by your side is impossible. 'Romantic love is nice but it is superficial, and what's left once it's gone is far more important,' says David. 'The more we share the closer we get, and that then becomes indistinguishable from love, and if for some reason Katrina died and I had to start again that would be the biggest issue for me. You can find someone who is attractive, but to lose this kind of closeness and shared life? That is just a horrible thought.'

Love is feeling understood. 'It's having someone know you almost better than you know yourself,' says Jaya, who has been with her lover Charu for twenty-five years. 'There are so many things that I never need to say, she just knows intuitively. It feels like coming home. I can be completely myself. She is the one who has made me believe in myself, and I know that without her I would never have achieved most of what I have done in my life.' Love is friendship. 'I was infatuated with him when I first met him twenty years ago and obviously that doesn't last,' says Laura. 'But it's an enduring, respecting friendship, and I still want to talk to him more about most things than I would anyone else, and I will certainly advise my children to marry a good friend.' Love means you never feel alone. 'You are taken, and that is such an amazingly secure and lovely feeling that it cuts you off from a whole area of sadness and longing and loneliness,' says Stella. 'I have this great thing, she is the love of my life. Billionaires would spend their billions trying to get this if they didn't have it, and yet it is not quite what you expected in the romantic sense. It's like success or fame or any other ideal, in that it just seals you from the opposite emotion, which is very bad. It so reminds me of having that best friend at school.' Love is feeling at peace with someone. 'Sometimes we just spend an evening with him reading over there, and me reading here and we don't have to say anything to each other, or even go to bed at the same time, but there is this deep sense of companionship,' says Evie, who is in her fifties and has known her husband since she was a teenager. 'It's fantastic, so comfortable, priceless and I am really glad that we found our way through the really difficult times because I always had this sense that companionship in later life would be lovely.' Love is about sharing the day-to-day minutiae of life: 'Those everyday routines which unite us more than the clamour of passion,' as Isabel Allende writes in her memoir *The Sum of Our Days*. 'When we're apart it is this silent dance we miss most. We each need to feel the other one is near, always there in that intangible space that is ours alone.'

The trouble with romantic love is that there is little room for ambivalence, for the rough and tumble, for the shifts in power as circumstances change. It is too rigid, and does not afford each a sense of their individuality, as distinct from their life together as a couple, when it is those spaces between your love which allow it to flourish into something deeper and lasting. The myth that we each have a soul mate, a perfect match to our every need doesn't help. 'Our edges do not fit together so neatly as two torn halves of a stick of wood or a broken plate,' writes Robert Solomon in his book *About Love*. It is the differences between us which create dialogue and make life and love more interesting.

Love isn't a given; it is something you earn by giving, some-thing which can grow through adversity with enough heart between you. Tim and Rose went through two very dark periods in their marriage when he left her, in the throes of a midlife crisis, for another woman. That period is now referred to by both of them as 'That time when I lost my address,' says Tim. 'When you go through an experience like this together, even though you do it separately, in the end it is a shared experience, it is so painful that when you come out the other side and feel exactly the same about each other as you did before, it's like glue, a further dab of Evo-Stik, which reseals the relationship in a stronger way.' Jaya and Charu's partnership was also severely threatened by sexual infidelities. They had always hoped that their relationship would be open: 'As fiercely independent women, neither of us wanted to stop the other from doing what they wanted to do,' says Jaya. But when Charu got very involved with another woman, Jaya found herself so jealous that they had to reassess and renegotiate everything between them. 'I think the key to our longevity is that we have given each other absolute and complete freedom to be who they are even when that has been threatening to the other, and I think because we took that risk with each other our love now feels so solid. We trust that it could sustain us through anything. After twenty-five years we have watched each other grow and have supported each other through difficulties with our families, illnesses, the ups and downs of life, and consequently she is somebody I feel completely and totally at one with. It's a blessing. She still makes my heart skip. She just has to smile and I feel blessed.'

'I thought that love would suffice to smooth the way,' writes Anne Roiphe after thirty-four years of marriage in *Married: A Fine Predicament*. 'I thought I was up to anything life could toss at me. I wasn't. We have had many crises and troubles along the way and our love for one another did little to prevent them. What it did do was to hold us together, make a safe place in each other's arms where we could float and drift and find our way.' All of these wonderful things that a loving partner can offer do not come from some external magical force, from the bolt of romantic love or the rituals and vows governing marriage ceremonies. Simone Signoret got it right when she said, 'Chains do not hold a marriage together, it is threads, hundreds of tiny threads which sew people together through the years.' Alice feels that the love she enjoys with her husband of twenty years has been stable because they started off as friends. 'We never felt we were each other's soul mate. But there have been times when I felt I needed more emotional support than I did when I got married, or I do now. I was a bit of an emotional wreck after my father died, and I wanted him to talk and engage emotionally with me. But he couldn't really, and once I understood that and accepted that I couldn't change him, then in a funny way the battle stopped. I would have been quite nervous at that time about saying I felt secure in my marriage and that it would last, but now I feel that he is just a very nice person to live with, a good father, a good friend, funny and there is just this huge feeling of security about him. You would appreciate having him on the deck of the *Titanic*. I think there is also an age thing in that between the ages of thirty-five and forty-five there is a real moment when you think there is a chance to live another life with someone else. But after forty-five, that's harder, and it's not particularly tempting. Lying on a beach looking at this god of a new husband? It just doesn't work.'

There are times when people fall out of love with each other. 'To be perfectly honest there have been times when I haven't loved him very much,' says Imogen, who has been married to Gareth for thirty-four years. 'He behaved quite badly and had an affair when the children were small, and that has an effect on the emotional ground between you. It goes through different intensities and reinventions at different times. We had a passionate affair once, but now it's more of a companionable relationship with an affectionate respect for each other, which is a different kind of love, but it's still a love.' There are times when love shifts subtly into a different gear. 'You go through seven marriages, not just one,' said the Canadian campaigner Jane Callwood in her last interview before she died in 2007. She had been married for sixty-three years. 'There's the romantic one at the start, but that doesn't last. There's the busy one with kids, then there's the one where your career blossoms and now there's so much tenderness, it's just so sweet with lots of hugs and cuddling. To end the marriage and break up the kids – I know a lot of people do it, but if they do they miss all this. Marriage can have boring times, periods when it's very irritating but if the basics are there it's worth holding together. He said to me the other day, "Don't die, you've got a great bum." That's about as romantic as it gets now.'

'Increasingly, the individuals who want to live together are, or more precisely are becoming, the legislators of their own way of life, the judges of their own transgressions, the priests who absolve their own sins and the therapists who loosen the bonds of their own past,' write the German sociologists Ulrich Beck and Elisabeth

Beck-Gernsheim in their book *The Normal Chaos of Love*. 'They are also becoming, however, the avengers who retaliate for injuries sustained. Love is becoming a blank that the lovers must fill in themselves, across the widening trenches of biography, even if they are directed by the lyrics of pop songs, advertisements, pornographic scripts, light fiction or psychoanalysis.'

Romantic love has assumed unparalleled importance in our marriages and lifelong relationships, raising a whole new spectre of risk and cynicism which underwrites all our presumptions about relationship and all that it entails: sex, having children, how you fight and learn to respect each other's autonomy. Love is precious, and we have to take charge of it if we want to make it last. We have to walk into it with our eyes wide open.

'Love from its very nature must be transitory,' writes Mary Wollstonecraft in *A Vindication of the Rights of Woman*. 'To seek for a secret that would render it constant would be a wild search for the philosopher's stone or the great panacea: and the discovery would be equally useless, or rather, pernicious to mankind. The most holy bond of society is friendship.' In any significant relationship, falling in love is entirely different to the love that sustains you through time. Passionate love is exhilarating, absorbing, magical, transforming and irrational. The world beyond disappears for a while. But it doesn't last, and it is not necessarily the best reason for a long-term relationship. Yet from those seeds a different love can grow that is rational and roots us as individuals with a sense of safety, purpose and belonging. 'If falling in love is like taking off or flying, then love is like landing,' writes Ayala Malach Pines. 'Falling in love is flying high above the clouds; love is standing firmly on the ground. Falling in love is like a flower; love is like a fruit. The fruit comes from the flower, but they are two different things.'[24]

3

FIGHTING FOR YOUR LIFE

Some couples row once or twice a year, others once or twice a meal. 'There are couples who dislike one another furiously for several hours at a time; there are couples who dislike one another permanently; and there are couples who never dislike one another; but these last are people who are incapable of disliking anybody,' writes George Bernard Shaw in the preface to his play *Getting Married*. 'If they do not quarrel, it is not because they are married, but because they are not quarrelsome.' Argument is normal, healthy and cathartic. It helps to clear the air with honesty and restore balance. Argument helps us to see our weaknesses, to shake us out of complacency. 'My idea of hell would be us agreeing on everything. I don't want an ordinary life,' says Philip. 'We row a great deal about organising our lives; it's finding a balance, bashing a balance into place.' All couples have problems; it's how you deal with those disagreements and the incompatibilities between you that marks the difference between lasting stability and a downward spiral of deeper discontent which can lead to separation.

In unhappier relationships, each takes a stubborn position where the problem is always the fault of the other person. Minor hurts and irritations escalate gradually with time into major resentments and hostility, at which point neither feels able to acknowledge their part in the emotional dynamic between them. Unhappier couples become locked in a negative loop which can be difficult to break. They vent all their rage and disappointment with life on to each other. They bicker and lash out, airing resentments in front of other people, lobbing snide remarks through embarrassed third parties. 'Sometimes it's as if husband and wife were making a long-distance call to one another on faulty telephones,' says Marianne, a divorce lawyer in Ingmar Bergman's *Scenes from a Marriage.* 'Sometimes it's like hearing two tape recorders with preset programmes. And sometimes it's the great silence of outer space. I don't know which is most horrible.' The triggers may seem trivial to outsiders but for each estranged couple, a long history of difficulty feeds every insult. Every display of lack of love or understanding adds yet more salt to highly sensitised wounds. Each feels more sinned against than sinning. Each hits out angrily to avoid acknowledging their own mistakes, fighting for the right to take charge of their own life, or to control the other.

'You're probably past resolving things when winning matters more than anything else,' says Relate counsellor Paula Hall. 'It doesn't matter what the cost is, your partner could be lying in pieces on the floor, so long as you win.' We think of divorce and separation as something which, fingers crossed, we can avoid with luck, when the seeds are almost always sown near the beginning as minor differences escalate subtly into major disagreements, or outright and persistent hate. We trust everything to love and the romantic myth that 'we wouldn't fight if we loved each other', instead of approaching relationship pragmatically and establishing ground rules for the type of intimate talk which helps strengthen relationship. In unhappier relationships resentments are often fuelled by our own disappointments with life. One hates the other for not changing into the person they would like them to be, for not being rich enough, helpful enough, successful enough, loving enough or sexy enough. Rows are always about what the other person doesn't do, for not giving them that special something which they may never have been capable of providing in the first place. As couples grapple with the shared responsibilities of home and work, it has never been more important for couples to learn how to listen, negotiate, articulate their needs and desires to strengthen that partnership from the inside.

Argument is a natural consequence of two individuals who have different histories, emotional temperaments, dreams and expectations living in very close proximity. 'There must be a dumb, dark, dull, bitter belly tension between a man and a woman,' writes Stella Gibbons in *Cold Comfort Farm*. 'How else could this be achieved save in the long monotony of marriage?' It is, of course, the differences between us as individuals which make life more interesting and force each partner to change and grow. All couples, even happy ones, argue about the same things – money and what constitutes legitimate expense; children and how we bring them up; housework and who does what and how; the in-laws and the shadow they cast upon our relationship; and sex – when they can talk about it at all. But there is a world of difference between argument about daily difficulties, where each feels able to air their grievances and then, if they are lucky, see them resolved, at least in theory, compared to those arguments that are being fuelled by some deeper resentment or unhappiness.

It is accumulated grievances which tend to lead to divorce, not one-time events such as infidelity. John Gottman has studied hundreds of couples over a period of years in his 'Love Lab' in Seattle. He has observed distinct behavioural differences between more contented couples and those heading for divorce, and has identified what he calls the 'Four Horsemen of the Apocalypse': Criticism, Contempt, Defensiveness and Stonewalling. Couples row, but there is a big difference between expressing a specific complaint ('You forgot to get some milk on your way home') and complete character assassination ('You're always doing that, you're so stupid/selfish/lazy'). Contempt is even more destructive. It leads people to be defensive, covering up their true feelings because exposing them might lead to yet more humiliation. People in unhappy marriages can be brutal to each other. In Ingmar Bergman's *Scenes from a Marriage* Katrina tells her husband, in front of the two main characters of the play, that he nauseates her so much: 'I mean physically, that I'd *buy* myself a lay anywhere at all just to wash you out of my sex organs.' When couples express such outright loathing of each other, they create such acute stress that any rational resolution becomes impossible. Defensiveness may seem like a natural response to being attacked in an argument, but often it doesn't reach any sort of acknowledgement of a grievance or compromise. Stonewalling, or simply withdrawing from engaging in an argument, which can be a typical male response (as against criticism and contempt which are often female characteristics), also prevents any sort of positive resolution. While every relationship degenerates from time to time into using these tactics 'When all of the Four Horsemen are present during a conflict discussion', writes Gottman, 'we are able to predict divorce with 94 per cent accuracy, even with newly-wed couples.' Couples with this level of conflict between them tend to divorce earlier in their marriage, most of them within seven years, while those couples who allow their relationships to atrophy slowly by disengaging from each other emotionally, while everything seemed fine on the surface, were more likely to divorce between seven and fourteen years.[1]

Ursula recognises, now that her divorce is well and truly behind her, how some of the seeds of unresolved conflict were sown near the beginning of their seventeen-year marriage, although neither of them saw that at the time. Her ex-husband is a high-earning workaholic whose career always came first, and Ursula had to accept early on that she would have to leave her job, beloved friends and family in Toronto for London if she wanted to stay married. 'I will never forget it. He was standing in the bathroom peeing, his dick in his hand, and he started talking about this new job that he was almost certainly going to get and he said, "You know it is going to be in London eventually." We argued about that for nearly a year because I really didn't want to go, and he knew that.' They eventually relocated, had four children and Ursula gave up her own work to look after them. But she continued to resent how little he was there as part of the family, and how she felt like a single mother with a husband. 'He worked seventeen hours a day and said that when he was made partner we would have more time together. I believed him, but then when he was made partner it never happened,' says Ursula. 'His working life gave him everything he needed materially, a social and professional life, but our marriage started to fall apart because of the corrosive effects of that kind of job. I was angry a lot of the time. Nobody likes it but anger happens sometimes, and you have to be able to express it, and if you don't feel that whatever is making you that angry is even being acknowledged, as I did then, it never goes away. As far as he was concerned my anger was my problem, and if I had to characterise one thing that tore our marriage apart, that would be it.'

It takes two to row but it also takes two to resolve the row, and Ursula found that difficult because her ex-husband refused to acknowledge or take responsibility for his part in their deteriorating relationship. In some ways he was incapable of it, and emotionally inarticulate. When Ursula had four young children, early evening was full of the rituals of bathing them and getting them to bed, all at the top of a three-storey house. 'It sounds like nothing, but he started forgetting to take his key, so I would have to go downstairs and open the door for him when he came home, leaving one or all of the children in the bath and it would start with me saying, "Could you please remember to take your keys with you?" When he repeatedly didn't, it ended with me screaming, "Could you take your fucking keys, how many times do I have to ask you?" We separated for a bit that summer and I went to Cape Cod with the kids. Max came out to see us at one point, and I remember we took them to the beach and it was this really foggy day. We sat down with them and said, "Look, we're having some problems and we are trying to sort them out and you must be aware of that, so is there anything that you want to ask us or talk about?" The eldest one said, "I don't know how you expect to fix your problems, Dad, if you spend all your time playing chess on the computer." Max just stood up and walked off into the fog and left us there, leaving me to try to reassure the kids that everything was going to be just fine. I was so preoccupied with the kids that I didn't see what was happening right in front of my eyes. Looking back on it now I can see how I was selfish in my own way. I would say things like, "Don't you see how hard it is with four small children?" and, "You said you would do this or that and you didn't." I was hard, and I didn't manage the conflicts between us very well. I had such faith that we could just dig our-selves out of it, it never occurred to me that the harsh way I was feeling could be as corrosive as all of the other things that hap-pened between us. Some of my friends and my mother were able to say to me at one point, "Don't be such a bitch." I can see that in retrospect, but when you are in that kind of pain it gives birth to such anger. I can't imagine anything making me as angry again as that sense of one's family falling apart.'

When someone feels resentful, they can withdraw, unaware how that merely exacerbates the difficulties in their relationship. 'I got angry with him all the time and he would just stare at me, which drove me to complete distraction,' says Lydia, who has sep-arated from her husband after years of entrenched difficulties. 'He is very powerful, and I have to say that I was lousy at managing it. I would do the same thing over and over again. I would scream at him, expecting that I would get something back, but he would just look at me or walk out and nothing would ever change. He sees himself as this benign presence. He just sits there and says, "I can do whatever I like. I can screw up however I like, and you are just going to have to deal with it." I sit there and think, Why should I deal with it? Why should I have to manage my emotions in front of the children because of what *you* do?'

Beatrice has been married to James for long enough to understand how her husband disengages from her whenever there is high emotion because of events from his own past. His younger brother died in an accident when they were teenagers and he felt responsible. When their daughter was severely ill as a baby he found it so difficult that he never went to the hospital. 'When he distances himself like this it makes me feel really anxious, so I go in closer to try to engage him in conversation, which makes him withdraw even more and often with alcohol,' says Beatrice. 'My preferred way of sorting things out is to talk; his is to avoid conversation altogether. His self-esteem is so low that if I criticise or blame him for anything he just closes down.' She tells me a story from the previous evening to illustrate the typical pattern of dialogue between them. She had bought herself an iPod, which she uses whenever she has to commute on the train into Manchester. Her son helped her to download her favourite music, and it gives her a great deal of pleasure. Her husband borrowed it, and she had asked him to put it back where he had found it when he had finished so that she didn't have to hunt for it early in the morning when she next needed it. 'I'm getting my bag ready, knowing that I have to leave home at six the next morning and my iPod isn't there. I ask him where it is and his response is not to help me find it or say anything. So I ask him when he last used it and he says Tuesday, but that is all the response I get. So I have to ask another question like, "Where were you when you were using it," and then it begins to feel like an interrogation because again I don't get an answer which helps me to find it. I eventually find the iPod, but the headphones aren't with it, so then it's like trying to get blood out of a stone and he is getting cross and blaming someone else for taking them. I am trying to stay calm but actually getting really cross because if he had put it back like I had asked him to there wouldn't be a problem. But his response to that is, "Well, I will never borrow your things again. You are so mean about lending things," when that's not what it's about at all. It's about respect, returning my things and charged up, preferably.

It's all very childish and not fair because if it had been the other way around I would have engaged and tried to help instead of taking this kind of crossed-arms position.'

Women tend to define intimacy in terms of verbal interaction, and typically press for greater intimacy and emotional engagement than many men are able to give. Men tend to like expressing intimacy by sharing activities, and typically withdraw in a passive-aggressive way as a powerful means of attack. But it is a very dangerous one. It almost always gets worse as women push harder to the point of nagging to get their needs met, which forces men to withdraw even more. It is, according to marital experts Howard Markman and Scott Stanley, 'One of the most powerful predictors of unhappiness and divorce'.[2] American professor of psychology Edith Mavis Hetherington's landmark studies of divorce in America have identified five basic types of marriage based on the way that couples express emotions, solve problems and communicate. What she calls the Pursuer–Distancer Marriage, where women in the main push for more intimacy and communication while men stoically reject the need for emotional expression, is not just the most common type of marital relationship, it is also the one most prone to divorce.[3] Beatrice felt so estranged and unhappy at one point that she began to raise the subject of separation, but her husband withdrew even from discussing that. 'It is incredibly hard to think about how we might move this forward if he refuses to have any conversation about it. I know that if I make the move unilaterally he will blame me. I will become the bad mother for breaking up the family. But I am not a bad mother. He needs me to be the bad mother because of his own family history.'

Whether it is gender per se, or the socialised roles associated with each gender, which forces women in particular to react in a more vociferous and hostile way, is simply difficult to say without more research. Two studies of homosexual relationships in the 1990s found that gay men did not show a greater tendency to withdraw or distance themselves from conflict than lesbians, who in turn did not show a greater propensity for confrontation than gay men.[4] When people are distressed they tend to react in one of two ways – fight or flight. The chances are high that each person will have very different temperaments; indeed it is that difference which may have been attractive in the first place, with the more inhibited, for example, often naturally drawn to the more emotionally expressive. When it comes to arguing, that can make things difficult as one presses for dialogue and the other withdraws. When both have similar backgrounds over tolerance to argument, it can be easier to row and still get on. Robin and Hilary both come from large families where they used to have to fight to make themselves heard. 'Hilary is extremely stubborn and she will not give an inch, ever, which means that our kids have also had to fight it out to grow up. But I also think it has helped us to be more confident and open with each other,' says Robin.

Others grew up with so much terrifying screaming and shouting that they avoid conflict whenever possible. Ralph's grandmother and great-grandmother lived with them when he was a child in rural Ireland. 'All of these relationships were fraught. They were always at each other's throats, and I never knew who was not talking to somebody. I found myself excluded from these conversations for weeks, and my father used to withdraw and go into the front room and write. I felt in later life that the only mistake my father made was turning right into the front room – he should have carried on out the front door!' Ralph married young, and as his second partner Madeline commented when I met them, he spent most of those twenty-two years with a woman who became like his mother. 'To some extent that is true,' says Ralph. 'There was always something that you couldn't do, like you couldn't go for a pint after work and you couldn't go to the match on Saturday, and that just builds up resentment. Given the baggage I carry with the complexion of women I grew up with, the only way to cope with this constant nagging was to withdraw. It took me a long time to stop all that and say, "I *am* going to the match on Saturday." I know what needs to be done. I don't need to be shouted at because my instinct then is, "Well, actually, I am a bit busy at the moment." The big difference now is that Madeline is nice to me. My mother, my sister and my wife were not. There was always an angry issue.'

Juliet recognises that she and her husband often have a row at night – usually about the domestic chaos – when Philip has had a difficult day and been unable to let off steam in any other way. She becomes the punchbag. 'The other night I was sitting with the kids in front of the fire doing a jigsaw puzzle, having a really nice time, and he came home all critical and unreasonable about how I ought to keep the house a bit tidier. Instead of just swallowing it I go mad and then he says sorry. It's usually because he has had a bad phone call with his mum, or something has really got to him, so he takes it out on me. His dad has dementia and his mum has a pretty hard time with him, so she often rings him up to moan about it and he just has to take that. He never says "boo" to her but then he comes home and knows which buttons to push to make me furious, and he doesn't mind pushing them. But then I can't row with my mother, either.'

Unless resentment is openly discussed and acknowledged, unhappiness is more likely to erupt in what John Gottman and his associates have called a Harsh Start-up, which moves very quickly from neutral to negative because irritations have simmered for too long. 'We had tremendous arguments all the time, where we each fulfilled the other's negative predictions,' says Rajani. 'He has this idea that all women are nags. So I would make a perfectly reasonable request, which he wouldn't do, so I would ask him again and he still wouldn't do it so I did turn into a nag even though I was asking for something reasonable. It was always over something small to do with the children or money. And then he would say something, put me down, and I would just be so strung-out by that point that I would swear at him and then he would say, Why are you talking to me like that?'

Adanna deeply resents the fact that she has had to give up a professional job she loved because she had an impossibly long commute to get to work, and the company she worked for wouldn't give her a part-time contract. With three small children she decided to give up work completely. 'I never thought I would give up working, as a mother. I loved my work. I spent seven years studying to be a professional and I know there is more to me than just looking after the kids. I even thought about being a child-minder. We argue a lot more about money. We do try to sort things out but sometimes that just doesn't work, and all the anger and resentment comes out in our arguments. He's doing really well at work, and I don't even know if I can hold an adult con-versation any more it's got that bad, but he is out there in the world talking to other adults. Sometimes I really want to get my own back. He will say things that really annoy me, and I will wait for situations where I can throw everything he has said back into his face.'

Eliza has been married for nearly twenty years and is also honest about her resentments and the way her husband doesn't acknowledge them, but says they rarely argue. 'It's my own fault, I suppose, in that I will do anything to avoid confrontation. When I have tried to address the issues he is just so stubborn it's not worth it, so I will store things up instead and then have a dig so that I can't be accused of arguing or nagging. I just say things at opportune moments. It's always stupid stuff, like putting out the rubbish. Instead of saying, "For God's sake, can you put the rub-bish out," I will huff and puff and then about three weeks later I will say something like, "I did an experiment to see how much the bin would overflow before someone actually put it out." I can't bear to nag, and then there's the stress of having to check whether or not it's been done, and then asking again and then checking again, by which time you've wasted all your irritation on that and you might as well have done it yourself.'

When men find themselves at home doing more of the domes-tic work, they can feel equally unacknowledged and taken for granted. Diana works full-time while Sam is part-time and at home more with their baby and two teenage stepchildren. 'We tend to have a really big row about every six months, a good old

scream-up to clear the air a little bit,' says Diana, who acknowledges that he is a brilliant, hands-on, active partner but finds it
hard at times to say that to him because of her own history. Her
father expected her mother to do everything for him. 'Sam can be
quite selfish emotionally, although he doesn't think he is. He will
say things like, "I don't know what you'd do if I wasn't here," and
I'll say, "Well, we managed before you came along." Or he will
complain about doing all these things and no one's noticed or said
thank you. He seems to need thanking the whole time for everything he does, and sometimes I just can't be arsed. I don't want
to be married to a martyr. I don't want to have to live my life
saying thank you the whole time for something I didn't ask him to
do, for wiping down the surfaces again when maybe I would have
got round to it myself in ten minutes, or for not noticing that he
has moved the desk further over in the sitting room to make more
room. Yeah, it's great now that you have pointed it out, but I can't
be made to feel that I have to say sorry the whole time for being
who I am, for not noticing or not being more grateful. I could lie
like my mother would do for an easier life, but I have this fear of
being like my mother who lost her entire sense of identity in her
marriage, so I feel I have to fight with Sam to be who I am.'

'I could say something which sounds completely benign to
somebody else, but to him it is like a red rag to a bull, and there
will be an argument because there is a history,' says Adanna. 'I
could say something like, "Could you put the vase over there,"
and he will take it as, There you go, telling me what to do again,
or that I think he has put it in the wrong place. Or he will ask me
something obvious like, "Is this Babygro wet?" When my reaction
to that is, "Can't you tell? You're the one holding it!" It's like he
doesn't want to have an argument, so he just asks me what to do.
I know that's probably because I have inevitably told him off for
doing things wrong in the past, but it just drives me mad and it's
usually the really petty things, like he can't put the kids to bed
without calling up to me to ask me where something is. I just
think, For God's sake, you have had these kids as long as I have.'

Women berate themselves for nagging, and as Gottman's research suggests, a softer approach where the problem is explained in personal terms as to how it affects you is more likely to produce change and compromise. But that is only possible if men really listen and engage. A great deal of research suggests that the more a man accepts his partner's influence, and the more aware he is of the emotional dynamic between them, the happier they will be together.[5, 6] Women need to be happy for a marriage to be happy. Some research seems to suggest that they are more adversely affected physiologically by hostile argument than men, with blood pressure more elevated and increased levels of stress hormones, which remained elevated long after the argument had subsided.[7] It is usually women who decide to leave a relationship after years of dissatisfaction, while men seem to have a greater tolerance for bad marriages.[8] A quarter of the men in Edith Mavis Hetherington's studies of divorce said they had no idea that their wife had been thinking about leaving the marriage. 'Any man who isn't sold on the need to accept his wife's influence should consider the many pluses,' writes Gottman in *The Seven Principles for Making Marriage Work*. 'Studies have shown that marriages where the husband resists sharing power are four times more likely to end or drone on unhappily than marriages where the husband does not resist.' A more poetic slant was offered by Dustin Hoffman, who has been married for twenty-eight years, on the *Jonathan Ross Show* in 2009. When asked how he had stayed married for so long he replied, 'On a fundamental level you have got to be scared shitless of your wife.'

For couples to be able to argue constructively there has to be a sense of equity. Without that fundamental sense of respect for each other, an argument can soon turn destructive. When one partner feels out of control, they tend to try to control the other, which almost always translates into a subtle form of emotional manipulation. There is a fine line between control and abuse, which can be emotional or physical. Wendy met her husband when she was very young, fell madly in love and got married 'so quickly that I didn't really know him, but I felt that I wanted to be with this man for ever and ever'. She soon realised that she offered Ian a stability that he had never known as a child because his mother had walked out on them when he was small. 'I remember he would shout and get aggressive and it wasn't really physical at first, but he would smash objects like doors and tables. But what was more dangerous than the violence was the insidious level of control, a sort of enforcement of petty rules, a creeping tyranny, which can be anything from how you wrap the cheese when you put it in the fridge to how you put something in the rubbish bin, even to how you close the door. You think, I really love this guy and I want to make him happy so I will put the cheese in a plastic bag before I put it into the fridge because it's such a small thing, what do I care? If you try to argue with every little thing you are on a losing wicket in any relationship, but then you also apply that to the whole emotional spectrum of what goes on between you.' As the years went by, happy years mainly, Wendy began to realise that Ian often treated petty incidents with an explosive rage which she felt was inappropriate, and that by giving up on so many of these smaller issues she had in fact given him a means to control the entire relationship. They moved house when he wanted to. He had holidays abroad alone because he said he needed them and when she went away for work when their children were small she always sent them to their beloved childminder because he wouldn't look after them, even though he adores them. Wendy ran her own business as well as their domestic life. Things got progressively worse, and eventually Ian became physically abusive, hitting her and pulling her hair. 'We had huge rows. I remember there was one time when the children were in the car when they were small. He broke the car door by kicking it out and hurt my arm in the process, and he just kept saying, "I know you're going to leave me and you're going to take the kids," and they were sitting listening to this. He was just pushing and pushing me to do just that, even though I said, "No, I am not going to leave you." But actually I used to think about what it might cost to rent somewhere. Then when I did earn enough to be able to leave, I couldn't with any ease because I really wanted the kids to have the sort of stable, happy childhood, that feeling of safety that I had had. That is what mothers do. I put myself last. The arguments were never really about all those petty things, like not wiping the dogs' feet before they came into the house or putting the glasses into the dishwasher when he felt they ought to be hand-washed. They were always about all the other, deeper stuff, those fears that he couldn't verbalise.'

The line between someone being over-controlling and abusive is often hard to detect. Every conflict is in some sense about anger, and few things can exasperate us more than the irritating habits of a person we have to share the bathroom with. But in some people there is a deeper anger which is always present and 'one seemingly small issue after another is used to justify the expression of infantile rage. Disagreements become opportunities for vengeful assault,' as Marion Solomon writes in her book *Narcissism and Intimacy*. 'Rage wells up in response to lapses in approving or affirming responses. The experience of being failed and of psychic injury is much greater than the partner or an outside observer can fathom.' Deep feelings of betrayal or self-loathing, which stem from childhood, resurface as they relax into the security of an adult relationship. It is hard enough for any warring couple to settle on some sort of peace but, with a turbulent emotional history, a person's ability to resolve conflicts successfully can be even more compromised, simply because they have rarely experienced that themselves. Those with a more insecure background seem to be more likely to indulge themselves in uncontrolled bouts of anger and to be less forgiving of a partner who has hurt them, interpreting those wounds entirely narcissistically because they are less able to understand things from their partner's perspective. Adult attachment studies have consistently found that those with a more secure family background are more likely to be able to find ways of enhancing the relationship through stressful times with more supportive communication and compromise. Those with a more insecure family background either find it hard to prevent arguments from escalating or simply distance themselves to avoid engaging in the argument at all.[9, 10]

Long-term conflict bordering on emotional or physical abuse was a common factor in many of the unhappier marriages and relationships I encountered. Some experienced horrific violence, like Rajani who was hit regularly, had cleaning fluid sprayed in her face and was left haemorrhaging in the bath after a miscarriage because her husband refused to call an ambulance. 'I was three months pregnant and had given a bottle of milk to my son,' says Rajani. 'It was empty and he wanted more, so I put the bottle at the top of the stairs and asked my husband if he could get some. He said, "Why can't you do it," and when I said I was tired he started shouting at me so I threw the bottle down the stairs, I was so angry. He came up the stairs, dragged me down and pinned me to the wall, twisting my arms painfully. It was always something small which triggered such an extreme reaction.'

Others, like Jan, had to tread lightly around emotionally volatile and mentally unstable men for the sake of their own health and that of their children. 'Very early on in our relationship he would say, "Back off, don't try to change me," and I would say, "I am not trying to change you, just have a discussion." What happened was that I became the shock absorber of what he was incapable of addressing in other people. I always had to take responsibility for everything: working, earning the money, sorting the boys because there wasn't anyone else to take that strain. I was on my own. He wouldn't travel and take work outside London because he didn't want to be on his own. He wanted me exclusively, and as the children have got older we have rowed a great deal over how to bring them up. Mostly, though, we row over his intense jealousy of the attention that I give to them. When things got too much I would get sick and collapse because I couldn't express all that rage and resentment which had built up over time. I have got much better at saying things, but I still think I shouldn't have to say them, that he should know.' Matthew drank heavily and could get very aggressive, and at one point Jan left with her two sons and moved in with her parents. 'Things were really extreme, and some of the things he said were pretty frightening. It was self-loathing and self-destructiveness projected on to me and the boys, but it was scary. I went back to him because he said that he would do everything he could to be less aggressive, including giving up the drink, and that he would let me take the lead on what I thought was important for the family.' She kept trying, kept faith. 'It's the history. I'm not willing to give up hope because that's what it would be to say there are no more pleasant surprises. I have seen and experienced everything there is to see and experience with this person.' They have now separated.

Power inequities and issues over control, typically along patriarchal gender lines, are believed to be critical factors in aggressive marriages. Abusive husbands never accept influence from their wives, and while women can and do intimidate their partners, it is usually the other way around. The British Crime Survey shows that at least one in four women are victims of domestic violence at least once in their lifetime, compared to roughly 15 per cent of men.[11] That can mean anything from grabbing, pushing and forcing their partner into unwanted sexual activity to severe assault. Nearly half of all women murdered in the UK are killed by their partner or ex-partner, as opposed to just 8 per cent of men, and in many of these crimes conducted by women the violence perpetrated came after years of severe mental and physical abuse where they feared for their own lives.[12] Domestic violence can be emotional or psychological as well as physical. Humiliating put-downs, frequent yelling, intimidation, threats, refusal to communicate, provocative sexual interactions with others or extramarital affairs, unreasonable jealousy and extreme moodiness and dictatorial control over the family's finances are common in unhappy relationships and just as damaging as physical violence. These behaviours are unacceptable in any relationship, and have to be challenged and stopped. They are determined attempts by one to dominate or gain power over their partner, and often they will take care not to show this side of their relationship to the outside world, making it that much harder for their partner to question. These patterns of abuse are not solely confined to heterosexual relationships. Studies seem to show that between 25 per cent and 30 per cent of gay and lesbian relationships suffer abuse at some point, a similar percentage to heterosexual partnerships, which indicates that the causes are similar, irrespective of gender. All abusers typically suffer from very low self-esteem, personality disorders, antisocial tendencies, high levels of anger and hostility and are overly dependent on their partners.[13] They are also more likely to have grown up in either a violent or an abusive home. Often, when one partner tries to control the other it is because they are overly sensitive to being controlled, usually because they have experienced a very controlling and powerful authority figure in the past.

Wendy put up with years of argument, unhappiness and occasional violence, aware that her husband's family history influenced the dark side of their relationship. His mother left them when he was small because of the abuse she experienced from his father. Even Wendy's closest friends had no idea how miserable her marriage had become until Ian had an affair with a much younger woman, just as Wendy hit the menopause. That form of abuse was more than she could bear. 'I was so angry and hurt I just wanted him to die, to crash the car and not end up as a paraplegic because I wasn't going to look after him. That was the big betrayal, not the physical abuse. Go figure!' Wendy's anger was palpable when I first met her. They separated for the best part of a year, the full truth of their relationship became known to their friends and she found support from those around her, determined to continue alone unless her husband was prepared to change. When I met her again just nine months later the anger had vanished. She had regained a sense of her own value by standing up to his behaviour and now they are back together on an entirely new footing. 'It is possible to come back from the brink, and I never thought that would be the case. The key was that he didn't want us to split up, so we had lots of big conversations and he went into therapy, which denotes somebody who is prepared at least to look at changing,' says Wendy. 'When you have this kind of an explosion it gives you permission to say an awful lot of things that maybe I had kept quiet about. We had this really interesting conversation about what he used our relationship for, which was a real journey in itself, and he was obviously emotional and upset. But I felt empowered by it rather than upset because one of the things I wanted was respect, to be able to say, "You have to allow me to be who I am and not bully me around." Knowing that we were trying to work it out together really helped, but the whole thing made me realise how much I had hedged bits of my life to avoid his disapproval, which meant that I had ceased to enjoy being myself. He has put a lot of work into trying to be a nicer person, because it's not the content but how you say it which can be really destructive and painful. I think he has become more accepting of the dimensions of my character which don't exactly match the dimensions of his.'

Irrespective of whether a relationship borders on the abusive, we all have a tendency to assume that our partner's expectations of marriage will be much the same as our own. Most argument springs from a refusal to accept the other's right to be different. Too many couples live a life of quiet desperation, overly compromised to the point of being subsumed by the other because they are terrified of confronting the divisive issues between them or unable to let go of past difficulties, accept what they cannot change and move on. Couples in distress communicate very badly, often to the extent that they will avoid arguing altogether, believing mistakenly that any form of disagreement is destructive. Instead of talking, which, according to the directors of the Center for Marital and Family Studies at the University of Denver, Howard Markman and Scott Stanley, can resolve up to 70 per cent of a couple's difficulties, they express their resentment in critical, overtly hostile and unsympathetic ways. They can become so lost in blaming or attacking the other person that they enter a different state of mind, where it is almost impossible to reflect on what might actually be going on, or to read all those non-verbal signals that couples give to each other as reassurance of their love.

The romantic myth that 'we wouldn't fight if we loved each other' can make couples feel as if their relationship is doomed if they do row. 'You're fed this idea of how beautiful a relationship should be, where you say "darling" and you never argue, particularly in front of the children,' says Adanna. 'That's the bit I find really difficult. I don't understand how you can possibly hold in all that anger and wait until the kids are in bed, or you feel a lot better and have calmed down enough to be able to say, "Today I found it deeply annoying that you told me you earn the money so therefore you decide." Surely nobody can really live their lives like that, and that just makes me feel like I am failing.' Notions of idyllic, blissful contentment within the nuclear family die hard. By simply returning time and again to the basic truth that we are separate, autonomous and entirely different beings who have voluntarily engaged in this intimate relationship, we take hold of ourselves rather than react instinctively, in rageful ways. Anything that helps to soothe that immediate eruption such as counting to ten, as with a small, irritating child, or breathing deeply, will increase the likelihood of being able to resolve difficulties in a calmer moment when we can really listen to each other.

Relationships wouldn't be nearly as exciting if we were with someone who behaved and thought exactly like us. Oliver and Jerome have been together for ten years. Oliver is dynamic and fiery; Jerome is slower, and has helped Oliver to control his quick temper a little better. 'Our main point of conflict is the kitchen – so I cook – and driving. He is a very slow person, really slow. You say, "OK, turn right," Four . . . five . . . six . . . and it's gone, he's missed it, so there are countless arguments over that type of thing. I guess you do want them to be more like you, but it would be disastrous if there were two of me, and if there were two of him we wouldn't be where we are right now.'

Destructive argument is bad for our health, suppressing the immune system and raising blood pressure. In unhappier relationships each is more vulnerable, and suffers more, when it comes to coping with life's stresses. Couples with 'ongoing marital difficulty have high rates of psychological disorder, particularly depression in wives and alcohol abuse in husbands.'[14] Nor is it good for children. Attempting to hide hostility behind closed doors will not work, for children are highly sensitive to their parents' moods. A substantial body of research indicates that children and adolescents exposed to frequent and intense parental fighting experience negative consequences when it comes to their own health, behaviour, school work and relationships with friends.[15,16] Up to half of the emotional and behavioural difficulties of children and adolescents such as depression, aggression and withdrawal is thought to be caused by living with ongoing conflict in their parents' relationship.[17] When parents are unhappy or living with relationship difficulties, they are often less sensitive to their child's needs, or signs that they are themselves stressed. Conflict between parents and children can get worse as parents become more hostile. Sometimes parents scapegoat or blame a child for their difficulties. Other parents over-invest in their child emotionally, compensating for the lack of intimacy in their own lives, which isn't good for healthy development in children either.

Children don't get used to conflict, they grow more sensitive to it. Their emotional stability is rocked to the core by uncertainty, and they are highly likely to blame themselves for their parents' difficulties. They need their parents to be a calm and stable presence, and are often far more aware of that importance than their parents are. A survey of young people's attitudes to parents in 2007 found that seven out of ten teenagers considered parents getting on well together to be one of the most important factors in raising happy children, while only a third of parents felt the same way.[18] This may be an old-fashioned view, but if we are adult enough to bring children into the world, we ought also to be adult enough to be prepared to do whatever it takes to minimise the conflicts between us in order to protect those we love who have no part in our personal battles. Learning how to nip disagreement in the bud doesn't just improve marriage, it also eases the process of separation should that relationship break down completely. According to Edith Mavis Hetherington, who has conducted more than thirty years of research on divorce, the emotional turbulence of an angry marriage full of argument is likely to mean that the divorce and post-divorce years are full of argument, too.[19] In many cases children really are better off living with divorce if their parents cannot face their own demons head on and resolve their difficulties. But judging that moment isn't easy for parents, either. Is this just a dip, for all lifelong relationships wax and wane, or is this a more permanent emotional disengagement? How unhappy do you have to be to leave? Libby has been married for forty-one years but her husband has been depressed, argumentative, grumpy and abusive, humiliating her in public for the past fifteen years. 'If I'd realised then that this was how we were going to end up there's no way I would have stayed this long, but you always think it will be better next week. No one tells you how to do this bit – is this normal?'

So how do we assess the argument stakes in our relationship? Happier couples find ways to break negative loops of conflict before they become entrenched, with apologies, acceptance of some responsibility for their part in the disagreement and constructive discussion, which tries to resolve their differences. They are more able to edit their responses with an eye on long-term goals rather than short-term retaliation. They manage a running banter, often lanced with humour, where everything is aired gently, nudging each other towards amending their ways. Sureena and Spike learned how to talk to each other early on in their relationship because they had such huge hurdles to surmount just to be together at all. Sureena is a Muslim who was expected to enter an arranged marriage; Spike is white and eventually converted to

Islam so that they could be together. 'Because of all that, we had to talk about things like how we might live, or having children,' says Spike. 'One of the things we said early on was that we would always be honest with each other. Whatever was going on with us or with other people we would always tell each other, and that is what we have done.' Sureena chips in with a joke at this point. 'I am very opinionated and I am always right . . .' 'And that can make things very difficult,' continues Spike. 'But we sort it out, we never seethe. Why waste your life seething for a week when you can sort it out?'

Honesty in a relationship takes effort. 'Speaking your mind to someone you care about is something I have only recently learned to do,' says Charles, who now lives with another divorcee in her late fifties. 'Maybe it's all that conditioning as a child that you have to be nice to people. Jilly speaks her mind, and that's very refreshing.' Happier couples feel safe enough within a trusting, cherished partnership to be truthful without losing love. 'If we slip into slightly diggy mode,' says Robin, who has been married to Hilary for more than twenty years, 'then we just say things to each other like, "Don't talk to me like I am a kid," or, "I don't want you to undermine me in front of our friends." That usually works. It's having complete trust in the other person, knowing that we can say anything. We can say, "You are really pissing me off," to each other without taking it personally.'

When happier couples fight they tend to push each other up to a point where the warning signs flash, indicating that the argument is spinning out of control, and then retreat. Men typically get defensive or physically agitated and attempt to withdraw when they feel overwhelmed by an attack, while women tend to show fear or sadness.[20] Even in the most heated arguments they will allow completely irrelevant topics into the row – breathers, an olive branch of peace – which allow each to take stock, calm down and agree on something seemingly trivial before they resume discussing that deeper disagreement between them. Unhappier couples tend to interpret this strategy negatively, accusing the other of not listening or caring by changing the subject. Most importantly, happier couples show each other that they care enough about 'us' to attempt to reach some sort of compromise, even though they may fiercely disagree. They attempt to understand their partner's position so that they stand a chance of reaching some solution. David and Katrina have been together since university, but now that they have a baby, as well as two full-time careers, 'There are a few more disagreements because we both care about him, and the differences in our expectations show, so sometimes we have to talk about why something is important to us now,' says Katrina. 'Ten years ago I would have found it really hard to understand why Katrina might be doing something which caused us to row,' says David. 'But now that I know her so well I can put her reaction into a context and she will say, "Look, I want it done this way because I need to know . . ." And that means we usually find a way to reduce the tension. Katrina is very organised and I am a bit more spontaneous, so occasionally I do feel that home is the place where I really want to let go – let's not plan every fifteen minutes and just wing it for once – but that's because we are different people.'

Having children toughens happier couples up. There are acres of possibility for argument, but their commitment to each other because of the needs of the children overrides other concerns. Richard and Carol have been married for eight years and have two daughters aged one and three. 'We almost don't have time for rows, and there doesn't seem much point,' says Richard. 'If one of us says something which is over the mark or does something which is perceived to be unfair, I think it's more of a case of just trying to get on with it because of the kids, maybe saving things up for a chat later. Now that we know each other so well, we can put the problem into a wider context. It might just be that we're both tired and haven't had much sleep. There are moments when we both say things we don't mean in the heat of the moment, but we do try to sort out those smaller problems before they snow-ball.' Happier couples continue to reveal understanding, admiration and respect for each other, as well as pride in the way they have survived difficulties in their past, together. They can say 'I hate you' and mean it at that moment, and then find ways to lance that rage with humour.

'We usually end rows by laughing because one of us will admit to being a complete arse,' says Katrina. 'We usually get to the point where we will have some sort of perspective on our behaviour because it's mostly that one of us is being unreasonable about something, or because we're grumpy and tired or ill.'

There are plenty of common pitfalls which can lead to unnecessary rows. Couples often find it hard to remember to exchange simple courtesies, the small kindnesses integral to sharing or caring for someone, let alone talk when something major has happened to disrupt the equilibrium. We just expect the other to know, by osmosis, that we are pissed off. We almost dare them to guess because we are so scared of giving voice to our feelings. 'The only thing that drives me mad is that she doesn't talk,' says Ella. 'I get a sense of what is going on in her head but way too late, and by that time we are at boiling point. Perhaps I don't notice things enough or I can't read how things are going, but all of a sudden I realise that I have basically been pissing her off. I don't get pissed off by little things. I really can't be bothered to have an argument about them, but what annoys me is that she doesn't vocalise things at the stage when it's not a big deal.'

Sandra and Jane are in a similarly happy relationship. Jane acts as a calming, stable balance to Jane's greater volatility. 'We never row. Jane getting angry means she will raise an eyebrow and then two weeks later she will say, "I was really angry with you." My reaction to that is, "Can you tell me that in future? I can't read eyebrows." I am not argumentative but sometimes I feel that issues are not resolved because we don't have a heated argument.' Sandra understands that Jane finds it hard to show her emotions because her parents don't much either; she has never seen them row. But what that means is that Sandra can't get cross without it causing a major ruction. 'One night I had cooked dinner and Jane was on the phone and wouldn't get off it, so I took her dinner upstairs to her and slammed the door behind me and shouted something, and she got so upset that she left the house. I stormed off in the car and came back thinking she was in the spare room, so double-locked the front door. She then couldn't get into the house and had to go and sleep in the local Travelodge, and you'd swear she thought it was the end of the relationship, all because I had raised my voice.'

Florence feels that they almost always argue because some tone of voice sets the other off rather than the subject matter. 'People in straight relationships might think it must be lovely to be having a gay relationship with your best friend, and that it must be so much simpler, but sometimes we're both so emotionally hyper-sensitive that we could do with an emotionally inarticulate man to calm us down. We are so in tune with each other we think we can read each other's minds when of course we can't, and at times we are too thin-skinned and too bloody articulate, everything has to be discussed.'

We have such busy lives, particularly as working parents, that we tend to put off important conversations about 'us' until we have the time. We put our relationship at the bottom of the list of things to do when it should be at the top because so many other aspects of our health and happiness spring from that base. Sarah feels more able to analyse her own part in the break-up of her marriage now that she has some distance from it, and enjoys a far more nourishing relationship with someone who makes her talk and won't let things fester. 'In the long term I think I had a role to play in terms of communication. I was equally to blame in that we didn't talk about things enough right from the beginning, and that kind of built up. That's so easy, especially when you have children, and sometimes even now I feel like I'm bottling things up. I have to make a conscious effort to tell myself not to do that but to say something before it festers.' It is often only when couples part that they can begin to look back on their time together with some sort of objectivity. 'The fact was, the man to whom I was once married, and I both did a poor job of treating each other with love, a poor job of being partners to each other. We knew nothing of stepping outside of our own stories with sufficient imagination and compassion to recognise what the other person's story might have been,' writes Joyce Maynard in *The Stories We Tell*. 'What he offered I didn't value. What I offered back he also missed. We were two people who loved each other, I think, but we had such different ideas about how to express it. The other people we sought out (both long gone from our lives now) were really just a way of making the connection, somewhere, that we couldn't make with each other.'

Major relationship horrors such as failing to turn up at an important funeral or leaving your children on a train are rare. It is the habitual minor insults and injustices which tend to trigger conflict. Then when some significant and tangible crime happens we hurl all our hostility there. 'That's the catch about betrayal, of course: that it feels good,' writes Nora Ephron in *Heartburn*. 'There's something immensely pleasurable about moving from a complicated relationship which involves minor atrocities on both sides to a nice, neat simple one where one person has done something so horrible and unforgivable that the other person is immediately absolved of all the low-grade sins of sloth, envy, gluttony, avarice and I forget the other three.'

When you dissect the anatomy of a major argument, it is usually something seemingly small which triggers an immediate nuclear reaction because it touches a raw nerve, some deep fear or sensitivity about being left, or unloved, or not in control. The wounded one then lashes back to protect that vulnerability and makes things worse. When life is stable and we feel in control, all of the more fragile aspects to our personalities remain hidden. As soon as life gets stressful they surge to the surface. It's easier then to turn our partner into the villain as a form of defence, avoiding the need to confront our own latent desires or disappointments, which have emerged because of something they did or didn't do. The longer couples find themselves locked in this form of

attack–defence, the more they distort the emotional landscape of
their relationship and make honesty less possible. One blames the
other for their behaviour; the other accuses them of overreacting.
Both may be right but each occupies such an entrenched and
polarised position that neither has enough distance from the problem to be able to view it objectively. 'There are no victims or
villains – or saints or devils – in marriage,' writes Maggie Scarf in
her classic book *Intimate Partners*. 'There are instead only active
colluders, each carrying a disclaimed area of the spouse's internal
territory as part of what is a mutually agreed-upon, unconscious
arrangement.'

It is incredibly hard for most couples to know how to solve the
larger ructions that can occur when so many of us lack the psychological or diplomatic know-how to solve even minor disputes.
There is now an industry of therapists, self-help books, agony
aunts, websites and charities on hand to help us when we get into
difficulty, and many of them are lifesavers. However, the implied
assumption is always that there is a higher marital standard which
many of us are failing to reach, and that relationships are fixable
from the outside, like houses, by professionals who barely know
us. We turn to strangers with no knowledge of our history, our
emotional make-up or our partners when we cannot solve the
problems or the divide in our lifelong relationship ourselves. All
of these outside agencies can be helpful, particularly if couples
turn to them at the earliest hint of trouble in their relationship,
before they find themselves locked into patterns of conflict where
the destructive bickering is masking deeper resentments or
unhappiness. Many find that therapy helps them to see how their
own pasts are influencing their relationship, and extrapolate what
is really going on in the emotional dynamic between them. The
trouble is that so few people consider it a viable option. A survey
conducted by the BBC in 1997 found that 75 per cent of married
couples had experienced serious problems, but only 8 per cent
had tried to resolve them with the help of a counsellor.[21]

Gareth and Imogen hit a major low in their thirty-year marriage when Gareth had an affair and left when their children were small. When he wanted to come back, he did so on the understanding that they both went to counselling together. 'It was incredibly helpful because we didn't have the skills to unravel the problems, and we certainly didn't have the language to talk about them. I had an affair for all the obvious reasons in that we had two small children, had got used to each other, and I felt Imogen was more in love with our son than she was with me. There were all these feelings, but talking about them was too difficult. The therapy helped us to realise that we could address difficult things without that becoming terminal. The unhappiness we both felt at the time was because neither of us felt like an equal partner, and I still haven't worked out how it can be that both of us gave the impression of being the dominant partner while actually feeling as if they were the inferior one,' says Gareth.

Imogen also feels that couple counselling helped them to communicate better. 'The resentments and frustrations we had were laid out on the table and we were able to see what we wanted from each other, which is one of those questions that you don't ask yourself very much. There was no doubt in my mind that I felt everything was on my shoulders and that he was just swanning around having a nice time. The therapist also helped me to see that you don't have to be afraid of all the nasty things you feel within a relationship, like anger and rage. Gareth's family was much more robust in the way they resolved conflicts, and he isn't aggressive but he has a punchy way of debating things or arguing his case, whereas arguing was a big no-no in my family. You couldn't express an opinion, you just had to listen to authority. The things that cause friction between us tend to be low-grade things which hover in the air and we don't really address them very well. Sometimes it takes something else to break those issues out into the open. We had very different ways of dealing with things and that difference was brought out by a therapist.'

For a great many other less fortunate couples, by the time they have acknowledged to themselves or to each other that they need outside help, it is too late. Some researchers estimate that it can take couples five to seven years to seek help for their difficulties.[22] People are often reluctant to admit that they have problems they cannot solve themselves, particularly in the early stages of their relationship, when marital therapy can paradoxically be most beneficial. The more distressed the couple, the less likely counselling is to work. They have become so emotionally disengaged from one another, their arguments so entrenched, that it takes a miracle to prevent them from separating. Often one partner is aware of that, and simply needs an outsider to support and help them come to terms with the end of their relationship.

The little research that there is indicates that therapy helps prevent breakdown in less than one half of all couples.[23] There is even less research when it comes to the long-term effects, but one small study found that 30 per cent of those who found marital therapy helpful subsequently separated two years later, and another study found that 38 per cent of the sample had divorced four years later.[24] It takes time for a professional to get to know you both as individuals, as well as the emotional dynamic between you, time one or other of you may not have. A survey conducted for Relate of 2,000 people found that 38 per cent terminated counselling after the initial assessment interview, and a further 33 per cent ended the sessions before their therapist thought they should do so.[25] Therapists may not necessarily have any solutions or, indeed, be any good at their job. When people are in great personal difficulty they are often very clever at disguising their contribution to the dynamic in their relationship.

Lydia says that Paul was always charming and charismatic with her family and friends: 'Everybody adored him. I can remember therapy sessions where I could see the therapist thinking, "What is this woman talking about?" because he would come across well, he talks the talk. He would sit there and tell her that the only thing that really concerned him was his children. He would be frank and lucid, and you would think, I have finally got through, and then the next morning, bang! It's back to square one.'

Therapy can, in some instances, unsettle the foundations of a relationship and make it worse, particularly when one of the pair is reluctant to disclose their true feelings in the first place. Treating older couples and those with traditional gendered divisions seems to be harder than helping younger couples, or those with more flexible attitudes. Studies also indicate that only a minority of couples with a depressed partner recover their relationship with marital therapy, for depression can be far more destructive to relationships than the events which triggered the depression in the first place.[26] Couples rarely presume to question the therapist about the various techniques available and which s/he intends to use, or their attitudes to marriage and relationship, when these are inevitably influenced by their own personal history. It can also be difficult for therapists to distance themselves enough from the impact your marital difficulties have on *them* to be of much objective use to *you*. Distinguishing between marital and individual psychological difficulties is never easy, and I have heard several examples of bad advice given to couples in trouble, of therapists taking sides and passing unhelpful judgements on their partner.

Intimacy is not something you can learn easily from books or counsellors. We learn how to improve the way we relate to lovers largely through experience. The onus has to be on us as individuals and as couples to face divisive issues head on, however painful that may be. There is no one right way to have a relationship. The modern emphasis on having a high-quality relationship, coupled with an industry of professionals offering 'treatment' for marital difficulties, easily translates into the notion that all marital problems are solvable. Many aren't. It is only when we accept that each of us brings a whole raft of different emotional temperaments, past experiences and expectations of intimacy to the relationship and can talk honestly about them that we can begin to understand that precious third party – the chemistry that we create together. Few of us enter marital therapy to change ourselves; we are usually seeking ways to change our spouse. 'We seek out simple tips, techniques and benedictions that tell us how to communicate and be compassionate,' writes David Schnarch in his book *Passionate Marriage*. 'But techniques can't dissolve interpersonal problems – only changes in us can do that.'

Key aspects to resolving arguments, or preventing them from snowballing to the point where they become entrenched, lie in understanding the influence of our family histories and the importance of individual integrity and self-respect. But so too is the courage of honest communication. 'Whether we opt for the familiar trio of accusation, blame and coercion; the evasive tactics of avoidance, minimisation and denial; or a more subtle strategy of putting up defensive barriers and striking back through passive resistance, we end up not being heard and not feeling safe in a sanctuary that should be safe for both of us,' write psychologists Andrew Christensen and Neil Jacobson in their book *Reconcilable Differences*. It is only when each can articulate their resentments and face their fears that some sort of resolution can be found.

Evie's three children are now teenagers, but money troubles when their children were small provoked one of the greatest strains on their thirty-four-year relationship and they argued much of the time. Neither of them earned much, but it was only when they borrowed a friend's house in France for a holiday and her husband's bank card was cut up in front of their eyes that she realised the extent of their financial difficulties. He had a county-court judgement against him for a small amount of money owed on a credit card, which meant they were blacklisted and couldn't borrow money to buy the freehold on their house when it was offered to them at a very reasonable price. 'If I had known about this small debt, I would have borrowed the money off my parents and we needn't have got ourselves into this ludicrous situation. It was a complete nightmare because he was so difficult about it, he just withdrew and wouldn't discuss it.' Their relationship hit rock bottom before Evie realised that the only way forward was for her to take complete charge of their finances. 'He comes from a very traditional working-class background where his father never discussed money with his mother, so that was what he did with me. I might not be very good with money, but he was clearly absolutely hopeless. I don't like having to do it but at least now I know where I stand. I also insisted that he got a proper job with a regular income because we had a mortgage and two small children and he did do that which really helped our relationship as well as our finances.'

The signs of hidden resentments fuelling argument are helpful. When you find you are having the same conversation or argument over and over again without making any headway; when trivial issues seem continually to trigger an explosive reaction; when sarcasm begins to dominate, or both of you are avoiding certain topics of conversation or levels of intimacy at all times; when one of you seems to keep a running score of who does what – these are valuable signals of the need for a bigger talk about what you want from life, and each other, in a calmer moment. When one feels the need to talk about something, there can be so many other distractions: noisy kids, all those things that need to be done nagging in one's head, tiredness, boredom, inattention to what the other is really saying, the feeling that you've heard it all before, that the other doesn't focus properly, which then gets picked up as indifference or rejection. All too often it is easier to attack in the heat of an argument than it is to listen and consider how we might be contributing to the problem. Indeed, argument is often a way that couples try to reconnect intimately with each other because they haven't got the time to do so any other way.

Dusty and Frank have been married for twenty years and have a contented working partnership with four children. 'There aren't any deeply divisive issues between us, nothing bad has ever happened, but we do have terrible escalating rows,' says Dusty. 'You get hit in a vulnerable spot, so you just hit back. Neither of us is very good at taking criticism, and we aren't great at saying sorry, either. There's no one to prick the bubble, although now that we have the kids, teaching them to say sorry means that you learn how to do it yourself. You learn how to stand back from situations a bit more. You know when someone has said something true but hurtful, and I have got better at acknowledging that truth rather than just feeling hurt and hitting back with something equally hurtful. Sometimes we have face-offs, and then Frank decides he needs some sex so he says sorry and then it gets better.'

Some psychologists recommend couples carve a set period out of their busy lives without phones, books or any other distractions, to dedicate to listening to each other. For many this feels uncomfortable. They have used life's distractions to avoid talking to each other for so long that they have to breach hours of silence before they can begin to communicate. For others it feels risky. They might discover things about themselves, or about each other, which they have been resolutely avoiding. It could spell the end of their relationship. But perhaps it is better to know what each really feels and wants than to continue feeling emotionally dead to love. More often than not couples find that by making a positive effort to break down the walls between them, they bridge gaps and forge a deeper intimacy.

If you find yourself constantly blaming your partner, or expecting them to fix things when they go wrong, then it is perhaps time to work on yourself rather than on the relationship. Get some distance from the relationship, assess it from the outside almost scientifically in order to try to get some perspective on the whole truth. Think perhaps of how you might have come up against similar difficulties with other people, or how others might behave in a similar situation to see how you could be contributing to the problem, and lose some of that righteous indignation. Resolving arguments is only possible when both partners accept the need for the smallest change. If you find yourself vehemently disagreeing whenever your partner criticises something about your behaviour, that is a useful sign, a pointer to an aspect of your own personality you are unaware of and therefore over which you have the least control. When you find yourself taking things personally, ask yourself why. Forget about the idea that the relationship is something other that has to be worked on. It is made up of just two people, and you are one of them.

When couples are prepared to go to the brink, when they are able to find enough distance between them even through a temporary separation, they are more able to change the rules of their relationship if they are to come back together. Tim and Rose met at school and have been married for forty-two years. They separated twice when Tim had affairs with two separate women. 'We stopped talking to one another, just like my parents did. Their marriage was terrible; they didn't speak to each other for the last thirty years,' says Rose. 'I was doing a really stressful job and I know that's no excuse, but I would come home and go to bed, so the sex stopped and the talking stopped.' After Tim left, Rose found greater self-confidence because she had to do things without him. She went to India on her own, did an abseiling course to master her fear of heights and the house was much tidier, the way she liked it. Now that they are back together, Rose has found that her depressions have eased, 'Because I know I can live on my own and rely on my own resources. It's stronger because we talk more. Now I tell him when I am unhappy about something rather than brood about it for weeks, and we are both more honest. If only he had told me that he didn't like me fat. It's ridiculous not to be able to say that, and of course the moment he left I lost four and a half stone. I also discovered that he didn't like me going to bed early – it was as if we were in different time zones. He gets up very early and I hate mornings so now I try to be nicer to him in the mornings and he tries to be nicer to me at night. Although he doesn't come up to my standards of tidiness, at least he tries now. I feel much stronger, more grown up, more in control, and we are both more honest. You can't ever take a relationship for granted, that's what counselling has taught me because when you take it for granted, you stop talking.'

There is a big difference between being honest about what irritates you or makes you erupt angrily, and cruelty – using that honesty as a weapon in your arsenal. Knowing the difference between the two, between helpful and harmful forms of speech, can make a big difference to the nature of the relationship. Often people are more brutal than honest, letting rip emotionally in uncontrolled, hurtful statements disguised as constructive criticism. 'We never row. I don't think we have ever had a row in twenty-two years,' says Alice. 'I scream quite a lot but it's never a row. I always thought that was a huge failing in our relationship, not having that kind of openness, but the other side of not having rows and talking about our feelings is that you don't destroy things, you don't say really damaging things which can never be unsaid. You may be thinking them, but that's very different to saying them. On the few occasions when I have really exploded and said something hurtful, that has shocked him into realising things. But I am glad that these have been rare.'

Marcus was happily married for nineteen years until his wife died of cancer. Even though they were honest and open with each other 'I held back on certain things. She always felt there was a better life with more money, and she was accused by others of being a workaholic. In the heat of an argument I would say that too, because that's what marriage is about – you have to give your partner crap when there is crap to unload. It was like a cleansing process if she was uptight about something, and then things would get better again. But I also kept my mouth shut a lot of the time to keep the peace. There has to be a sensitivity which works both ways. Why make waves when you don't have to?' Louise has been married for fifty-five years and says they hardly ever row because she has kept a lid on her irritations, particularly now that her husband is so frail and consequently even more irritating. But she has been shocked in recent months by the way he has been unable to hide his true feelings. 'He has told me not to talk so much in front of other people, and I have put on a lot of weight, like my mother did at this age. I think he can be quite critical about how much I eat and how I don't look after my figure enough. Isn't it interesting how you remember the hurtful things that people say? He once said that he felt cheated if I didn't look nice and I thought, I don't want to be loved for how I look. But I didn't say it.'

Couples build up a marital bank account over time, where every loving and positive gesture adds to the balance and every display of contempt or hostile criticism is tantamount to a withdrawal. The more they draw down on the account, the more destructive their arguments are likely to be. Words may be important to communication, but so too are the tiniest gestures of care and respect. In John Gottman's Love Lab, happier couples were generally nicer to each other, offering on average five times as many positive interactions as negative ones, responding to 85 per cent of their partner's attempts at connection even if that was just with a smile.[27] 'Positive engagement seems to envelop the couple like Teflon,' write American psychologists Benjamin Karney and Thomas Bradbury. 'Couples with relatively poor problem-solving skills will achieve marital outcomes that are no different from couples with relatively good problem-solving skills, provided that they display high levels of affection, humour and interest. It is only when spouses display relatively low levels of these positive emotions that poor skills appear to be detrimental.' What might appear to the outside world as a troubled and antagonistic relationship is quite possibly rock-solid, simply because each feels cherished through the millions of other minor, wordless ways in which couples daily express their affection for each other. They don't ignore each other. They turn to each other and engage over seemingly trivial things. They are more playful and teasing of each other's differences and drawbacks. In John Gottman's Love Lab happier couples interacted in this way up to seventy-seven times in ten minutes, while the more distressed couples only managed ten to twenty types of connection. The more they connect, the greater the intimacy that builds between them, which helps to buffer their relationship during the more stressful times.

The ideal relationship consists of two adults. Real grown-ups are autonomous. They are able to take care of themselves. When

they are anxious or stressed they look to their partner for understanding and support rather than expecting them to sort things
out. They have a clear picture of who they are within the partnership, someone with limitations and shortcomings who is able
to deal with the anxieties and issues which arise from their own
lives, family backgrounds or circumstances. This ability to hold
on to who you are changes how you interact with your lover. It
means you place less stress on the marital bond and consequently
make it more stable. It means you are more able to avoid negative
interactions and turn them into positive ones. A sense of personal
autonomy means that you are less likely to feel the need to match
your partner's angry temperament during arguments, or become
low when they do. It means you are more open to being influenced by them because your sense of self is resilient enough not
to be so shaken by what they say that you become defensive or
compromise too much. You do not misinterpret argument as
falling out of love but acknowledge that ambivalence, irritation
and sometimes even hate are integral to love. You can accept your
partner as different with opposing views on some subjects without seeing them as a threat to the relationship, and become a little
more self-aware as a consequence of their honesty and the mirror
they hold up to you.

But that's not easy. It isn't easy to accept criticism, to change
habits, to challenge our insecurities and fears. It isn't easy to retain
a sense of autonomy as an individual when so many aspects of
sharing a life with someone encourage you to give that up. You
have to be self-conscious. If the problem is his rage, then refuse
to bear the brunt of it and absent yourself until he has calmed
down. If the problem is her 'nagging', then why are you so determined to avoid meeting simple requests, which might stop the
harassment you find so irritating? If the problem is money, how
do your own values, expectations about earning power or failed
dreams fuel that conflict? If the arguments centre around work,
are those long hours away from home really necessary? Is that
tension being fed by a deeper jealousy of the other's triumphs or

freedom? If it's sex, and there are differences in desire, is it that you really don't find your partner that attractive any more? Or are you withholding sex because of another unexpressed or unre-solved resentment which needs to be aired or put firmly in the past?

When you stop trying to change your partner, or give up rail-ing against a seemingly intractable problem between you, the pressure eases and other perspectives are more likely to present themselves. That doesn't mean you are giving in. It means you are attributing to your partnership the value it deserves and are pre-pared to confront aspects of yourself that you would probably rather avoid. Relationships are more resilient when there is enough space between people for each to reflect on their own needs, that of their partner and the relationship as a whole. 'In marriages that work, the partners have learned to understand and respond to each other's underlying needs in a mutual exchange without either one feeling diminished,' writes Marion Solomon in *Narcissism and Intimacy*. 'Each uses the other at times as an "object" for restoration, consolidation, transformation and organ-isation of internal experience in order to maintain or regain feelings of cohesiveness.'

Forgiveness is easier when you accept that all relationships have bad times and that people make mistakes. By refusing to forgive, the wronged one maintains the higher ground, the ultimate in scorekeeping and therefore continuing cause for conflict. Forgiving is not the same as forgetting. With forgiveness people demonstrate their dedication to the commitment they have made to each other, a conscious choice to put the past to rest. 'I made a decision that I wouldn't bring it up all the time or castigate him,' says Rose, after she accepted Tim back post-affair. 'It wasn't that I didn't want to know. I just didn't want to rub it in all the time how he had been such a shit. I had to let it go because that was the only way we were ever going to move on and I think life is good now, damn good, and I am sure he would say the same.'

Relationship cannot always be happy, equable and nourishing

for both partners. There will inevitably be differences which you simply cannot fix. The key, as almost every person within a stable partnership has told me, is being able to recognise the difference between issues worth fighting over and those best left alone. Prevention is so much more effective than cure. People draw up prenuptial agreements to protect their financial assets now that divorce is a statistical probability. But no one thinks it necessary to draw up an emotional agreement, for those times when the stability of relationships is bound to be threatened, which could prevent them from separating at all. Happier couples build a bigger picture of their partnership as more good than bad, and keep their eye on that picture rather than on smaller losses or retaliation when there is conflict. 'Philip's mother said to me at one particular low point in our marriage, "How do you feel when you hear his key in the lock at the end of the day?" which was quite sweet, because I always feel OK about it. If you feel a sense of dread when the person you are living with comes home, that's quite significant, isn't it?' says Juliet.

With time, as we grow older, traversing life's adversities together, many couples learn how to accept each other's imperfections, and that there are some issues over which they will never agree. 'We may have fought like hell when the kids were young but whatever it was we were fighting about, it wasn't worth splitting up over,' says Tom. 'It would be yet another thing to have to get through. You're just arguing about stuff, there's no murder being committed. Lots of people we know separate because it's usually the bloke who thinks the grass is greener, it'll be easier elsewhere, something else will be better, but I never thought that. It was always quite clear to me that the grass would be a lot browner and shittier.' His wife Carol agrees that even though there were desperate times, particularly after their second child was born, 'I couldn't see myself with someone else. It wasn't like I was thinking I could have done better, or I have made a mistake. And the bottom line was there was nowhere else to go. We couldn't afford even to think about it. We've got a friend who has gone through exactly the same sort of rows and rifts that we went through with small children and she wants to leave, but who is that going to be better for? The child? I told her better the devil you know. Work through this shit with him because he is the father of your child rather than think you can start all over again and somehow it's going to be better, when it isn't necessarily. Sure enough, that's exactly what's happened to her when I think they could have worked it out.'

Often couples simply grow tired of fighting. 'I think somehow over the years we have learned to be more gentle with each other about each other's passions and preoccupations,' says Imogen. 'There were times when we were younger when we were quite unkind to each other, working out tensions and conflicts. But over the years we've learned how to focus on the good bits in each other, and not to become too infuriated by the bad. I'm sure we're both exasperated with each other at times. He definitely exasperates me, but somehow that's become affectionate rather than a furious, brittle kind of thing.' The sharp edges of difference between people get sanded down to something close to an equilibrium where each can breathe. 'I know our relationship works,' says Alice after twenty-two years of marriage. 'But that's only possible when you realise that you don't have to get everything from one person. Infinitely more important is ease, which seems like such a low-key demand but that's how I feel, easy when I am at home with him. It feels like a safe haven, comfortable.'

Fights are an essential aspect of love's dynamic, forcing each to show the other that they care enough to compromise and accept that the other person has separate needs. With poor communication skills, lack of self-awareness, unrealistic expectations of love and happiness and of each other we will be lucky to leap the first hurdle of sharing a life together, let alone the greater adversities that life can deal. But if you allow each other the space to air the dark side of human experience – rage, hate, anxieties, mistakes and disappointments – within the privacy and safety of your relationship, without resentment, and each can do so honestly and without hurting the other, then you stand a chance of creating something unique and as close to heaven as we can be. These are skills that cannot be learned from a book, but only from living within an intimate relationship. Often that takes time, and several attempts. 'Friends who marry, like me, having coped with first-time disappointments and the fears that failure engenders,' writes Phyllis Raphael in *First Thoughts On My Second Marriage*, 'exhibit in midlife marriage the characteristics that sages have told us for centuries are the secret to contented lives: a sense of humour, the willingness to let go of the unimportant and an awareness of the fleeting nature of time. These can't guarantee a successful marriage, but they almost certainly tilt the odds. The ability to live in concert with another human being may be a skill we learn not at first, but at last.'

4

BETTER THE DEVIL YOU KNOW

When you meet someone you think you might want to spend the rest of your life with, take a good hard look at their parents. Familial influences can be of such profound importance that they permeate adult love in all sorts of insidious ways. They affect our choice of partner, how far we trust, how we talk to each other, sexual behaviour, the way we fight and the lengths each of us can go to try to control the other. It isn't just that each partner brings their presumptions about how life in a relationship should be because of the model they witnessed in their parents' marriage, or that each becomes more like them as they age. With time, as emotional armour is stripped away, the quality of intimacy touches something visceral and reminiscent of the love that was experienced in childhood. 'People live in the present, and if you are twenty-five and fancy someone like mad,' says Peter Bell, Head of Practice at Relate, 'the last thing you are going to think about is that whatever happened to that person when they were seven or twelve could resurface years down the line.' There is no route map to tell us how our lover will cope when something major happens such as the birth of a child, a second child, a midlife crisis or the death of a parent. Psychologists call it 'recycling'. I was staggered by the numbers of couples I met and interviewed for this book with difficulties rooted in family history.

Research into the psychological processes of relationships over the past thirty years has come up with some enlightening and reassuring thoughts. We know a great deal more today about the formative power of these processes. Childhood security appears to affect the whole of the romantic process, from that first date through marriage and commitment, to divorce. That a child needs oceans of unconditional love, support and guidance to grow up well is now clearly understood. It was only in 1987 that the first links between infantile and adult experiences of love and longing were made with Cindy Hazan and Phillip Shaver's study at the University of Denver.[1] There have been few longitudinal studies, and there are still some pieces missing from the jigsaw, but empirical findings are beginning to support clinical observations which show that emotional attachment is a primary human need that may begin in infancy but that certainly doesn't end there. We are shaped by those we are closest to until the day we die. Those with a more secure background in childhood tend to exhibit more trust, less jealousy, infatuation or game-playing. They are more able to communicate sensitively and find compromises to problems. They don't get as angry when their partner behaves unreasonably, and seem more able to accept and support their partner in spite of their faults.[2] Those at the highest point on the security spectrum tend to be more able to retain a sense of their own separateness as they form close emotional connections to other people. They tend to be better at taking responsibility for themselves, are more flexible to change and are open to criticism. Perhaps most significantly of all, they seem more able to maintain a sense of their adult self when they are with their parents, for it is those who can really grow up and separate from their family of origin who tend to form the most stable partnerships.[3, 4]

Those closer to the other end of the spectrum, with largely unsupportive or negligible caregiving, tend to be more 'anxious', while those with rejecting parents veer towards 'avoidant' behaviours in their adult relationships. 'The more intense the unresolved issue, the more intense the experience of falling in love,' writes psychologist Ayala Malach Pines, 'with incredible highs when the infantile needs are satisfied and incredible lows when the infantile needs are frustrated, the way they were in childhood.'[5] People often fall deeply and quickly in love with someone who resembles the parent with whom they had difficulties, unaware that they are unconsciously trying to master and eliminate those deep hurts by punishing their partner for the sins of the parent.[6, 7] The more 'anxious' can then become overly dependent, clingy and controlling very quickly, and if the relationship fails, the rejection confirms what they have known all along – that they are unlovable. The 'avoidant' often find it hard to commit at all. They can be emotionally volatile, jealous, sexually promiscuous and find it impossible to trust that love can last.[8] A large body of research also suggests that abusive men tend to be insecure and therefore overly dependent on their partners, and that jealousy or fears of separation are common triggers for abusive episodes.[9] If you feel so entwined that you do not know how you would survive alone, that prospect becomes a threat and a major torment. That romantic couple we perhaps admire or even envy because they go everywhere together and seem to be so in love, may well be clinging to each other out of a deep need for security. Or, as the novelist Mary McCarthy puts it in *The Company She Keeps*, 'Some failure in self-love that obliged her to snatch blindly at the love of others, hoping to love herself through them, borrowing their feelings as the moon borrowed light.'

People are often attracted to those who are at similar points along the parent–child attachment spectrum. Peter Bell at Relate says that it is not uncommon to find couples mirroring each other's pasts in the consulting room. 'It's almost comic, sometimes. If the wife tells you that her parents split up when she was eleven, the chances are high that her husband's parents also split up, or that they both have familial skeletons in the cupboard.

Relationships start with fancying someone, but what's really interesting is that they seem a bit like you, they feel similar but you
can't see how at the time.'

Like Narcissus, we appear to be drawn to our own reflection
not just physically but also to those who resemble us in age, education, socio-economic status and values. 'It was like a sixth
sense,' says Amy, who met her husband of eleven years when she
was thirty-four. 'Almost knowing what he was thinking, or we
would both look at something and say or notice the same things.
It turned out that his mother had worked for someone in the
1950s who married my father's best friend and my father was
their best man. Both of our parents were at the same wedding,
and it all felt very familiar, I suppose.' Evie met her husband at
school, and they had an on-off relationship for years until they
married in 1984. 'I love the fact that he knew my grandparents
and I knew his grandmother because we were childhood sweet-
hearts. We probably know more about each other's family than
most.' According to studies conducted at the universities of
Aberdeen, St Andrews and by Dr Anthony Little at the University
of Liverpool, it isn't vanity which makes us attracted to those who
look a little like us. We are drawn to faces that appear to offer stability through familiarity, and people who look like us also look
like family members because of the genetic link.[10] 'From the
moment my dad died suddenly in a car crash, my first relationship deteriorated because he didn't show any understanding,' says
Molly. She then went on to marry someone she had been at
school with, the son of a friend of her mother's. 'Gordon wrote
such a nice letter of condolence. Then when we met again a year
or two later there must have been something about his similarity
to my dad which got to me. My mother says that everything about
his manner and his irritating habits are just like my dad. It does-
n't sound very sexy!'

For those with less stable childhoods, opposites are more likely
to attract as people find themselves drawn to what they most
lacked. For example, a person who experienced a great deal of

rejection as a child is likely to be attracted to someone who found their family engulfing and needs in turn to experience greater autonomy.[11, 12] All too often we unwittingly put ourselves in a position where the quality of emotional intimacy we experienced as a child is re-enacted – a woman who felt unloved as a child falls for a man who does not show love and therefore confirms she is unlovable. Or a man who was made to feel inferior as a child chooses a critical and judgemental partner. But that doesn't mean we are destined to repeat that pattern in perpetuity. Adult love can soothe and even heal some of the emotional hurts of the past. David is the only child of a divorce who spent much of his childhood looking after his mother, who had bipolar disorder, alone. When I asked him what had initially attracted him to his wife Katrina, he replied without hesitation: 'Her happy, friendly nature. She is outgoing and laughs, and is interested in everything as well as being extremely bright. But that is a response to my own nature as well as to my childhood. I am not a very positive person, and there is a long history of mental illness in my family: Katrina is such a sharp contrast to me, it's just overt happiness.' Katrina's family live in America and David describes them as 'perfect. Mine is completely dysfunctional, and hers are all very healthy and happy with two parents and grandparents living close by. But I think she needed to get out of that and experience something different. She needed to expand her horizons rather than resorting to the tried and tested, which was why she came to England, and then met me.'

We even appear to have a tendency to replicate our sibling position as a child. The psychologist Walter Toman has found that couples are less likely to divorce if they marry someone who mirrors their birth position within the family, an older brother who marries a younger sister, for example. Each partner can then slot into a familiar way of relating, while two firstborns are more likely to fight over who is in charge, and two youngests may struggle over who gets to lean on whom.[13] 'We're both one of four siblings and we've formed the kind of family, bought the kind of house and lived the kind of life in exactly the same way as my parents did. We go to church and so do both our parents,' says Juliet. 'You must pick up vibes from people. You are probably sorting out in your mind is this a lover or marriage potential? We must have recognised in each other someone with long-term prospects because of the similarities – you know they come from a family you like.' Robin and Hilary are the same age. 'We both come from Australia with the sun on our backs and big skies, and we just have so much in common that the vernacular is the same. There is so much that we don't have to talk about. We've even been able to trace that we've probably been in the same room together before we met, so our roots are intertwined. We both come from big families, which meant that even once we had two kids, we never questioned that we wanted more. Two kids is just too perfect. We both wanted a bit more anarchy because that was what we had growing up.'

Sometimes people repeat the pattern of the marriage they were born into in uncanny ways. Ursula's mother was a Canadian professional who loved the city. 'Then she fell in love with my father, who had a bit of a temper. But he was hardworking and a country boy, so they moved to the country, which was about as far away from what my mother knew as moving to England from Canada has been for me. It's a fine parallel, and when I say country, I mean triple-nipple cousin-fucker-land. It's 350 people, two of whom went to college, and they were my parents. My father died after seventeen years of marriage leaving her with three kids. When I married Max, he knew I didn't want to move to London; my entire life in terms of work and friends was in Toronto. We moved for his job, and then things deteriorated. He was never around. So after seventeen years, the same length of time as my parents' marriage, we started splitting up, and here I am with four kids in their home but far away from mine. It's spooky!' Ursula wasn't the only person I interviewed whose life course seemed to echo that of her parents. Camilla knew that her parents had two very close friends, but 'I didn't know how good these friends were until my mother sat me down when I was twenty-one and told me.' Her mother had had a long affair with the other man, with her father's approval. 'My sister was shocked and didn't want to hear it, but I was fascinated.' Camilla now actively pursues open relationships herself.

Mary's father died when she was twenty and she has a very strong-minded mother who appears to want to control much of her four daughters' lives. 'Dad was twenty-three years older than my mum and not very hands-on, more like a grandfather-figure, and most of my boyfriends have been a good ten years older than me. My mum was always in charge – still is, and none of us can really argue with her.' Mary got engaged to a man she didn't love at the age of twenty-nine, the same age at which her mother had got married also to a man she didn't love. Mary managed to extricate herself from that engagement only to fall into a string of relationships with men who were unlikely ever to commit to her because they were either married or too unstable as a result of their own problems. She now has a baby fathered by a friend with whom she would like a closer relationship, an older man severely shy of commitment himself. I couldn't help but feel a sense of foreboding as I sat there watching her breastfeed and cuddle her own daughter, listening to her talking about how it was all going to be fine now because they had each other and she didn't need anyone else. It felt to me as if she was throwing all of her own need for love into loving her daughter, just as her mother had done.

The greater the damage in childhood, the more volatile the relationship is likely to be. 'You look at the person and you don't see the baggage,' says Mick, who spent sixteen years with the mother of his two children. She had never known her father, and had been sexually abused as a child. 'It was very much about me looking after her while she grappled with her identity. She went to therapy and we did lots of really good things together, and the communication between us was brilliant on one level but not in a way that made things change for her. It didn't make her happy.

Having children made her happy, but it threw up huge things in her past, and I was then both her saviour and her demon. If we had an argument I would be like every other man, and we argued about everything. The baggage plants itself on your doorstep, and then you realise how much there is. You try to clear it away and more turns up, and then there's so much that you begin to understand that it will never go away. I wasn't strong enough to be able to deal with it. I didn't know how. She was so beautiful and lovely, but she had so many issues just to do with her existence, and then towards the end of our relationship she started self-harming and distancing herself from everything, even the kids, and went on Prozac. It got to the point where we were living separate lives. At that point I thought, I just can't take this any more, I have got to live my own life. I felt like such a failure.' Mick was visibly upset as he described the deterioration of the most powerful relationship of his life, even though they parted years ago. 'There is no doubt that she has had the greatest influence on me, and I still love her and she still loves me. To share something like that with someone and then for it not to be there any more is very painful, and I will never live with anyone again.'

Tim and Rose fell in love at school over forty years ago. 'We both came from unusually unhappy households and we never talked about it then, or were even able to identify it as such. But I think we always found some comfort in one another's joint sadness, which made us close. We both had one desire, which was to get out of that environment to something better,' says Tim. His father died when he was seven and five years later his mother married an alcoholic and violent man. 'The worst thing was the unpredictability; he was always drunk, and that was terrifying for both my mother and me because you never knew whether he would come home and say, "Why did you wait for me to start dinner?" or throw his weight around with, "Why didn't you wait?"' Rose's father was also alcoholic and violent. She remembers calling the police on several occasions, and once saw her father hold a knife to her mother's throat. 'I remember going to

the cinema when I was about nine with a friend and forgot to tell
my parents,' she says. 'I remember walking up this really long,
dark road worried that they would be cross with me because I was
late, but when I got there nobody was home. Nobody had cared
where I was.'

Tim and Rose have spent the best part of their marriage doing
everything together, and have depended upon each other for the
support they lacked as children. 'We cleaved to one another
during our early years,' says Rose, 'and that isn't an adult relationship. We were replacing the parents that we didn't have with
each other, but that closeness, that support did help to heal
things.' Tim supported Rose through her darkest moments of
near-catatonic depression, and Rose forgave him two affairs. As
such they are unusual, for research shows that couples where both
have emotionally insecure backgrounds tend to have less constructive patterns of communication and are more likely to
separate when they face deep emotional difficulties in their relationship.[14] But research also shows that all it takes is one person
with reasonably secure roots for some of those wounds to heal,
provided there is a glimmer of insight and a willingness to separate from difficult relationships with parents and move on.[15]
Nothing is fixed. You can't change the past, but you can change
how you think and feel about that past with the love and support
that a partner can offer. 'Spike is like a lighthouse, my rock
because he is so solid,' says Sureena, who had a tumultuous relationship with her absconding father. Spike grew up in a much
more stable home with both his parents. 'It's a long and not very
happy story, but that was then and I am so determined that won't
happen now. It really annoys me when people think that if you
come from a broken home you have to repeat that past. I believe
in the power that relationships can have when it comes to giving
people different choices.'

When people settle into an established relationship, family
echoes can distort everything from the most casual request, which
triggers a defensive response from someone who has had too

much demanded of them in the past, to profound anxieties and problems trusting that the other will not leave because they experienced divorce or bereavement in childhood. Some find that each person has very different ideas of what it means to be together. Jackie had two major relationships with mildly abusive men who smashed her self-confidence and milked her pay packet, before she spent six years as a single mother. Then, just as she hit forty in 1990, she met Bill, a kind and solvent man ten years younger. They have been together ever since, and had two children of their own. 'He would like me to talk to him more about how I feel about things. I do, but I am not as open on that level as I appear. He can't understand why I can talk to my girlfriends about things but not to him. He wants to be closer to me, he wants us to do everything together, but part of me thinks, You're as close as I want you to be, not because I don't love him but because I selfishly want to keep a bit of me to myself. You have to divide yourself up into so many sections as a wife and a mother.' Jackie had a difficult relationship with her mother as the youngest of three daughters. She was effectively an only child from the age of eight after her two sisters had moved out. 'We used to fight about everything. She didn't like me having friends or going out, and she didn't like any of my boyfriends. I could barely breathe, and my father always took her side. He would take me aside and say, "Just do what she wants for a quiet life." I think that had a knock-on effect in my relationships because I was always too passive. It was always about what they wanted, not what I wanted.' Jackie also felt that her mother never listened to her. 'I then spent eleven years married to someone who didn't really want me to talk at all, who made me feel stupid, worthless, as if I was speaking Cantonese. Conversations after we married were basic: "What's for tea?" or, "When are you getting back?"'

Some find that family issues affect levels of honesty. 'Sam has a thing about people lying to him because his mother died when he was twenty after she told him she was going to survive,' says Diana. 'So he has this really irrational thing in that if you tell a white lie he goes nuts and I have to say, "Stop putting me on a pedestal, I'm bloody human, for God's sake!'" Paul and Amar have been together for sixteen years. Paul comes from a liberal family where politics and culture were discussed round the dinner table and his homosexuality has always been accepted. Amar comes from an army family. 'It was controlling but very caring. They are fairly right-wing; you did things the right way and nothing was discussed or analysed, and there was a time when I couldn't talk to them much at all. I was a little frightened of my father, unnecessarily probably, but I knew I was gay and my parents would never have accepted that so I lived with this deep secrecy as I grew up.' Paul earns more money than Amar but is happy for him to spend it. 'I don't have a materialistic bone in my body, but there was a time when he would tell huge porky-pies and that produced a bit of a crisis. He kept taking money out of the account and not telling me – he was scared he would get into trouble. It wasn't the money that mattered, it was that he wasn't being honest with me, and I have managed to stop him doing that now.'

Money is a common flashpoint when people's childhood financial backgrounds can be so different. Both David and Katrina earn enviable salaries, but while Katrina enjoyed an affluent childhood David lived with his mother on state benefits. 'He worries about not having enough again, whereas I take it for granted that I will always earn,' says Katrina. 'We do row about that sometimes because he thinks I am spendthrift. I will buy something I want, like organic apples, without looking at the cost, and he wants to go through the bank statements again and again to make sure that nothing will bite him. He makes us both sandwiches to take to work because otherwise I would spend five pounds a day on lunch, when actually I would much rather buy something. But I can't say that.'

Some find that they have to tread sensitively around their partner because of a particular aspect of their upbringing. 'I have noticed over the thirteen years we have been together that if Dean feels that I am in any way trying to tell him what to do, or being even slightly critical, he has flashbacks to his mum and the way she treated his father,' Sue told me, with Dean listening by her side. 'It doesn't provoke a row, but he might snap or refuse to do something quite innocent like bring me something from the kitchen when he is in there anyway.' Dean describes his mother as rather distant and cold emotionally, wanting children to be seen and not heard, and certainly not allowed to play ball games in their garden. 'It wasn't a tactile relationship, and she can be very manipulative,' says Dean. 'Materially we didn't want for things but there was a kind of emotional starvation, and even now if I give her a hug she doesn't know how to handle it.' Dean has picked a woman seemingly at the other end of the emotional spectrum – a warm, cosy, maternal woman.

When couples have children the template of family life begins to resemble aspects of their upbringing even more. Philip and Juliet come from very similar family backgrounds but each grew up with a different attitude to argument. 'I never saw my parents row much, so when they did it was really scary,' says Juliet. 'I remember my dad kicking a hole in a wall once and my mum in tears saying, "I suppose he stays with me out of duty." It was such a massive deal that I remember it vividly, whereas in Philip's case they were always yelling at each other and then telling each other that they loved them, which was another thing my parents didn't do, tell us that they loved us. Somehow that was too big a thing to say.' Philip's mum was an obsessive house-tidier, and he too wants everything in his own home to be immaculate and beautiful, which isn't easy with three young children. 'Every so often he will come home and be completely vile, unreasonable and critical,' says Juliet. They also clash at times over how they bring up their children. 'He will keep them up later than they should be and indulge them, whereas I am the one setting the rules. I always felt that his dad was jealous of the children and that his mother was the strong one, like a mother to them all. Consequently Philip pushes me into being the responsible one. He thinks I am excessively cautious about the children and I can see that my parents are too, but that's just the way I was moulded, so we row about that a lot as well.'

Florence and Grace also argue a great deal about issues of safety and danger when it comes to their children. 'Grace is very controlling and fearful in quite a bossy, neurotic way. That's partly a legacy of being Kurdish because even though her parents were born here, many of their parents' generation were murdered by the Turkish. While I am entirely understanding because it has of course been proven that the world is out to get them, when she extends that to me and the children it drives me mad. I only have to walk out the door and she tells me to be careful.' Florence acknowledges that her main problem is being too critical of Grace, which stems in part from her own childhood and her difficult relationship with her mother. 'She really didn't like me, and utterly favoured my brother. Looking back with adult eyes, I think she basically projected all her own self-loathing on to me and found me threatening because I was slimmer and academically successful. She wasn't particularly affectionate, and I think I do feel echoes of that when I feel threatened by Grace and react by being too critical of her. I don't like her loudness because my mother was loud. But Grace has helped me to see that it isn't personal, and that the era my mother was brought up in and her relationship to her own parents bear a lot of the responsibility.'

Others find that their family history affects their levels of tolerance and commitment. Imogen is the eldest of four girls and has been married for thirty-four years to Gareth, who comes from a family of boys. 'There have been a number of points in the marriage when I could have said "that's it" – and it wasn't. I think that comes from my family as well as from my Presbyterian background, where you don't make a fuss and you put up with things. That's not the way I feel about things deep down, in terms of one's integrity as a human being. I probably ought to have stood up for myself more than I did,' she says, 'but I didn't have the confidence.' Imogen traces some of her lack of self-confidence back to the fact that her mother had a stillbirth two years after she had given birth to Imogen, and became so depressed that she lost interest in her. Two years later she had another daughter, 'Who was a very engaging and lovable child, and still is, whereas I slightly detached myself. There is this story of me being the one who was OK on her own and not needing much attention, and I think I have carried that on some deep level into my marriage. I don't look back and wish I had done things differently, but I do think that I have rather deliberately put myself at the bottom of the queue. I think you carry your past with you very much, like a snail.'

Gender can play its part in this cocktail of childhood experiences, affecting the nature of adult relationships. 'Observed marital interactions are more positive and less conflictual when the husband has a secure model of parents; the security of the wife's model does not seem related,' conclude Wyndol Furman and Anna Smalley Flanagan in the academic relationship bible, the *Clinical Handbook of Marriage and Couples Intervention*. When it is an emotionally inarticulate, insecure man, however, paired with a more secure woman, the combination is likely to be much more volatile. As his emotional defences melt with time, her strength resembles that of his mother. He then feels emasculated within a relationship where he is supposed to be in charge. He feels old hurts and betrayals bubbling to the surface once again, but has fewer outlets for a whole range of powerful and disturbing feelings because men rarely talk intimately with close friends in the same way that women do. Men who are unable to separate fully from their family of origin, who idealise their parents, minimise the significance of their past or avoid it completely are likely to have the greatest difficulty establishing a contented, lasting relationship. Some men seek out women who they perceive to be more nurturing and accepting than their own mothers. When these women fail to match those expectations, when they feel all of the old wounds of rejection surfacing once again they can get very angry, controlling and even abusive.[16] Without having to look very hard I encountered wounded men in several dramatic and destructive relationships: men who collapsed emotionally within the security of a relationship, expecting to be mothered, and then punished their wives for failing to be that mother they never had; men who had affairs or spun out of control when their wives had a first, second or third child, depending on where they were placed in their own sibling hierarchy; or men who had breakdowns when a close family member died, triggering suppressed memories of an earlier loss.

Some very insecure men present an overly assured and self-sufficient manner, which women mistake for strength and confidence, thinking that here is someone they can rely on to take care of them. 'Everybody liked Paul. He was handsome, charming, incredibly well educated and he had money,' says Lydia. 'But he was packed off to a Jesuit boarding school in England when he was seven. His mother lived in Kenya and his elder brother became his guardian, but there was no proper family life here to speak of and he has suffered from that emotional neglect all his life.' Lydia recognised how needy he was from the beginning but never thought it would be a problem. 'I thought I could help him. I suppose, like most women, I thought I could change him, and I was desperate to have a baby. It was pure baby hunger.' Jan also found herself similarly attracted by the confidence and talent of her musical husband, who, like Paul, was packed off to boarding school at the age of seven. 'Matthew has this veneer of charm and confidence which I fell in love with, but actually it was arrogance. I mistook that for the real thing, a real sense of self. I admired him, we worked together and I realised, I think, that he was quite rigid about his work. He would freak easily if people didn't respond in exactly the way that he wanted them to.'

Jan and Matthew married soon after they met so that they could be together in this country, for Jan is South African. She was also pregnant with their first child. 'There were so many warnings, I should have been listening,' says Jan. 'His mother was very much against me. I remember when I first met his family at a party his godparents were warm and welcoming but his mother didn't even move to greet me. I was expected to make all the running and it has been like that ever since. One of the first things she said to me was, "Family is very important to me and by that I mean the family he comes from." She insisted we went to see them on the day before our wedding so that she could give us her presents, so we had to stop all the preparations for her and all she talked about was how ill her husband had been and how they had had such a difficult summer, and I was furious. I wasn't going to let her hijack something that my family had put a great deal of thought and effort into. When Matthew saw that I was about to say something he clipped me on the shoulder as if to say, "Back off." From then on it was absolutely clear to me that if push came to shove he would side with his family – his birth family.'

Soon after they married, Matthew gave up trying in his creative work and allowed Jan to take responsibility for them both. She got jobs and gave piano lessons while he stayed at home with the baby. His depression grew after his father died, when Jan was pregnant with their second child. 'The shock waves that sent through his family were extraordinary.' He became withdrawn, aggressive and demanding. He also started to drink heavily. 'We tried counselling at one point, but he gave it up. He talked for ages about his father, and then when the therapist asked him about his mother he said, "I don't have a problem with her." Listening to him talk about his family, it was very clear to me that he has no role models for how to be in a relationship, he has no empathy.' Jan continued to work, while Matthew avoided all musical work, in spite of his talent, and took up jobs as a painter and decorator. 'I was the major breadwinner and that was accepted, but I have also continued to work in the creative industry he used to love, so that makes it very difficult for me. The sadness in our marriage is a kind of loneliness in that he relies on me a hundred per cent to be the person on whom he dumps, the shock absorber for everything he was incapable of addressing in other people. I hadn't realised how from the very beginning he was freaking out about having got married and having a child and went into a very frightened, catatonic state. He was offered a prestigious job working with an orchestra but he wouldn't take it, and I couldn't understand why. I didn't realise that he couldn't cope with that level of responsibility on top of marriage and having a baby. He kept saying, "They are going to find out that I am a fraud," and then I realised I had married someone who was crippled by insecurities. So over the years I overcompensated, I took on too much, and that has been very stressful.'

After fertility problems, one stillbirth at six months and a miscarriage, Lydia and Paul finally had their longed-for first baby and she looks back on those days as being very happy. They set up a business together, had another baby and Lydia found herself doing more and more to keep home and the business running smoothly. When their eldest child was eighteen months old he had a febrile convulsion and was taken into hospital. Given her past fertility problems, plus the unfortunate prediction of a palm reader who had once said she could see several dead babies, Lydia panicked and thought that he too would die. 'From that moment on something happened to Paul. There is a history of clinical depression in his family, and from that point on I would say that he lost all motivation. He became depressed and started drinking more. He'd always been a dope smoker and I hate the stuff, but from then on he started smoking it every day from early in the morning. It was a nightmare because we were working together and I was having to deal with someone who was now making appalling decisions, but I didn't want to emasculate him so I didn't say anything. I would have to clear up the mess behind him as well as look after two small children. We always had a good time together when there wasn't responsibility involved and he didn't have to do things, but he is very insular and egocentric and has no idea how to be a team player.'

Lydia was committed to the marriage and determined to see things through for the sake of her children, but at times she was so exhausted balancing both the business and home life that she would collapse, in much the same way that Jan did, forcing her husband to pick up the reins. 'As soon as it got to the point where I couldn't get out of bed, Paul would be fantastic, cooking, looking after the kids, bringing me up stuff, it was almost as if all of my energy had gone into him. I had to be on the floor and utterly vulnerable – that was the only way he could deal with me. You get so sucked into this dysfunctional way of behaving that you fail to see how bloody warped it is.' When the children were ten and eight, the business spiralled down into bankruptcy and Lydia was diagnosed with breast cancer. She stopped working completely to have chemotherapy and Paul fell apart, drinking heavily. 'It got to the point where he was making no contribution at all, either with money or the children, and I was carrying him and I couldn't go on. I asked him to leave and he refused. I didn't know what to do because I didn't have any money, at which point my dad said that I could have my inheritance early and bought me a flat. I moved out with the kids.' Lydia was subsequently diagnosed with secondary cancer and went through yet more treatment while her children stayed with her brother and his family. Paul had become so depressed that he was unable to look after them. 'He came to see me in hospital and told me that sometimes he felt so depressed that he wanted to end it all. I had to say to him, "Look, I know there isn't much point in telling you to pull yourself together, but how can you sit there and say that to me? I mean, who is actually dying here?" To which he replied, "Don't you think your cancer has affected me?" It was always all about him because he is stunted emotionally, and has never had an ounce of support from his family, with a stiff-upper-lip dad and an utterly neurotic, depressive agoraphobic mother. Not once did she pick up my babies. I think he is mentally ill – you can't reason with him.'

Beatrice has known her husband since childhood, for he was

her brother's best friend, and they have been married for twenty-five years. For the first fifteen years they were happy, life rocked along and they had two children. Then James lost his job and his sister-in-law died from breast cancer. 'The whole family went into deep grief but for James I think it brought back the fact that his brother had died when he was a child and he became very depressed. He withdrew from me, from everybody, and he wouldn't talk about things. That's how he deals with anything that is difficult emotionally because that's what happened when he was a child. They never talked about his brother's death, and he blamed himself for it because he was there when the accident happened. His absence was so powerful; he wouldn't respond for days on end if I talked to him, and he withdrew from the kids, which was even more painful to watch.' Beatrice had no previous warning that her husband might change so dramatically under stress. 'When I met him he was very parental towards me and I fell madly and deeply in love with this man who I had idolised in my childhood. But looking back now on our years together, I can see that there have been other times when he withdrew. They thought our first baby might be brain-damaged and he couldn't even come to the hospital with me. His family always called him "Baby" and he was always slightly protected by them and considered fragile, but he didn't seem that way to me. But he did revert to "Baby" under crisis, and he married a nurse – I am sure that wasn't chance. He picked a professional carer as a partner, and I forget about the fact that when I first met him he was depressed. I was sent by my brother to cheer him up because his girlfriend had cheated on him, and I think that's why he fell for me. It was almost like an unconscious agreement that I would take care of him so that he didn't have to deal with his own deep emotional issues himself. I went in there and made him feel better than he'd ever felt in his life.'

Sons with manipulative and controlling mothers can find it hard to leave them behind when they marry – their mothers won't let them. Rachel and Adam have been married for twenty years and have two children. 'We have the mother-in-law problem,' says Rachel, 'in that she still treats him like a child and I don't like the person that he is when he's with her. We argue about that more than anything. He admits that he doesn't have a good relationship with her but he won't stand up to her. She tells him what to do and he does it, and there are times when it impacts badly on the whole family. She recently told us that we all had to go with her on the *Orient Express*, without any consultation, without asking me whether it suited, whether it was OK with work or whether the children would be at school, and because he is the dutiful son he just says, "Three bags full." Whenever there is a problem between us it always comes back to her, and I have never felt part of that family. We talk about it, but it's an instant cul-de-sac because he has lived with it for so long and he hates confrontation. But what's interesting is that he doesn't think it odd that his mother should order everyone on to a train.'

Wendy and Ian fell madly in love when they were both twenty-three. They had known each other for just two weeks when they started living together, and decided to get married less than four months later. 'It was love at first sight. I wanted to be with this man for ever and ever,' says Wendy. 'I had always been told by my mother that when you meet the right man you will know, which is a pretty fatalistic way of seeing things, but that was the way she had felt about my father, and they had a very happy marriage. Ian was good-looking and good in bed – what else do you want when you are twenty-three? What else do you see? It never occurred to me that his background would influence what our relationship would be about. I think I realised he had been through stuff, and that I offered an escape route. But it's only now, twenty-eight years later and after everything we have been through, that I can see he saw in me someone who was this optimistic, bright hippy chick from a stable background, and he needed that because his mother had walked out on them when he was small.' Ian's mother left the family when he was two and his younger brother was just a baby. In the early days of their marriage, Wendy never felt that was an issue. 'We were very happy and there were loads of good times: dinner parties, holidays, getting drunk with friends, going off to the country at weekends. It felt equal, Ian was out there in the world, and when I look back at the photos there is a real sense of us doing things together and sharing the same sense of joy in things.'

Wendy got pregnant with her second child when their first child was less than a year old, and although she sensed that Ian wasn't happy about it, she was over the moon at the news. 'He kept on saying, "This is damaging for Anna," but what does Anna care as a tiny creature if another tiny creature comes along? What he meant was, this was damaging for him. His children reflected his childhood, whereas my experience as a child was that the love between my parents and the love they gave to us was always balanced. It was only after Sid was born that it became clear to me that this was a big issue for him and I couldn't cope with it, I really couldn't. I had two very small children, a business to run and I was exhausted. I expected him to make sacrifices for the sake of the family, like my father had done for my mother.' Ian decided to give up work at the age of thirty-eight – he had run a highly successful business and earned a great deal of money. 'But what that meant was that he wasn't doing anything. He didn't help with the babies, he didn't help round the house, he didn't help with the move. He was always ill. Essentially he was having a nervous breakdown, driving himself insane with all this stuff about not having two babies. I couldn't deal with it, and I think I started to withdraw at that point and told him to go and see a professional.'

Wendy says that, looking back on their marriage, she now recognises what she calls an 'insidious creeping of tyranny, a petty enforcement of rules' through the earlier years. It could be anything from how you shut the car door to not putting glasses in the dishwasher. Once the babies were born, Ian's attempts to control Wendy escalated into a pernicious form of tyranny and abuse. He would wake her up if he heard a baby snuffling and tell her to deal with it rather than going himself, for that was her job, he said. He became more controlling about how and where they lived, and the rows escalated over the years. 'The arguments were about all the other things that he couldn't verbalise, really. I felt he was very much programmed to destroy, to destroy us all, and I was determined not to let him do that.' Occasionally he vented his anger on Wendy physically, hitting her and pulling her hair out, or threatening violence as he attacked their possessions: 'If I weren't smashing this table it would be your face.' It was a pattern of behaviour that ran through his family – his mother had left because of the verbal and psychological abuse she had endured from his father, and his aunt had a violent husband. 'I think I offered him something that was stable and satisfied his needs, but then his psychopathology wouldn't allow him to enjoy that and grow within it. He had to try to destroy it, but it wasn't me he was really fighting with, it was his mother.' Ian had a second breakdown when the children were older. 'He just couldn't cope and would freak out over minor incidents with desperate cries for help. He would say things like, "If I were one of the children you would solve their problems, why can't you do the same for me?", and I would say, "But they are children, I can make things better with a plaster or a kiss. I am not your mother, and you need professional help." But of course because I am a woman and a mother, I did mother him to a degree. I ended up taking on all of the responsibility for everything because he couldn't, and I couldn't leave him, either. I couldn't leave him in crisis, and I wanted to give the children the same sort of stable family life I had had.'

Wendy is aware now that she was attracted to what was dangerous in Ian because she came from such a stable, safe home. 'He was like a South American drug dealer, dark hair and sparkly earrings, and my parents wanted me to marry the boy I had been going out with from school, like my sister had.' She believes that marriage is a commitment for life and that you make sacrifices. 'My father made two major sacrifices in his life because he loved my mother – it was about them together, and not just him, and I suppose that was what I expected from Ian and didn't get.'

Beatrice and Lydia are aware now after decades of marriage that they picked men who resembled their fathers in some ways. According to Beatrice, 'My dad was always absent emotionally, so as the only girl with three brothers I spent a lot of time trying to please him to get his attention. When James withdraws from me and retreats into this depressed silence, my anxiety levels leap and I find it really hard to bear, and he knows that.' Lydia feels completely let down by Paul. 'It's like an ongoing leitmotif in my life, that I married a man who would turn his back on me just like my father did. All my life I have never really felt heard by him.'

The women in each of these relationships spent years putting up with their lot, unaware of how they were contributing to the negative downward spiral between them and their partner. Too often women accept too much: we acquiesce and step back, putting ourselves last to allow a man space. Or we expect him to take care of us, which merely reinforces the problem. 'I went into busy mode,' says Beatrice. 'I managed everything, and told him to take the time he needed. When he said he didn't want to come on holiday with us I took the kids away alone but all that did was reinforce his position of not being needed. It would probably have been better if I had done more earlier on to try to hoik him out. But then the more emotional I got with him the more he disappeared, so that wouldn't have been easy either.' Now that they have been separated for several years, Lydia can see how, in some ways, she made the problems worse by not facing them earlier. 'He is never challenged, so he thinks he is always right and he isolates himself so that he doesn't have to be challenged.' Jan is also separated after years of struggle. 'He used to get very anxious about me travelling away from home, even though I told him that the more he tried to imprison me the more he would push me away. I went away recently for work. The first day I got back from the hotel there were thirteen messages from him, all desperate, wondering where I was. He imagined I was swanning around when actually I was working. I am certain now that long-term I will be on my own because I rediscovered something in myself which has been dormant and it was too much fun, too important, too enlivening not to have it again. This is the first time I have been able to talk about it without crying because I have come to an objectivity about it now. There are factors well beyond Matthew's inability to change. The shadow of his past hangs over him, but what's liberating is the recognition that that shadow doesn't have to hang over me.'

Wendy feels she spent too long allowing the abusive pattern of behaviour between her and Ian to continue before she challenged him. 'I didn't talk to him about how unhappy I was and I didn't ask for help because I felt he wasn't able to give it. He was so fucked-up and depressed, so I coped. I am extremely good at coping, which in some ways is a good thing but it is also a bad thing. Ultimately you always end up feeling responsible and invisible. I cleaned up the mess when he smashed things and I did things the way he liked because it was easier, but I should have stood up to him years ago. I didn't because I believed he would change or because of the children – there were all sorts of rational explanations, but I regret them deeply. I want to prove to him that it can be made to work, that all his family conditioning that says marriage doesn't work because the woman will always leave you isn't the case. I don't just want to prove that I was right but to prove to him that he can transform his experience within the family that he now has with us.'

We think simplistically that everything would be better if only the other person would change, if only they were different because it is all their fault, when our own behaviour has also contributed to the gridlock. By changing how we react, or how we choose to live, we can disrupt the entrenched and often negative dynamic between us, as all of these women have done. For some that has meant separation; for others it has meant changing how they behave, standing up to what they cannot tolerate and being prepared to walk away if need be. Often we don't need to change very much, merely reorder our priorities, putting the health of the relationship above our own intransigence. If we examine our

reactions when they are extreme or when an anxiety is permanently uppermost in our minds, that can be enough to pinpoint
one aspect of a deteriorating relationship and change the elements
of it. Men may be more prone to dumping down expectations
that women will mother them, but women can in turn find it hard
to accept that men are human and are consequently prone to
periods of weakness. Lestor has been unemployed twice during
his twenty-five-year marriage to Ruby, and their relationship got
close to breaking point during the first period of joblessness. The
more she questioned him about what he had done to find a job,
the more angry and inadequate she made him feel. When Lestor
became unemployed again Ruby wondered whether she could
stand the strain. But this time she looked into her own history to
try to understand why she found it so difficult and was consequently being so unsupportive. 'My father was declared bankrupt
on more than one occasion and my parents divorced because of
it, and when I realised how much my own ingrained insecurity
was feeding into the conflict between us, I backed off and tried to
calm my own anxieties before saying anything. I literally took hold
of myself and took responsibility for my own emotions rather than
blaming him for them. I am not sure whether that helped him find
a job – although he did – but it certainly made things less difficult
between us and with the children because I was being less critical and demanding.'

It can take years to understand how familial trauma from the
past resonates through an intimate relationship. I spent the first
ten years of my marriage saying, 'You won't leave me, will you?'
because my father had left the family home when I was five. It was
only when we were well into our second decade of married life
that we both realised I had finally trusted the relationship enough
to cease this refrain. Tim feels, looking back on the dark days
of Rose's deep depressions, that he tiptoed around her for years,
unable to soothe the emotional hurts which were rooted in
her past. 'Sometimes the depressions were so bad that she would
literally be locked to a chair for two or three days at a time. I tried

to get through to her – men like to solve problems – but there was seemingly no way I could solve it. I think there was this deep sadness in her, and if you move from that sadness in your past into an environment where in theory you should be happy, it is difficult to understand why you're not. So I would say, "What can I do to help?" and she would say "Love me," and I would say, "I do." She would say, "But you have got to hold me," and I would say, "I do." She could never get enough affection from me. When we went to America I put it down to homesickness. When we had children I put it down to the fact that she wasn't going to work. She would always say, "You have to accept me the way I am," whenever I tried to talk about it. In the end I felt that this had gone on for too long. She was blaming me silently for everything when I had no idea what I had done. Somehow I just had to burst this great bubble of tension and anxiety. So I would say something that would really upset her, and then we would talk about it, and then after a few hours we would be back to normal. It was very strange. Maybe if I had done that earlier on, her depressions wouldn't have got so bad. It's a double-edged sword, being tolerant, because it can mean putting up with things for too long.'

Rose wanted to feel held, and needed Tim's love to soothe the insecurities of her childhood, but she also admits with hindsight that it was only when she was forced to do things for herself after Tim had left her for another woman that she began to take charge of her own feelings. Their lives were so fused during the first twenty-five years of their marriage that she had no real hold over who she was. They did almost everything together, talked to each other on the phone at work at least once a day and collected each other from work events. They have grown to look very alike, and their handwriting is almost indistinguishable. 'I was very moody then, sometimes I was just unhappy and sometimes I would take offence for some ridiculous slight and not speak,' she says. 'I hate the way he thinks he knows me better than I know myself – I don't want anybody to know me better than I know myself. He will say things like, "You always do this, Rose," or, "This is what happens

when . . .", and I don't want him to say those things. My mother
sulked all her life and I think I must have got it from her, but in the
end it doesn't get you anywhere. Tim would ask me what the
matter was and I would say I didn't know when I did. Now I say
when things bother me, and I have grown up a little more and
learned that there is no point in sulking or getting depressed. I also
think I was more like his mother at that time in terms of the caring.
I was like a mother to all three of them, and I don't do that now. I
don't know why I have always tried to please him but then I have
always felt that people wanted me to change, that I wasn't good
enough for them. I felt that other people accepted each other warts
and all, but that was never the case for me.'

You don't need to be a qualified psychologist to understand the
influence of your family of origin on the dynamics of your relationship. An element of insight into your emotional hard-wiring,
and the way that might clash with your partner, is often enough
to be able to differentiate between personal and relationship problems. At Relate they sometimes get couples to draw their own
emotional family trees to look at patterns of behaviour. Other
counsellors illustrate negative syndromes by showing how people
can move between being the persecutor to the victim and then
back again without realising it, while their partner steps easily into
the role of rescuer. By disrupting the stasis, individuals are forced
to take a long, cold look at themselves and the defences they have
erected because of the hurts of the past. 'The best counselling I
think we had was probably with each other,' says Sam, whose
mother died when he was twenty-one. 'It was a close-knit family
with aunties and uncles and it was all very safe, but when my parents died that security was just blasted away. The family didn't
step in, and I just went AWOL and lost touch with people. Diana
had her own skeletons, with her own parents and her divorce, but
the one thing that really brought us together was that we talked
stuff out. All I can remember initially is spending hours talking
over countless bottles of wine, and for the first time in my life

being completely honest with someone about who I was. I felt I could talk about all the things I didn't like, what scared me and what I wanted from a relationship.'

Florence says that her difficult relationship with her mother led to a string of inappropriate relationships with older women. 'I had to go after unattainable people who were already attached to someone else. I didn't even notice that I was setting myself up to fail until someone pointed it out to me. Then I got involved with someone who was emotionally and physically sadistic. She was horrible, loony, she should be clapped in jail, and again she was in love with someone else. I got tired of it all, I genuinely couldn't bear it any more.' Florence consciously broke the pattern when she found herself falling in love with Grace. 'She was different, a good person and exciting, too. I couldn't believe it. I thought you had to be nasty to be exciting. But I carried on doing myself down for a long time, and for years I would say something and Grace would say, "That's the bitch talking, not you." Grace has been immensely healing. I trust her with my life, and it is such a privilege to be able to say that I am really loved. I have never felt that before.'

Madeline spent so many years married to an unreliable man who could never be trusted to fulfil the simplest promise that it took several years for her to believe that her new partner Ralph was different. 'Sometimes it's not so much going back to the family as to our previous marriages. I always say to Ralph, "Have you got the keys?" and it drives him crazy because of course he has got the keys, but I was married to a man who couldn't even get himself on to a train – he left the kids on one once. He got off to get a newspaper and the train left without him. I really try hard not to say, "Have you got the keys?" but it isn't easy because that's what I am used to.' Ralph's reply to that when I met them was, 'I always feel like saying, "What keys?!"'

Our sense of identity isn't fixed in concrete; we are not clones destined to repeat the same patterns in perpetuity. We are shaped by life as we follow our own individual ambitions, influenced hugely by our experiences in the world, but most importantly by the emotional connections we forge with other people. 'The key thing to realise is that people are not computer programs,' says Peter Bell at Relate. 'You don't have to live that script for ever. People do heal within relationships, but if that childhood damage has been severe it can only be recovered from, not repaired, in much the same way that some people have to learn to live with the gene that causes asthma. You will always be influenced by your childhood experiences.' There is a child in every adult, and one of the great joys of a close, loving relationship is the way in which we can learn and mature from our partner and their past experiences of intimacy when they are good. 'Frank is an incredibly supportive and positive person, and has given me a lot of confidence,' says Dusty. 'I grew up in a family where that was knocked out of us the whole time – my parents were very definite about not letting us get too big for our boots. Frank has a typical Jewish mother. I met her once before we started going out, and someone mentioned France and she said immediately, "Oh, Frank is very good at French!" I think I have been good for him too, in that I give him a healthy dose of realism, bringing him down when he is a bit too up himself.'

Dean has found that the warmth and love he now feels from his thirteen-year relationship with Sue highlights the emotional starvation of his childhood. 'It's a good and a bad thing because it throws up the oddities and peculiarities of my own upbringing even more. You question it more.' Florence feels that Grace's 'Love for me has been so solid and unconditional that she has helped heal some of those primal hurts about my mother. I can talk about it now without crying. It still hurts, but a few years ago I couldn't have talked about it at all. I have always felt that Grace's love for me echoes the love my father had for me when he was alive, in its flavour. I knew my mother loved me but I always felt judged by her, whereas I knew my father really loved me and her love echoes that in that it is non-judgemental. There is real understanding between us and I can completely be myself. I am so childish and silly with her – I can laugh, say stupid things and just mess around with her in the way that I used to do with my father.'

Sandra's mother was an alcoholic, and she remembers covering her head with a pillow as a child and crying herself to sleep regularly as her father assaulted her mother downstairs. Her first committed lesbian relationship was extremely volatile. Her lover had an equally unhappy childhood and Sandra was forced into a caretaking role in the relationship that she wasn't able to sustain. 'Both of us had so much emotional baggage that it was explosive,' says Sandra. After seven years together they separated painfully, fighting over every single possession they had accumulated together and Sandra tried to kill herself. Then she met someone completely different on the internet and they have been living together for five years. 'Jane is the kindest person I have ever met. She's very calm, very together and knows how to handle me because I can be a bit of an emotional roller coaster. My need for approval comes from never having had that as a child, but Jane's parents couldn't have been more supportive of her. I told her after our first night together about my suicide attempt, expecting her to say that she didn't want to get involved with me, but she just said, "That's the past, and this is now," so straight away I got that feeling of acceptance even though I didn't feel I had done anything to deserve it. I am a lot more confident in myself because of Jane, but I still worry that she will go off with someone else, and question whether she loves me, and that's because of my past.'

With kindness and reassurance that a partner is strong enough to take the load, a person's deepest fears can be lanced. 'I think he always felt that he couldn't rely on anyone,' says Katrina about her husband David. His parents divorced when he was young, his mother is bipolar and he too has been through two or three bouts of depression. 'He was very sad, scared and anxious, and he was on medication for about a year at one point. I read lots of books and talked to doctors and just tried to be as calming, loving and reassuring as possible, so if he couldn't sleep at 2 a.m. I would say,

"OK, lets chat, let's breathe, lets do things instead."' David says that Katrina's love and positive attitude has made him much more positive, and that he hasn't had a depressive episode in over five years. When Sarah's marriage broke down after fifteen years she had a lot on her hands looking after three small children and earning enough to keep them all by working as a childminder. She was devastated emotionally by her husband's betrayal with the woman she considered her best friend, and never expected to meet anyone else. But two years later she met Mark and they have been living together for nine years. 'It's completely different in that he won't let me fester. I keep everything tucked inside and it has to be dragged out of me. He will do that, and that's what I need. The kids say I am much calmer now. I may get short-tempered but they say I don't shout or fly off the handle any more, and that's because Mark makes me talk to him.'

The idea that you lose yourself to love couldn't be further from the truth in a good lifelong relationship. We cannot flourish as human beings in a vacuum of solitude and self-obsession. We are defined and affirmed and come to know ourselves better through those who care for us, who really know us. 'You get a lot of confidence from having somebody there who believes in you,' says Sureena. 'You don't look in shop windows so much.' We cannot help but be profoundly influenced by someone we love, absorbing their more enviable characteristics over the years, and as we learn to accept their faults and less attractive traits, we too become more able to accept our own. 'I like myself more when I am with him,' says Molly. 'I feel so loved and supported that I am more confident and able to air my neuroses,' says Florence. 'I can show my real self to her, and I don't feel like I am putting on a mask or disguise to try to impress her.' Tim says there isn't a word for it in English but that in German it would be *Gemütlichkeit*, 'Just being so at ease with somebody that you feel you can be totally yourself, and there is no one else I can feel that way with, not even my children.'

We cannot avoid the deep, tenacious links between the families

that we come from and the family that we create together. Two
families and an extended network of people connected to both
hover in the wings of every committed relationship. With just a
glimmer of insight into the hold the past has over us, we can
get rid of some of the more destructive elements and do things
differently. As time goes by, the dependency that we once had
on our family of origin dwindles. As we watch our parents age and
then die, a whole new set of issues arises out of grief, and often
couples find they grow closer once their dependency on each other,
as orphans, is sealed. Charles and the mother of his children were
divorced over twenty years ago and after most of a lifetime as a
single man, he is now living happily with another divorcee who
is also in her late fifties. Charles's parents died eight years ago.
'One of the many joys of being with Jilly is that her mum and
dad like me a lot. They are so pleased that she is happy again and
it's like having parents back and I adore them.' Just as women
feel themselves mutating at times into their own mothers, couples
occasionally glimpse their relationship in the same light in
which they once saw their parents' marriage – boring, conventional,
trapped in routines. 'Hilary and I have this ongoing joke between
us,' says Robin. 'She says that if I turn out like my father who had
dementia, then before it gets too bad she is going to take me down
to the bottom of the garden and shoot me. And I say if you turn
out like your mother, I will take myself down the garden and shoot
myself. It's a joke, but there is an element of truth to it. If someone said to you when you got married at thirty that with average
life expectancy you will be together fifty years – what will you
look like then, and how healthy are you and what things will
happen along the way – maybe it would make people think a
bit more about what they were committing themselves to.'

'At its best marriage becomes a crucible for psychological
growth,' writes Helge Rubinstein in her introduction to *The
Oxford Book of Marriage*, 'allowing the individual to break through
inhibitions and self-imposed limitations, and provides the most
nurturing, healing and fulfilling area of a person's life.' We can't

change our past, and we cannot expect our partner to heal the wounds of that past. But if we are prepared to listen to the uncomfortable truths that emotional intimacy raises about ourselves, if we are prepared to abandon pointless efforts to change our partner and seek, instead, to understand why their behaviour causes us such discomfort, we can both change. 'Marriage teaches you how to put yourself in someone else's shoes, it helps you to mature,' says Rachel, who has been married for forty-five years. 'Then as you get older it gets easier both to do that and, consequently, to be married.'

5

BALANCE OF POWER

Sally met Joe in her last year of university at the age of twenty-one. They fell madly in love and got married a year later, but almost immediately Joe changed, spending every weekend out on his own getting drunk with his friends. Sally changed too, putting a promising career as a trainee lawyer on hold and second to her marriage. They argued almost all of the time and separated after just two years together. 'I think the problem was that we got married! He panicked; he just looked at his life and thought, Oh my God, I have got a wife and a mortgage and I am only twenty-three. He used to be so loving. He used to say, "I can't wait to be married to you," and then just a few months later he couldn't wait for Friday night so that he could get away from me. I guess he thought that being married would stop him from being who he wanted to be. But I wanted to be his wife, I loved him and I wanted to be there for him. Before I got married I didn't think things would change that much, but then once we were married I felt I needed him more and I am quite an independent person. I am always the one who organises things and does things and from then on I wanted him to look after me and he didn't seem to want to do that. It's only now I look back that I can see that I did lose a lot of my strength, trying to be what I thought I should be as a wife.'

There is an implicit bargain or deal to every long-term relationship, and the nature of that deal changes with time and circumstance – with children and good or hard times. In more traditional, heterosexual marriages men were expected to provide financially while women did all the caring. Now that is rarely viable or desirable. Women have career ambitions. Few families can survive on the income of the male breadwinner alone, and a whole generation of men want to be more hands-on and closer to their own children than they ever were with their own fathers. Yet the assumptions associated with those older gendered roles linger on and affect the nature of relationships. So does our socio-economic structure, which still hasn't adapted enough with policies to support working families. Consequently, rising numbers of couples may be living more rounded lives, with a fairer balance of power between them, but they need a pioneering spirit to get there. Without clearly demarcated or prescribed roles, everything has to be negotiated often on a daily basis, and that takes courage, imagination, initiative and unprecedented levels of tolerance. Traditional gender templates still have a deep hold over our psyches as the only 'right' way to be. They affect young couples like Sally and Joe, who were just starting out on a life together, and others further down the timeline. When so many other aspects of life have to be carved out for ourselves, it feels much easier to slip into the safety and routine of the prescribed roles of 'husband' and 'wife'.

Issues of gender and unequal power are at the root of most marital distress. 'Marriages go bad not when love fades,' writes Phyllis Rose in the introduction to her portrait of five Victorian relationships, *Parallel Lives*, 'love can modulate into affection without driving two people apart – but when this understanding about the balance of power breaks down, when the weaker member feels exploited or the stronger feels unrewarded for his or her strength.' Inevitably there are periods, such as during illness

or unemployment, when one of the pair gives or takes more.
What matters is a deep sense of fairness rather than a uniform,
bean-counting parity, as well as enough honesty when one is feeling put upon, resentful or needs space to breathe. What also
matters is flexibility about gender rather than rigid notions of
masculinity and femininity. Those who feel comfortable dabbling
in both their masculine and feminine sides – for nobody is either
all one or the other – are more likely to find a common ground of
understanding. The trouble with traditional relationships is that
they tend to be inflexible and less able to accommodate change
when we live at a time when change has never been more a feature of our lives. With the new deal, couples have to construct a
kind of bespoke relationship with less rigid gendered roles. For
couples to thrive they need a healthy balance where neither feels
swamped by the needs of the other, or merged to the extent that
their entire sense of self has disappeared; where there is just
enough distance between them to feel that each has to reach out
to the other. The problems with the new deal come when we
forget to reach out, or don't want to because of some unexpressed
need to preserve our sense of self within the relationship.

'Marriage can turn people's head in no time,' says Peggy,
who has been married twice, 'and it terrifies the life out of me. I
have seen it happen. You don't know on the day of the ceremony
whether the person you are marrying is going to be one of those
people. It happened in my second marriage. He liked me being a
free agent who resisted getting married again, for years. But I
soon became his "ball and chain" when I finally relented. I only
realised it on the day I married him, and that I should never have
given in.' Years after her marriage had failed, Peggy embarked
on a relationship with a man whose relationship was in tatters.
'I remember asking him once what had happened, and he just
started to sob because the woman he had married changed immediately from a friend and lover to someone who wanted to be
a proper housewife and in charge, and he didn't want that. I
completely understood how he felt and how horrendous it is

when that happens, that you can go from a friend you want to hold hands with through life together, to these ghastly roles.'

Men can change, too. Rajani says that her husband was happy to do housework before they got married. 'I thought, Great. Here is a man who will share things equally. But then as soon as we had children I became the housewife-cleaner-childminder, even though I was still working and earning more than him. He began to do things like drop litter all over the floor, and he became like a child. I even had to clean the loo after him.' When she discovered extensive email exchanges between her husband and the woman he was having an affair with, she was shocked to discover how he saw her as this nagging, asexual wife. 'He just went on and on, complaining about his life at home and how I made him do things like wipe the table or the floor, and how the kids were shouting and crying and driving him round the bend. He called me the "OL", the old lady, while she was "kitten" and he was "Tom". I had tried so hard to think like him and speak like him. I wanted to be a good wife. I tried wearing the clothes that he wanted me to wear, doing the things he liked, until I realised this wasn't me. I was just dismissing myself as nothing compared to him, and I fell into the trap so easily. I am never going to do that again. From now on it has to be an equal relationship, and they have to be in my league.'

Marriage seems to hold a transformative power. 'I was driven mad on our honeymoon because Sam suddenly decided he would be in charge of the money, and every time we crossed a road he would either stop me or put his hand in the small of my back to push me on,' says Diana. 'I kept thinking, Being married doesn't mean I have lost the ability to cross the road. I am thirty-seven. I earn my own living. I can look after myself. It definitely changed, and it took us about eight months to get used to, but now it's no different to when we were living together. Sam must have thought, This is how I am supposed to be as a married man. That made me think, Well, what am I supposed to be, then?' If a newly married woman feels that she is changing and that she might slowly, as Mrs Millamant says in Congreve's *The Way of the World* 'dwindle into a wife', it can be terrifying. It seems to be that, despite a vast change in the way women perceive themselves, it is still too easy for women to be their own worst enemy and slip into stereotypical assumptions of being the 'good wife', caterer to the needs of others, in the belief that that will make them both happy.

Molly is a successful publisher who has always earned her own living. She has been happily married for four years, and she and her husband have a baby daughter. 'It suddenly felt incredibly grown up being married. During the first two years I slightly tiptoed around him, wanting to be the right wife for him, and gradually I relaxed. But even now that we've shown our true colours and know each other inside out, and I am working too, I constantly try to be as good as, if not better than, him as a house-wife. Sometimes I think he demands a lot of me. But then I also bring a lot on myself, in that I want to keep a perfect house. I feel bad if he comes home and I haven't unpacked the dishwasher or the shirts are still stuck in the tumble dryer. I'd love to get a hot meal on the table by the time he comes home, but nine times out of ten I don't.'

Old-style notions of what it is to be a good wife or good hus-band die hard. Over time, unless one is alert to the shifting balance of power, partners become entrenched in separate male and female spheres, with much of the power over decision-making sliding into the domain of the highest earner, usually the man, particularly when there are children. We know how to enjoy marriage the old way. Yet most of the research evidence suggests that in the healthiest, happiest marriages and lifelong relation-ships, couples grapple, often fiercely, for a more equal partnership where their roles are regularly up for negotiation, choosing a divi-sion of homemaking, breadwinning and childcare that suits both of their individual needs at different times. The American soci-ologist Pepper Schwartz has conducted large-scale studies of couples and coined the phrase 'peer marriage' for those relation-ships where there is roughly a sixty–forty split on household and childcare responsibilities, where work is given equal weight in each person's life and where each has equal influence over important decisions and the family economy. 'These couples were distinguished by more than their dedication to fairness and collaboration,' she writes in her book *Love Between Equals*. 'The most happy and durable among them also had refocused their relationship on *intense companionship*.'

While most 'peer' couples tend to be dual earners, those where one had a salaried job and the other stayed at home also managed to reap those benefits provided that money, influence, decision-making, childcare and domestic duties were shared. There is everything to gain from attempting to instil a sense of fairness and consequently mutual respect into a partnership: a more tenacious and committed intimacy based on genuine empathy for each other because of everything they share. With that greater intimacy it then becomes more possible to alter the balance of power when it veers dangerously towards unfairness and resentment. Almost every contented couple I interviewed said that friendship was one of the main reasons why their relationship worked because with friendship comes trust, a respect for each other's opinions, their individual differences, their need for personal privacy as well as a greater willingness to negotiate as soon as they developed difficulties.

But it's hard to cast off gendered roles in a relationship and accept new roles, where each retains a sense of their own separate individuality, when the law has defined marriage as the merging of two people, the absorbing of the female into the male, for so long. As the eighteenth-century legal commentator Sir William Blackstone puts it: 'By marriage, the husband and wife are one person in the law: that is, the very being or legal existence of the woman is suspended during the marriage, or at least is incorporated and consolidated into that of a husband: under whose wing, protection, and cover, she performs every thing.'[1] Romantic fiction distorts this notion of one merged unit as something magical and life-affirming. 'I *am* Heathcliff,' exclaims Cathy in Emily

Brontë's *Wuthering Heights*. 'He is always in my mind – not as a pleasure, any more than I am always a pleasure to myself – but as my own being.' Notions of true equality, where two separate individuals come together and remain separate, still feel as if they are only skin-deep. Not so very long ago when a woman married, all that she owned, from goods and money to land, became her husband's, under the common-law doctrine of *coverture*. She could not keep her earnings, sign contracts or make a will, defend herself in a divorce or sue or be sued unless her husband was also party to the suit. Her husband could sue for the restitution of conjugal rights, and their children belonged to the husband. 'In the past, English society was brutal, and a husband had almost unlimited power over his wife,' writes Maureen Waller in her history, *The English Marriage*. 'He could demand sex as a right, chastise and beat her, subject her to life-threatening violence, dissipate her fortune, starve her, banish her from his house even if that house had been purchased with her money, forbid her to see her children, imprison her or incarcerate her in an asylum.' The ideal woman was 'Weak, submissive, charitable, virtuous and modest,' according to historian Lawrence Stone in *Road to Divorce*. 'Her function was housekeeping and the breeding and rearing of children. In her behaviour she was silent in church and in the home, and at all times submissive to men.'

It was not until the Married Women's Property Act of 1882 that the courts had to recognise a husband and wife as a separate legal entity and the Custody Acts of 1883 allowed a woman to keep her children up to the age of sixteen after divorce.[2] But the model of man as provider and head of the household and woman as the weaker, more subordinate vessel continued, influencing even the fabric of the welfare state established after the Second World War. 'On marriage a woman gains a legal right to maintenance by her husband as a first line of defence against risks which fall directly on the solitary woman; she undertakes at the same time to perform vital but unpaid service and becomes exposed to new risks, including the risk that her married life may be ended prematurely by widowhood or separation,' wrote William Beveridge in his report of 1942. The resulting social security legislation gave married women the right to a pension based on their husband's contributions and a widow's pension if he died before she did, but denied her the right to claim unemployment benefit. Income tax was also combined until the 1980s.

While these institutionalised endorsements of the family breadwinner model are no longer with us, money and who earns it is still so often the central pivot to the balance of power in a relationship. The notion that a man's wage is more important than a woman's hasn't disappeared, particularly among the older babyboomer generation brought up by parents who believed in these values. A man's entire sense of self-worth is still wrapped up with his ability to work and provide, and women tend to get disillusioned very quickly when men cannot contribute. 'He sees his life very much as going out to work; he earns the crust, in that he earns more than me. But he doesn't see what I do as being particularly serious work, even though I am full-time too,' says Elizabeth, who is in her late forties and a family lawyer. When her husband was made redundant, she upped her hours and expected him to take on more of the responsibility for their daughter. 'But he hated picking her up from school because of all the other mums. He sidelined himself and didn't talk to anyone. Work is very important to him and without his income we could never afford to send her to a private school, but when I suggested that we went and talked to the head about our situation his male pride was so injured at that point that we didn't go. I would go to work and he would be sitting at the computer, and then when I came home he would still be sitting there having done nothing around the house. But I couldn't say anything or tell him off, or say things like, "Gosh, if I had some time on my hands I would . . ." because I could see that he was just terrified and depressed.'

The distribution of assets in relationships has changed radically in the past few decades. Research carried out in the 1950s in southern England showed that 70 per cent of men gave their wives housekeeping, 16 per cent touchingly handing over their whole pay packet, while just 14 per cent of mainly younger couples pooled their income. By the 1980s, with many more women working, pooling money in a joint bank account became the preferred option of the majority – 56 per cent according to research conducted at the time by Jan Pahl. Another survey in 1986 found a similar figure of 54 per cent with just 2 per cent of couples saying that they managed their finances independently.[3]

The idea that it wasn't 'his' or 'her' money but 'ours' is a sweet, romantic idea and may just conceivably have been a way among some couples of levelling pay inequities at a time when feminism still commanded media presence and debate. A cynic might interpret this change rather differently: when men are the sole breadwinner they hand out housekeeping; when women earn too, everything should be pooled. The lack of a level playing field in terms of earnings and opportunities between the sexes meant that many could present a façade of equality without really challenging the stereotypical assumptions that lurked underneath. Most men felt that, as the higher earner, they had more rights when it came to deciding how to spend it and most women allowed them that right simply because they had worked for it. Even to this day, when many women earn a reasonable wage they still find it hard to spend it on themselves, and the vast majority of all women's earnings go on their children.

Rebecca and her husband both work full-time, but Rebecca earns considerably less in local government than her husband, who runs a successful business. A major cause of resentment for Rebecca is the amount of weekends he spends away pursuing an expensive hobby – motor racing. 'I reckon he probably spends the equivalent of what I earn in a year on a hobby, and that's quite irritating. All our money goes into a joint account, so it's a bit galling that, when I'm here busting a gut at work and other people are using their bonuses to pay off bits of the mortgage, he is taking money out of the house to pursue a hobby which I have no interest in. Every now and then I might have a dig about that, but it's my own fault in a way because I don't want the confrontation, and he thinks it's justified because somewhere in the back of his mind he thinks he has earned it so he can spend it. He's not mean. I think if I tried to buy something big he would be quite pleased, but I wouldn't dream of doing something like that because I haven't earned it.'

The inequities inherent to the man-as-provider model remain, forcing women to become dependent on a man's magnanimity, needing to seek permission for expenditure and reluctant to challenge a husband's decisions too much in case they push him away, however good the marriage. Adanna felt she had no choice but to give up work after the birth of their third child because they couldn't afford the childcare. Once her partner became the sole breadwinner, they began to argue a great deal about money. 'Not because we didn't have enough, but because he now feels that he should be able to spend more on, say, lunch because he earns it, and I am the one saying it all adds up. It used to feel much more equal when we were both working. We would both come home and sort things out round the house, and the children. Now we argue a great deal more about the house not being tidier because he thinks I should be doing more, and about how we spend our money because he thinks he has more of a right to decide that. But if you met him you would think he was the sort of new man who would be very understanding of all that.'

I met many other professional, educated women who had always earned their own living and settled with men into what they assumed would be equal partnerships, only to find the balance of power slipping back into traditional roles where the man controls the money. Kate had a prestigious job but gave it up to look after their three children because her husband's job involved extensive trips abroad. 'We have a joint account and he has his own bank account, and for a long time I thought he was very together with money until about a year ago when we reached a crisis point financially and I realised he was putting his head in the sand about the bills. He shoves everything into a drawer

unopened, and when I opened them and discovered that he had
run up this massive overdraft I went ballistic. I did at one point
think, Why can't I be in charge of all the bills? But I resisted for
years because I really didn't want to know about his life insurance
policies and pensions. I'd like him to look after that. I don't want
to have to do that as well as everything else. You think, Well, he's
a man. He can do that. I've spent months trying to get him to go
through his standing orders and cancel things, but he just thinks
it isn't much money here or there, which makes me furious. I
don't go and meet people for lunch on expenses like he does, I go
to H&M once every three months and treat myself to a T-shirt,
in order to save. I rented out our son's bedroom to a lodger when
he was away to get some extra cash. I don't want us lumbered
with this massive debt.'

Increasingly, according to Jan Pahl's research, younger couples
want to retain a sense of their own personal autonomy with their
own bank account, contributing a fixed amount, sometimes on a
percentage basis, of what they earn into a separate account for
joint outgoings. Others prefer not to share an account at all, and
divide up their expenditure with each taking responsibility for a
particular area. A survey conducted by the Alliance & Leicester
building society in 2004 found that 38 per cent of couples had an
individual as well as a joint account, 34 per cent managed their
finances through one joint account and 28 per cent maintained
completely separate financial arrangements.[4] It may not sound
very romantic or family-minded to have such a divide, but it
means couples argue less about what is necessary or wasteful,
they are more likely to nurture respect for each other as separate,
autonomous beings and they have to talk to each other regularly
about their joint financial needs. It is so easy to resent the other's
expenditure, keeping a running mental account, when they come
home with a new pair of shoes or the latest high-tech gadget,
unless both are completely honest about their income and joint
needs.

I know that I am not alone in fearing that I might one day

become a bag lady, shuffling from bench to bench with my belongings, even though my husband reassures me that he will be there too tucking me in with a nice crisp copy of *Metro*. Women are perhaps more aware of how vulnerable they are economically because of pay inequality between genders, maternal ambitions and the fact that so many opportunities both professionally and personally still seem to depend on looks and sex appeal, which are fleeting. Savings and pension arrangements are negligible for women on average earnings, and more women than men haven't even been able to pay enough in the way of National Insurance contributions for the basic state pension because they have taken time off work to care for others. It is understandable, perhaps, that so many women, even when they earn good money, should yearn at times to be taken care of, and that pay differences between couples where the woman earns more might feel uncomfortable. 'I have always earned more money than him, and at certain points that has made me feel very insecure in that it means you can't ever give up working,' says Alice. 'But on the other hand I do feel that I get my way. I decide who we will see and what we will do, and he seems to be happy with that. I think I would know by now if he wasn't, which is why it's tough when I am feeling fragile because then I just want him to manage everything. I have come to a certain understanding after twenty-five years, in that it is perhaps unrealistic to expect him to fall in with everything I want when I am feeling in control, and then want him to become a more masculine caretaker and take charge when I am not.'

Nancy's husband took a unilateral decision to give up work completely in his late fifties, eight years ago, during what she now believes was a mild and unacknowledged breakdown. 'The very dynamic person who I thought on some deep level was going to take care of me turned out to be a sort of reconstituted hippy, who gave up everything without a pension when we had two children and I was running a business. It actually works now because he looks after my aged mother and does things at home, but I still deeply resent being pushed into the position of having to keep everybody. I have never really forgiven him for it because it wasn't a mutual decision; I had no say in it. What's horrible is that he has boxed himself into a corner and I have become more powerful, which isn't what I wanted at all. It feels really wrong, somehow. If he had an accident, or got ill, or expressed some desire to be a hill farmer or something, then I would have been completely supportive, but it was unilateral, and I remember saying at the time, "This is going to destroy everything." You need space in a relationship, then each can bring something fresh back to talk about, but you can't talk properly when there's this much resentment.'

When both are aware of the financial constraints and are able to air their frustrations and feel heard, they can jostle their way towards a more equable playing field. Carol and Tom married in 1984, and say they argued weekly during the first ten years of having children because they never had enough money. 'We were young and on benefits while Tom was trying to build his career as an artist, and I had no skills whatsoever,' says Carol. 'I would keep pushing him to go out and do stuff to earn money.' Tom chips in at this point: 'And I didn't respond well to being pushed. I remember saying at one point, "When are *you* going to start earning some fucking money?" I needed a biro, and walked into Smith's and they were 24p, and I only had 19p in my pocket. I thought, Here I am in my mid-twenties and I can't even afford to buy a bloody biro. It's a real pressure for blokes, having to do all the earning.' Carol gained some qualifications and eventually found work as their children got older and their financial burdens eased. But they have always been open with each other about their earnings and their liabilities. 'Carol might say "We've got a bill for this or that for £250 – have you got it?" and I would say I had, or didn't have, or I might have in a week.' They have separate bank accounts. 'It's nothing to do with any feminist principles, it's entirely pragmatic,' says Carol. 'If we've only got one bank account, we've only got one overdraft.' Tom chips in again, 'And with two accounts each, we've got four!'

More and more men like Tom welcome the fact that their partner works. David is in his early thirties and says he cannot imagine being married to someone who stayed at home, even though they have a child. 'Being the sole breadwinner would certainly put me under a lot of pressure. I like the fact that we both work. It enriches both of our lives. It's good for both of us, and it makes our relationship more balanced. It is more stressful for Katrina, in that there are these stereotypical expectations about being a mother, and there are undoubtedly people who think she must be an egotistical, career-obsessed maniac, but we both know as older parents that it would be harder to get back into work at the same level if one of us stopped completely. Plus work becomes part of your persona, so it would be like losing a part of yourself if you stopped.' David and Katrina have high-powered, successful careers, and David acknowledges that he has at times found it difficult that Katrina earns more, and is identified by her company as a high-flyer. 'If anyone did have to give up their career for some reason it would probably be me. I think I oscillate between being slightly competitive with her and enjoying seeing myself reflected in her success. Since Thomas's birth it's definitely more of the latter, in that her success is now my success and I am happier to step back and do everything I can to help her realise things in her career. Our professional lives depend upon the other one being there to pick up the slack at certain times, and we are an inseparable unit now because of Thomas.'

The ability to look after each other comes easily and willingly only when the power balance in the relationship is roughly equal. When couples share more of their lives together, when men soften and become more emotionally intuitive through caring for their children, when they appreciate and admire their wives' energy, ambition and achievements, when they understand how important their partner's happiness is to their own and when women share the economic burden and find new freedoms to be themselves rather than just 'wife' and 'mother', couples fashion a stronger foundation. It's a foundation based on respect for the

other as well as greater flexibility when it comes to an understanding of what is fair, which goes way beyond superficial
arguments about who last did the washing-up. Each looks out for
the other's welfare. Partners are more open to criticism and are
more prepared to change because they value the quality of their
relationship. Pepper Schwartz's research in *Peer Marriage* has
found them to be less high-handed, dismissive and disrespectful
of each other. They share a common vision; women feel able to
assert their needs and men are able to acknowledge how much
they have gained by being in a more equal partnership. Perhaps
most importantly of all, children gain in spades from this type of
relationship. There is greater stability at home, greater emotional
investment in their welfare from both parents, making it that
much harder for men to leave or abandon their responsibilities,
and a great deal harder for working mothers to let that loving,
helpful man go. How could they deny their children that kind and
involved father? Children grow up witnessing healthy patterns
of relationship and understand that they are part of a marriage
rather than being the whole point of it as in more traditional relationships, where women often have no choice but to over-invest
in their children. As children begin to grow up, parents in more
equable partnerships find it easier to slip back into the companionship that has always been there between them, and consequently
ease their children out of the nest and on to their own two feet with
fewer complications involving guilt or loyalty.

With greater fairness over responsibilities and assets, couples
are more likely to fashion a steadier domestic balance of power.
Few, however, find they just slip easily into these new ideals
without a great deal of argument, setbacks, resentments and
difficulties. Arguments usually flourish around housework, with
survey after survey consistently showing that women do a great
deal more, even when they work full-time. Yet even though levels
of conflict have risen, surveys in the US show, comparing marriages in the 1950s, when marriages were far more traditional, to
those of the 1970s, when more women worked and feminist ideas

rocked our minds, it was found that people were much happier with their marriages in the 1970s.[5] Another study comparing relationships in 1980 and 2000 found not only that levels of equality over decision-making had increased but that this factor was one of the strongest correlates of marital happiness and stability.[6] Relationships are slowly but surely becoming more equal and consequently more content. Diary data collected in 1975, 1987 and 1997 by the Institute of Social and Economic Research at the University of Essex has found a substantial increase in the amount of time men contribute to cleaning, cooking and childcare across all social classes.[7]

'We try to share things equally, which is why the relationship works, but that's also why we fight,' says Philip. 'We fight all the time about the domestic chaos and who is going to do what, but that's because we both work.' Men are learning how to be more domesticated. The received wisdom, the semi-humorous banter among women, is that men just don't see the dirt or care about it when they do. But the truth is that men often lack confidence: they consider themselves 'bad' at housework, clumsy when it comes to dressing babies, inept at cooking. They resent the way they are expected to do things 'her' way. Their sense of autonomy is undermined by consistently being seen as the sous-chef, a junior partner in the home epic when it is their home and their children, too. More and more men are prepared to take responsibility for 'women's work', provided their women are prepared to relinquish those roles and be clear about what they want. It is then in men's interests to meet those needs head on. Women drive relationships, but they also tend to be the ones who break them. When women ask for more help, for recognition and appreciation, it is foolish to see this as a threat to masculinity. Instead it is a request for greater closeness, for the shared life which reaffirms masculinity simply because a man likes to feel needed. Research seems to indicate that the whole stability of a relationship often depends upon how much a man is willing to accept his partner's influence, for it is women who, in the main, initiate separation and divorce when they feel disillusioned, unloved and diminished. Research conducted by John Gottman in the US indicates that when a man is not willing to share power with his partner, there is an 81 per cent chance that his marriage will self-destruct.[8] 'When I look back on my other relationships, I think we always went wrong because we assumed that we had to take on certain roles and accept that things have to be a certain way just because this woman was my girlfriend,' says Sam. 'Now, in my relationship with Diana, I know that we are two very different people. There is no reason why we should get on; it's only by approaching things as a team that you can get through things. The key thing is respecting that we are two individuals, and that there is a barrage of differences between us. Everyone has their ups and downs but we're on a breeze, we've got it right compared with what some people I know live with. I wouldn't want to be married to any of my mates' or cousins' wives.'

Diana had a more traditional gendered split with the father of her two children before he left her for another woman. 'He drove me mad all the time. He was just so messy, and never thought about what life must be like for me at home with two young children. I remember being really unhappy, isolated, alone, unappreciated, tired and like a doormat.' Now that she is married to Sam and they have a baby of their own, 'It's totally different. I've always wanted to be with someone who would phone me up and say we need more bleach for the toilet, and I've got that man!' Diana works full-time while Sam is a part-time teacher and musician. He had a steep learning curve from being single, with far less challenging girlfriends, to having a ready-made family with two stepchildren whom he took to school every morning and cooked for most evenings. It is Diana who sets the pace, clear about what she wants from him because her previous relationship was so destructive. 'Sam is the sort of man who can do the shopping and not come back with a load of crap. He can paint a bedroom in an afternoon, put the baby to bed and get the dinner on the table. It's not perfect – no relationship is – but I don't want to have the whole domestic responsibility on my shoulders. He enables me to work, which enables me to fulfil myself, which keeps me a happy person and he's very loving and supportive. He's great with the kids and he's funny and amusing, and we work well as a team. That's really important to me because it means he doesn't take me for granted and just expect me to do certain things as a woman. It means I feel very free within the relationship, and I don't feel ground down.'

Diana, like many other working mothers, has found that the simplest way to manage the home front is to hand over whole chunks of responsibility – in her case, to Sam. Equality does not mean that every task from cleaning the lavatory to washing the sheets has to be shared and logged on an invisible running account. The happiest couples just pitch in with whatever needs to be done. One cooks, the other clears up; one does the washing, the other takes charge of the rubbish; one gets up with the children on a Saturday, the other on a Sunday. They build a sense of fairness into their relationship which evolves with time, individual needs and changing circumstances. That sense of fairness is harder to achieve in a more traditional relationship, where the daily lives of each can be so different. Kate is honest about how much she resents the fact that her husband is away a lot on business, and she has had to compromise her professional life to care for their three children. 'I hate the fact that I have given up my whole life and he hasn't, and that pisses me off to this day. I still don't think he gets it. He just sort of thinks there is no way round it, so why get worked up about it.' Like many women, she finds it hard to lay all of her cards on the table about the balance of power in their house, or to ask for the small things which will make her feel more cherished and respected as an independent person. Kate loves running, and took part in the London Marathon, but it took a friend to tell her husband that he ought to be there to watch her do it. 'His response was, "Why? I can't. Her friends will be there, I don't think she really cares that much and anyway, I'll be home on Wednesday." It was my friend who said, "That's not the same, you should be there." He did come, and it did mean a lot to me, but it's really weird that he didn't get that . . .' Diana wouldn't hold back from making sure that her husband knew exactly what she wanted. 'I have no problem with that whatsoever. Take Mother's Day. I know what I want, so two weeks beforehand I said, "I want a cup of tea in bed, and then I want you to go away and leave me for an hour and then you can come back with another cup of tea and some toast, and then we can open presents. Then we can all go to church and out for lunch." That's what I got, and I was as happy as Larry. If you expect them to come up with something you are going to be disappointed. Just tell them.'

Trouble tends to start when couples feel so wedded to the more traditional roles that they get lost within them. The line between feeling diminished within gendered roles and abused is a fine one. Deborah knew fairly early on that her marriage wasn't working. 'He got very aggressive with me one weekend soon after we met. He didn't hit me – that came later in front of the children – but he was just very threatening, shouting and pushing me around, and I should have pulled out then. But you only know that looking back. One of the biggest mistakes was that we got married very quickly, before we really knew each other. He proposed to me three weeks after he had met me and I was flattered, I suppose, swept away. Once you start making wedding plans it is that much harder to pull out of it, somehow.' They were married for nineteen years and after their first child, Deborah's husband persuaded her to give up a career she adored in the police force. He became very controlling, moved them all to the country because he wanted to live there and gave her very little in the way of housekeeping money. 'He wanted me at home and under his thumb. I would have to ask for anything I wanted. I remember once my bras were falling apart, and having to ask him for fifteen pounds to buy a new one and thinking, I shouldn't have to do this.' When they finally separated Deborah was left penniless with two children and her self-confidence in tatters. She now lives with her new partner and his older children, and has found her sense of self restored, 'Because it is equal and that's the bottom line, in that we both support each other in whatever it is that we want to do, even if those are separate things.' They have separate personal accounts and a joint house account, and Deborah has a new career in education. 'I've been going for interviews for promotion and he has been supporting me a hundred per cent whereas my husband would have undermined me. I feel totally secure now. We're both utterly committed even though we are not married, and I see our future together whereas with my husband it was never knowing what he would be like temper-wise, or even whether he would be around from one week to the next. I would have to pick my moment to bring something up, usually money, and if I picked the wrong moment he would fly into a rage. I remember that feeling of walking on eggshells as horrible.'

Shahira's story reminds us of the triumphs of feminism and how privileged we are to be able to forge a relationship based on partnership and mutual respect. Her family comes from Kashmir, but she grew up in Leeds, went to university to study English literature and loved her job working in a library. Shahira's mother came into the sitting room when she was watching television one day and told her that they had found somebody they would like her to marry. 'She made it clear that that would make them happy so I agreed, which was stupid in hindsight but at the end of the day I was afraid to say no to them.' Shahira and her family flew out to Kashmir and the first time she met her husband was after they had signed the marriage papers. They then flew back to England to start a new life. She had never had another relationship. 'It was scary and very difficult to be the "wife". I was supposed to be running a house and making sure there were meals but my idea of a meal is getting a sandwich, and I don't see that it is my responsibility to make sure that he eats. He wants a clean house and unquestioning support, someone who is willing to listen to him all the time, someone to be there to attend to his needs. If he wants something I should be able to fetch it, if things need washing, ironing or mending I should know that and he believes that this is how marriage should be.' Her husband was also homesick, at sea in a foreign culture with very little English, and they were just scraping by financially with her job and his at the local café until she gave birth to her baby and had to give up work. With a child to consider, Shahira felt even more trapped and miserable in a loveless marriage with a man who found it hard to accept that she had friends, interests and a life of her own.

'He doesn't like me reading, which is odd. He doesn't understand the concept of personal space. He doesn't want to be alone but with me all the time, and finds it irritating when I am buried in a book and not talking to him, whereas I like being on my own.' Shahira likes to escape from her unhappiness in books. 'But that's probably not as helpful as I think it is because it's feeding some notion of a romantic universe where love wins out, when it doesn't. Seeing other people being happy can be difficult, too. Most of my friends are single and miserable. It's just this feeling that there must be something better out there – better versions of this – but equally I want to make it work, I don't want to be a bad wife. I feel bad about complaining because my problems are really quite insignificant in a way, when there are other people out there starving and dying. I am not destitute. I also feel awful about breaking rank and not towing the whole "my marriage is fine" line. It's all very well when you are out with friends and pretending things are OK but at the end of the day you still have to go back to that house, and that can be a lonely place to be. You kind of feel that there is nowhere to go which is really yours. You need to get out because home is a place where there are all these expectations of you, all these things that you are basically failing to do. I don't think I am as happy or as confident as I used to be. I feel very oppressed, really, tense whenever he is around, and then I feel bad about not being particularly nice to him when he is thousands of miles away from his family. To a certain extent it may be my upbringing, but you do expect personal fulfilment to go out of the window as a woman. You feel selfish thinking about yourself because your marriage and your children should come first, so it becomes all about other people and how to fulfil their needs, not your own.'

Shahira has tried to talk to her mother about how she feels and she is supportive, but her view is that nobody has an easy time in marriage and that you have to make the best of it. 'You are expected to manage your husband, to know when to pick your moments and choose your battles, but that's not easy when you lack the emotional skills.' Shahira also knows that leaving, or taking her problems to an outsider for help, would be considered an even greater crime. 'I'd have to be strong enough to leave both my husband and my family, and I am not. There are some who get divorced and just about manage to stay within the family but it's not the done thing. There are huge ructions every time it happens. That's what your family are there for, to arbitrate when there are problems. I had a cousin who was being beaten so badly by her husband that he perforated her eardrum and put her in hospital. She chose help with her baby son from the social services rather than from her own family, who were horrified by what he had done. But once she was back they started to turn on her, saying that perhaps she hadn't been telling the truth. You stay in a marriage, however bad, and if there are problems you sort it out with the family. Even though my parents are fairly enlightened, I cannot ever really know what would happen if I chose to leave or if something happened like that.'

When I asked Shahira how bad it would have to get for her to consider leaving she said that physical violence might be enough of a trigger. 'But even then I'm not quite sure what would happen. I would tell my parents and they would talk to him, and then I would go back to him, that's what would happen. I think death is probably the only way out of it. I don't know why I am laughing because it has to be a competition as to who dies first, really.'

An essential aspect to the new balance of power in relationships is a respect for each other's right to privacy and a life outside the relationship. The great hidden danger of the new deal in more equable partnerships is the romantic fantasy that we should want to be involved in every aspect of each other's lives. In most middle-class Victorian marriages, men and women occupied very separate spheres, and relations were much more formal and distant. There was no expectation that every confidence should be shared, and marriage manuals of the period counselled against it. Now the ability to talk intimately is considered crucial to a healthy relationship, and people feel guilty for having secrets or for wanting to keep some element of private space to themselves. Couples who juggle the demands of work and family on a daily basis often find it hard to voice that need for some sense of separateness within their togetherness when there is so little free time even for each other. 'Privacy as a couple is really important, but so too is private time for me in my own mind,' says Philip. 'I really need that, and I would love to know that Juliet needs that too, but it's not easy to talk about it.'

Jackie found herself unexpectedly pregnant again at the age of forty in a very loving and happy relationship after six years as a single mother. 'The domestic scene was imposed on me again, and I found it really hard to give up that sense of having my own personal space.' Her first child was a teenager, and she herself liked to get up between 2 a.m. and 4 a.m. to write. 'I am a night owl, and I love that time when everyone else is asleep and it feels as if that time belongs to me. But when the baby came along and this new, lovely relationship, I couldn't do that any more, and I have this feeling that I have to find me in all of this, find where I am.' She had a third child soon afterwards. Her husband is caring and adoring, but he never goes out on his own with the boys or pursues individual interests outside the home. He likes them to do things together, as a couple. He once asked her what her ideal holiday was, and when she answered truthfully that it would be meeting up with old girlfriends who now lived in the States, he got upset by the fact that her ideal holiday was not going to some romantic paradise with him. 'The kids were quite young, and at that time what I needed was to go somewhere where I could be me, Jackie, and not his wife or somebody's mother, where you had no responsibility except for yourself. I wish he wanted to do more stuff on his own; perhaps then he would have more of an understanding that this space I want to occupy is sacrosanct rather than making me feel so selfish for wanting it. I worry that talking to him about it will make him think I don't want him. That's not what it's about at all – it's about having somewhere to rediscover who you are because it's so easy to forget that as a wife and mother.'

The idea that we should be all things to each other is new. Not so very long ago men and women occupied very different worlds. Men didn't just go out to work, they went out to play as well, at the football, in pubs, clubs or the garden shed. Research by Ann Whitehead in Herefordshire during the 1970s found that the amount of time husbands spent drinking triggered unhappiness, rows and violence but rarely divorce. 'Some young wives found that the marriage they dreamed of, with evenings spent in front of the fire with a chosen companion, turned out to be a succession of evenings spent alone with the television and the baby and the husband's dinner drying up on a plate over a pan of simmering water.'[9] Many men preserved their tough, masculine image by not going home, by not being seen to be under their wife's thumb. Diana Leonard's study of marriage in Swansea in the 1960s found that it was only when couples were courting that they spent substantial amounts of time in each other's company.[10] Thankfully, those days of separate worlds are dying out as the working lives of men and women become more similar. Young couples are much more likely to go shopping or to the football together now than with friends of their own sex. 'We don't do very much apart,' says Katrina. 'I would rather come home to David than go out and have a drink with my girlfriends, which is probably sad, but I work really long hours and that's enough. I just want to come home. I have known him for most of my adult life – we met two months after I left home – and we sometimes feel like it's the two of us against the world. We have to cope and sort out our own problems because our families are abroad and neither of us has anyone else to turn to.' David feels similarly. 'We are each other's closest confidant in every respect, and that closeness has just increased with time to a point where it becomes indistinguishable from love. We are very private, in that we only share things with each other.'

The downside to this new sense of intimate togetherness is that personal, individual needs can get squashed out of the equation. 'If you're in a relationship then you want to spend time with them,' says Megan, who is in her early thirties and lives with the father of her baby daughter. 'But the biggest change for me was this sense that my social circle was dissipating. I remember feeling a bit of grief – here I was, in this really nice relationship, but also withdrawing as a couple from the bigger social network. I am more focused on the here and now and my relationship than on going out tonight, which used to be my favourite thing. A lot of my old friends have also had children and moved out of London, so it's that much harder to see them. You can't just pop by. You make new friends, but there is something false about that because you don't know them at a deeper level, you only know these people because they have babies of the same age. What I miss is the opportunity to see and talk with my old friends, and I just don't have enough of those now . . .' Megan comes from a large family and she was used to big gatherings when she was younger, which she also misses. Her parents live three hours' drive away, so they have to make plans to visit. She would love to have hordes of siblings and cousins staying with her for the weekend, but her partner tends to resist both these ideas.

Research seems to confirm that couples are being thrown more and more on to each other for support as their working lives get busier. A study conducted by sociologists at Duke University in North Carolina compared the numbers of 'confidants' people felt they had in 1985 to 2004. There was a sharp decline in close relationships with family members, co-workers, neighbours and friends, and the numbers of those who had nobody to confide in at all tripled. The only relationship where there was a rise in the number of people who said they could talk about important matters was marriage. The number of people who depended solely on a spouse for close conversation almost doubled from 5 per cent to 9.4 per cent. Most of these were younger people who had lost touch with university friends and become overwhelmed by the demands of work, maintaining a loving relationship and then having children.[11]

It may feel like a bridge too far, keeping any kind of life outside a relationship going, but that is one of the most important ways we can make the relationship last. It is dangerous to insist that love means always being together, giving up solitary pursuits, friends or a sense of ourself as an independent person. When relationships become this exclusive, individual identity is compromised, any difference of desire becomes harder to negotiate without being seen as a betrayal, one partner feeling abandoned or lonely. Couples are supposed to confide solely in each other, but to do so with complete honesty might hurt a partner's feelings. They harbour secrets which they feel they shouldn't have. They covertly carve out space for individual pleasures, which couples in more traditional arrangements take for granted because their worlds are less entwined. In fact, we strengthen our relationships by not expecting them to be the sole refuge from the pressures of work and modern life, and the happiest couples seem to find complete trust in the spaces between their togetherness. The more secure they are in their love, the more separate and different they can be. Neither feels diminished or overly compromised, and each is consequently more able to argue constructively and cogently to make sure their needs are met. 'It would be impossible for me to lose myself in this relationship because of who I am, so strong in myself I can't be lost,' says Oliver, who has been with partner Jerome for ten years. 'It's like a wonderful raspberry swirl ice cream: it has a light pink whirl which is us together, but there is still the dark pink and the white. But we were fully formed adults when we met.'

The emphasis on romantic togetherness is so strong that often people presume that there must be flaws, difficulties or unhappiness in a relationship where partners holiday or do things apart. When I asked Evie why she thought her marriage had lasted for nearly thirty years with three grown-up children, her reply – 'We don't see a lot of each other' – may have been meant as a light quip but there was more than an element of truth to it. She works late three nights a week and has always enjoyed socialising and late-night drinking; he teaches music and likes to compose in solitude while she is out, and then go to bed early. They have total respect for each other's needs as individuals. 'I know that what matters to me is my own sense of personal space. I can't bear to feel controlled,' says Evie. 'We're both people who need separate private space and neither of us resents that; there is very little jealousy. I don't begrudge the fact that he is doing his own work or off travelling, and I have never felt suffocated or controlled by him and I really appreciate that. But other people seem to assume that your relationship must be unloving in some way, or that he doesn't care, but that's just not the case. We have a really deep sense of companionship and that's fantastic, it's so comfortable and priceless. We like spending Sundays together, and we love going on holiday together, and if you can do those two things happily then you really do have the basis for an ongoing relationship. But I like late-night drinking and socialising, and he doesn't. A long time ago I used to go out drinking with a friend from work and have crap conversations about politics and the meaning of life with others, and this friend kept saying to me, "Are you sure your husband doesn't mind?" No matter how much I said that he didn't I could see this man thinking, This can't be right. Then one night my husband met me there and I introduced them, and he shook this man's hand and said, "Thank you so much for giving me so many nights when I could go to bed at a reasonable time," because he hates the very idea of sitting in some bar in Soho with dodgy toilets where you have to queue. My friend from work was completely gobsmacked!'

'We always go off and do separate things with our friends, and that's very important to us,' says Carol. 'Otherwise you end up as this boring couple who always do the same stuff together all the time. We both have separate interests. I'm not interested in going to gigs or the football, and Tom's not interested in girly things. But we've both been shocked by the number of comments we get like, "So Tom doesn't mind you going out, then?" Well, why should he? Or it's, "Tom out tonight too, then?" "Well, no, actually I think he's watching television."' Like many happier couples where both are working, they have learned that this sense of separateness works not because they are distanced from each other but because it allows them to come together. 'You have to learn how to give each other space and stop making the other account for things. We know each other so well that there is no point in trying to make each other into something we're not, and we don't feel the need to give each other permission. We're actually more interested in each other, in who we met and what they said. It means we've always got something to talk about.'

'My belief reinforced by twenty years of practice is that in the course of establishing security, many couples confuse love with merging,' writes Esther Perel in her book *Mating in Captivity*. 'Love rests on two pillars: surrender and autonomy. Our need for togetherness exists alongside our need for separateness. One does not exist without the other. With too much distance there can be no connection. But too much merging eradicates the separateness of two distinct individuals. Then there is nothing more to transcend, no bridge to walk on, no one to visit on the other side, no other internal world to enter. When two people become fused, when two become one – connection can no longer happen. There is no one to connect with.' When each has a life outside the relationship, as well as the knowledge that they have enough money of their own to be able to leave it if need be, they choose how to live together and they fashion a partnership which more readily suits them as individuals. 'We can be different,' says Sureena, who has been married to Spike for thirteen years. 'We can allow each other space because I know that fundamentally we want the same things. We share the same values about how we live in that we want to be good parents to our children, we value education and we don't want to be overwhelmed by consumerism.'

We are in the unique position of being able to tread new ground, establishing a balance between home and work, where our sense of self as an individual isn't swamped by what it means to be a couple. Inevitably, when there are decades together rather than just years, there are times when the power balance between two people feels unequal, when one is more dependent upon the other. A long and contented relationship is built on the basis of fairness: neither owns the other; each must continue to be their own person, connected to the wider world by a range of interests and a history of their own.

Imogen and Gareth have been married for more than thirty-five years. There is a great deal of respect and affection between them, even though there have been times when the power balance between them has been distinctly unequal. When their children were small, Imogen took on most of the responsibility for their welfare as well as her job in local government, and Gareth had an affair, which led to a temporary separation. Then, when he was in his early fifties, Gareth had a stroke and was unable to continue working, and Imogen became the one with a lot more power in the relationship, as well as a new high-profile job of her own. 'There have been times in our marriage when the shifts in the balance of power have been immense. I have grown stronger through the marriage, and now I have all the power I don't much like it because I don't see myself that way. I am now earning, and he isn't, but we have always shared our money so it isn't an issue. We are quite compatible in that we each adapt a bit to what the other likes, but we are also quite comfortable with the other having a set of things that they are interested in. I have no interest in football or golf, and he does. I love my work, and the fact that I now have to travel for it, even though that can be difficult because he isn't that good on his own. I think we have reached an equilibrium over the years, but not without some cost. Sometimes there has been too much separateness and sometimes one or other of us has had to suppress a bit too much of the "me-ness" of "me".'

The strongest structure is a triangle. We may be each other's most important person, but that does not mean we do not need anyone else. If we see ourselves as standing on one corner of that triangle, reaching out not just to each other but also to another point outside that relationship, we are reminded of who we really are. There are so many ways in which we can all be sucked into the vortex of coupledom and need to find ourselves again. Ruby remembers the first time she went abroad with one of her children, but without her husband. 'He had always held all of the passports, and after ten years of never having even to think about that I was suddenly very apprehensive of all that responsibility again and whether I was up to it. Which was of course mad, given that I had spent years travelling as an independent woman before we married.' With time, we get so used to being with somebody that we can almost forget how to be on our own.

Florence has been deeply in love with Grace for years and they have one child. 'They went away for a few days, and being on my own for the first time was a revelation. I was scared, and didn't like the noises at night. It was pathetic given that for years I lived on my own happily. So I started hitting town and making sure I saw all my friends, and it was like, "Oh my God! I remember this," wandering around Brighton at 2 a.m., and it's exciting. There's a much greater intensity of thought when you're on your own, and when you're in a live-in relationship with a child that just gets smothered. Your sense of self does disappear to a certain extent without you noticing, and then you think, Does that matter?' Florence's relationship was so intense and satisfying that she never considered herself outside the relationship until she developed a small flirtation with someone else. 'I have been utterly faithful, I haven't done anything wrong. I haven't even snogged someone else, and I wouldn't because I am hugely committed to Grace and would chase her to the ends of the earth if she left me. But this little distraction just makes me feel young and desirable again. It's like having a renewed sense of self because somebody else finds me attractive and I don't want to lose that, even though we can't talk about it. I think it's healthy, that reminder of what it feels like to be a bit more autonomous, that there is and always will be that bit of me before I met her.'

With that sense of otherness, the reminder that each has integrity as a human being, we are less likely to take the other for granted. There is always someone, or something, which could potentially seduce one partner away. The emphasis is on us to engage and behave, and consequently build more tenacious, respectful and fairer relationships, able to withstand the normal stresses of change through life as well as adversity if and when it strikes. The longer we spend in a 'good enough' intimate relationship, the happier we are to be defined by it. The more secure we feel, the easier it is to acknowledge that we can have separate lives without it threatening our union. 'As I get older it becomes more obvious that that's the way to be,' says Hilary, who is in her forties. She adores Robin, has been married to him for most of her adult life, but regularly goes out alone or with friends to the theatre and cinema. 'When you start out you want to do things together and be together, but then you just become more and more yourself and possibly more selfish. Robin works long hours, so when he comes home he just wants to chill out, watch the news or the rugby all afternoon on Saturday. I am much more accepting of that now, and that gives me more freedom too.'

Robin feels the same way. 'Hilary and I have acknowledged for a long time now that we have different interests. I work hard and she goes out with friends and that's fine, but people have said to me, "Why don't you go along too?" And, "That's so peculiar!" Why would I want to? I have never thought of that as peculiar. If it was something that we were both interested in then great, but often I am tired. I like going to the movies but on my own terms. If she says, "I am going to see a film in ten minutes, do you want to come?" and I haven't thought about it or put it in my diary, I don't want to go even if it's a film I want to see. Sometimes she will go and see something by herself or with friends, and then so will I on another night and we talk about it three nights later.' They have also broken down the high walls of the nuclear family by bringing elements of the outside world into their home with a series of lodgers. 'Our house is a good haven for us, but it's not a refuge from the world. We don't need to scurry home and huddle,' says Robin.

Equable, companionable, loving lifelong relationships are forged by two people arguing their case and standing up for themselves; they are not born merely out of love or by slipping into the prescribed traditional roles associated with the marriages of our parents. More often than not it is women who challenge these presumptions because they are less willing to roll over into subservience. Feminism and the changing role of women has done more to strengthen the quality of heterosexual relationships than anything else. Women now expect to work, to be as socially and culturally integrated as men, and they have forced the men in their lives to soften and express more of their intuitive side. Our lives have become much more similar; our roles at home and at work are more interchangeable. With a sense of separateness within their togetherness, each partner grows to respect the other as an individual. 'A good marriage is that in which each appoints the other guardian of his solitude,' writes Rainer Maria Rilke in one of his letters.[12] Consequently togetherness is born of choice and rarely threatening. It was an ideal imagined for herself by Virginia Woolf; she wrote in her diary in 1917: 'It's as if marriage were a completing of the instrument, & the sound of one alone penetrates as if it were a violin robbed of its orchestra or piano.'[13]

6

THE DOUBLE BED

'Marriage is a result of the longing for the deep, deep peace of the double bed after the hurly-burly of the chaise longue,' the actress Mrs Patrick Campbell, who died in 1940, once famously said. The double bed is the symbolic emotional epicentre of a marriage. But it is not just an arena for the intimacies of complete sexual abandon, or those erotic-free cuddles and caresses. It is the seat of family security, home to sick or sleepless children, often the place for the opening of birthday presents, Christmas stockings and the Sunday papers. Because it is such a private place it can become a dark or lonely wrestling ring when things go wrong. Resentments get brought to bed and flare up in the middle of the night with insomnia and a marked reluctance even to touch, as angry couples lie at the furthest edges of their half with an imaginary barrier between them. 'I know what it is like to be in a double bed with someone and feel lonely,' says Holly, who went through a difficult period in her marriage after the birth of her second child. 'And that's horrible, more horrible than being on your own.' Nevertheless, leaving that double bed for the sofa feels like an act of betrayal. Fantasies of sleeping alone or of separate beds, one in London and the other in Manchester, surface with the rage.

Good sex is the glue that is supposed to hold marriages and relationships together. Bad sex, boring sex or no sex at all is now considered a good enough reason to leave. For centuries sex was compromised by a whole range of issues, from fear of pregnancy, the power of the Church, ill health and rampant, untreatable venereal disease, to overcrowded housing and lack of cleanliness. Now we don't have to marry to get laid and we can experiment endlessly with a wide range of partners before we settle down. However, new sexual pressures and expectations have surfaced which throw up new problems and compromise lifelong relationships and our attitudes to fidelity, commitment and happiness.

Sex is difficult to talk about. For many it is something shameful. A survey of over eight hundred people by netdoctor.com found that a quarter had been brought up to think of sex as something 'dirty'. It is so private that often we don't have the language to convey our innermost thoughts or sexual desires even if we are lucky enough to know what they are, yet the little research that has been conducted shows that the more couples talk about sex in general, the better the quality of their sex lives and the happier they are together both in and out of that double bed.[1] Sex was inevitably the one great area of difficulty in the countless interviews I conducted for this book. I was aware of having to brace myself to ask questions about it and push through our mutual embarrassment to try to get at some sort of truth. Surprising numbers of couples in long-term, stable relationships said that they could talk about anything to each other, but then went on to say for the first time in each other's company that they were aware that one of them – always the man – wanted more sex than they got. Even those who have been prepared to go to couple counselling admitted that it would be hard to take their sexual problems outside the relationship. 'I'd be too embarrassed to do that with sex,' says Florence. 'In a way it would be good, but ugggh . . . It would also be admitting something that you wouldn't want to air, and I haven't got time in my life. There is something to be said for the shut-up-and-shag attitude, just

don't over-analyse it so much! What throws me are all those surveys which indicate that people seem to be having much more
sex than I am.'

Without honesty, we cannot help but compare our relationships with a romanticised, mythical image of constant explosive,
sexual compatibility, and feel inadequate. Cultural imagery almost
always presents sexual pleasure as youthful, heterosexual, immediate, electric and mutually satisfying, with vaginal penetration
and orgasm as its goal. It's always intensely enjoyable rather than
occasionally messy, painful, unwanted or boring, for sexual desire
fluctuates through the course of a relationship, and reflects
how we feel about ourselves as well as each other. The sex we
see usually conforms to male rather than female interpretations
of what is sexy. We never see old people or fat people enjoying sex
in their own way, and anything that might vary from 'vanilla sex' or
the missionary position, such as the acting out of fantasies, verges
on the perverse. Handbooks may be explicit and offer practical
advice about how to do it, but the art of sex, the grace and pleasure
of sex we absorb from the pervasive, semi-pornographic imagery
of film, television, magazines and advertisements. It is only after
years of experience with a loving partner that we can begin to free
ourselves from this imagery and relax enough to enjoy it our way.
With a plethora of sexual imagery around us, it is no wonder that
so many people have blinkered, ignorant views about the way that
sex changes over the course of a relationship. 'I remember one of
my husband's close friends saying to him soon after we met, "This
may be what you want sexually now, but that doesn't last for
ever,"' says Ursula. 'When he told me that I remember thinking,
It doesn't?'

As soon as there's a lull in our sex life, the assumption is that
everyone else must be having more sex and better sex than we are,
but the research evidence suggests otherwise. Those who are married or committed to a relationship have better sex, and more of
it, than those who are not. Single men are roughly twenty times
more likely to be celibate than married men.[2] A recent large US

survey found that sexual activity among the general population is far less vigorous than one might imagine, with just a third of American adults having sex twice a week or more, another third having sex once or several times a month and the final third a few times a year or not at all, with interestingly no variations across race, religion, ethnicity or level of education.[3] The largest survey of sexual behaviour in Britain conducted in 2000 found that married women between the ages of sixteen and twenty-four had had sex six times on average in the past four weeks, and that fell to twice in the past four weeks in the forty-five to fifty-nine age group. The equivalent average for men was seven times in the past four weeks, dropping to three in the forty-five to fifty-nine age group.[4] While the frequency of sex within an established relationship drops the longer the relationship continues, both of these large surveys found that married couples are still having more sex and better sex than those not living with a sexual partner. The American survey found that people in more casual relationships reported considerably lower rates of physical and emotional satisfaction than those in established relationships. They worried far more about the future of the relationship and sex was the main focus, with fewer other means of communication and support, whereas for those with trust in their commitment to each other, sex was just 'one of many avenues of exchange'.[5]

Many presume that the best sex is the intense, passionate lust when we first come together and that once that has gone the relationship is over. There is no doubt that sex with a new body can be delicious. 'Waking up with your arms tied in a knot around each other because you have made love four times on that night alone . . . I do miss that energy which comes from being intimate with someone new,' says Lawrence, who has been with his partner Jane for five years. But sexual novelty is just one small aspect of a wide palette of sexual experience. In the early stages of love we can afford to fuse and lose ourselves in each other's bodies, stare into each other's eyes for hours or lie locked in each other's limbs after orgasm because we are entirely separate beings, and such physicality bonds a relationship we want to work. Once your lives are linked in other ways, when you have seen each other in your least attractive moments, the urge to pull away can be more powerful. We need to retreat at times, in order to preserve our sense of separateness. And staring into each other's eyes? Well, it's just plain silly, isn't it? 'I think sex means different things to people at different times,' says Robin, who has been married for twenty-five years. 'There's the intense, passionate-relationship sex, which keeps it together and which is essential, and infidelity at that point destroys it. Then there is recreational sex, which is a one-night stand, or masturbation. Then possibly there is reproductive sex, which is slightly special and different again. Then you can have routine sex in that you're in a relationship, you're in the same bed, you hadn't planned it but what about it, it's familiar and nice in its own way. The problems come when people are having different kinds of sex – I'm having recreational sex, but the other person is having relationship sex, or, God forbid, reproductive sex . . .'

The intensity of that early passion disappears for a good reason: it would be impossible to sustain over the course of a lifetime. As couples settle down, with time and commitment they get to know each other better and that sense of physical idealisation and sexual hunger wanes. Our body chemistry changes after about two years in a relationship as the passion-inducers, neurotrophins, are replaced by higher levels of what is known as the cuddling hormone, oxytocin. 'Ordinary life, the rising in the morning and the setting the coffee on its way and the picking up of the paper and the waiting for the bathroom,' writes Anne Roiphe in her memoir *Married: A Fine Predicament,* 'are all part of the erosion of romance, the end of excitement, the dulling of the erotic factor.'

The longer a relationship lasts the greater the likelihood that one or both partners should find their sex drive diminished, or opportunities for sex compromised by circumstance. Illness, injury, stress or exhaustion in our workaholic culture, childbirth and caring for children, depression, anxiety, mental health problems, drug or alcohol use, family difficulties, grief, lack of time, prolonged separation for work or family issues, ageing, menopause – all are common factors which affect the delicate sexual chemistry of a relationship. In fact, it's a minor miracle that so many people in marriages and long-term relationships manage to have sex at all. Ruby says that when her husband was out of work for a while, 'He was unable to motivate himself enough even to look for it. I was so angry with him for letting us down, I could barely get into bed beside him, let alone touch him.' Sam says that 'As soon as Diana got pregnant, for the first time in my life my sex drive disappeared. I just wasn't interested at all, and suddenly it was me saying, "I'm a bit tired", and I don't know whether it was biological or just some switch going off – you've created a baby so there's no need.' Katrina says that when David was on antidepressants, 'He went off sex completely for about a year and that was a real low point. I found that very hard because I felt unattractive and I missed the sex. I didn't think for a second that he was interested in anyone else; he wasn't interested in me, and it might have affected the intimacy between us because I am much more tactile than he is. Of course now that we have a baby there is no sex at all – we're both much too tired. I have taught him, though, that we have to cuddle before we go to sleep, then everything is OK.' Jackie says that sex was a huge part of her marriage, 'Until I hit the menopause and my libido dropped. But I found it very difficult to talk to Bill about it, which was odd since I can talk to him about everything else, and I felt huge guilt. He put a lot of pressure on me to have sex when I didn't want to, and I am sure he thought I didn't love him any more. It was only when he suggested that we took the issue out of the double bed and went for walks in the middle of the day instead that I could really talk about how I felt so that he understood that it was me, not him.'

The explosion of explicit sexuality in our culture is recent. Few had much in the way of knowledge or experience of sex until just a few decades ago. Geoffrey Gorer conducted two large-scale surveys of attitudes towards sex and marriage in people under the age of forty-five in 1950 and 1969. He found surprisingly high levels of sexual inexperience in 1969, in spite of the Swinging Sixties, with 26 per cent of married men and 63 per cent of women virgins until they wed. A further 20 per cent of men and 25 per cent of women went on to marry the person with whom they first had intercourse.[6] Even the word 'sex' was considered offensive, called instead 'the intimate side of marriage' in the problem pages of *Woman's Own* until the mid-1960s when 'intercourse' was finally openly referred to.[7] There was widespread ignorance about sex and its pleasures. 'Certain things your husband will require of you,' was a mother's advice in Lincoln during the 1950s on her daughter's wedding night. 'It's not nice, and you will just have to put up with it.'[8]

The sex advice literature of the last century was written in the main by men, and consequently presupposed female complicity with a male view of sexual pleasure. L. B. Sperry's popular *Confidential Talks with Husband and Wife* published in 1900 said that sex should be mutually pleasurable, but there were no descriptions as to how, or guidance as to how much sex was permissible, although men were exhorted to cultivate restraint. And as for a woman's pleasure? Well . . . *Nature's Revelations for the Married Only*, published in 1904, assumed that as long as a woman had not been subjected to a 'Mistaken sense of manliness on the wedding night and was not the victim of selfish husbandry excess, mutual pleasure was a matter which needed no instruction.'[9] The idea that a woman's pleasure was irrelevant or secondary began to change slowly with the pioneering work of the birth-control movement and books such as *Studies in the Psychology of Sex* by Havelock Ellis, also published in 1904, the first writer at that time to point out that good sex was a conjugal art which had to be learned. Havelock Ellis researched literary and medical resources from Ancient Greece to early modern Europe and discovered, to his amazement, that women had been thought to enjoy sex more than men, and that it was nineteenth-century Puritanism which had sought to protect them from wanton sexual abandon. But it was the publication of *Married Love* by Marie Stopes in 1918 which fundamentally changed thinking about sex within marriage. She talked about women's desire: 'So widespread in our country is the view that it is only depraved women who have such feelings (especially before marriage) that most women would rather die than own that they *do* at times feel a physical yearning indescribable, but as profound as hunger for food.' She described a woman's anatomy during arousal, and the cyclical nature of desire in relation to menstruation in extraordinarily explicit terms for those times, and she blamed ignorance in men for failing to seduce properly. 'It should be realised that a man does not woo and win a woman once and for all when he marries her. *He must woo her before every separate act of coitus*, for each act corresponds to a marriage as other creatures know it.'

With the birth of 'sexology', sex emerged as a recreational pastime. Orgasm, particularly women's, became a prerequisite for good health and matrimonial harmony and dozens of new books were published to tell you how. E. F. Griffith's *Modern Marriage* went into nineteen editions between 1935 and 1946. He gave lectures on the importance of marriage, and believed that sexual problems were the most common stumbling block. But with this spotlight on the importance of sex and sexual pleasure within marriage there was, 'A new emphasis on getting it right, in the right place', writes Roy Porter in his book on the history of sexual knowledge in Britain, *The Facts of Life*, and a whole new set of anxieties in relationships were raised. These pragmatic, empirical and reassuring manuals, 'Not only disseminated, but recreated sexual knowledge,' continues Porter. Normal sex was now defined, and narrowly at that. Dutch gynaecologist Theodor Van de Velde's *Ideal Marriage: Its Physiology and Technique* was published in 1926, went into forty editions, had twenty-five pages on coital positions and stated knowledgeably that 'The bridal honeymoon should blossom into the perfect flower of ideal marriage', as a woman's desire is awoken, Sleeping Beauty style, by the man. Normal and perfect sex was defined as heterosexual, excluded the use of sadomasochism or artificial devices and had simultaneous orgasm through intercourse as its goal, for 'The man's orgasm begins and sets the woman's acme of sensation in train at once.' A staggeringly inaccurate account but an enduring myth prolifererated by a man who left his wife for a twenty-eight-year-old patient and based his theory entirely on his own love life.[10]

There is now a stark contrast between our culture, where everything screams sex, and the reality of people's love lives, which are often inactive or difficult. It is easy for individuals to feel as if they are failing when it is conceivable that these new pressures are exacerbating their sexual problems, as it can seem that sex has to be a transcendental experience, with both experiencing delicious orgasms, for it to be considered worthwhile. 'I have a low sex drive, but I think there was always this sense of inadequacy, that I should be enjoying this because this is what other people do,' says Lawrence. In just a few decades sexual relationship had been completely redefined from a religious duty to a necessity, a fundamental key to our health and well-being, with a whole new emphasis placed on mutual sexual satisfaction. In 1955, agony aunt Mary Grant's reply to a reader in *Woman's Own* who said she had been married for fourteen years and didn't like sex was, 'Your husband has a legitimate grievance. However good you are in other ways, you are failing in part of your duty to him.' In 1980 her reply to a woman who had been married for twelve years and felt the same way was, 'You and your husband need sexual intercourse as an expression of your whole selves and your love for each other.'[11]

The new sexology of the twentieth century defined an active, regular and mutually satisfying sex life as central to a healthy and happy marriage, without much in the way of solid research to go on. Difficulties with sex research are legendary given that human beings are one of the few species that needs privacy to perform. It wasn't until Alfred Kinsey published his surveys of human sexual behaviour in the 1950s, and Masters and Johnson studied live copulation in humans rather than animals in the 1970s, that we began to understand more about human sexual response. However enlightening, these observations cannot be extrapolated from the burgeoning sexually explicit culture of the late 1960s, where being able to say 'yes' made it harder for women to say 'no', and the new *Penthouse*-style soft porn defined the nature of 'good' or 'normal' sex in much the same way as the sex manuals of the early twentieth century had done – still male in its interpretation. Women's bodies were exposed and overtly sexed up as they pouted at the camera for male consumption. Female submission and sexual purity had been replaced by an equally inhibiting need for female sex appeal.

The reality today is that substantial numbers of couples experience sexual difficulties or indifference at some point in their relationship. According to the largest British survey of sexual practices, 35 per cent of men and 53 per cent of women with one heterosexual partner in the previous year had experienced at least one sexual problem lasting a month. Men commonly experienced lack of interest in sex, premature orgasm or anxiety about their performance, while women complained of painful intercourse or an inability to experience orgasm.[12] A similarly large study of 27,500 forty- to eighty-year-old people in thirty countries published in 2001 found that 25 per cent of women were unable to achieve orgasm for several months in the past year, 33 per cent reported lack of interest in sex for several months or more at least occasionally, and more than 30 per cent of men suffered from premature ejaculation or some other sexual dysfunction. A high percentage of both sexes also claimed that they didn't have sex often enough.[13] The modern medical ethos of fighting disease with drugs leads us easily into the delusional world of defining these difficulties as disorders which can be treated from the outside, with lubricants and Viagra – goldmines for the pharmaceutical industry – rather than as symptoms of deeper relationship difficulties, or a sense of inadequacy because of the cultural pressure to have constant, meaningful sex.

Sex is never just sex. It is intricately linked to our emotional and psychological states within a relationship, yet we disassociate the two and diminish their significance by seeing sex merely as a physical act. According to psychologists, sex gets complicated because the intense intimacy of commitment is reminiscent of the family we grew up with. 'The same fears that draw us to our partner in the hope of mastering unfinished psychological business may also provoke the defences that inhibit our sexuality,' write psychoanalysts Stephen Goldbart and David Wallin in their book *Mapping the Terrain of the Heart*. Prolonged sexual difficulties such as impotence, premature ejaculation, vaginismus and consistent failure to reach an orgasm are likely to have roots in childhood or family difficulties. 'When the past rears its head in the present and we see in our partner reflections of a parent, our sexual interest may diminish, because sexuality now has "incestuous" overtones.' You don't have to be the victim of profound physical, sexual or emotional abuse to find these echoes from the past inhibiting. 'All of us see ourselves in the mirror of our parents' response to our childhood sexuality and our body,' continue Goldbart and Wallin. 'Were they comfortable holding and nurturing us physically? Did they enable us to feel good about our body? Were they relaxed about our flirtation with them or with others?' We learn about sexuality from observing our parents' attitudes to sex and whether or not they were physically affectionate or withdrawn, and intuit that sex is either bad, mysterious or not to be talked about.

'Sex was never discussed at home, and my mother had a weird attitude towards it. She thought it was dirty, and I'm sure that's why it's always been difficult for me to talk about, even with my therapist. It's just so embarrassing,' says Jackie. Mark and Rebecca have been married for twenty-five years and they have two daughters. Mark is one of two brothers, brought up by a terminally ill single mother who died when he was twenty-one. 'His respect for his father is zero. You can see that when he talks to him because his father didn't do the one thing you expect a father to do, which is to look after your wife and children rather than run off with other women,' says Rebecca. One area of tension between them is that he wants her to wear feminine clothes, skirts and high heels all the time, even at the weekend. He buys her beautiful jewellery and notices when she has done her nails or hasn't had her hair done. 'Some of my friends think that's very nice that he notices, but I feel it's too much pressure, it's what's inside a person that matters, but he thinks it means you are still interested in your husband finding you attractive. I don't know whether it's to do with his dad's infidelity,' she asked me. She paled when I suggested that he might be frightened of not finding her sexually attractive any more because that would take him to a dark place, closer to his father's experience in having to resist temptation. 'Considering the infant training that the majority of people have had,' writes A. S. Neill in *Summerhill*, it 'is a matter for astonishment that there should be any happy marriages at all. If sex is dirty in the nursery, it cannot be clean in the marriage bed.'

Merging with and opening up to another person is both the pleasure and the problem of sex. A healthy sense of attachment to another human being isn't just important to us as children, it extends throughout life, as chapter four has shown, and inevitably affects the nature of our sex lives as we reveal more of our deepest selves in that double bed. A person who has grown up secure in the cradle of their parents' love tends to find it easier to operate independently and doesn't need to cling to their partner to shore up a fragile sense of self. Consequently, during sex, 'They have sufficient trust that the merger will not annihilate their individual identities. For the man, the ecstasy associated with fusion, and the early stage of elation in the mother–baby relationship, can coexist with the aggression needed to penetrate his partner,' write Christopher Clulow and Maureen Boerma in *Sex, Attachment and Couple Psychotherapy*. 'For the woman, the prospect of bodily fusion and aggression in intercourse does not unduly threaten her security, or evoke feelings of being intruded upon or being invaded in ways that threaten her sense of integrity.'

Both can experience a sense of letting go, of losing conscious control over their bodies, which makes sex more exciting and fulfilling. Those with more insecure, 'avoidant' attachment patterns can tend towards avoiding the emotional intensity of a close sexual relationship with one-night stands and prostitutes, while the anxiously attached can use sexual activity to forge close relationships with others through promiscuity.

Many 'disorders of desire' can be linked to attachment issues. 'In order to risk being fused with another in intercourse, the boundaries of the emotional and physical self have to be firmly in place,' write Sandy Rix and Avi Shmueli in *Sex, Attachment and Couple Psychotherapy*. 'Loss of sexual desire might be thought about as a protection of those "self" boundaries for the couple when, despite conscious desires for the contrary, they are too fragile to tolerate any fusion, however momentary.' A man who has an erection during masturbation or oral sex but regularly loses it during intercourse may fear his own aggression. A woman who feels insecure in the relationship because of childhood issues may find it difficult to relax and open up enough of herself to be able to orgasm. A man who was kissed regularly on the lips by his mother cannot stand to be kissed by his lovers. Most of the time we never stop to consider why we might like or dislike something sexually, but psychologists believe these blocks can develop because we need to protect our most fragile parts from danger. It takes a conscious desire to try to master them with someone we trust.

For those with early emotional difficulties, insecure childhood attachments or even deep disappointment in love during adolescence, power and powerlessness can become the emotional currency between a couple during sex rather than a loving respect for each other's autonomy. Sexual intimacy can feel so threatening for some, that 'perversions' such as sadomasochism provide ritualistic protection against the way love can permeate their sense of self as well as a means of channelling their own rage. In abusive relationships sex often becomes ugly – 62 per cent of sexual

assaults against women are committed in relationships.[14] There
are higher rates of sexual aggression in established rather than
casual affairs as partners assume they possess the other physically.
The monthly sexual frequency in American marriages with violent husbands is two and a half times higher than those with
non-violent husbands.[15, 16] 'Our marriage was intensely sexual but
there was no love,' says Rajani. 'One weekend he had sex with me
twenty-six times and I couldn't walk for two days I was so sore,
but he boasted about his sexual prowess to his friends.'

Just a glimmer of insight into the way our emotional history can
be replayed in the double bed can prevent sexual relations from
spiralling insidiously into a pattern which is abusive. That sense
of awareness or psychological introspection is more important
than ever now that overt imagery of sexualised violence and
gender-specific roles in heterosexual sex pervades our culture. We
grow up with huge assumptions about how we should behave
sexually as men and women: that men should initiate sex; that
a sexually forward woman is still considered unfeminine; that
women are passive rather than active, the sexual givers rather than
takers, objects of desire rather than desirous. Often sexual blocks
are linked to gender conditioning, with men finding it harder to
surrender the assertive role to their female partner and women
masking the less aggressive aspects of their eroticism to protect
their partner's ego. 'I've discovered that I do find it difficult to
reach orgasm if I am not in control, if Ann is, say, giving me a
hand job,' says Lawrence. 'Five years ago I would have had difficulty telling anyone that because I couldn't think of it as normal.
But now I can talk about it with her, she has made me come that
way and I've realised that it doesn't really matter what's normal
because we're all different. I think Ann in her way has had problems thinking that vaginal sex has to be the goal and anything else
is just an approximation of that. It's a conditioning, isn't it, that
that's the only sex worth having but we've managed to shake that
off with time, too.'

The assumptions that we make about loss of desire also tend to be gendered and stereotypical – men always want more sex than they get, while women tend to go off it. It is considered a female condition, an individual problem rather than a manifestation of a relationship problem. Low sex drive among men is usually disguised as a physical condition such as impotence or erectile dysfunction. Masculine staglike stereotypes and the pressure to perform can be so great that it is much better to protect a man's pride by medicalising the problem as treatable with Viagra, prescribed or bought privately by millions of men each year. Women are routinely depicted as – and describe themselves as – less interested and therefore less threatening to a man's sexual self-esteem rather than simply bored by their partner's ineptitude or the intense, almost sibling-like nature of their presence after so many years. 'I think I have always been undersexed,' says Alice. 'You want the release of orgasm, but you also know perfectly well that you could achieve that by yourself. We don't talk about it, though. He makes advances and obviously we do have sex, but sometimes it is quite scary how little it's a coming together of two people wanting something, and how it's nearly always because I think, Poor Theo hasn't had any for a fortnight. But there was also a period when Theo found it hard to get aroused, and I did think that was particularly unfair because they have this pressure to perform, and me lying there like a lump doesn't help much.'

There has been far more research and money invested into the treatment of male sexual loss of desire than female, which seems remarkably short-sighted given that it takes two to tango. With the plethora of cultural images, which always equates slim, youthful beauty with sex appeal, it can be hard for a woman to crank up desire whenever she feels fat or as close to looking like Nicole Kidman as the earth is to Pluto. Finding someone who you consider attractive enough to have sex with is often secondary to concerns about whether they find you sexually appealing as a woman.[17] Adanna has found that her partner wants more sex now that she is slightly bigger after three children. 'He likes my build a lot and I don't, and that is mainly the problem. At one point when I was getting bigger and bigger, he was finding me more and more attractive and wanting to jump me all the time. I could not understand how he could fancy me when *I* didn't fancy me.' Feeling sexy can also be intricately linked to a woman's hormonal cycles. Dozens of studies have found that female sexual desire peaks in mid-cycle and that after the menopause, those mid-cycle spikes in libido disappear.[18]

Jackie enjoyed an active sex life with her second husband until she reached the menopause. She would avoid the issue by going to bed early or she would just shut down. 'He would say to me that he didn't feel I was really there, and when I thought about how that must make him feel it was awful. I thought, I have to find a way to talk to him about this. But part of the reason why I went off sex was that I put on weight. My mum was very big, and I had such a difficult relationship with her. I was changing shape, I wasn't happy with my body and I didn't want him to come near me, and that must have been quite bewildering for Bill, when previously I had always been happy to throw off my clothes.' Bill had always been comfortable with his body and with hers: 'He was even happy to have sex with me during my periods, which was something I couldn't do.' She is a decade older than him, and this was the first time in their eighteen-year relationship that she had felt the age difference between them. 'If you can't find that sexy person within yourself, it is very hard to create it. When I was younger I would get dressed up and go out and think, Yay, go, girl, but it wouldn't cross my mind to think like that now. I do get dressed up but my first thought is not, Am I a sexy woman? but, Do I look like mutton dressed as lamb?' An awareness of the way in which we are so profoundly influenced by the ubiquitous images of youthful, sexy, beautiful women doesn't necessarily help. It just makes women feel more inadequate and vulnerable for not being able to rise above it. 'I say to Bill, this is how shallow I am in that it is my feelings about my body which get in the way of our sex life. If I thought I looked fantastic in a bra and suspenders I would wear them, but I see myself as a short, fat person, not a long-legged siren. I am sure there are women out there who feel confident about their sexuality in their fifties, sixties and seventies, and I would love to be one of them, but I don't know how to get there.'

'You can have non-intimate sex on a regular basis and some people only have non-intimate sex,' says sex therapist Sally Openshaw. 'A lot of women say they do it just to tick it off the list and that they would rather be watching *Coronation Street*, but that it's worth it because doing it is better than not doing it. You can use sex as a distance regulator or as a connector because if you have sex with them, the chances are they are going to be nice to you and warmer the next day.' There will be times in any life-long relationship when there is no sex or less-than-good sex. The question to ask is, is this just a passing phase, the product of circumstance such as the exhaustion of having small children, or is it the manifestation of some deeper malaise? Often we unknow-ingly torment our partners sexually because we cannot express our resentments or disappointments with the relationship in any other way. We withhold sex, engage in selfish or aggressive sex, give ourselves only partially to sex with 'mercy fucks' or prema-ture ejaculation. Reduced sex drive is a recognised symptom of depression, and for good reason. Our need to feel desired is an affirmation of our sense of self, and when we feel diminished by mood or swamped by circumstance, it is hard to feel worthy of sexual attention or willing to expose ourselves further through intimacy. But instead of thinking that it is anything to do with our own shortcomings in the relationship or the defences which surface as intimacy deepens, we may instead blame our partner or assume that we simply don't find them sexually attractive any more.

Jan's husband went to their doctor to talk about the fact that she didn't want to have sex with him. 'He talked to the doctor rather than to me, but that did at least provoke a conversation where we could discuss how I really felt. He wanted to know why our sex life couldn't be like it used to be, but there have been horrible

times in our relationship when we have had no physical relationship at all, and there have now been so many bad times that I
cannot remember the good times. It is hard to separate the two,
which is what I used to do. For a long time I had a semipermeable
membrane that would filter things out, but I don't think that's a
good thing to do, it's a form of self-deception and that's what
makes sex difficult. But there is a huge obstacle between us now –
it's my own rage – and I've been sweeping it under the carpet for
too long so that it has become a mountain. It isn't going to go
away overnight.'

Rebecca has felt resentful of her husband's privilege and control over their marriage for a long time, and she acknowledges that
sex between them is difficult because it is one area where she can
still hold the power. 'I am not as interested in sex as he is and I
know that's an issue. He has said that it just makes him feel worthless and rejected, always to have to make the first move, and that
if it's reciprocated, it's quite dutiful, which is true sometimes.
Quite often I think, Just get it over with and do what you want to
do and let's go to sleep, which must be horrible. Sometimes I
don't even pretend any more. But then if he feels that way, why
bother at all if it's that bad? He would perceive that as me holding all the power in the relationship, which in one sense I do, but
actually I feel quite disempowered. I feel it's the other way around
because if you don't respond even half-heartedly he just gets
grumpy and moody. I do it in a grudging way, which makes him
feel belittled, so we are both in this downward spiral and it's hard
to know how to get out of it.'

Couples often attribute their sexual difficulties to exhaustion,
differing lifestyles and not having enough time together, when
these factors can be disguising a deeper gulf between them.
'Ethan is often too tired from work and he likes to go to bed and
get up early, whereas I'm a late person and like to work on the
computer after the children have gone to bed,' says Amy, who is
busily preoccupied running a campaign against a local phone
mast. Ethan feels the pressure as the sole breadwinner, and while

he likes the fact that she has found an interest outside of their children, 'She spends every sodding night until one in the morning on the internet, fantastic, but in the long term it is wearing. Of course I agree with it, it takes someone to be the suffragette to lash themselves to the railings, but it's a shame it's my partner.' Their sex life is non-existent but Amy thinks the lower sex drive lies with Ethan because of some physical difficulty, rather than resentment. 'Maybe he has low testosterone or something. I always think it is his fault because he didn't want it as much as I did in the beginning, and I totally blamed him for it. If it's the other way round a man can persuade her, but if it's the woman making the running, he should just sort it out. He's so sensible, sometimes too sensible. He has never even had a one-night stand and he is very respectful of women, which is of course nice, but sometimes you just want him to be a little more risqué.'

It is hard to break out of that negative tendency and be more proactive. 'Rory's a terrible slumper in front of the TV which really annoys me so I go to bed, and then I am up before him in the morning. You get to a point where you just stop having sex. It's quite hard to have sex with someone if you're never awake at the same time in bed,' says Kate. 'It worried me, and then I talked to some girlfriends about it and most of them were sort of the same, you know, birthdays and Christmas, although I did have the world record in that we hadn't had sex for a year.' Her husband has been abroad a lot with his work, they have had financial worries and Kate has found herself deeply resenting the fact that he has been away and eating out every night on expenses, while she has been at home with the children, budgeting. 'When I tried to bring it up once and said, "Do you realise we haven't had sex for a year," it was almost as if he hadn't noticed, which I found a bit weird. I don't think he has ever had a particularly high sex drive, or maybe he's been shagging women all over the place, but I don't think he is. I miss the sex, but how can you find that mystique when they fart in front of you, and now that he has grown a beard, I'm sorry but I don't fancy that at all.'

People give often to their own detriment. The needs of others, particularly children, are so paramount and can be so draining that their own needs feel swamped, their sense of self sucked dry. The idea of exposing or giving even more of yourself through sex leads to a clampdown. Men and women can have different sexual needs, yet all around us it is the thrusting, explicit nature of a more male sex drive that is promoted as the norm. Women tend to prefer the slow, intimate build-up to sex; more often than not they like time to connect emotionally as they construct erotic and romantic stories in their head, while men tend to be much more able to cut to the quick and like to connect physically in order to feel loved. Interestingly, many of the men I interviewed assumed I was referring to their sex lives when I asked them how the love had changed through their relationship. 'He has always wanted more sex than me,' says Adanna, 'but a lot of it is about his approach, which can be like a schoolboy, and I want to be with an adult. I don't want to be grabbed or groped or told that I am tasty. OK, I might be doing the cleaning in my bra and knickers, but that's not an open invitation – I want to get the cleaning done! But maybe he could say some lovely things to me and make me feel sexy, then maybe when I have finished the cleaning I might feel like it. But I can't stand being pawed when I am doing something else, when I am busy. He says we only have this time, but I don't like fitting it in when the kids are out playing. I don't feel sexual in ten minutes, and he does, so in a sense we have different agendas.'

Two basic portraits of sexual activity emerged from Masters and Johnson's pioneering research, observing sexually active heterosexual and homosexual couples during the 1970s. There was efficient sex, often skilful and goal-directed, but the best sex, the most amazing sex was far slower, as couples took their time, teased each other and became as aroused by what they were doing to their partner as what was being done to them. 'The best sex going on in Masters and Johnson's sex lab was the sex being had by the committed gay and lesbian couples,' writes Mary Roach in her history of sexual research, *Bonk*. 'Not because they were practising special secret homosexual sex techniques, but because they *took their time.*' They lost themselves in each other and in sex. They tended to move slowly, lingering at each stage of response, appreciating each other. Yet all around us it is this intense, genital, quick shag fixation, which saturates everything from films, television dramas and soaps to advertising and pop music. 'I remember one of the first things he said to me was, "Don't ever fake it, I want this to be real,"' says Ursula of the man she was married to for seventeen years. 'But then all he ever wanted was penetrative intercourse, and I like that too, but that doesn't mean you don't like to mix it up a bit as well. Sometimes he would say, "I want you to come at the same time as me," and I would think, Whoa. And look at my watch and think, When are you going to come? What time is it? OK . . . 8.15. That means . . . but . . . Talk about pressure! Which means,of course, that you don't come. I tried to make him understand that this was porno magazine stuff, but he wouldn't have that, he said it was possible. In twenty years together I could count when that happened on the fingers of one hand.'

Sex may lead to children, but having a child does not necessarily lead to more sex. Childbirth can be traumatic both physically and psychologically, and sex is usually the last thing on a new mother's mind. Yet today the cultural expectation is not one of reclusive rest, but of bouncing back into an even sexier image as a mother who has no difficulty reconciling her new role with her sexual self. She is sleep-starved, slobs round the house exhausted in one of her partner's shirts, her breasts are engorged, she spends hours bonding with her beautiful new baby, wondering where the rest of her life has gone, but the celebrity new mothers in magazines look entirely different, so sexualised it's hard to believe they have given birth at all. Megan's one-year-old son still sleeps in their bedroom. 'Plus I had an episiotomy, and I was very sore for quite a few months. It was the last thing I wanted to do. I remember Charlie overheard a conversation I had been having with some other new mothers who were also saying

"No way," in a sort of jokey way, and he got quite upset that I had been talking about our lack of a sex life to them when actually it was good to know that we weren't the only ones.' Women also find it harder to focus exclusively on sexual activity among other distractions, particularly when there are children around. 'We didn't have sexual problems, but we started to have problems finding a good time to have sex,' says Ursula, who has four children. 'He would get aggravated with me at the weekends because I got up. I didn't mind him staying in bed because he had been working hard all week, but after you hear enough noise in the morning, with four small kids banging around the house, you have to get up. I found it distracting but I didn't realise until later on how much that bothered him at the time. He wanted me to stay in bed with him.' In *Bonk*, Mary Roach says that women get more easily distracted during sex than men. They worry more, about things like turning him off rather than on when they take their clothes off and not moving in the right way. But 'If it's any solace, even rats find it hard . . . I give you my favourite sentence in the entire oeuvre of Alfred Kinsey, from *Sexual Behavior in the Human Female*: "Cheese crumbs spread in front of a copulating pair of rats may distract the female, but not the male."'

The reality of life with children is that there is rarely enough privacy, energy or time for the rampant lust couples feel they ought to be having, and men often feel sidelined. 'People joke about the husband becoming the extra child,' says Anne, 'but maybe that's why women go off sleeping with them. I mean, why would you sleep with your surrogate child?' Mothers are sexually invisible in our society, and no longer available. Women usually need intimacy for sex to be really arousing, and if they lack that in their marriage they replace it with the immense intimacy they get from their children and their friends. When women feel wrung out by the demands of working and mothering, children and their incessant needs can provide an essential respite from the pressure to have sex. When Alice and her family went on an extended travelling holiday driving through Europe, all four of them ended up sleeping in the same room together to save money. 'I found that incredibly restful, like having a couple of chaperones with you all the time,' says Alice. 'It is interesting the subtle ways you can create situations in which you are not saying "no", because nobody likes saying "no". It's insulting and really rejecting to be saying, "I don't actually want to do this with you."' Ruby has found her sexual appetite returning now that her children are older. 'When the children were small I couldn't muster the slightest hint of eroticism if I could see a toy or any residual evidence of one of the children. But actually I think I just didn't want to be touched by anyone. I didn't want to have to give myself over to anything other than wallowing in a hot bath or a book. Just the thought of sex was exhausting, but now that the children are out of the house a lot and I am less tired, I definitely want sex a great deal more.'

We are terrified of losing passion because that threatens the intimacy of our relationship with distance and the possibility of infidelity. 'I know that communication broke down in my first long-term relationship, so the sex did as well. At the beginning we were swinging from the chandeliers, but he zapped my confidence in a lot of ways. I stopped eating and got thinner for him, I hated my body. I was a bundle of insecurities, and in the end I had so little confidence in myself that I didn't want to have sex. For a long time it was just a token shag,' says Molly. 'I do worry sometimes that the same could happen in my marriage. I'll be a bit moody and I won't know why, and then we'll have sex and I'll feel better and it wasn't that I wanted to have sex, I just wanted it to happen so that it felt like our marriage was healthy and that quota was being fulfilled. Or I'll jump him and he's tired or it isn't the right time, and then I'll get upset and he'll know something's bugging me and he'll ask what, and I will say, "You don't love me because we're not having sex enough . . . Even if you were tired you would want to have sex with me if you loved me." He will say, "Don't be silly," and then probably force himself to have sex with me the next night just to keep me happy. So we talk on those levels but not in a more up-front, vocal way by simply saying, "I want sex," or "Could you do it like this not like that." I think sex in relationships is a massive issue for men and women in that they often find it easier to talk about it with other people than with each other.'

We may be living in sexually enlightened times but sex is still the great taboo subject. We don't even have the right words to describe the sensuality of the act: 'sex' is too biological; 'sleeping with' not very accurate; 'making love' sounds wet and is also not necessarily accurate and 'fuck' is not only considered rude, it is used pejoratively as a form of aggression. People might confide in friends when they are having problems with their children, or marital troubles when pressed, but few talk about what they actually do or can't do with each other in bed, let alone out of it. Consequently there is no measure, no ballast against the onslaught of the romanticised fiction of permanent sexual bliss. Couples rarely talk to each other honestly about what turns them on, their fantasies and whether or not they want to share them, the fact that they still find others attractive and what constitutes infidelity even though these boundaries are more important than ever before if a sexual relationship is to flourish and last a lifetime. 'Sex is absolutely essential to a marriage. Without it you are only brother and sister at best,' says Philip. 'I think men feel that other men's wives must be more interested in sex than their own wife is. I'd love someone to give me some data on that. Men have greater sexual appetites, so why wouldn't they try to redress the balance by making comparisons? We are quite prudish when it comes to talking about sex, particularly around the children. We might walk about in the nude – I could be shaving in the nude while my nine-year-old daughter is cleaning her teeth – but we don't talk about sex, pornography, masturbation. We don't go there, and it doesn't bother me, but I reckon other couples do. I also really hope that Juliet finds other men attractive. I would love to hear her say that because then I would know that she finds me attractive, that she was interested in me and in men, because most of the time she is so preoccupied with work and the children. If we're driving along, my eldest daughter spots it immediately if I find a woman on the street attractive. She'll say things like, "Do you love Mummy, Daddy?" when of course I do. She needs to see us as a very tight unit so I have to keep my eyes straight on the road, but any man who says they don't look at a beautiful woman is lying.'

When we get bored, when sex begins to get repetitive, when there is, as Mrs Patrick Campbell suggested, such 'deep, deep peace' within the double bed that one would rather sleep, it is not just hard to find the right words to express what we want – 'I can't imagine saying, "Put your hand here, not there, and I want it rhythmically," it takes all the romance and the surprise out of it,' says Adanna – it is harder to say anything at all, in case it should be interpreted as rejecting or insulting. 'When he rolls over and puts his hand on my leg in the way that he has always put his hand on my leg for the past twenty years, it just makes me shiver because you can't just switch it on,' says Alice. 'In fact it's the only time I have ever really exploded, but all I said was, "Can't you at least put your hand on something different!"' Couples quickly settle down into their own sexual routines, and sex with the same person tends to mean always the same sex. 'It's hard to change patterns because if you've only ever done it in X or Y positions, and then you come home and say can you put this rubber suit on, it's not going to go down well unless you've managed to talk about it and gone to the shop together to buy it,' says Hilary.

'It's almost like the meals you cook – after a while you think, I just can't do these same things any more' says Ursula. 'So you have to consciously open up the cookbook and find something new, see a film, get a new idea into your head or go somewhere new.' People easily slip into a sexual rut, and the two largest surveys on sexual practices suggest that a great many of us are still surprisingly conservative in that double bed in spite of the sexually explicit culture in which we live. In the largest US survey of sexual practices, the overwhelming majority of respondents said they found vaginal intercourse 'very appealing', while only 28 per cent of women and 27 per cent of men could say the same about oral sex. Lots of people, it seems, can't bear to put their mouths where they put their genitals, which are still considered 'dirty'. Masturbation is still considered secondary to 'real' sex and scorned as somehow amoral, with more than half those who masturbate regularly saying they felt guilty about it. The idea that using a vibrator or watching others having sex could be 'very appealing' fell to less than 5 per cent.[19] The largest British survey found that even though oral sex was more practised by younger generations, it was far less popular than vaginal intercourse and there was a poor understanding of the meaning of non-penetrative sex and mutual masturbation.[20]

Sometimes it isn't just that we lack the vocabulary to talk about sex, it is that we are scared where such a discussion might lead. 'I don't go there,' says Rebecca. 'He does occasionally if I have been particularly uninterested, and then I will think, This is really hurting him – I must make more of an effort. But I don't bring it up because if I was being really honest I would say that I don't want sex at all any more and I don't want to know where that might take us in our relationship. His response might be something that I wouldn't particularly welcome.' When I brought up the subject of sex in a conversation with Dean and Sue, Sue told her husband for the first time that she knew that 'It's not often enough for you, and when we do it I think, Why don't we do this more often? But if you didn't suggest it for another month I probably wouldn't think about it. Women need to get really worked up to want it.' Dean replied that he wasn't surprised by her comments, 'But it is a sort of rejection in a strange way, and that might be an insensitive thing to say but I am being honest. Maybe we don't talk about these things because in spite of the closeness, we don't want to expose ourselves. Once you start that sort of a conversation, you don't know what the other person is going to say next.'

The more traditional the marriage, the more traditional sexual relations are likely to be, with men and women stepping into the active and passive roles which reflect their relationship. 'Women who have looked for male leadership in marriage tend to want it to continue in their sex life; men who hold the senior position do not generally give up that role when it comes to sex,' writes Pepper Schwartz in *Love Between Equals*. Schwartz has found in her research that when couples have a more equal basis to their relationship they both feel able to initiate, suggest different positions and refuse sex. Deborah married her first husband when she was twenty-six, in the early 1980s. They hadn't known each other long, and the nature of their relationship changed soon after they married – her husband became aggressive and controlling and made her give up work. Deborah stuck with it for nearly twenty years because of their two children and because she believed she had made a commitment. 'The sex wasn't good, it was his sex, the way he wanted it, the positions that he wanted, and then he would reach a climax and that would be the end of it for me. I hardly ever climaxed, but you don't know how different it could be, do you? You read stuff about orgasms in women's magazines but you don't honestly know what's expected of everybody, or what the norm is.' After they divorced in 2002, Deborah met another divorcee with his own children. They now live together in a much more equitable relationship and the sex is entirely different. 'I have got my confidence back and my sense of self-esteem, which my husband had whittled away over the years, and we both really enjoy the sex life that we have now. We both reach a climax most of the time and I never think, I can't be bothered.' When there are difficulties in the more traditional relationship, women are more likely to use sex as a salve to try to heal things between them. When Ursula's husband was deeply depressed and on Prozac, it affected his ability to have an erection. 'As if things weren't bad enough. So I thought, OK, I am going to help you, however long it takes, because I realise now in retrospect I so badly wanted to rescue him. I loved him. I was his wife, and physicality is a great way to do that, it's so relaxing and he always said that colours seemed brighter when you've had sex.' Ursula succeeded in getting her husband through that particular physical block, but there were so many other difficulties between them that her marriage had reached irretrievable breakdown. Their sex life had become so detached that 'I could have been anybody lying there, there was no emotional connection and that was sad and made me start to ask questions about what was going on. You imagine a million different scenarios – is it because of me, or is it because you are fucking someone else, or is it because you don't love me any more, or because your mind is on your work – all those things go through your head which make it much harder to enjoy the sex.' Ursula's seventeen-year marriage ended in divorce, and she has now found a much more equable new relationship with someone who respects her and is prepared to take his time in bed. 'To really enjoy sex I have not so much to trust the person as to be able to let go enough that I have disengaged any thought process that might get in the way of it, and this is so completely different – gentle, relaxed – it's an expression of a feeling that you have for that person, and you just go with it.'

Eroticism requires a respectful distance. The more fused we feel with our partner, the more likely we are to find sex dull or repetitive. Experiencing our lover as separate, as someone who has to be seduced and who perceives us similarly, is essential for passion. 'After a honeymoon and the blaze of passion and desire, we settled into a life of pleasant routine,' writes Susan Cheever in her essay 'In Praise of Married Men'. 'Over a few years that routine gave way to mutual irritation and lack of appreciation. We owned each other, so we could relax. We didn't bother to dress for each other or to keep each other away from our most repulsive and intimate grooming rituals; he watched me tweeze my eyebrows, I saw him deal with his hemorrhoids.'

The modern emphasis on love as a state of complete togetherness where every secret is shared, every physical blemish or ailment revealed, and where we look to our partner to soothe all our anxieties about the uncertainties and difficulties of life narrows the erotic divide between us. Our need for stability in relationship dampens desire, which thrives on a longing, a craving for something you do not have. In gay circles it's called Lesbian Bed Death: 'We're so in tune with each other, so incredibly similar that we could easily drift into being flatmates in our nighties,' says Florence. 'Often we can't have sex because we're much too busy laughing and talking, which is sweet, but sometimes I think we need more difference between us to push us into having sex. There isn't a man with a thrusting erection demanding it.' We're goaded on by handbooks and magazine articles to spice up our sex lives to keep our marriage alive, and while experimenting with the odd fantasy or sexy bra can be great fun, that cannot be the whole answer. There is a ludicrous artificiality to the idea that sex within a committed partnership has to be novel to be exciting, when its most precious strengths are the ease of being together – where the touch and smell of someone you really care about feels as familiar and reassuring as your own; where you can laugh over the silliness of the sexual act as well as enjoy its pleasures; where style and performance matter far less than the expression of a loving physical intimacy.

Sex is just one small part of the rich tapestry of a relationship. However, it doesn't just happen magically when the elusive time or place is right; we have to take responsibility for making it happen, for keeping the spark alive by changing the way we think, often in subtle ways. When you let go of the illusion of certainty in love and think about how anything could threaten the relationship, you automatically create distance and that partner of old immediately seems more alluring. When you feel overwhelmed by their least attractive habits, draw back – give them more privacy and try to see them as others do. Ask yourself, how much freedom you really give the other to be themselves within the relationship? If you injected more distance between you, would the relationship really suffer that much, or gain in spades when you come back together? Familiarity can breed contempt. 'I would like to marry someone who can act as if he is married to someone else, even though he may be my husband,' writes Susan Cheever. 'I would like to treat and be treated with the kind of passionate respect I remember from having married lovers.'

Some create that distance with separate hobbies or holidays; others with separate beds. 'I told him that I wanted him to actively court me, to ring me up and invite me out to dinner so that I know he wants to have a relationship with me for who I am now, and that I want to have a relationship with him for who he is now and not for who he was when he was twenty-three,' Wendy told me, after her husband had ended an affair with a young, sexy Spaniard. He was and still is determined to make their marriage work. She never got that date, but has found that a physical separateness within their home has helped to build their relationship once again. 'We have had separate bedrooms for a while now. I don't like sleeping with him because we have totally different temperature needs and he claims I snore. He gets up five or six times in the night to pee and I can't cope with that, it just doesn't work, and I love having the whole double bed to myself. But what that has meant is that we have had to consciously rebuild the physical affection between us, which started with the reinstitution of the good-night kiss, so in a way it was like dating again.'

With those great expectations of constant togetherness and fulfilment in a loving relationship, more and more people appear to be escaping into the privacy of 'solo' sex such as masturbation, telephone or cybersex as a means of self-preservation because it is unlikely to threaten the health of their relationship in the same way as infidelity could. 'We know that today's young men and women are far more likely to masturbate than earlier generations were when living with a steady partner, apparently because it is a refuge for self-determined, freely available, autonomous, secret and refreshing sex,' writes Gunter Schmidt in his essay 'Sexuality and Late Modernity'. You don't have to consider anybody else but yourself. You can escape the high standards of sexual etiquette, which are now expected in making love with another. You can imagine all sorts of alternative freedoms and experiences for yourself. When couples can find those same freedoms and experiences with someone they love and trust, sex within commitment becomes anything but dull.

You are allowed to break all the rules in bed and get down to the nitty-gritty of the real differences between you. 'Sexuality is more than a metaphor for the relationship – it stands on its own as a parallel universe,' writes Esther Perel in *Mating in Captivity*. In sex we are allowed to play with and consequently expose all of the elements of ourselves and the relationship which necessarily get hidden. Good sex is often ruthless, aggressive, daring, even ugly as we play with issues of power and control. Each needs to focus on their own sensory needs as well as giving pleasure. Each needs to be allowed to let go, to fuck and ravish as well as be fucked and ravished without feeling compromised by notions of masculinity and femininity or gender politics. When sex grows into something this intimate within a committed relationship, it is too delicious to let go.

It is easy to get stuck in a sexual rut. Sometimes all it takes is for one of you to decide to step back from the sexual routines that have defined you both for so long and to change things in subtle ways, for the sexual dance to change completely. Your partner has little choice but to follow, or to refuse, which means you have to begin to talk about what is really going on between you. There are all sorts of ways in which couples can inject new excitement into their sex life, from toys and pornography to role play. 'Fantasies are maps of our psychological and cultural preoccupations; exploring them can lead to greater self-awareness, an essential step in creating change,' writes Esther Perel. It's a testament to the power of the imagination that we can weave stories to peel back the blocks to sexual pleasure, which are so often rooted in negative emotions of shame, rejection and guilt. There are numerous sexual enhancement techniques such as focusing solely on one person physically one night, the other the next, recalling moments of sexual desire in the past, or not being allowed to touch each other's genitals for a prolonged length of time. If your sexual difficulties feel entrenched and damaging, then sex therapy can, with time, work wonders.

But all of the focus on sexual novelty is meaningless unless you are using it to reconnect emotionally with your partner. 'Sometimes when I look at those sex manuals and they say get the massage oil out or the candles, I think, Well, if you're not really into that person, it's not going to work,' says Hilary. 'It's all a bit false: get some sexy underwear – but if you've never worn sexy underwear before, would he even notice? If he did, he'd more likely think that something was up.' Sexual technique and experimenting with positions may be important but they are always secondary to the deeper intimacy that we build together. Simply deciding to re-engage with the person you love and slowing everything down so that you really feel them when you touch, responding to their pleasure rather than withdrawing to focus on your own sensations, can be enough to build a deeper, more intimate and erotic sex life. David Schnarch, an American psychologist, maintains that emotional intimacy can be enhanced by opening your eyes during foreplay, as you stare into each other's souls and allow yourself to be truly seen, and that those who manage to keep their eyes open throughout manage a more powerful orgasm. 'It's not about how your body looks or how you position it, it's about your frame of mind and emotional connection with your partner,' writes Schnarch in his book *Passionate Marriage*. 'It's not about frequency of sex; its about eroticism. It's not about techniques; it's about integrating your head, heart and spirit with your genitals.'

When you just don't feel like it for weeks on end, when you look at your partner and wonder where all the lust has gone, question what you might be holding back and why, rather than assuming that the eroticism between you is dead. The best sex is not as our wider culture suggests, about youthful bodies, staggering sexual technique and the ability to have a thrusting erection for hours of intercourse. You can never regain that hot, lust-filled time when you first met and wanted to have sex five times a night, but you can move on to something much more satisfying, liberating and even rejuvenating if you approach sex differently and recognise that you can think yourself into wanting sex rather than simply waiting for physical or hormonal triggers. 'There have been times when we've had terrible sex, or no sex at all, but the sex we have now twenty years into our marriage is far better than any of the sex we had when we first met because I know myself now and I really relish what my body can do,' says Ruby. 'But I have had to consciously think myself into a different head space at times because otherwise you just focus on his hairy back or your flabby stomach and feel you'd rather do something else. That private, intimate space between us feels so dense and important that I cannot conceive of ever being with the most youthful and beautiful man in the same way as I am now with my husband.'

David and Katrina have also been through their fair share of sexual difficulties as a result of fertility treatment, and loss of sexual desire when David was on antidepressants. 'The five times a day when you can't contain yourself disappears at some point, which is a sad thing to admit but it does get supplanted by something else,' says David. 'You can see a lot of women who might cause a hormonal surge but this is in a totally different league. It doesn't touch it, it is immaterial because what you have in your relationship is on a completely different level. I find Katrina more attractive than I did before, I don't know why. It might be corny in that she is the mother of my child and there is a different bond between us now. Also I have always been adamant that the one thing I will never do is get divorced because I am a child of divorce. I don't think I suffered, but it's not something I want for our son, so perhaps that deeper attraction is born of a deeper level of commitment too.'

Good sex is a valuable asset to any relationship because it

serves and deepens intimacy. It makes us feel good about ourselves and each other, for touch and physical connection send
surges of feel-good hormones around our bodies and root us,
relax us. 'I don't think that sex has to be an expression of love,
necessarily,' says Lawrence, 'but it is, in the end, the ultimate
aphrodisiac. Just watching someone you love enjoying themselves
is enough to get you off too.' When sex is good we feel secure
enough in the relationship to be able to disclose, to push arousal
to its most extreme limits without worrying that your lover might
be either overwhelmed or appalled. The more known we feel, the
more profound and intense those experiences can be. Each of you
needs to be strong enough to take all of each other, and that is a
very erotic as well as a comforting thought. As intimacy deepens
with time, early passionate sexual chemistry shifts subtly into
something far more nourishing and fulfilling. With trust and a
sense of safety in each other's arms, familiarity with each other's
bodies, sexual flexibility and greater sensitivity to each other's
desires, sexual satisfaction can deepen.

'We've got better at communicating over the years about what
we like, fantasies that turn us on. The sex gets better in a way
because you know what buttons to press; its kinkier but it's also
more honest and open,' says Lawrence. 'The animal excitement
is almost totally gone now,' says Oliver, who has been living with
his male lover for ten years. 'But there is such tenderness and
accuracy now, and it's so satisfying that here we are, two guys in
our mid-forties getting that achievement of feeling like you're an
attractive adult, which is entirely different to when you're in your
twenties.' And for those who have spent the best part of two
decades raising children, the freedom of being alone again once
they have left home is an aphrodisiac. 'Sex is better now than ever,'
says Philippa, 'because you don't worry about getting pregnant,
and I've finally got the work–life balance right. We're home at the
same time, and I'm not constantly tired, so we don't have that
thing of one wanting it and the other being too tired and turning
over saying, "For God's sake, sod off." Plus the kids are at uni so

we don't even have to worry about whether anyone is going to come in and spoil it all – that's liberating too!'

The deepest sexual pleasure stems from intimacy and honesty, not from the firm, perfect flesh and acrobatics of romantic sexual ideals. Countless people find that their sex life gets better as they get older. The ageing process may slow everything down a little, but provided that their health is still fine, older lovers make up in style what they now lack in stamina. A survey in *Saga* magazine of 10,000 over-fifties found that 65 per cent were still sexually active, and that many older men and women report the strongest orgasms and the most meaningful sex of their lives. It takes time to mature sexually, and while hormonal drive may be integral to sexual desire, it is certainly not the whole story. After half a life-time of sexual successes and failures, experiences such as pregnancy and childbirth and witnessing the slow physical ageing of each other's bodies, couples can grow to accept their weak-nesses and find it easier to relax into a deeper sensuality steeped in feelings. It may be harder to find yourself turned on by the froglike way your partner's midriff swells in midlife but your own body sports its own failures as it ages, too. 'I'm lucky in that we're both so short-sighted now we just take our glasses off,' says Evie. As women mature and feel less threatened by the tyranny of youth and beauty or the need to please a man, they are more able to sink into their own sexual pleasure and explore meaningful ways to orgasm which they now feel is theirs by right. 'A mature man no longer needs to have all the answers in bed, and is less threatened by a partner who is a sexual equal. And he can let someone hold him,' writes David Schnarch in *Passionate Marriage*.

'The sex has been good throughout. It has lessened as we have got older, and I will probably need some help with Viagra as I have blood-pressure problems but it has been good because we don't take each other for granted. I am happy to give Rachel the stimu-lation she needs whether I perform or not. It's a pleasure because I love to see her happy sexually – it's not a chore,' says Jack, who has been married and faithful for more than forty years. 'Sex is not necessarily just coitus. We enjoy sexual intercourse, social intercourse and intellectual intercourse,' says Adam, who has been married for more than fifty years. 'It's a male living in harmony with a female, and vice versa. We enjoy touching each other and usually sleep in the nude, for there is nothing that creates more quality "opposite-sex awareness" than bumping into your partner in the night without being shielded by nightclothes. I happen to think that my wife is more beautiful than ever – nude or fully clothed.'

'When you have been together this long,' says Tim, who is in his late sixties and has been married to Rose for more than forty years, 'sex is the icing on the cake, a physical act which is still lovely and pleasurable but secondary to the much more important relationship between you, which is based on love.' With decades of commitment to each other, you take your entire sexual and emotional history to bed with you each night: your partner's physique, the way your bodies fit so easily together, the familiarity of their touch and smell triggering deep, visceral memories of how things used to be. You can still see the younger person you once fell in love with and have shared so much of life with. It's a time of precious, sweet intimacy, a time of cherishing the physical comfort between you which keeps people bonded as their health grows more fragile. 'He's had a heart operation and I have had health problems too,' says Rose. 'We do still have sex but we cuddle each other more now than we've ever done in our lives, so the balance has shifted to fondness and touching. Before, it was much more about intercourse rather than foreplay.' As sex dwindles with old age, intimacy becomes that much more prescient. As Alice Munro writes in her powerful short story, 'The Bear Came Over the Mountain', 'They had usually prepared supper together. One of them made the drinks and the other the fire . . . this was their time of liveliest intimacy, though there was also, of course, the five or ten minutes of physical sweetness just after they got into bed – something that did not often end up in sex but reassured them that sex was not over yet.'

7

THE DOUBLE BED PART II: INFIDELITY

'I don't think fidelity can ever be a compulsion or a resolution. You can never promise anyone fidelity,' says Marianne in Ingmar Bergman's *Scenes from a Marriage*. 'Either it's there or it isn't. I like to be faithful to Johan, therefore I am faithful. But naturally I don't know how it will be tomorrow or next week.' Marital affairs fascinate us, and appear as constant themes in fiction, films and news coverage of celebrities and politicians because of the richness of the ingredients – sex, excitement, romance, risk and the dramatic potential for heartbreak. We know that infidelity could threaten us at any time, so we shore up our marital castle by expressing profound disapproval of those who stray around us, rather than acknowledge that sexual transgression is common and consider what we might do should it happen to us. Surprising numbers of those I interviewed said that both of them knew sexual infidelity was not acceptable but had never discussed it. Plenty of those I met had had an affair or a casual sexual encounter which had remained hidden from their partner and their friends.

It's an odd paradox that the more sexual activity and availability is explicit and celebrated by society, the more faith people seem to place on the value of fidelity and monogamy within committed relationship. Patterns of sexual behaviour among the young are changing. They have more sexual relationships earlier in life than previous generations but they appear to value monogamy in those affairs more. 'Being faithful to each other is not bound up with an institution (marriage) or even a person, but with one's feelings for this person,' writes Gunter Schmidt in 'Sexuality and Late Modernity'. 'The partners expect and pledge sexual exclusiveness only as long as they regard their relationship as intact and emotionally satisfying.' Sexual fidelity has absorbed a new sanctimonious power, forging couples together now that lifelong marriage can no longer be trusted. Sexual transgressions have become the great unforgivable sin against commitment, sometimes provoking separation in what are otherwise loving and compatible relationships. Consequently many have little choice but to be more deceitful – which can be more destructive to a relationship than the sex itself – because the research seems to indicate that not only is infidelity common, it is on the rise. Hard statistics are thin on the ground. Few people are prepared to admit even to sexually unfaithful thoughts when the moral emphasis on monogamy is so great, but adultery remains the most common reason for divorce. Most of us believe fidelity is important and intend to remain sexually faithful when we first marry or commit to another, and if some statistics are to be believed, we succeed. Laumann's study of 13,000 Americans in the National Survey of Families and Households in 1994 found that 25 per cent of men and 15 per cent of women had had at least one extramarital sexual liaison, and that figure was even lower when they were asked about extramarital sex in the previous year.[1] Other statistics from both sides of the Atlantic indicate that rates of infidelity could be as a high as 50 per cent of all married women and that up to as many as 65 per cent of married men have had at least one lover by the time they are 40.[2]

Historically, sexual fidelity, along with virginity in women, was crucial to the institution of marriage to protect the legitimacy of children, the transfer of property and the honour of men. Adultery was theft of another man's wife. A woman's body was not hers to give as she pleased. Infidelity in men, however, has always been more acceptable. When so many marriages were arranged rather than the result of choice and attraction, the taking of lovers was common and bastards were not hidden. Husbands in countless marriages had mistresses or slept with servants or prostitutes to minimise the threat of pregnancy with their wives, or because their wives were already with child. When divorce was difficult to obtain, sexual affairs were less threatening to the stability of marriage as an institution or to a wife's status. But as love and romantic notions of permanent togetherness became central to marriage, sexual exclusivity within that union began to take on a whole new semi-religious significance. Monogamy has become the new sacred cow of the romantic ideal, a marker of commitment and our individual specialness within the marital union – I have chosen and been chosen; others have been denied.

With more liberalised attitudes towards divorce and sexual behaviour, monogamy became, as Christopher Clulow writes in his introduction to *Rethinking Marriage*, 'an achievement of moral work that involves renunciation, sacrifice and tolerance of disillusion'. Infidelity betrays the fundamental basis of romantic relationship and defines marriage in absolute terms – you can't be just a little bit monogamous. It is an all-or-nothing achievement and a difficult one at that, given the average life expectancy of a relationship, the changes couples live through both individually and together, as well as the constant lure of sexual novelty and erotic pleasure from the wider, more 'permissive' world. 'Both of us have been unfaithful to other people before, so we have talked about it,' says Molly. 'We know how easy it is to overstep the line. There's a kiss that is a sinful kiss and that's it – there's no going back. You start doing something, and then before you know it you've done something you really shouldn't have and then you think, That was easy, and do it again. I know that if I was to take that step I would really bugger things up.' Sam and Diana hit a low point in their relationship when they had difficulty conceiving, and the truth dawned on Sam that he might have to choose to leave if he wanted to have a child of his own. 'I started talking to another woman friend and ended up having to confess this to Diana, which was strange because nothing happened but I was scared. We had stopped talking to each other about it, so I had started talking to someone else because I felt vulnerable and the thought that we could start to go our separate ways worried me. I could see how easy it would be to get too drunk, wake up in bed with someone else and think, That's really done it.'

Infidelity is easier than ever to initiate with internet dating sites, chat rooms, mobile phones and email. 'The internet has allowed people to do whatever they want to do,' says Robin. 'If you like sex a particular way you don't feel quite so isolated or embarrassed about it. You can Google "spanking" and find myriad options and opportunities.' There are countless ways now for people to seek partners for no-strings-attached sex; attempting that with people within your own social circle would be far too risky. People feel more sexually empowered these days, as if sexual excitement and novelty is somehow their right, but they also believe in the importance of fidelity as a symbol of romantic love and togetherness. Such a sharp contradiction can cause confusion and guilt. It forces people to become that much more deceitful and secretive, which feels like a double betrayal when everything in a modern relationship should also be honest and open. The betrayer feels shame for not being able to maintain the monogamous ideal, and sexual activity continues to be hidden as something naughty, which either cannot be enjoyed because they are wracked with guilt or is enjoyed too much because of it. 'The guilt gnaws away at you because you have been such a shit,' says Gareth, who had an affair over twenty years ago when their children were small. 'In my case I felt very guilty for years. That's gone now, but I still know I did wrong. I have said my Hail Marys, and we all make mistakes.'

Sex is sold as a constant nirvana, with Viagra, Botox, cosmetic surgery and HRT to shore it up, challenging the reality of the slow decline of passionate sexual relations into a more intense and companionable love. Within such an explicit and sybaritic culture many find it easy to justify sexual fulfilment with someone outside their relationship with 'I need more sex or love than I get from my marriage'. Surprising numbers of people never tell their partners that they have visited prostitutes or used pornography, for these are excused as meaningless casual physical encounters. 'It was always when I was away from home for weeks,' says Tim, who travelled extensively for work. 'You're having a drink or breakfast, someone's next to you, you're both lonely, you would much rather be at home than stuck in a hotel room, and for me it was just wanting to be comforted. Whether or not you can allow people to be comforted in that way, I don't know.'

Women who work away from home, even just once a year, are nearly three times as likely as women in general to have had two or more concurrent sexual relationships during the past five years.[3] 'When I go to conferences there's a lot of sex going on. Often it is unfinished relationships or going back to something that makes them feel younger,' says Beatrice. 'If I think of my closest friends, I would say that all of them have had some sort of sex outside their marriage. I haven't . . . yet . . . but most of my friends have had a fling, and for all of them it was opportunity that motivated it – the fact that they could. And it was flattering in some ways, receiving that kind of attention.' Anna embarked on a 'brief and very intense affair' with a married man she used to have business dealings with abroad. 'Now that it's over, I just think how unattractive and annoying he is when I run into him. What the affair highlighted for both of us was how terrified we were of losing what we had, and that makes me feel quite jolly about my marriage. Affairs hold no attraction now that I know that something which seemed to be so intense at the time was actually impossible.'

People have sexual liaisons for all sorts of reasons, and not just because they are not getting enough sex in their marriage. In fact, there is some research evidence that suggests that it is often those who enjoy good sexual relations with their partner who have more extramarital sex. Affairs are not necessarily a reflection of an unhappy marriage, although that is more often the case for women. Dr Shirley Glass, an American psychologist who has been studying infidelity for more than twenty-five years, has found that 56 per cent of men and 30 per cent of women who had been married for more than twelve years were happy with their marriages even though they had been unfaithful.[4] Men seem more able to compartmentalise their sex lives as separate from their marriages and justify their exploits as meaningless, while women tend to link sex with love more and excuse their affairs by citing a lack of love and affection from their spouse. Those who believe wholeheartedly in the myth of romantic love as the principal foundation for a monogamous relationship can justify their infidelity with the belief that they fell 'in love', and rewrite their own marital history, now denying that they love their spouse. Some need affirmation of their sexual potency or desirability, and sexual infidelity is then justified by that person's narcissistic needs: they are improving their marriage because 'I'm very sexual and need lots of variety'.

But equally, and particularly if they are workaholics, those who stray could be the ones who are not investing enough in their relationship. They already have one foot out the door, and affairs can serve as a means of escaping intimacy and avoiding commitment to anyone. When relationships hit difficulties, some use infidelity to exact revenge on their partner. Others feel so lonely and abandoned in their relationship that they simply need more love, and the pull of romance is too hard to resist. Tim and Rose have been married for forty-two years but Tim left Rose for another woman twice, once when they had been married for twenty-five years and then again, ten years later. 'Rose was going through a tough time. She was depressed, and would come home, sit in a chair and then go to bed early, and I just think I got a bit lonely. I've never stopped loving Rose, but I worked with this other woman and she flattered me in the sense that I suddenly realised that I was attractive to somebody. She was very affectionate, and I needed that. Sex pulls you away but it is love that brings you back.'

The overriding reason for most infidelity, though, is the thrill of the secret. Both sexes enjoy the sexual frisson of the illicit, even if that is just in their imagination when they feel confined by safety and the unrealistic expectations of the nuclear family, or bored by the repetitive nature of a long-term relationship. Infidelity springs from discontent, but increasingly people feel discontented merely with the ordinariness of marital contentment when romance and risk seem to offer something much more exciting. The great appeal of an affair is that it is an escape from reality. When people work long hours and also feel that they have to conform to the roles inherent to family life, sexual liaison offers reclusive relief for pleasure, a place where they can simply be anonymous, or be themselves. Evie had a six-month affair when her children were two and four years old. Her husband was withdrawn, difficult and grumpy for months, and 'That put us under a lot of pressure. Having small children is a hard time in any marriage. I just felt I wanted to be something else other than a wife and a mother. It was ridiculously stupid, all about meeting up for a couple of hours in bed in the early hours of the morning. The guy was a brilliant saxophonist, and this was a period of stolen romance. He knew nothing about me and we talked about music and literature, so I think it was about wanting to feel that sense of separateness, a sense of individual identity away from being a mother.' When people feel as if their lives are too controlled, comfortable and responsible, sexual infidelity is a foolproof way of feeling spontaneous, chaotic and irresponsible. It's a deep, dark secret that only the two of you share, and the knife-edge possibility of discovery keeps you permanently alive and on your toes. Infidelity is an extreme sport which threatens the established order with either destruction or great change, for, as Stephen Brook writes in the introduction to *The Penguin Book of Infidelities*, it 'lobs a rock into that placid pool, whipping up waves and cross-currents in waters previously unruffled. It disturbs us not only because it nearly

always brings pain to those involved, but because it is by definition an unpredictable element that shatters the uneasy truth of
marital sexuality.'

Sexual infidelity wrecks many marriages because it betrays
fundamental trust in the safety of the relationship and violates
a couple's sense of private, protected space. The rejection can
trigger monumental self-doubt in the betrayed, for clearly they
were not attractive, sexy or interesting enough to keep their
spouse interested. After years of living in an abusive marriage,
Wendy found her husband's affair – and affairs are often a form of
abuse – with a 'younger, very plastic Spaniard' when she was
going through the menopause more than she could bear. 'I told
him I didn't want to even breathe the same air as him because
it completely destroyed my self-respect. Being hit should produce
the same result, but it was the affair which made me feel so
terrible. It's a complete betrayal. It makes you feel like a complete
nothingness, even more invisible than the menopause does. I
remember feeling as if I wanted to tell everyone from my mother-
in-law to the dry-cleaner. You want to hold this man up as a liar
and say, "He is not who you think he is."' Now that they are back
together, Wendy acknowledges that with hindsight she played a
part in their difficulties. She had been pushing him away, mentally
absenting herself from the relationship until their children were
old enough that she could leave. He wanted to come back to their
marriage enough to be prepared to change. Even so, Wendy feels
that her confidence can be easily undermined and that her affair
antennae can be oversensitive. 'We went shopping recently in
a department store and he went off to the men's section and I
went somewhere else. Then I saw him talking to this tall, thin, very
attractive blonde and of course I thought, Who the fuck is that?
but I didn't say anything. Then at supper he said, "Oh, I bumped
into Clare today when we were shopping," and I didn't say,
"Yes, I saw you and it sent my heart rate up," I just said, "Oh, did
you?" and it turned out she was the estate agent who had sold us
our house and she is really nice. So it would have been completely

stupid to air my suspicions. You pick up patterns of behaviour and think, This is very similar to what happened before, and then you go a little mad. You start overelaborating, imagining something which doesn't exist, so you do have to take charge of your own insecurities a bit.'

If the affair has continued undetected for a while the betrayed can also feel like a fool, deeply undermined by the deceit. All the assumptions they held about their partner or their past together are destroyed, and on top of the physical rejection they also face disillusionment with the romantic, exclusive dream. Iris and Gerry met each other twenty-five years ago after each had lived through a failed marriage. Not long after the birth of their first child, Gerry had a nine-month affair with someone he met at work. He was in his early forties. 'She was attractive, very confident and she sort of controlled me,' says Gerry. 'I'm not using that as an excuse because I should have had the strength to say, "no thank you". It was purely physical, I couldn't control myself.' Iris was devastated. Gerry's first wife had been unfaithful to him, and she believed that having lived through such pain he would never inflict that on her. 'I never thought he would be unfaithful, not just to me but as a person. I thought so highly of him. It takes away all your dreams, your dreams of togetherness. I didn't leave him because I was ashamed. I didn't want anybody to know. You can't have a second marriage fail, and also it wasn't easy to go. Where do you go with a fourteen-year-old and a one-year-old? And we'd just moved here, this was my home. But I also know that if he had left me, I would have been all right. It's not that I find it hard to forgive, it's just that he's not the same person I married any more and he hasn't changed back, in my eyes. It's not that I dislike him; we get on with the day-to-day. The really hurtful thing is the emotional side. How dare he tell things to another woman about the way he feels when he's supposed to do that with me? That's what's always really got to me. All I ever wanted was total emotional expression, a soul mate, and if you go off and do that with someone else that's ruined for ever, isn't it?'

Those with a history of betrayed trust in childhood can find this newer trauma and the threat of abandonment within an adult relationship especially merciless. The symptoms of many betrayed spouses are strikingly similar to the post-traumatic stress reactions of those who have suffered emotional, physical or sexual abuse. Some feel numb and avoid the issue entirely; others have nightmares, flashbacks, insomnia, become irritable, easily angry or intensely jealous. They constantly monitor their partner's behaviour and find it difficult to think about anything else. Rose had a difficult childhood with an alcoholic father and an overly dependent mother, and was devastated when Tim left her after twenty-five years of marriage. 'It was like a constant gnawing pain. You can't think fully about anything else. I'd drive around or walk somewhere and see him everywhere. I started turning off the answering machine because I would come home and expect a message from him, but there wouldn't be one.' It's a pain that is never completely forgotten because the fragile balance of trust and loyalty and the expectation of complete commitment have been irrevocably damaged. Tim came back, and then two years later left again for another woman. 'All that insecurity came flooding back, all of it, and I couldn't stop crying. Finally it was my daughter who said I had to get some help, and I phoned a counsellor on Christmas Eve, such a family time. But even then with all that pain I think I knew he would be back, that the story wasn't over, and I couldn't have known that so completely the first time. The pain wasn't quite so bad as it had been the first time because I had learned some lessons.'

Couples often survive the excruciating pain and betrayal of sexual infidelity but their relationship can never be quite the same again. 'The affair was very difficult and it took a long time to rebuild a sense of "me" and "you", and of course it doesn't ever really go away. It's always in the background,' says Imogen, whose husband had an affair with a childless and glamorous actress when their children were small nearly twenty years ago. She went to visit her husband in hospital after minor surgery and his lover was there too, and she just knew. 'I made him leave, and then he finished with her and said he wanted to come back. I was furious. The betrayal was compounded by the fact that I was working hard and looking after the kids and your sense of self is so precarious at that time, anyway. I didn't think that the right thing to do was to separate. He was a good dad and I didn't feel that our relationship had burnt itself out in spite of what he had done. We had counselling and as the years go by you do stop thinking of it in terms of blame, rather as something that just happened. But even now if I see her face in a magazine or something it still makes me furious.' Juliet's husband 'got too close to someone at work' after the birth of their second child, although 'To his credit, he knew that he was in dead-end territory, but it unleashed a year of hell with rows. My first instinct was to protect the family unit. I didn't want to lose him, but that was my main concern – the family package. It's an unspoken rule between us that he couldn't do that again. I wouldn't tolerate it. It hurt, but I realised how strong I was, and I think it is strong women who save relationships and make marriages work. I felt so disdainful of him for behaving like a kid – like, who gives a shit how he's feeling emotionally because he's an adult. The whole thing made me feel rather superior, and still does, which isn't very good.'

Monogamy matters so much to modern relationships that sexual infidelity is complete infidelity and disapproved of more than divorce. Often we would rather keep up the fiction of a monogamous marriage by turning a blind eye. Several of those I met maintained a little too forcefully that their partner's dalliance had never been physical. Some use an affair to bring an unhappy relationship to a close and move on to something more fulfilling, but many feel that they have no choice but to separate, urged on by their friends to protect their pride. British and American culture is especially condemning of sexual infidelity. A Gallup poll in 2006 found that Americans were happier with polygamy and human cloning than they were with infidelity, and even a one-night stand is often considered completely unacceptable – one fall from grace, one silly, zipless fuck and you're out the door. But that isn't necessarily what we want. A great many of those who separate because of sexual infidelity regret the decision later. Less than 10 per cent of extramarital affairs end in marriage between the two lovers, and three-quarters of those who marry their lover divorce again.[5] 'I often say to him, "I hope to God she loves you because if she can leave her own children, she can leave you,"' says Marjorie, who was devastated when her husband of more than twenty years told her that he had fallen in love with someone else. 'But he didn't want to leave. He said he knew it was mad but in an ideal world he would like her to move in. Everything became very intense, and in a strange way it also made me feel alive. I became incredibly wired up and lost a huge amount of weight, determined to keep him. But then I got to the point where I just couldn't fight any more. I got annoyed because he wouldn't leave her for a week to come on holiday with us, so I asked him to go, and if I hadn't said that I am not sure where we would be now. I still love him. I am sure I won't ever not, which frustrates people hugely. All my friends want me to slate him, but how can I when we have had all those happy years together?'

A great many marriages and long-term relationships survive affairs, but they need to be able to flout strong social expectations to do so. 'I loved him enough not to want others to judge him badly, and they would have done even though I was also to blame. There were reasons for it. I was preoccupied and I probably did neglect him for a while,' says Juliet. 'I took him back because I knew why he had left in the first place,' says Rose. 'We met so young, and I think I was even waiting for it to happen. But I never thought he would leave. I thought there would be sex, not love and that's when it really hurts. All my friends said you have got to accept that this is the end, and get out into the singles market and find somebody new. Even our children were hard on him and told me to change the locks and not be such a doormat. The counsellor I saw told me that I had to make him really work for it, so that he would beg to come back, but I couldn't do that to him because I could see he was in such a state. I loved him and I knew he loved me, that he belonged with me and that he would be back. I think lots of people take umbrage and feel deeply offended when actually there is perhaps more to be pitied than scorned. Yes, he has hurt your pride and all sorts of other things about you, but actually he is still the person you married underneath, and probably going through hell.'

Rose also recognised that there were ways in which she had contributed to the breakdown in their marriage. She was depressed, they had stopped talking to each other and their sexual life had ceased as well. Tim had the classic midlife crisis affair with his secretary, and kept leaving and then coming back to Rose for the best part of a year. 'I should have seen all the signs. He was reading Proust and there was a lot of introspection,' quips Rose. But she acknowledges that there are all sorts of ways in which Tim's two affairs have challenged and improved their marriage because it is now more equal. Rose has had to fathom deep reserves of independent strength that she never knew she had, and now feels more able to assert her needs in the relationship. They talk about things, and she now knows to the penny how well off they are because she has made a point of taking charge of their finances rather than leaving it all to Tim. Their sex life is more fulfilling than it was before. 'He learned a few things while he was away, so why not benefit from them? I bought myself a rabbit dildo, which shocked him when he came back but why not, I said, "I'm a healthy woman!" The sex is now much more thoughtful rather than the wham-bam it used to be. Sex is very important to Tim. If he didn't have it twice a day he would think he was hard done by and if I didn't feel like it I wouldn't say. Or I'd say, "Just pretend I am a hole in the wall, that it's necrophilia," which is a terrible thing to say. I wouldn't do that now. I say if I am not in the mood, or I try to make myself more interested. There have been times even in the past five years when we've been to see a particularly randy film and had sex in the car on the way back because we have both been turned on, and then there have been periods when we have had no sex at all. Either way, it's good now.'

There is also a sense in which sexual infidelity can force a couple to go to the very extreme edges of their relationship and talk honestly about how they really feel about each other and what matters to them, often for the first time. 'I had an affair for all of the usual reasons,' says Gareth. 'We had two young kids, Imogen was exhausted and didn't want sex and I did, but actually we were both feeling neglected by the other. It was only when we went to counselling and began talking about everything at a much deeper level that I realised how jealous I was. I thought that Imogen loved our son much more than me, and and discovered that that was to do with my upbringing. I was a second child, and resented my older brother.' Evie had already stopped her affair when her husband discovered it by steaming open a letter. 'I stopped it because I didn't like lying. I think the dishonesty is the worst thing. Once you start lying you are going down a very different path in terms of your own self-respect and I couldn't do that. I behaved badly, I know, and he had a right to be really furious and bitter about it; the rowing and talking about it went on for months. It went on for so long that at one point I did think, I can't be dealing with this any more, it's too exhausting. But there was never any question that he would leave or kick me out. But it meant that we talked through everything, about all of the other stuff in our marriage, not just the affair. I made him realise that my love for him has never been in question, and I think people can tell when they are truly loved. I have also got much better now at initiating sex to pull us closer together even when I am not feeling like it, because he gets grumpy and withdrawn sometimes and that's the only time when we can really talk about things.'

Jaya and Charu met over twenty-five years ago and decided at the very beginning that they should have a more open relationship and not stop the other from seeing other women if they wanted to. Jaya travelled a lot with her work, and they occasionally saw other women. 'We were both fiercely independent, so we wanted that caveat in our relationship,' says Jaya. 'But actually I started the whole thing because I had never really played around, I wanted more sexual experience. But then when Charu began to get serious about somebody else, that was tough. It was very, very difficult for me, I got so jealous and didn't behave in a controlled way at all. That started a domino effect in that it meant we had to reassess our whole relationship and our commitment to making it work.' Neither of them wanted to throw down ultimatums because they didn't want to grow their relationship on any kind of resentment. Unsure of what to do, they went to couples counselling, and after the second session discovered that they both hated the therapist. 'We thought, We don't need her, and it was extraordinary because it was like falling in love with each other all over again. It was as if after a certain amount of time we had just stopped listening to each other, we were taking each other for granted. It was like rediscovering a new person, and we are now completely monogamous. We feel blessed, but I think it is perhaps because we took that risk with each other and with our love, that it now feels so solid.'

If, like Jaya and Charu, Evie and her husband or Tim and Rose, you can survive the emotional body blow of sexual infidelity and rediscover the deep love, respect and trust which unite you as a couple, then you can probably survive everything else married life throws at you. Relationship counsellors and psychologists seem to agree on the best way to foster recovery after an affair. Contact with the extramarital lover needs to be severed completely and there needs to be as much open conversation as the betrayed partner wants to help him/her recover from the trauma, even if that means going into painful detail about exactly what sort of sex took place, where and when. Those who have been betrayed typically turn into inquisitors. Sexual infidelity shatters a person's sense of safety within the relationship and, as with any traumatic event, recovery comes only when the story has been retold so many times that it becomes a story that the two of you share together. It takes time to rebuild trust, but something far stronger can emerge when you can arrive at a mutual understanding of the meaning of the affair and show each other the depths of love and commitment through actions rather than promises. Blame and self-blame is understandable, but when we understand that there are huge societal pressures on people, that monogamy is a rare and precious gift, that sexual infidelity is always a possibility through the life course of a relationship, perhaps we can be a little easier on ourselves and on each other. No marriage can be immunised against affairs. 'I now always feel that he could bump into some absolutely fabulous musician at any point,' says Evie. 'Our marriage is rock-solid for so many reasons, but if someone decided they wanted to blow his mind, it might happen. You just don't know what the future holds and if that were to happen I probably couldn't do anything about it.'

The damage that can be wreaked on relationships by not talking about the affair can be great indeed. When Iris discovered that Gerry was having an affair twenty years ago they didn't discuss it. 'We didn't row because we never row,' says Iris. 'He just said, "It doesn't matter. She doesn't matter." I kept saying, "Why did you do it?" and you go through all these silly things in your mind, but he never wanted to discuss it, which meant that the after-effect was worse than the affair. He said it was finished, when it wasn't finished for me. It was the aftermath that caused the really deep problems between us because he carried on lying, he pretended that it was platonic. How could he think I was such a fool as to believe there had been no sex?' Gerry says that he avoided the issue because he felt that talking about it would make things worse. Gerry believes it might have been easier to talk at the time if Iris had got really angry with him. 'Then maybe she would have dragged me out of my safety net and I would have thought, Well, I have to tell her just to stop her going on about it. With hindsight that is what we both should have done but I didn't want to make things worse, make her walk out or get really upset. I didn't want to lose what I had, what I love, which is Iris.'

It was clear when I interviewed Iris and Gerry that the pain caused by his affair was still raw twenty years after the betrayal, and that she still hadn't forgiven him. Iris sat in her chair hidden in an alcove in front of the television, angled in such a way that they couldn't see each other, and masked the upset she clearly still feels about the affair with jokes and put-downs at his expense. She said she couldn't love Gerry in the same way but had married him two years later, tricking him into going to the register office – he thought he was attending a friend's wedding – because he had always said that one of the reasons why he had had the affair was because he felt she wasn't committed to the relationship. 'I thought we could make it work, that you just have to keep trying, you can't just give up. I thought that if I proved to him that I was committed, things would change.'

They have stayed together but, looking back, Iris says she now feels that those were wasted years. She is adamant that she doesn't and cannot love him in the way she used to, and feels she could have done other things, like build a career, if they had separated. Gerry deeply regrets the affair and has spent years trying to make amends, to keep her happy by buying her things. He believed that Iris must have loved him because she had married him. Then, three years ago, they went away on a three-week holiday and started to talk about the affair properly for the first time. 'I just asked him something and he answered it, and then I asked him something else, and for the rest of the holiday he told me every single detail about the affair. I wish I had reacted more when it happened – had a row, smashed things or left for a while, but that's just not how I am. I never react. At the time you think you're going to get over it.'

Relations have improved between them and they can joke about what happened, but Iris still feels a lot of resentment and inevitably that has affected their sex life. 'We were having sex once a month, and I knew she wasn't enjoying it most of the time,' says Gerry. 'I felt that if I put too much into it then he would think, Oh good, she's over it, we're going to get back to normal, and I couldn't let him think that because I am still so hurt,' says Iris. 'I know that passion does change over time but there must be times when you have had a good day together that you still feel that rush of passion. But I have never felt that, and mentally I can't go back there.' Iris has found it so hard to forgive Gerry that she is still punishing him sexually. 'The thing that really hurts me,' he said to me in front of his wife, 'is that when I make love to her I still love the person I knew twenty-six years ago, and I know that she doesn't love me, and that really bugs me because there is nothing better than two people coming together with that love. You know each other so well.'

Such is the emphasis on the pursuit of monogamy as emblematic of true, noble romantic love that we are not just overly hard on each other and on ourselves when we transgress, we are also confused as to what actually constitutes infidelity. Is it full penetrative sex, or just eye contact, or that electric shiver as hands touch over a cup of coffee? A conversation with someone can be more exclusive and intimately charged than sexual intercourse. Are sexual fantasies about someone else a betrayal, or is what goes on in your head yours alone? And what about naughty text messages, flirtations at parties, masturbation when you are alone – are those allowed, or just as hurtful a betrayal as physical sex with someone else? Is there a subtle double standard between you in that you do all of the above but would feel upset if you discovered your partner indulged in similar behaviours? In *Adultery: An Analysis of Love and Betrayal*, Annette Lawson's classic study, she discovered that 40 per cent of those she surveyed had had an emotional connection with someone else which they considered adulterous even though there was no sex. 'I have had crushes, and that feels disloyal to a certain extent,' says Florence. 'It's pure distraction, diversion and flattery. I've been utterly faithful. Snogging fidelity counts as well, and obviously I don't intend to do anything, but I also feel bad because I know I am not being completely honest about my crushes. I have told my old straight best friends, and we even text, but I haven't told my girlfriend.'

For some, discovering that their spouse has been looking at porn feels like a betrayal. Others think that a casual sexual encounter while away from home, or paying for sex does not count as real infidelity. To some extent this modern confusion as to what constitutes infidelity is part of a wider uncertainty about the integrity of our individuality within a relationship. We want certainty, stability and committed love, but we cannot ever own another's body or their sexuality. Monogamy cannot be enforced or expected; it is an expression of loyalty, which is given freely by someone with an independent sexual past and a very private sexual space within their heads which they are entitled to keep to themselves. Experiencing our lover as different, separate, someone who has to be seduced or teased into sexual abandon, and who perceives us as similarly autonomous and in need of seduction, helps to keep enough distance between us for passion to ignite.

'Here's the thing about the other woman,' writes Pam Houston in her story 'Not Istanbul'. 'She lives inside your head. She may live on the next street or in the next town or halfway across the world; she may be five-two or five-nine; she may be rail-thin (never skinny) or voluptuous (never fat). But however big or small she is, however much space she takes up in the world, will never compare to the amount of space she'll take up in your brain.' Sometimes that third person is vital as an imaginary tool; it helps us to see our partner as someone who could be attractive to others. 'I do still think he is cool,' says Alice. 'So many of my friends' husbands have become quite old and Theo hasn't changed. That's important, feeling proud of him when we are out. You want your partner to look like someone that other people might want to sleep with even though you don't feel like it yourself.'

Infidelity is, as the statistics show, a real threat to relationship, and the assumption that marriage immunises against that threat is naive in the extreme. You commit yourself to monogamy, but you cannot hold a partner to the same promise with threats and you cannot hold them responsible for the fact that you no longer sleep with other people. We're surrounded by such temptation, such promise of greater sexual riches elsewhere, that the fragility of contented monogamy feels like a precious fruit that neither person wants to bruise or spoil. Talking about it isn't the same as doing it, but it just might be enough to help rule out misunderstandings. A new sexual thrill might divert for a while but, like many, I think that it is superficial and selfish compared to the deeper sense of self-respect that comes with loyalty, love and the ability to put someone else's feelings before your own. Sexual satisfaction may feel like a physical need, but so too is the security and sense of place that comes from a committed relationship. Nobody is perfect. It is easy to find shortcomings in our partner to justify sexual infidelity, but far harder to live with the damage that the deceit and dishonesty of such a betrayal causes. 'I find other men attractive in the way that lots of men find other women attractive, but that doesn't make me want to go to bed with them,' says Jack, who was gay before he settled into a monogamous marriage with the first woman he slept with over forty years ago. 'You don't have to follow it through but you do have to think about what following it up would involve. Maybe you could get away with it and maybe no one would know, but you would know, and in my case it would hang on my conscience.'

Most couples still value monogamy as a symbol of their commitment and togetherness, but it is by no means the only way. A small but growing number of people take the principle that they cannot stamp a sense of ownership over their partner's body to its logical conclusion by establishing more open sexual or 'polyamorous' relationships. Some are bisexual and do not want to have to stifle that aspect of their sexuality through monogamy; others may have sexual needs which are not being met in their long-term relationship. Even though their relationship is more open, the idea of coupledom, of being special to someone, is still king. The term 'polyamory' emerged in the 1990s and means having more than one loving relationship at a time. It can be sexual but it doesn't have to be. 'It's being faithful to the promises you've made,' says Anna Sharman, author of a pamphlet on polyamory called *Open Fidelity*, who is bisexual and practises what she preaches. 'So if that is, "I will always tell you before I have sex with someone else" and you keep to that, then you can be non-monogamous but still faithful. With me, its not that I am desperate for sex with lots of people, it's just that I don't want that option to be blocked off for ever. It feels so restricting. Some people go to the football, other people go and have sex with some-one else. It's actually not that different, if you really think about it. Huge numbers of people have affairs because monogamy is hard in long-term relationships, and lots of people say that when their partner had sex with someone else it wasn't the sex that mat-tered as much as the way they had handled it – it's the betrayal that's worse. Maybe allowing people greater freedom within rela-tionships makes them stronger because you remove that threat.'

Like Anna, Lawrence and Jane are young, in their mid-twenties, and arrived at polyamory early on because neither of them felt able to limit themselves to lifelong monogamy. They love each other and their long-term commitment is not in doubt, but both feel they are taking less risk with their future together by being more open and flexible. 'I don't have a great track record for being faithful to people and I have always hated the deceit,' says Lawrence. 'But with Jane I feel I can say anything, even when I find someone else attractive, and she's cool with that. I like to feel that we're free to do what we want and that our relationship is deeper than who we do or don't sleep with. It doesn't even nec-essarily have to be about sex, but about having connections to other people outside the relationship.' Both approach relationships pragmatically rather than romantically, and Jane feels that their love has been cemented by the fact that they talked about what they both wanted from the start. They share similar ideals and, 'We are happy for each other to have other relationships as well as flings because love isn't limited. It's certainly working so far, but if either of us felt that it wasn't working we would hopefully be able to talk about it because the whole point is that nothing is hidden. We're as committed to living our lives together as far as is humanly possible, but that doesn't necessarily include sexual fidelity, and some people can't handle that.'

During their first five years together Lawrence and Jane each had one or two casual sexual encounters outside the relationship. Then, not long after I first met them, something far more serious happened. They embarked upon a 'quad' with another couple who had previously been completely monogamous. Each of them had two partners of the opposite sex and swapped on alternate nights. 'Years ago we thought we would just want random sex with people, but actually we both prefer sex with people we know,' says Jane. 'It has made our sex life more varied, and Jane has been able to delve into aspects of S&M with the other guy which she seems to need and doesn't get from me,' says Lawrence. They recognise that it is an unusual arrangement but say that all anyone else is interested in is the sex. 'But it's not about the sex, it's the intimacy,' says Lawrence. 'If I had to choose to drop from my life either sex with these two people I love or the time I feel able to spend being close to them and feeling loved and important to somebody, knowing that they care about me, I would drop the sex.'

As people get older, with a relationship history that has failed to live up to the monogamous ideal, some consciously adopt much more flexible sexual and living arrangements. Mick lived with the mother of his two children, who are now in their late teens, until the relationship fell apart. He has a close relationship with both his children and their mother and has decided that he doesn't want to live with another woman again. He is in his mid-forties, is exploring his bisexual tendencies and has an ongoing relationship with two women, Lucy, who lives nearby, and another woman who is married and lives in Paris. He sees her every couple of months for a few days when she comes to England, with her husband's approval. 'Needing and only having one person to deal with every aspect of your life has been my main problem. It becomes a burden, and you're only scratching the surface of some areas,' says Mick. 'There are times when Lucy and I are together and times when we're apart, but what gives anyone the right when we are apart to say what I should do? It doesn't feel as if I am taking advantage of anyone because I am being completely honest and I love them both. I couldn't give any more of myself to Lucy if my other lover wasn't there.'

Lucy is a successful businesswoman who was married to the man she met at eighteen, and thought of as her soul mate, until she realised at the age of thirty-three that the romantic illusion of 'till death us do part' had evaporated. She then spent the next seven years in a relationship with an abusive man she hoped she could have children with, but when they failed to materialise she realised that she could now do what she wanted with her life as a single woman. She sees Mick most weekends, adores him, sees him as her life partner but is adamant that she doesn't want to live with him. In both of her previous long-term relationships she had had affairs, and found the kick of the deception exciting. 'I didn't know myself, really, in either of those relationships. Loneliness, convention and insecurity were driving me down the wrong path, thinking that I had to be the same person as everyone else, ticking all the boxes, trying to fit into nappy valley. I would have been a serial adulteress but I don't need that now because I have all these other kicks. Sex-wise, this is a great window for women in their forties. I always thought I was quite wild when I was young and doing blow jobs in cars when nobody else used to, but Mick has pushed me into areas I didn't realise I could go.' He has introduced her to a whole new world of sexual experimentation and taken her to sex shops and clubs. 'I know now that I was always trying to please men sexually when actually it's enjoying a cock, really feeling it and getting into the sensuality of it unselfconsciously, not caring about wearing any make-up or having a shower immediately afterwards. Every week something new happens. Last week I had this amazing vaginal orgasm where I was shaking for about half an hour. You think youth has all the sexual thrills, but this has so much more excitement and solidity to it.

Obviously I do feel jealous sometimes but when you look into those feelings, what are they actually about? I am learning to really trust, and once you trust your relationship it just flows, like skiing when you don't have to try. I trust us, I trust him, I trust what we're doing and I can't see any new person coming into this relationship and driving a wedge between us.'

Another couple I met embarked on a no-strings-attached aspect to their sex life in midlife after half a lifetime of monogamous marriage. They met as students, moved to this country from Australia, established their careers and have three teenage children. Hilary and Robin have always had lodgers, and when Robin became aware that Hilary was particularly attracted to one of them he suggested she should seduce him. 'The rule had always been you can look, you can fancy, you can tell me who you're fantasising about but no touching,' says Hilary. 'Once near the start of our relationship, he came home from a weekend away working and told me that he had held this girl's hand and I remember feeling completely gutted and thinking, That is a complete no-no. But he was the one who, years later, said, "There is so much stuff in our marriage that is good, there are a thousand other things that hold us together and that incredible passionate lust ended a hundred years ago, so just have sex with him." That really threw the ball back in my court. Where do I start? But if I've got permission, I'm out there, boy, and you know what? First-time sex is bloody delicious, and World War Three didn't break out. Our sex life has got much better because Robin likes to hear about it all, he finds it exciting. It's added a certain frisson, but neither of us could have predicted that.'

Hilary now actively pursues no-strings-attached sex through websites and small ads, and has had several flings since her first extramarital sexual liaison seven years ago. There have only been two or three men whom she has really liked and most of the men she has met for a drink she hasn't wanted to go to bed with. Often they were not being honest with their wives, and that has simply highlighted 'What a great guy Robin is, in that I am always really pleased to go back to him. He's not perfection, but compared to some of the men I've met he's Christmas. I couldn't be married to anyone else.' Hilary says she feels much more self-confident and stronger because she has been able to enjoy this freedom to play. 'Reaching forty was a big turning point for me, and as Robin says, life is too short never to have this sort of lustful sex again. It makes me feel better about myself, more confident in my skin and it's made me much more tolerant of Robin's fetish – he likes wearing women's underwear. It used to drive me mad waiting for him to choose the right pair of knickers but now, because I have been given licence to do what I want, I feel I must actually concentrate on his proclivity *and* I have the best lingerie in town.'

Hilary looks enviably fantastic on it: self-assured, relaxed and contented. She oozes a sensuality which must make other women think, 'I want whatever she's on.' Few people know what she gets up to because she can't trust them not to tell others or to make absurd assumptions. When she told her sister, she warned Hilary that this was bound to wreck her marriage. Others have leaped to the conclusion that Robin must be gay or sleeping with somebody else – he isn't – that they're not sleeping together or that there is something wrong with their marriage. The fact that this extra dimension could be enhancing their marriage is too threatening for the majority who adhere to the monogamous ideal. 'It is exciting if she phones me up and says she is going somewhere to have her brains fucked out. It's like sending someone a rude text at the beginning of a relationship,' says Robin. 'I think fidelity is about honesty, not about penetration, and if fidelity is physical, what does it mean? Holding hands can be very intimate, but what about snogging someone under the mistletoe and sticking a bit of tongue in there, is that infidelity?'

Hilary and Robin have made their relationship work by being very clear about where the boundaries lie. Robin says he only got jealous once when he discovered that Hilary was planning to go away for the weekend, which he felt was 'A step too far, from just shagging to spending time wandering round Paris together.'

When he told her this, she didn't go. Lawrence and Jane have regular meetings with the other couple as a foursome to discuss how they are feeling, whether there are any resentments or jealousies building up, with someone feeling as if they are not getting enough time with one person, or on their own. 'A lot of couples who decide they are polyamorous put rules in place about what's OK and not OK,' says Lawrence. 'Some people say that they can only have other lovers who are out of town, to preserve their individual reputation. Others say that there have to be clear distinctions between their primary commitment and a secondary one. We decided that was all a bit artificial and that we wanted much more pragmatic golden rules like safe sex, honesty comes first and if in doubt, ask. I also feel that I would like to have priority over the house we're paying rent on, so I don't actually want someone else using my bed if I want to.'

The idea of discussing bespoke boundaries in relationships has been central to many gay relationships, where casual sex is far more acceptable and very much part of the gay scene. When Oliver first fell in love with his partner more than ten years ago, 'We still went clubbing, and there were a couple of times when he'd see me looking at someone and he'd smile and say, "Go ahead," or he'd pull me back if he didn't want me to. But we don't go clubbing now, we're too tired and it must be five years since I've gone outside the relationship. The boundaries are that we can't do anything else on a Friday night without permission because that's our night to collapse together. It's about respecting each other, being honest with each other. We are monogamous, but we also have fairly light feelings towards it because there is only one life to live and if something wonderful came his way and he wanted to scratch that itch, I would let him. I would prefer it to stop at a certain point, and I also know that you can risk losing control of the situation but it is so wonderful to feel like you have still got that sex appeal when somebody flirts with you.'

Roy and Juan met twenty years ago, and now that Roy is retired they live together on the Spanish island of Majorca. There is a beach close to where they live, which is a well-known cruising spot for gay men. 'I think sex is a bit like sneezing,' says Roy. 'If he wants to go to the beach and have a quick fiddle with somebody, I really don't care. I had a grope with someone on the beach once. It just happened, nothing serious. We don't talk about it because it isn't serious. But it would bother me if he met someone on the beach and then they went out for dinner without me. Sex is physical, but for me it is not a reason to jettison a relationship.'

All relationships have to contend with the fact that a third party could cause severe disruption at some point to a lifelong relationship. The knowledge that sexual or emotional infidelity could threaten us at any time means that we cannot afford to take each other for granted. It means you have to respect each other's differences and make an effort to be kind and loving to keep them by your side. It means that you are more alert to the signs that a partner might be wandering, and make more of an effort to look and be your best. It means understanding that you can never own another, and that they too have connections to a wider community of relationship just as you have. If we expect relationships and marriages to last a lifetime, we cannot avoid or legislate against the possibility of sexual infidelity. There can be no hard-and-fast rules, only ones each couple is happy with. By focusing on sexual fidelity as a symbol of the purity of that relationship, and one which necessitates separation or divorce when broken, we perhaps set the stakes too high, when there are many other aspects of a loving relationship that matter more than sex. A bonk is just a bonk after all, and often not a very good one at that, and worse things happen in a marriage which never prompt divorce. There is a puritanical righteousness about sexual fidelity in Britain and America, in particular compared to other countries – one strike and you're out – and this assumption that our partner must and will always be faithful creates a paragon of romance which can lead to deceit, betrayal and yet more sexual shame and guilt.

A great many couples manage to maintain the religiosity of monogamy within their relationships, and build upon that intimacy with pride. 'We agreed a long time ago that sexual fidelity matters to us because we know how painful infidelity would be, and there is a way in which our love and our sex life have got deeper because of that agreement,' says Ruby. Partners in many other relationships dabble covertly with extramarital sex, and maintain the fiction of monogamous stability by never talking about it. I remember a woman who had been married for nearly forty years putting her husband firmly back in his place at a dinner party. They have had their ups and downs, like all married couples, but are happy, well matched and still have an active sex life together. When he announced rather drunkenly that their increasing number of dogs were so troublesome that they should get rid of them, she replied, 'Darling, you have mistresses; I have dogs,' and the table was silenced.

Louise has been married for fifty-five years. They have lived through a great deal together – four children, illness, severe postnatal depression, grandchildren, the death of one adult child and severe anxiety when another adult child went missing. Just before her husband's ninetieth birthday, a letter arrived from a woman he had met at university. 'He had liked her, I think, and had taken her to the college dance but had never had the nerve to do anything about it and she married somebody else. He got quite excited when this letter arrived and wanted to write back, so I am now the scribe for a regular correspondence with this old girlfriend. He dictates and I write it out for him because he can't really do that any more. It's all very sweet. It gives him a little thrill in his old age, and she is obviously a very nice person. How can I possibly be jealous now?'

8

THE LONG GOODBYE

People can spend more time extricating themselves from bad marriages and long-term relationships than they spend together. Often it takes years to accept that separation is inevitable, and even longer to unravel a shared life together. 'We were married for thirteen years, and I would say that for ten of those years I put up with a great deal of unhappiness. It took me five or six years to really recover from it,' says Madeline. 'Meeting Ralph, my new partner, was a huge help, but it was still a year or two into that relationship before I felt myself again.' Divorce is, as George Bernard Shaw once said, 'Not the destruction of marriage, but the first condition of its maintenance.' Nevertheless we never expect or dare think that it could happen to us. The effects can be life-shattering, and many are still haunted by their ex-partner years after the decree nisi has come through. The Stanford Custody Project in the US found that 26 per cent of all couples were still locked in hostile relations three and a half years after they had divorced.[1] It's hard to throw off dreams of togetherness. 'Everybody says it takes two years but it's much longer,' says Marjorie, whose twenty-year marriage ended three years ago when her husband told her that he had fallen in love with someone else. 'I thought it was for ever; I thought I was the only person he loved, and I still love him. I am sure I won't ever not.'

Media gossip pages lead us to believe that people lack commitment, that they ditch and swap partners at the first hurdle with the speed of celebrities featured in *OK* magazine, simply because they can. Divorce may be easier now than at any time in history but that does not mean people approach it lightly. Every person I met while writing this book went through years of agonising attempts to salvage their partnership, committed to the idea of commitment and the principle of 'For better, for worse', whether or not they were married, before they finally accepted 'irretrievable breakdown'. When I asked those I interviewed if they knew of others who had simply shrugged off their responsibilities without an apparent care in the world because of the new freedoms associated with no-fault divorce, not one case came to light.

Divorce is an essential human right in a civilised world. But it is so recent that we are still adjusting to its existence. It was only with the Divorce Reform Act of 1969 in Britain that married couples could legally separate after two years' separation or by proving adultery, desertion or unreasonable behaviour, and only in 1996 that the Family Law Act removed the age-old notion that someone had to be at fault for the break-up of a marriage. Even so, most find it hard to decide whether to push through such a dramatic change to their family life without the certainty of greater happiness at the end of it. It doesn't matter whether you are the one doing the leaving or being left – the end of a long relationship is a devastating decision, rarely made rashly. The stigma associated with relationship breakdown may be marginally less now that it is so much more common and talked-about, but for each individual involved the sudden aloneness, the sense of failure and of failed hopes can be traumatic. 'Divorce and suicide have many characteristics in common and one crucial difference,' writes Al Alvarez, who attempted suicide after the break-up of his first marriage, in *Life After Marriage*. 'Although both are devastatingly public admissions of failure, divorce, unlike suicide, has to be lived through.'

On the scale of stressful life events developed by Holmes and Rahe, divorce and separation come second and third after the top scorer of death of a spouse.[2] When you consider that the end of a major relationship is fraught with other known difficulties and traumas such as moving, reduced financial security and sole responsibility for children, particularly for mothers, loss of day-to-day contact with children for the non-custodial parent, increased argument with their partner and in-laws, as well as greater social isolation with the inevitable loss of friends who take sides, the numbers on the Holmes and Rahe scale add up to a major life crisis. Divorce increases the risk of death in every age group, particularly among men.[3] There are few statistics gathered for those who cohabit, but there is every reason to suppose that separated partnerships suffer in exactly the same way. Divorced or separated men and women are about 35 per cent more likely to consult their GP than married people. They smoke, and drink more alcohol, and morbidity statistics consistently find that the divorced suffer from a great many more diseases, depression and mental illness than married people.[4]

Family breakdown affects children profoundly. However, children vary widely in their experiences, and can fare better than children with both parents present, for there is overwhelming evidence that it is the way that family functions which matters, more than family structure, to a child's well-being. A range of studies have found a small but persistent lower score on a variety of aspects from academic achievement, behaviour, psychological adjustment and self-concept for some children of separated parents.[5] Often it is the consequences of divorce, such as increased financial hardship, high levels of conflict and parental psychological distress, which determine whether or not children fall into the majority group who adjusts well, or suffer long-term. When the children's needs are given proper consideration and priority, the fallout can be minimised but that takes a level of maturity and sensitivity which parents living with such a high level of emotional personal trauma are not known for. In such circumstances it is hardly surprising that people try so hard to salvage what they can from their relationship and take an inordinately long time to part completely. 'You do see some couples where it is clear that they will only remain whole if they split, they have become so imprisoned by the dynamic that has grown between them,' says Pam Fawcett, a relationship counsellor. 'But more often people want to find a way through. It's such a major crisis, breaking up, and people want to avoid it if they can. I have been touched by those who have made it through when I didn't think they would.'

Statistics are crude measurements, and in the case of divorce, blanket use of the 'one in three end in divorce' to predict the end of marriage as we know it is greatly misleading. Divorce rates began to rise in the US and in much of Western Europe with a sixfold increase between 1960 and 1980, a natural consequence of more sexually liberal and feminist shifts as well as changes in the law. Comparisons with pre-war statistics are hardly useful, when few could afford the privilege before the advent of legal aid in 1949. The divorce rate has been broadly steady for the past twenty to thirty years and even saw a slight fall in Britain, parts of Europe and Canada from 2005 onwards. Britain now has the lowest divorce rate since 1981 with 11.9 divorces per 1000 married men and women in 2007.[6,7] Some of that stabilisation is accounted for by the rise in the number of those who cohabit rather than marry. Many of those are testing partnerships before they commit to marriage because they believe in its permanence, not because they think they can exit a failing marriage quickly by divorcing. But it is also possible that, after just a few decades of readier divorce, we have only now begun to arrive at a true picture of marriage where a substantial number were always destined to fail. These are lifetime statistics, masking the fact that almost half of all divorces occur within the first seven years and that after twenty years of marriage, only 15 per cent are likely to end in divorce.[8,9,10]

The nature of life has changed profoundly in less than a century, making divorce much more important and more common. Death used to end most marriages; now we live longer than ever before. The chances of finding one person who will change with you and meet enough of your needs through that longer lifetime are inevitably reduced. The steady rise in divorce statistics through the twentieth century is largely accounted for by the extension of the right to divorce to every social group, rather than its being a privilege of the rich. The figures include second and third divorces, which means that some people are contributing more than their fair share to the overall figure, for second and third marriages are more likely to end in divorce than first marriages. The statistics cannot calibrate the socio-economic factors that impact upon relationships, for those in disadvantaged circumstances are more at risk. The reality of lifelong relationships and people's attitude to commitment cannot be measured by statistics alone. It is my view that people's desire for lifelong commitment within relationship is not diminished by the presumed ease of divorce; rather, it is stronger than ever.

There appear to be three key stages in the life of a relationship when it is most prone to breakdown – at the very beginning, then when children are young and finally in midlife. Divorce rates peak at three years into the marriage, with the sharpest drop in marital relations occurring between years one and two. Many of these relationships will have gone wrong the moment the romance died and insurmountable differences emerged, but take years to get to the point of separation. 'We often see people for just one visit,' says divorce lawyer Kim Beatson. 'They come to check out whether they can even afford to think about it, and then they come back two years later even though they have probably been miserable all that time.' Jackie found herself being seduced by a mutual friend just as a ten-year-long relationship with her first boyfriend ended, and four months later they were married. 'I woke up the day after we got married and it was as if someone had dropped a bottle of cold water on my head and I thought, What have I done? But then I thought, Well, I have made my bed, I had better lie in it. I always felt that marriage was for life so I was determined to make it work.' Her husband stopped talking to her and went away often to teach at summer schools, refusing to take her with him. One day when he was away two policemen arrived at the door to arrest her for unpaid parking fines. Several days later the phone was cut off. Jackie worked full-time and had been giving her husband housekeeping money to pay the bills. She went into his office, found a drawer full of unopened post and discovered that they had a substantial overdraft. At that point she decided they should separate, but it took months, stretching into years, before she was able to achieve that objective. 'It's horrible living with someone when you are trying to leave. It was one of the most painful times of my life because I just wanted him to go, but he spent months bunking on the living-room floor.'

Deborah also knew near the beginning of her nineteen-year marriage that it wasn't working but had found it hard to extricate herself from it before there were children. 'He got very aggressive soon after we married, and I just smoothed things over and tried to make everything OK. Actually I should have pulled out then, but I never really knew when it should end. I always felt that because you had committed yourself for better, for worse that you just carried on doing it and working at it, but I don't think he felt that commitment at all.' Deborah lived in an unhappy and abusive marriage with a husband who whittled away at her confidence for years before the marriage finally ended when he found someone else. 'But even then he kept coming back and saying let's make a go of it. It took me years to get to the point where I could shut the door on him completely. One of the biggest mistakes was to get married so quickly. I think if we had waited just a year we wouldn't have got married. But it was only six months, and after four months we were already making wedding plans, so it was that much harder to pull out of it somehow. He proposed to me three weeks after he met me and it was too quick, but I was flattered, I suppose, swept away. It seems ridiculous now, but then I was twenty-five and I really felt that if I didn't marry him I could be left on the shelf.'

When people marry young they are more likely to separate in the first few years of their relationship. Divorce rates peak among twenty- to twenty-four-year-old men and women in both the US and the UK.[11] In a third of all the divorces that took place in Scotland in 2000, one of the partners was under the age of twenty-one at the time of their marriage.[12] People make mistakes, and it is good that no-fault divorce allows them to separate quickly and find greater happiness elsewhere. However, the sense of personal failure when romantic expectations of lifelong loving end so prematurely is huge. Studies have found that those with a strong belief in marriage as a lifelong commitment found divorce particularly distressing.[13] We invest so much hope in love, so much money and public display in lavish weddings and so much faith in the noble value of commitment that even when people know that they have made a mistake, that truth is clouded, making it harder for people to go public with their unhappiness. The boom in romantic notions of expensive, fairy-tale weddings and escaping dull reality by living 'happily ever after' inevitably plays a part in seducing young people into believing that marriage is the solution to everything.

'It was blind love. We couldn't spend enough time together and we seemed to want the same things in life,' says Sally. Her boyfriend proposed on her twenty-first birthday but they were married for less than two years before they divorced. 'I think looking back I wanted to be looked after. My dad passed away when I was eighteen and Joe offered that stability and security I needed. We talked about growing up together; everyone kept saying you are too young, but there was no doubt in my mind. I just trusted that I was making the right decision because I loved him, and I thought that whatever happened, if we were together and if we loved each other that was the main thing.' Their relationship deteriorated quickly once they were married, with Joe staying out late at weekends drinking away most of his earnings while Sally slumped into a depression, diminished by Joe's contemptuous put-downs and sudden unloving behaviour.

Sally gave up a great deal of her own life, including a career as a trainee lawyer, in order to give Joe what she thought he wanted from a marriage, and in doing so surprised herself by how much she had changed. 'There was no spark left, and when I left him I wanted to feel like I was when I was eighteen again, when I was happy, and just be around people I knew. I remember bumping into a friend who had had a run-in with Joe at one point because he was being so nasty to me, several months after we had separated. She said I looked amazing, that I had lost weight and looked like the old Sally again, and how at school everyone had fancied me and I just cried and thought, Isn't that strange. I can't believe I changed that much, that I lost so much of me and I look back now and think, What the hell did you think you were doing?' The pain of the breakdown is still raw and Sally cried when she told me her story, still hurt by the betrayal of a dream and astounded by the way a bad marriage could destroy so much of her sense of self. Getting her own name back and achieving divorce before her twenty-fourth birthday so that she could put the whole experience behind her became a symbolic priority. 'I was working at a solicitors' and they asked me if I wanted them to do a change of name by deed poll. I just knew that I wanted to do it myself to make sure that it had been done and there were no complications. I lost my rag with the bank several times because they kept calling me by my married name, and I begrudged having to pay sixty pounds to get my name back when I should never have given it away in the first place.'

Marcus's first marriage also lasted less than two years, and he too fell into profound self-doubt for having made such a cata- strophic mistake, which took time to recover from. 'It was the easiest divorce in history, in that there were only a certain number of towels and ashtrays to divide up and it ended reasonably ami- cably, but it was a hell of a body blow. I felt let down, I questioned my own judgement and felt fairly shell-shocked for a year or so,' he says. They had been together for two years before they mar- ried and were very much in love. 'We were very happy, but we didn't know each other that well and she didn't know what she wanted in life and thought it would be a good idea to get married. Once we were married she didn't like feeling tied down, but I was thirty-five and thought it was time to grow up. I had done all the bachelor stuff, so it was completely shattering for me emotionally. I looked back to when we had met and wondered, Were those doubts I had at the beginning real warning signs, or just the sort of perfectly normal doubts that everyone has? I had nothing else to compare it with. Unless you've been married eight times, how can you possibly know or judge it?'

In spite of the agony, both Sally and Marcus managed to end their marriages before that decision affected a child. Parenthood seems to provoke the second spike in divorce and separation statistics with roughly a fifth of all marriages ending within five years after the birth of the first child.[14] Youth may be the ideal time for reproduction physically, but it is not necessarily the best time to establish a lifelong partnership. People change profoundly when they become parents, and now that both work longer hours than ever before, they rarely find time for themselves, let alone for each other. 'Finding time to do our work was always a problem. Money was always a problem. Childcare was a problem. Sex was a problem. We communicated poorly. (I deluged him with words. He gave me silence),' writes divorcee Joyce Maynard in her essay 'The Stories We Tell'. 'Good enough', loving parents recognise that they have to shift the emphasis of their relationship for the sake of their children. Satisfaction now has to come primarily from sharing family joys and responsibilities rather than from each other. The fear is that they could put their relationship on hold for so long that there is nothing much left in common other than the children when they find time to be a couple again. Those who drift inexorably apart find that in addition to feeling a deep sense of failure in marriage, there is the intractable feeling that you have failed to create a happy family as well. Yet all of the evidence suggests that the more resilient parents are, accepting the end of their partnership quickly and with good grace, focusing together on their shared roles as parents rather than hurling resentment, blame and rage at each other, the more resilient and undamaged their beloved children will be. When parents adapt and move on, so too do their children, provided that their needs as children are always given priority.

The vast majority of those who separate as parents of young children do not do so lightly. It's an agonising decision, which takes even longer to arrive at because of the children. A great many parents still stay together for their sake. A survey of 2,000 people commissioned by the firm of solicitors Seddons found that 37 per cent were staying in a doomed marriage to spare both the children and themselves from going through the massive upheaval of a divorce, and that significantly as much as 59 per cent of the wives would divorce their husbands immediately if they knew that their future economic security was assured.[15] Many women especially are prepared to live with extreme betrayal and personal unhappiness because they understand their children's prime need for stability and do not want to impoverish them emotionally or financially by separating. Sarah was married to her husband for fifteen years and had three children when she discovered that he had been having an affair with her closest friend. 'She was like the sister I never had, we were that close, and then after a few years I began to feel claustrophobic, like she was moving in. We bought a sofa; she bought the same one. We bought an Espace; she bought the same car. We went on holiday to France; she tried to get into the same campsite.' Sarah and her husband had nursed this friend through a difficult divorce, and they had just moved away from friends and schools to another part of London in the hope of starting a new life when her husband admitted to the affair. 'I lost my husband and my best friend in one fell swoop. I would have stuck it through because of the kids; I wouldn't have denied them their father for anything. I begged him to stay, even though deep down I knew it wouldn't be right but I had to, I had to know that if they ever asked I could say that I did everything I could to keep it together. It took us three years eventually to part. I remember thinking then that I could see why they call it heartache because your heart really aches, your chest hurts. It's the crying, I suppose. My whole body just ached with it all.'

When it came to telling the children that they were separating, Sarah refused to allow him to give them the 'Mummy and Daddy don't love each other any more' line. She made him tell them the truth, that he was leaving because he wanted to. 'That was the worst day of my life,' says Sarah. 'All in all, the kids have coped really well but the thought of my middle son, the day he told them, still makes me cry. The youngest was playing with her Lego, Sharon was sitting with me, crying but Adam was on the floor with his face buried into the carpet sobbing "Please don't go, Dad, please don't go." And his father was saying, "It'll be all right," and "I'll still see you," and all this rubbish. After we had got through that and went into the kitchen, my husband said, "Well, I think that went all right, didn't it?" and I said, "Were you in the same room as me? You think it's OK to watch your son sobbing into the carpet, begging you not to leave? It's all right because that's what you want it to be."'

'For adults, divorce brings *a* world to an end; for young children, whose lives are focused in the family, it seems to bring *the* world to an end,' writes psychologist Edith Mavis Hetherington in her book *For Better or For Worse*. She has conducted one of the largest longitudinal studies on the impact of divorce at the University of Virginia in the US. 'In the short run, divorce usually is brutally painful to a child. But its negative long-term effects have been exaggerated to the point where we now have a self-fulfilling prophecy.' A large number of studies comparing the well-being of children of divorced parents with those whose parents were married to each other have found a small but consistent gap on measures of academic success, behaviour, psychological adjustment, self-concept and long-term health.[16] But how many of these children were affected by the way that their parents handled the break-down of their relationship, rather than the divorce per se, is far more difficult to ascertain. Anecdotal evidence suggests this to be the case, as does a review of the evidence conducted by the Thomas Coram Research Unit in 2009, and Hetherington's research. Hetherington followed 1,400 families through divorce and its aftermath over twenty-five years. She concludes that 80 per cent of the children from divorced homes were able to adapt to their new life and were 'reasonably well adjusted', while 10 per cent of young people from non-divorced families compared to 20 per cent in divorced and remarried families were troubled.[17] A much larger number of adult children described themselves as permanently 'scarred' by the experience at the end of her research than she found objectively to be the case. 'Most of the young men and women from my divorced families looked a lot like their contemporaries from non-divorced homes. Although they looked back on their parents' break-up as a painful experience, most were successfully going about the chief tasks of young adulthood: establishing careers, creating intimate relationships, building meaningful lives for themselves.'

It is the quality of relationship between parents and children which creates untroubled, happy children and not necessarily the number of parents present. Young people with difficulties tend to come from all sorts of homes, intact as well as divorced. It tends to be high levels of conflict, neglect and authoritarian, rather than authoritative attitudes which have the most profound negative effects on a child's development, not divorce per se, provided it is handled sensitively. For those who are escaping violent, abusive marriages, separation and divorce brings an end to the fear and misery of a heavily conflicted family life, and is often highly beneficial in the long run for both adults and children. While for other children, particularly those from homes where the marital conflict has been concealed, the sudden breakdown of that stability is far more damaging and harder to come to terms with, for it makes children question their past and themselves and can lead them to believe that they are somehow to blame. For both adults and children it is the number of stresses and protective buffers they experience through the process of family breakdown which helps or hinders how they cope with such a radical change in their lives. What is surprising, and rarely discussed, is how many women in particular, as well as their children, eventually find that their resilience and way of life has been enhanced by what has happened to them during divorce, rather than diminished by it.

The anguish parents feel when their relationship breaks down cannot be underestimated. It is highlighted, rendered more complicated, because of the children. Sarah was astonished by the length of time it took her to recover and eventually went to counselling at Relate to help her get over it. 'My sister seemed to think it was like going to a psychiatrist and that I wasn't mad, but you can't keep burdening your friends with it. I used to come out with my eyes red from crying for an hour but it does eventually get easier. Then I saw this man there who was devastated by his break-up, in tears every week, and you realise how much you have moved on, finally.' People discover things about their partner during the acrimony of separation and begin to question their own judgement and their years together – what really went on, and how could I have been so mistaken? For Ursula, it was the fact that she had to take her husband of seventeen years to court three times in order to get him to pay up for their children, even though he was wealthy. 'The man I knew before was like the tip of the iceberg because the man I discovered underneath was somebody very different. He fought me as if he was doing a deal with somebody he had never met, and I couldn't believe he could treat me and the kids that way.'

The break-up of their marriage was so tumultuous and drawn-out that it makes the average soap opera look tame. They separated and then came back together again. Her husband suffered from depression and used emotional blackmail, threatening to kill himself on several occasions if she didn't respond to his extreme demands at that very moment, even though he was the one who had placed the relationship under strain by having an affair, which he refused to end. After years of drama, trauma and uncertainty Ursula found that her sense of self was shaken to the core. 'It's a complete rocking of everything you are. I was scared, just trying to hold everything together, and there were long stretches of time when I didn't even know who I was because my whole being had been wrapped up with the family and with him. The only way to rebuild yourself is to start at the bottom and realise, I am not dead. I can see and feel and I am still standing. What doesn't kill you makes you stronger, that was how I got out of bed in the morning. I remember when I finally left court for the last time I thought finally, I can breathe and I haven't felt that way in years. Then it's like a whole new process of rediscovery of who you are and what you want and that's exciting, but it takes a hell of a long time to get to that point. He lied so much at that time that I am no longer sure what was really going on during the seventeen years of our marriage. I will never know, and he will never be able to tell me in a way that will make me believe him, and I can live with that if I just put it to one side in a box. It's the collapse of trust which is the longest-lasting canker for me because it pervades everything. I wouldn't trust him with my garbage, but I have to trust him with my kids.'

Divorce destroys the rhythms of family life, and when parents separate there is rarely a level playing field between them. It can be hard for both adults and children to adapt to their new circumstances; in one large-scale longitudinal study in the Bristol area, 26 per cent of single mothers were found to be depressed as opposed to 12 per cent of mothers with a resident partner.[18] Women usually suffer financially through divorce far more than men and are 40 per cent more likely to enter poverty than if they remained married. Only a quarter of the fathers in the Hetherington study met their financial obligations regularly, and even then their ex-wives often complained that it wasn't enough to meet their children's needs. Another quarter provided no financial assistance whatsoever and half provided inconsistent support.[19] Analysis of the British Household Panel Survey in the late 1990s found that women's net income declined by 18 per cent after divorce, with a larger decline among younger women.[20] Another study found that mothers with custody typically see a 36 per cent decline in their

standard of living, while non-custodial fathers typically experience a 28 per cent increase and overall a mother's standard of
living dropped to about half that of fathers.[21] Sarah was left with
three children aged three, six and nine, no income and a new
house which needed everything doing to it. Her husband worked
full-time as a builder and gave her £70 a week when he first left,
'Which he thought was a fortune, but after about two years that
stopped completely and I didn't bother him about money because
I knew how awful he was with it. We had the bailiffs round four
or five times in our last house.' Sarah started working as a childminder and then as a teaching assistant. 'You get tired of arguing,
and I knew I wouldn't get the money at the end of it so what was
the point? I'd only upset myself.'

She was not the only single mother I met who found herself in
difficult financial circumstances. Rajani finally left the family home
with her two children after years of physical abuse. She simply
couldn't stand it any more and wanted a fresh start. But what that
meant was that she left her husband in the house she half owns,
while she rents somewhere else on her income alone and now can't
get him out of the house to free up the money for somewhere else
to live. He shows no sign of moving or putting the house on the
market. 'Financially it has been difficult, he has been earning but
the mortgage he has to pay is low while I have been scraping by to
pay the rent on my earnings, and when I ask him for money he
says he hasn't got any. He said initially that he would give me 60
per cent of the house for me and the children, then he said he
would give me 70 per cent. Now he says he doesn't want to sell it
at all and that I am a bad mother for wanting him to do so because
it is our children's home. I am worried now that he is trying to
build up a case against me. He won't discuss things on the phone,
I have to email him now about everything and I never got it in
writing that he would give me 60 per cent of the house.'

For the growing number of women who are also the main
breadwinners, in some 18 per cent of all couples in the year 2006
to 2007 in the UK,[22] the no-fault divorce laws can leave them in

a tricky position financially. Marjorie would have loved to spend more time at home with her two children when they were small, but her husband was a writer and as she was the main breadwinner with a good full-time job they couldn't afford for her to. 'It used to upset me sometimes but I just thought, You are in this marriage, you love him, he loves you and you just happen to be earning the money. You don't look twenty years down the line because you think it is for ever.' Her husband fell in love with another woman three years ago and left Marjorie and their teenage children shortly after he had confessed to the affair. She had always thought of their house as their financial safety net, and imagined that once the children were older they would be able to downsize and have some extra cash for themselves as well as to help their children through university. Now the house is on the market so that he can buy somewhere to live with his new lover, and Marjorie's lawyer has advised her that he is also entitled to half her pension – she is in her fifties – and could even be entitled to some of her salary, even though there was a nanny when the children were younger, and he has not paid her anything for the children since the break-up. Their lawyers have struck a deal whereby he gets the endowment policy on the house so that she can keep her pension. Marjorie is left not just heartbroken by the man she loved and still loves but considerably poorer and angry at the way 'no-fault' divorce has seemed to cost them all so much as a family, through no fault of her own. 'All those dreams of that future that you imagined for yourself disappear overnight,' she says. 'It feels so unfair in that the law was meant to protect wives who had given up everything to stay at home to look after the children, wives who have nothing and no way of earning, and that's not the reality for us at all. He could easily earn a lot more money than he does.'

But it is the fact that her husband of twenty years has cut off his relationship with their son that staggers and upsets her the most. 'He has been terrible with the kids, and in many ways that has prolonged the whole agony of it all. He did this when the kids were so needy – it was just the most appalling timing with Jack doing his A levels. He is so selfish.' Her husband was at home for their children for the first fourteen years of their youngest son's life, and now rarely makes contact with him at all. For two consecutive summer holidays Marjorie's husband never got in touch or arranged to do something with their son while she was at work, even though they were both at home and just a few miles apart. 'He has never spent more than four hours with him, he has never taken him out and he has stopped communicating with him, even though our son really needs him and I have been pushing for them to be together. I have done a lot of reflecting over what has happened, and in many ways I always knew that inside this great teddy bear of a man there was someone who wasn't quite so nice. He never worked harder or took jobs that he didn't want to help me out when we were together. He never felt he should be sacrificing something for his kids, and I can see that now. But I can't hate him because that negates twenty wonderful years of family life. He could have made the past three years so much easier just by being kind and thoughtful to our son.'

Children cannot help but be affected by the emotional disruptions of their parents separating, but how parents manage such a traumatic change can make a world of difference when it comes to helping them cope and adjust. Children exhibit different symptoms of distress about divorce at different ages, from difficulties eating and sleeping as infants, to bed-wetting, excessive temper tantrums, regressive behaviour as young children, to being overly anxious and troubled teenagers.[23] Children of all ages become confused, worried and angry and can be overly clingy, whiny, demanding or disobedient, adding yet more stress to a single parent who is usually having to cope with more than enough difficulties of their own. But never underestimate the power of a parent, even as a divorcing one, when it comes to being able to put things right for them. There is substantial evidence that suggests that good relationships between parents and children, as well as flexibility when it comes to making contact arrangements, can reduce many of the potential negative effects on children of separation.

The health and well-being of a child is intricately connected to that of their parents. When parents manage to accept their loss or guilt and move on, when they can be civil to and about their ex-partner, they help their children to move on too. Easier said than done, I know, but by refusing to fall headlong into two of the most common pitfalls – diminished parenting as distressed adults rely too much on their child emotionally, and entrenched conflict between the separating parents – children stand a really good chance of bouncing back relatively unscathed. Divorce and separation is an inevitability for many families in today's changing world. For some, the dream of lifelong marriage is no longer an option. If everything else fails, when forgiveness, counselling, promises to change and trial separation do nothing to improve relations, separation and divorce are civilised solutions provided they are handled well by both partners, even the one who feels wronged. When children's needs are put first, when parents take steps to understand how to minimise the trauma, they can thrive.

That does not mean stifling one's own heartache; rather find-ing ways to come to terms with it away from the children by talking to friends, going for counselling, whatever helps you to be better parents to your children. Good parents tend to want to place their own emotional needs way behind those of their chil-dren, but often it is only when parents have settled happily into a new way of life that children can too. They sense parental unhap-piness without having to be told, just as they sense hostility between their parents without hearing rows and can feel doubly inadequate as a result, unable to ease their parents' distress on top of feeling personally abandoned and divorced too. 'I put all of my own emotions on hold, I felt I had to be strong for the children,' says Diana, who separated from the father of her two children after months of attempting to put their relationship back on track when he had an affair. 'I was prepared to stick it out and do any-thing to keep us together for the kids, but when he announced to the counsellor rather than to me privately that his new girlfriend was pregnant, I just knew then that there was nothing else I could do. I always said there is no way our kids are going to suffer because of our cock-ups. I was strong for quite a long time, I knew I had to keep it all together for the kids, and then after about two years I felt as if I was inside this wall looking out. I could literally see this wall crumbling in front of me, and I thought there's something going on here, and went to the doctor who put me on Prozac for a while. It was like after a bereavement, in that everyone thought I was doing fine and that I was really strong. Actually it was everyone else who had moved on, and I was still hurt and very angry but I had to keep up a pretence for the children. I was the one picking up the pieces for everybody else, including their father – I had to push him into doing the right thing by our kids because he is not very good at facing things and I really resented that at the time. But that's what you do as a woman left living with the kids, you pick up the pieces. It goes with the territory, it's about giving rather than receiving.'

Their youngest son was three at the time of the break-up and couldn't remember his father leaving. Even so, several years later he began to show signs of serious distress: 'When his dad came round he would hang on to his leg trying to stop him from leaving, and Nick didn't know how to deal with that so he would just shake him off and go. My son became quite depressed – if you criticised him in the slightest way he would run up to his bedroom in tears, and at one stage he climbed out of the window and said that he wanted to die. I remember being at my sister's once and she told him off for something and he went out into the middle of the road and lay down. He was a very unhappy little boy, so I got all three of us into some family therapy and we managed to turn it around, thankfully, by getting it all out into the open.'

A range of protective factors help adults and children get used to life after divorce. Children need exactly the same stable base, with good authoritative parenting, firm boundaries and rules explained, as they did when their parents were together, as well as a great deal more care, love and emotional support while their world is changing so radically. Too often a child's need for love and structure evaporates simply because their parents are consumed by their own emotional agony, by their sense of failure and guilt. Some parents neglect by their absence, others become overly permissive or spoiling because their child is already 'going through enough with the divorce'. Children need to feel listened to, consulted about decisions which affect their lives and protected by parents who keep their conflict levels to a minimum, and when they do row, resolve things constructively.

It is shocking that just 5 to 10 per cent of children feel that they know what is going on through their parents' separation and the conflict that often ensues.[24, 25] Children must never feel drawn into their parents' arguments, hear one parent demonise the other, feel responsible for supporting their parents through the upset, or feel to blame for the break-up of their family. They need repeated, age-appropriate explanations of what is going on. Research seems to indicate that it is these sorts of positive affirmations and practices, rather than the structural make-up of the family per se, which contribute far more to a child's welfare both in the short- and the long-term, and that it is inadequate parenting and ongoing conflict between parents which can have such disastrous consequences.[26] Children need as many other supportive adults around as possible: grandparents, teachers and family friends who can act as mentors, surrogate parents for troubled children to talk to, or even to run to, for nothing pushes adolescents away from their homes quicker than unsupportive parents riven with conflict. Children are not clones of their parents; they have their own individual strengths and weaknesses. Those with higher levels of autonomy, self-esteem, sporting or academic achievements, supportive friends and emotional maturity appear, according to longitudinal studies, to show fewer long-lasting problems after divorce, while those who were previously antisocial and felt more insecure and helpless before the divorce coped less well.[27] Children also have different temperaments, and the stresses associated with divorce seem to magnify the effects of that temperament on family relationships. An easy, agreeable child is more likely to stay affable, minimising difficulties for separating parents and making it easier for them to be authoritative, effective parents, while a difficult child is more likely to get more difficult and harder for a stressed parent to manage well.

The most constructive thing that separating parents can do to help their children is to come to a quick and cooperative decision over contact arrangements. Few things are worse for a child than not knowing when they will see that beloved father or mother who has left the family home, or watching them fight, often viciously, over how they will be spending weekends and who with. Children don't get used to conflict – they grow increasingly sensitive to it. While most divorcing and separating couples would clearly prefer to see as little of each other as possible, it is not necessarily in the best interests of children for parents to leave it to lawyers and judges to sort out arbitrary notions of fairness when it comes to dividing up a child's spare time. The most successful arrangements seem to be those that are arranged informally by parents with enough cool-headed maturity and flexibility to adapt arrangements around the changing needs of their children as they grow older, with the children regularly consulted in that decision-making.[28] The unhappiest children of separated parents are those who feel that they cannot talk to their parents about the arrangements and have no influence over how their time is parcelled out.[29]

There is no 'one size fits all' pattern to the aftermath of divorce, and what works for one family could be disastrous for another. Yet research indicates that only a quarter of parents manage to achieve that cooperative peace by arriving at their own solution, sharing responsibility and the planning of their child's life.[30] Edith Mavis Hetherington's studies have found that as many as a quarter of couples were still engaged in heavy conflict, undermining each other's relationship with the child and fighting openly in front of them six years after the divorce. When there is ongoing acrimony, typically fathers will retreat and reduce contact with their child to avoid argument and to defend themselves against their own feelings of guilt and powerlessness. There are fathers who simply walk out of a child's life and never look back. But equally there are other fathers who feel so ostracised and to blame because of the ongoing conflict that they think it is perhaps better to disappear out of a child's life altogether. Survey evidence from 935 divorced families in England and Wales in 2003 found that 23 per cent of children never saw their other parent.[31] Another study puts the figure as high as 37 per cent of fathers who lose contact with their child within two years of divorce.[32]

Too often parents retreat into their own misery, convinced that this is an adult issue and that children will either not understand what is going on or be affected by it, when the reality is that every certainty and source of comfort in their small world has been painfully shattered. Moreover the effects of divorce on children can be excused or minimised by the fact that it is so common these days that they will have friends they can talk to with similar experiences, and that there is next to no stigma attached to it any more. But for each child, losing day-to-day contact with a parent is a life-changing tragedy, and there is no evidence to suggest that the trauma of divorce for children has been diminished by rising divorce rates and a greater acceptance of relationship breakdown. If we are adult enough to bring children into the world, we should also attempt to be adult enough to minimise the conflict between us as separated lovers so that we can prioritise a child's needs when they have had no say over something so profoundly important to them. Both parents continue to play a monumentally important role in their child's life, provided they can find enough space in their hearts to allow each other in, and they don't have to be there daily to do that.

A small but growing number of parents are attempting to fashion their own solutions, oiling the wheels of a less nuclear family with flexible, shared commitment so that it trucks along with the minimum disruption for the children. Some choose to live near to each other so that their children can move easily between both homes. Others live further apart but manage to talk freely and regularly together about their children and their needs, and good relations between children and both parents are encouraged. 'We stayed on good terms, which was great. My ex-wife was great, and she did it for the children,' says Charles, who was divorced in the 1970s after twelve years of marriage. 'I got a good job up north, something I had always wanted to do, but Melanie dug her heels in and refused to move, so we just sort of drifted apart really. She allowed me unlimited access, and I spent most weekends with her and the children, and we always spent Christmas together. It was almost as if we were still married, even though we were technically divorced. I am really grateful to Mel for that because she could have poisoned the children with "Your father is a bastard", but she didn't because that's not in her nature. To this day I still feel guilty about the divorce because I chose my career over my marriage. I don't tell her that, but I think it is a measure of my affection for her that I still pay a court order for the children when the youngest of the three is nearly forty! It's a guilt payment, probably, and years ago she told me to stop paying her but I said, "No, this is for your pension."'

Some separated families even manage to go on holiday together, accepting early on that their relationship may have ended but that they still share a relationship as parents to their children. Alex and his wife were married for twenty years and have two sons. 'We were basically just so unhappy living with each other. We'd changed, I'd changed, and she had to cope with a lot because I had a drink problem, which I have now sorted. We tried several times to make it work but we wanted different things – most particularly she wanted to move out of London and I didn't, so we decided mutually to separate before either of us fell out or had an affair. I helped her move, helped get the kids into new schools and we are both much happier and the children seem fine. We like each other, and we're a huge part of each other's lives. When she comes to London she stays in the spare room. Our friends haven't needed to take sides, and we can't see any reason why we shouldn't go on holiday with each other for the children. But who knows how that will change once either of us finds someone else? In spite of all this, I still found the whole thing hugely traumatic. I felt I had really failed them all, and I recognise that Clare still has to cope much more than I do with the boys on her own. I have heard her buttoning her lip. She wants to scream blame with, "You don't have to deal with all of this every day like I do," but she can't because we decided to separate mutually and amicably.'

Madeline was the major breadwinner with her own successful business, while her husband moved from job to job and consistently got into debt. She knew that she would have to be careful when she decided to leave. 'I had the financial capacity to get myself out, which is what a lot of women don't have, so I rented a cottage and continued to pay for the upkeep of the house and my husband. I didn't care about the money: all I wanted was for my boys to come and live with me, and I thought if I just did everything slowly and backed off from every confrontation when it was about money to keep things on an even keel, then maybe that would happen. I was right in the long run because he just couldn't cope with the routines of normal family life. My solicitor felt I should have gone for more because there were policies which by rights I should have had half of, but I gave in on them – anything not to have to pay him alimony – and be shot of the whole thing.' Madeline and her husband went to great lengths to minimise the impact of the divorce on their two sons. 'We tried hard not to criticise each other and to keep things as amicable as possible. Of course they were damaged by it but it's not as bad as it could have been, and now I look at my sons and think they are very balanced young men. We really tried. I remember one of them saying to me once with great irritation, "Yes, Mum, I *know* it's not our fault, so will you stop going on about it." Whatever I think of my ex-husband, I know he loves them, even though he has a funny way of showing it sometimes.'

It can be hard for involved, loving parents to separate their own pain at the breakdown of the relationship from the impact that breakdown has on their children, and that is one of the reasons why it takes such a long time to recover. One's children are always there to remind you of what once was. Decades of memories are stored in the fabric of the things left behind. 'Every object, even those which had been hers, which he never touched, seemed to share his loss,' writes James Salter in his novel *Light Years*. 'That presence, loving or not, which fills the emptiness of rooms, mildens them, makes them light – that presence was gone.' For Marjorie it is the large chest of family pictures that she still cannot bear to open. 'I don't know what I am going to do with them. People deface pictures, don't they, but I can't because that's such a huge part of my life, and I hope to be able to look at them again one day. I was cleaning up Jack's room the other day and I came across this sweet little picture of us all together looking so happy, and you just think, how could anybody walk away from that?' Landmarks in the annual family calendar such as Christmas and birthdays become not just logistically difficult but poignant and upsetting reminders of all that has been lost. 'He emailed me about something a week after we had got divorced, on my birth-day, and forgot to say happy birthday. When that sort of thing happens it makes everything so sore all over again because for twenty-two years my birthday was a major deal – I was so spoiled. He was romantic and inventive, and gave me amazing presents. His forgetting just made me realise how far away he has gone, and that's so hurtful because he has this whole other life now.'

The break-up of a long-term relationship with children involves the break-up of a family, and that can be so painful that the only way to cope with the convoluted difficulties of trying to extrapolate why it happened is to find one simple answer and stick to it. 'Maybe because the actual events were so hard to live through, you stop revisiting them,' writes Joyce Maynard in *The Stories We Tell*. 'Instead, you revisit only the story you come up with to explain what happened.' During the first year after the break-up of a substantial relationship people tend to alternate between occasional bouts of euphoria at the freedoms associated with their potential new life and a more prolonged, depressive sense of failure, which for men can translate into sexual failure – rates of sexual dysfunction are 10 per cent higher in divorced men.[33] With deep feelings of anger and loneliness, physical appearance changes. Some become more dishevelled and put on weight; others channel their anger into a frenzy of self-improvement, changing the way they look with radical dieting, exercise, new hair styles, fashion makeovers and even cosmetic surgery. Others try to alter their work and home lives by changing jobs or moving away in order to attempt to create a brand-new sense of self and start afresh. For most, it seems to be the end of the first year which is the most painful, when doubts about the past and concern over the future reach a crescendo. A year apart seems to encapsulate a lifetime with those significant calendar events approached as newly separated people. Once these landmarks are revisited in year two, many couples have begun to accept the new status quo and moved on.

It is not uncommon for people, even those who have done the leaving, to doubt the wisdom of what they have done, and they are right to do so. Many divorced people admit to being no happier years later than they were when they were married.[34] Attachment and affection lingers on. The love that grows from spending years of one's life intimately connected to another person cannot simply be switched off because your paths seem to have parted irrevocably or one of you has fallen in love with someone else. In three-quarters of all the divorced couples in Edith Mavis Hetherington's study, at least one partner regretted the decision at the one-year mark and felt that they should have worked harder at their marriage, once the alternatives associated with freedom no longer seemed so attractive. Some studies find that unhappiness, depression and health problems have largely subsided two to three years after separation. Others fail to find an improvement unless a person remarries, and even then it takes time within that new partnership for the trust to build and the wounds to heal. Some never manage completely to get over the breakdown of their marriage.

Peggy considers the father of her second child to have been the love of her life, but their marriage soon deteriorated when he had what she now suspects to be a nervous breakdown. 'We were out with the kids one Sunday afternoon with a group of friends and as we were walking back he said to me, "I am not coming home," I thought he meant he was going somewhere else first but then he said, "No, I am leaving you." I had half a dozen witnesses who remember seeing my face crumble and realised something serious had happened. They scooped up the kids, but he wouldn't talk about it and just went.' Two of her friends decided they needed to track him down over the next few days, but failed, until Peggy remembered that he hated his name and had always wished he had been called Ian Fleming, and that he had a penchant for hotels because of their anonymity. Her friends found him in less than an hour. 'What followed was a long period of "It's not you, it's me, I didn't do enough of being me before we got together so I need to go off for a while," while I was so heartbroken I went down to six and a half stone and couldn't keep food inside my body,' says Peggy. 'Then we got back together again and I thought, This is fine, he has sorted himself out, but he hadn't and that went on for years and years, with him going away and coming back again.'

They eventually divorced and her ex-husband married again, but once that relationship started to go wrong he resumed a sexual relationship with Peggy. 'One day he got terribly emotional and told me that he needed me to know that he did not have a sexual relationship with his wife. I think he thought it would make me feel better but actually it made me feel worse, like some sort of prostitute that he called in on so as not to trouble his career-driven, too-good-for-him wife, so I stopped our relationship completely then.' They are still apart, and while Peggy has had other lovers and built a contented life for herself as a woman living alone, she also readily admits that her ex-husband still haunts her, unable quite to let her go. 'Of all the streets in Manchester he could have lived on, and he has chosen to live around the corner! That just makes me wonder whether I am going to be pursued again. Even the park feels different now because he has a dog and I could bump into him at any time.'

What seems to differentiate those who are able to move on from their separation and find greater happiness elsewhere from those who cannot, or who go on to repeat the same mistakes in their next relationship and separate a second time, is their ability to learn from their experience in their first marriage or lifelong relationship, and change. Women tend to find this a great deal easier to do than men who, more often than not, simply want to replace woman number one with woman number two. However, many women rediscover a great deal more about themselves and what really matters to them, even when they have been unwillingly left. 'There are all these more positive things which you don't think about much when you are going through the trauma of a divorce,' says Ursula. 'The first morning when I woke up without the kids I cried, and cried and then after a while you stop sniffing and think, Well, maybe I will go to the Royal Academy, or get a pedicure.' Diana had her first child when she was twenty-six, which severely curtailed her desire to party. 'You disappear sexually when you have children and I did find that hard, but when Mark left me I got all that partying out of my system and it was fantastic fun. Mark had the kids every other weekend and suddenly there were all these men asking me out, which was lovely, so I partied hard. I needed to, and I needed time for myself.'

Divorce feels like a devastating blow to a person's entire physical and emotional sense of self and well-being, but with time the trauma usually diminishes, leaving people in a better state than they were in a bad marriage. People in unhappy marriages are more psychologically distressed than people who stay single. A three-year study of married couples in which one partner had mild hypertension found that in happy marriages the blood pressure of the at-risk partner dropped when they spent a few extra minutes together, whereas for those who were unhappily married, a few minutes of extra time together raised the blood pressure of the at-risk spouse.[35] Divorce is better in the long run for the miserably married, particularly for women who have higher rates of depression, alcohol abuse and high cholesterol levels with twice the likelihood of heart attack or stroke as happily married or single women. At the six-year mark in the Hetherington study, the vast majority of divorced women were reasonably happy, their children were settled and they felt that on balance the divorce had been a

good thing, in spite of the financial difficulties experienced by a
great many of them. They had been freed from a dying relationship and had travelled down new paths of self-discovery, launching
themselves into jobs and opportunities that they would never have
seized had they stayed married. A large-scale study by the British
Household Panel Survey between 1991 and 2001 comparing outcomes for those who divorced to those who stayed married found
that divorce was usually traumatic in the short term, but that over
subsequent years the psychological well-being of men and women
improved considerably and they ended up feeling happier than
they had done two years prior to the divorce.[36]

The final peak in divorce rates occurs in midlife, with more
people over sixty now divorcing than ever before. Given the
length of time we all live these days, with our health and sexual
appetites less compromised than at any other time in history, it is
unsurprising that so many couples should ride the first two peak
times for separation and divorce, only to find themselves falling
at the final hurdle in midlife. Those who have stayed married for
the children find that there is little now to keep them together.
Often one partner will be more acutely aware that this is the case
than the other. The fundamental symbiosis between them has
never been openly discussed so it often comes as a great shock to
the other that their partner should want to unpack their relationship so suddenly. Those who haven't managed to face their
divisive issues head on, choosing to sideline contention for an
easier life, find themselves eyeball to eyeball with all the conflicts
once their children have left home. For others, their needs simply
change. We want a great deal from one partner through a lifetime:
passion and electric sexual chemistry when we are young, someone to share the joys and workload with through two decades of
parenthood, and then companionship in midlife as the prospect
of mutual caregiving in old age looms large. The chances of finding someone who can fulfil all of these criteria, who will adapt to
these major life stages at roughly the same time as you do and

where both can tolerate, let alone like, the way the other changes, are slim indeed.

Midlife crisis in marriage is a modern phenomenon and the result of a unique combination of factors. First, until the beginning of the twentieth century most marriages ended as the children grew up, with the average life expectancy of men and women hovering between forty and fifty years. Now the average married couple can expect to live for two to three decades after their children have left home. Second, couples devote so much energy to working and raising their children, sacrificing much of their own needs for the sake of the family within a climate where it is individualism and selfish pursuit which seem to matter most, that once they hit midlife they long to grab a bit more for themselves. Their children are less needy and suddenly there is more time, which raises the question, for what? Their own health begins to feel precious, their parents are ageing and in need of care or are already dead and their children burst with fresh promise and sexuality, prompting both men and women to reassess how they want to spend the rest of their lives, often with profound ramifications. Long-term relationship suddenly feels like a suffocating trap rather than a source of comforting security. The cracks in the relationship become all too apparent, wider than ever, now that there is less in family and working life to fill them.

'I was twenty-two when I got married, and when I look at the photos of the two of us I think, Why did nobody say, "Don't be silly, sit down and finish your dinner!"' says Ralph. 'There was this general sense of euphoria that I was settling down. I had come out of an era in Ireland when everybody did what they were told but from the very start I had doubts. We were together for about twenty-three years, and for the first ten of those years I would have said that we were blissfully happy and people used to hold us up as an example. Then I began to realise that she wasn't all that happy, she felt that her personality had been subsumed. For the last seven or eight years I just didn't want to be there. I hated walking up the garden path, and it got to a stage where the kids were fourteen and sixteen, so they were up and running largely, and I decided there was no reason why I had to be unhappy for the rest of my life. I had to stop this and leave. I moved into a flat, and I remember the silence the night I moved in and thought, This is good. She was a constant nag. Irish women tend to nag their partners with an expertise that I haven't seen in England. It's the vigour!'

Ralph didn't leave his wife to reassert his virility with a younger woman in midlife as many other men seem to do. He left choosing to be happier alone rather than in a bad marriage, and eventually found a more loving and equable partnership with Madeline, who is also divorced with two children. Many men at this time do a great deal of soul-searching about their work and their achievements. It's a time when they can find it hard to accept that they may never succeed professionally in the way they had anticipated. They may never climb the Himalayas or learn to sail a yacht as they had always hoped, and if they feel their relationship lacks emotional and sexual intimacy because their wives and partners have been so focused on the children and juggling their careers and family life, now is the time that men will seek it elsewhere. There are undoubtedly many men who fit the 'bastard' stereotype, deserting their wives and children out of vanity and the fantasy that they can find a more perfect life with someone else a lot younger. But there are many more who are genuinely lost, at sea and confused about what they want for themselves: 'Looking forward to the years ahead with the same sorrows as the years past provokes people to action, to leave, to start down new roads,' writes Anne Roiphe in *Married: A Fine Predicament*, 'to save themselves, or so they hope, from boredom, quarrels, isolation, unhappiness, their first mistakes which time has compounded and turned into grudges, resentments, lumps of coal in the Christmas stocking.'

For women, an entirely different perspective opens up as their children grow up and become less needy. They have spent so many years caring primarily for their young that they now want to focus more on work, friends and exploring their own interests.

Greater economic independence and the fact that fifty doesn't mean the end of the road any more has given a whole swathe of baby boomers a new vista on midlife, and if their partner isn't prepared to step up to the mark and go with her, many would rather go on alone. Freed from hormonal drives, the need for sexual or social approval and the imperative of keeping the family together, with careers, greater health and enough money in their back pockets to pursue their own dreams, more women are prepared to approach their last few decades with a whole new set of priorities. Sixty-five per cent of divorces in people over fifty are initiated by women. 'When I ask myself, is this someone I want to grow old with, I know the answer is no,' says Jan, who was on the verge of separation after years of unhappiness when I met her. 'I want the ages of fifty to seventy to be everything that thirty to fifty wasn't, and not to act on that wish would be foolish. Yet there have been some fantastic moments in this marriage. He is the father of two wonderful children, and that means a lot.'

'We're going to turn into wonderfully powerful old crones,' says Nancy, who is in her mid-fifties and has accepted life in a less-than-happy marriage for the sake of her children. She spends half the week in London, and feels lucky to be surrounded by so many women friends. 'What helps is knowing masses of other women my age who support each other. It's not as if there are hundreds of men out there who are more attractive. The only people I want to shag are thirty-five and they aren't going to be interested. But there's no stigma to being a woman on your own any more, and I felt such huge delight last summer going away for a week by myself. We had been swamped by visitors, most were his relations and it was full on, so I went to France and read books and went to art galleries and ate in nice restaurants every night completely on my own, and it was wonderful. Obviously it would have been more fun if I had someone entertaining to talk to, but it wasn't appalling at all, it was fine.' For those women who have got used to living alone over the years, the idea of having another person share that home feels alien. 'I have become extremely used to my own space and time,' says Peggy, who has two adult children and two ex-husbands. 'So when a boyfriend wanted me to stay the night I chose to drive an hour home instead so that I could wake up in my own house, and I thought, This is terrible, I have gone feral. For twenty-five years I have made all the decisions as to what I do over the weekend, and I really look forward to gardening or listening to a Radio Four play, and I really don't feel as if I am missing out on anything. Even the thought of someone else being here permanently feels weird.'

The assumption, buried deep in our psyche, is that someone must be to blame for being 'the bad one' if the relationship fails, when it can never be that simple. Divorce is often the result of a prolonged and complex combination of irreconcilable forces that might perhaps have been prevented with hindsight and greater awareness, but then again could have happened anyway. The need for a scapegoat, the adulterer, the demon who abandons the marriage selfishly or gets seduced away in other people's relationships, excuses us from examining the dynamics of our own too closely. Blaming others is playground protection, and stronger than ever today because feelings of failing at love in a highly romanticised world are far too hard to deal with alone.

Double standards between the sexes endure in that separated, single fathers are often considered heroes and are more likely to be offered support even though their higher salaries mean that they are likely to be able to afford to buy in help. They are invited for Sunday lunches and dinner parties by other mothers at the school gate, perhaps indulging in innocent romantic fantasies of rescue and escape from the routines and boredom of their own married lives. Single fathers are attractive; they don't seem to pose quite the same threat, or conform to the stereotypical assumptions of vulnerable single mothers who somehow smack of tarnished goods. 'There is a very nice café near here where all the middle classes seem to gather. I was the only dark face there one Saturday morning, and the only woman there alone with her kids,' says

Rajani. There were all these children with their golden bobs and Mummy and Daddy there, and I suddenly felt something very subtle. I was being given glances because my children were talking rather loudly about when they were going to Daddy's house and I just thought, I can't go there any more. I think it's because they are scared it might happen to them, or I am seen as a threat as a woman on her own because I am still reasonably well preserved and I don't want to have babies any more, so maybe it's the women protecting their husbands.'

'I used to think, I am a really bad catch, a single mum with two children on income support,' says Sue, whose husband went bankrupt just before they finally divorced after years of loneliness and unhappiness. She worked as a cleaner and a childminder to keep her children going. 'I thought I was worth nothing, it was desperate and I remember thinking for quite a long time that I was never going to break out of this cycle.' Diana found that people whom she used to think of as friends began to cross the road. 'Others would be really patronising. They would walk up to you, cock their head to one side and say, "How are you?" really gently with their hand pressed supportively under my arm, so I decided that I was not going to be a victim, or a femme fatale.'

'In the weeks after my husband moved out, I received an email from someone offering to help me clean the house or cook, an email that evokes images of dishes piling up in the sink, flies hovering over half-eaten peanut butter sandwiches, laundry accumulating,' writes Katie Roiphe in the *Observer* newspaper. 'Why would the departure of my husband launch me and my daughter into a life of squalor? Someone else writes: "There are no words for a catastrophe of this magnitude. I am thinking of you." And it begins to seem as if my husband has, in fact, not moved five minutes away but died.' Katie Roiphe is honest about the fact that the break-up of her marriage was emotionally difficult, but that the silver lining to this dark cloud was a new sense of freedom, a new energy and lease of life for a better future. 'One of the disturbing things about my marriage break-up,' she continues, 'is the feeling that I have lost a significant chunk of time to unhappiness. This may be why I don't want to give myself the "time" that people seem to think I need to recover. This may be why I don't want to wait for some ideal future when my attachments arrange themselves into a more conventional pattern. At a certain point all you have are these raw, transitional hours: this is your life, and you may as well enjoy it.'[37]

The age-old religious assumption that marriage cannot be dissolved except through death might have been liveable with when most people died at forty, but in today's world, no-fault divorce has to be one of our most precious human rights. We don't have to stay in abusive, miserably doomed marriages. We don't have to live with our mistakes like some sort of life-long, tortuous penalty charge and, given the odds stacked against us, particularly for working parents with small children, it is a miracle that so many couples stay together at all. There is a tendency always to think of divorce as something negative and damaging rather than liberating and life-enhancing simply because we refuse to let go of the romantic, happily-ever-after notion of matrimony. But there is no idyllic past where most couples stayed together for decades of marital bliss. The stable family life we assume existed in the past was disrupted as much by death, migration and poverty as contemporary family life is by divorce. 'The duration of marriage of the cohorts marrying between 1920 and 1950 when death rates of young adults had dropped precipitously and divorce had not yet taken on a major role, were historically quite different from those before and after,' writes Lawrence Stone in his history of the making and breaking of marriage in England, *Road to Divorce*. 'During those thirty years, fewer than 20 per cent were broken by death or divorce after twenty years, compared with over 30 per cent (by death) for the 1826 marriage cohort and 30 per cent (mostly by divorce) for the 1980 marriage cohort.'

The misery of being trapped in decades of unhappy marriage without the easy exit of divorce is the subject of countless novels and plays, yet still those few freak years during the middle of the twentieth century, where substantial numbers of people made it to their silver wedding anniversary and beyond, hold our imagination as the norm which we somehow fail to reach when our own marriages end. Divorce may feel like a modern disease simply because it is now available to all, but it has always been with us in some form or other, its merits and faults debated heavily by intellectuals and politicians, its power to undermine the institution of marriage controlled by State and Church. The new freedom to separate or divorce with ease sits hand in glove with the new relationship ideals which we value so highly. If love, companionship and personal happiness is now more important than the economic and social union of two families, or providing legitimacy for offspring, then a more sophisticated, blameless and liberal attitude to divorce has to be essential should those powerful dreams die. You can't have an obsessive cultural need for love without such an escape clause.

Up until the Matrimonial Causes Act of 1857, divorce could only be obtained in England through an expensive Act of Parliament, and while ecclesiastical courts could grant legal separations, neither partner was permitted to remarry. While far fewer marriages ended when divorce was more difficult to achieve, large numbers of people found ingenious ways of coping with the inevitability of irretrievable breakdown for many of the same reasons they do today. Many couples simply left each other, for with little in the way of transport and communication systems it was easy to set off for another town, never to be traced again. Huge numbers of women and children were left in poverty, just as they are today. A census taken of the poor in the city of Norwich in the 1580s shows that a tenth of all the women on poor relief were deserted wives, and that a full quarter of those on relief lacked husbands. Magistrates' orders for maintenance during the late Victorian period show that desertions were in the tens of thousands each year.[38] For what the historian Lawrence Stone likes to call 'the middling sort' of the seventeenth and eighteenth centuries – shopkeepers, bankers, merchants, farmers, small

tradesmen and clerks – with more to protect in the way of reputation and property, annulling a marriage was too expensive,
protracted and public to pursue in the ecclesiastical or common
law courts. Private deeds of separation developed from the late
seventeenth century onwards and were popular until the beginning of the twentieth century as the most convenient, quasi-legal
way to bring a dead marriage to a close. Marriage laws and rituals symbolising betrothal were so vague and ill defined that they
were open to reinterpretation, and until Hardwick's Marriage Act
of 1753 began to take hold it was often difficult for many couples
to know whether or not they were legally married at all. Even
then, large numbers of couples were still able to exploit the ambi-
guities, for the Act made null and void any marriage in which
there was the slightest mistake in the wording of the banns or
licence with respect to age, which opened up yet another avenue
for self-divorce. Between 1810 and 1822, sixty marriages were
annulled in this way in two London courts alone.[39]

For centuries adultery or desertion for seven years or more was
the only means of divorce, and both had to be proved publicly
with the blame laid firmly at the feet of the wife. Double standards
were rife. Unless an adulterous woman was protected by a private
deed of separation, she lost everything: her property, her income
and even her children if her husband decided she could no longer
see them. A man's adultery, however, was a lesser offence, forgiven as an acceptable male need and not grounds for divorce
unless a woman could prove an additional offence such as desertion or excessive cruelty. What mattered most was male honour.
The severance of a marriage because of a woman's adultery had
to be made public so that the man was no longer liable for
alimony or the support of any future children she might bear. For
the poor, a rather distasteful public handing over of responsibility for a woman evolved during the seventeenth century in the
form of 'wife sale', where the husband put a rope around his
wife's neck and took her to market to sell her to the highest bidder,
usually her lover, with all three in agreement.

Blame lies deep at the heart of divorce. It was only in 1996 that the idea that someone should be at fault for the breakdown of a relationship was finally removed from British law with the promulgation of the Family Law Act. We haven't got used to it yet. The notion of no-fault divorce sits uncomfortably within a culture which romanticises everlasting love so heavily, and where consequently it is more important than ever for someone still to be seen as guilty for abandoning that love. With increased individualism and greater freedom of choice when it comes to forming lifelong relationships, there is no one else but ourselves to hold accountable for a failed union, and that isn't easy to stomach. Easier by far to blame the other, when it can take years, and only then with the highest levels of self-awareness, for two people to begin to understand what really went wrong in their relationship.

An intact, two-parent family is lionised as the gold standard, and divorced or single-parent families are perceived as damaged or troubled when large numbers of single-parent, divorced and reconstituted families can and do flourish, with a great deal of love and high quality of care. Divorce rates are higher in those who grew up in divorced homes. Some of these divorces will undoubtedly be the result of the lack of a strong marital role model and growing up within a family full of unresolved conflict, where the children lacked enough love to be able to love themselves. But equally, for others divorce is an entirely positive choice. They have experienced it first hand and not only survived but thrived, and therefore consider separation to be a positive solution when their own lifelong relationship stagnates with insurmountable difficulties. We romanticise the past when divorce was rare as healthier and happier, when there is no evidence that this was the case. We believe that only the nuclear family will do, when substantial numbers of families throughout history have been disparate with emotionally absent fathers, working mothers, adolescents in service miles away from their own parents and babies suckled by wet nurses, or raised entirely by nannies. The notion that marriage is in crisis because of divorce is bandied about liberally but the average duration of marriages has in fact got longer in spite of it – half of marriages dissolved in 2000 lasted thirteen years or more compared to nine years in the early 1970s.[40] Yet still we punish ourselves for failing when all of the evidence suggests that divorce and separation are almost always the last resort in desperate circumstances.

There is a curious paradox in that we view other people's relationships as deeply private, that 'Marriages are secrets, shared only by the principals,' as Martin Amis writes in his memoir *Experience*, yet when a marriage gets into trouble or fails we revel in all the prurient detail as if it were a horror show, passing judgement, taking sides. Madeline was unhappy for years in her marriage before she finally plucked up the courage to leave. 'We did "couple" and "family" really well, which is the tragedy of it in that nobody really knew what was going on until we separated. I wish I had had someone to talk to at the time. You feel like you have lost yourself. It was only when it was out in the open and we were getting divorced that I started talking to people, endlessly in fact – then I couldn't stop! They were shocked by how he had belittled my confidence over the years, all the job changes and money problems, how he did nothing to help, and then they expressed surprise at the fact that I had stayed so long. What's difficult is that you have invited everyone into your life with a view, and then you are shocked by what they tell you they have observed about your relationship over the years and you think, Well, why didn't you tell me earlier?'

Marjorie's friends have been so appalled by the way her husband has left, and abandoned his relationship with their teenage son, that they have been vociferous about where their loyalties lie, inevitably pushing him further away from a family he still cares for. At a recent sixtieth birthday party of a mutual friend where her husband was likely to be with his new girlfriend, Marjorie said, 'I will see how strong I feel on the day. If I'm up for it I will come, if I am feeling vulnerable I won't. But then so many of our friends said they wouldn't go if he turned up, they weren't invited, which caused huge upset.'

When Rajani's marriage hit the rocks after years of abuse from her husband, his family never acknowledged that their son must have played a part in its demise. She was branded the villain and left unsupported, even though she was the mother of their grand-children. Her own family lived in Indonesia, unaware even that their daughter's marriage had failed. When her father-in-law died, her mother-in-law made it clear that Rajani and the youngest child were not welcome, left to stand outside the church while the eldest grandchild was allowed to read a poem inside to the assembled mourners. 'My name was also left out of the obituary because daughters-in-law are not part of the family but my brother in-law's girlfriend was allowed to sit at the front during the service,' she told me bitterly. She spent the first Christmas after their separation without her children. Her husband took them to his mother's, and friends formed during their marriage did not extend invitations. Luckily, new friends and neighbours made sure that she did not spend that first season of goodwill alone.

It's easy to think of divorce as a private failing, an isolated event, like illness, which hopefully won't happen to us. However, just like illness, relationship breakdown often comes as part of a large package of difficulties such as financial problems and unemployment, depression and alcohol or drug abuse. Old-style notions of how marriage should be die hard. Unemployment for men when their wives are working has a greater impact on the quality of marital relations than it does when it is the woman who is unemployed. Edith Mavis Hetherington has found that physical violence is twice as high in families with an unemployed husband than in families in which both work or only the wife is unemployed.[41] Contemporary pressures such as lack of support for working parents with affordable childcare and flexible work-ing inevitably affect levels of relationship breakdown as couples drift inexorably apart, exhaustingly juggling work and family life. Large-scale historical events such as the first and second world wars forced the divorce levels up in Britain in subsequent years, as soldiers came home disorientated to wives who had changed and grown stronger by working or had fallen in love with some-one else. Unexpected personal tragedies such as the death of a child can trigger relationship breakdown. Parents often become so consumed by their own individual grief that they cannot relate to each other's. The slow undermining grind of economic hardship puts troubled relationships under even greater strain. Money worries are one of the two main reasons why couples seek coun-selling – the other is sex – and during the recession of 1990 to 1994, divorce rates in the UK rose from 153,386 to 165,018.[42] Inevitably people from different socio-economic backgrounds have very different experiences when it comes to access to the legal process. When the rich want to separate they can afford the best legal support to battle over their considerable assets, while those on middling or lower incomes often find that they cannot afford to divorce at all. 'If you're a teacher or a nurse or someone who is just outside public funding, you could be in a terrible position when it comes to getting help,' says divorce lawyer Kim Beatson. 'I think there is a whole raft of people in the middle who really struggle legally and practically, and perhaps don't do anything because they cannot even get the will to do anything when they can't afford it.'

Those from the poorest socio-economic backgrounds seem to have higher rates of marital dissolution. Women on income support are roughly four times as likely as non-recipients to experience a partnership split in the coming year.[43] One study of the British Household Panel Survey in the late 1990s found that deteriorating financial circumstances in a given year meant a 50 per cent higher risk of relationship dissolution in the following year than those whose financial situation remained constant. For those whose financial circumstances improved, the opposite was true – their risk of separation was 50 per cent lower than for those who reported no change.[44] A large-scale study of first marriages in Finland has found that male unemployment increased the risk of divorce, and some studies in the US have found the risk of relationship dissolution to be higher among couples with lower incomes.[45, 46, 47] Education levels, which in turn affect economic prospects, also seem to play a part. A large study in Norway found that couples where both spouses had low levels of education were four times more likely to divorce than couples where both had been through higher education.[48]

Politicians and certain areas of the media lash out at the presumed selfishness of single mothers and absent fathers, when some of the research evidence suggests that for those on low incomes it is the external factors of poverty and job insecurity that are the prime culprits, destabilising the fabric of family life. Young inner-city fathers in the UK are less likely to marry and assume financial responsibility for their children when they lack job opportunities or face bleak earning prospects. Kathryn Edin, a sociologist, conducted in-depth interviews with 300 low-income American single mothers in 2000 and found that most hoped to marry one day but found themselves on the outside of raised marital expectations, peering in to a romantic dream that they couldn't possibly afford. They were also faced with a stark choice – marry someone with few marketable skills and a shaky employment history or not marry at all, fully aware that some unions could be more of an economic burden than a benefit.[49] A large-scale study of 5,000 children born between 1998 and 2000, largely to unmarried mothers in the US, found that the overwhelming majority – 83 per cent of them – were either cohabiting or romantically involved with their child's father shortly after giving birth. Five years later the break-up rate of the cohabiting couples is about twice as high as that of married couples, but the average income of the unmarried fathers is also, markedly, half that of the married fathers.[50] Professor Sara McLanahan of Princeton University, and one of the researchers on the 'Fragile Families and Child Wellbeing' study, in response to a question at a panel discussion, said that many of those they interviewed wanted to get married, but high standards prevented them from doing so. 'For them, nothing is worse than a divorce: they'd rather not marry than marry and fail. There are all these hurdles to jump before you can get married so that you don't end up getting divorced, like his infidelity, low income, economic problems – financial and emotional difficulties. The surprise is these couples don't think marriage is unimportant.'[51]

Divorce is a blunt instrument, an anonymous and rough legal template for ending a marriage. We are still adjusting to its presence after centuries of either no divorce at all or having to resort to proving that our partner has committed a crime against the sanctity of the marital union to escape misery, violence or child-lessness for the chance of a better life with someone else. 'Melanie rang me in floods of tears when we got divorced in the 1970s because in those days it had to be "unreasonable behaviour",' says Charles. 'Her solicitor told her she had to read out ten items of misdemeanour and they were pathetic, like shouting at one of the children when we were on holiday, or coming home late. She had to scrape the barrel, it really upset her and all she could say was I am so sorry, I don't mean any of it.' Divorce can be costly and hugely unfair. Perhaps if young couples spent just an hour dis-cussing their options with a lawyer before they lavished thousands of pounds on their dream day, fewer would enter marriage as an institution quite so easily. 'I would now counsel my kids to think seriously before marrying,' says Ursula. 'It's the first social con-tract you enter into which has serious consequences, and I will never marry again.'

No-fault divorce is an essential human right in today's world. People make mistakes and are allowed a second chance of hap-piness. People cannot know how they or their partner will change with time. Everyone must have the right to escape an abusive, humiliating or violent marriage. Commitment is important, but so too are searching questions as to what exactly we are committing ourselves to, for a bad relationship where one's sense of self as an autonomous being is badly violated is a false, unhealthy quest which is in all likelihood doomed. Relationships can only work if both want them to.

You cannot legislate for the numerous different ways in which couples want to be together today, or how they separate. We now have that freedom, and consequently a whole new swathe of responsibilities. It is up to us as individuals to manage that process as well as we possibly can so that the damage to children is minimised. The existence of divorce doesn't destroy families; we do, with blame and righteous indignation because of the deep, searing pain of abandoning and being abandoned by love and the shame of personal failure. We fight over money, houses and things, sharing our children's weekends and holidays with the same ferocious dedication to fairness as siblings sharing out sweets, screaming our rage at each other for failing to rise to unrealistic expectations of love, for having changed. The pain for many is understandably acute. It takes most people longer than they ever could have anticipated to recover and to rediscover their sense of self. The most successful divorces and separations are accepted with good grace and emotional maturity, calmly and mutually agreed upon, without the need for expensive lawyers to remind those separating of the need for fairness. However painful the breakdown of a relationship, we were grown up enough to establish a mature relationship, and have to be responsible enough to end it with dignity. In doing so, we not only do everything we can to ensure the welfare of those who have no part in our battles – our children. We also provide those precious children with brighter rays of hope when it comes to forming their own relationships in the future, with healthier role models of respect, self-respect and the knowledge that love is about so much more than romance. There is a broader love for a fellow human being with whom we once shared so much.

9

HAPPY FAMILIES

'I have friends who are about to have babies and I have been saying to them, "Be warned, it puts a strain on your relationship." It's wonderful, I would never say to anyone don't do it because having a baby is the most fantastic thing that can happen to you, but it brings you down to the bottom line of what your relationship is all about,' says Megan, who has a fifteen-month-old son. 'It used to amaze me that people could have kids together and then leave each other, but I totally understand that now. I am just thankful that we have enough in our relationship to carry on because there have been times when it has been so bad that I couldn't see how it could possibly work. I wrote a long letter to a friend who had a baby shortly after me telling her exactly how I felt, and she was so grateful to hear that from somebody else. Everybody had been saying, "You should be so happy and enjoying yourself," when basically her husband was behaving really badly. You think having a baby is going to be this life-changing experience in a completely positive way, when a lot of it isn't that positive.'

Few things change the emotional landscape of a relationship more than the arrival of that first child. Men and women move from being lovers and equals to mothers and fathers, with new roles and responsibilities and a host of different expectations based on their own histories. There is less time alone together, their days have a different rhythm and a precious and very needy child now sits between them. Life with small children is full of extremes and paradoxes, great highs as we relish the love, wonder and joy, as well as staggering lows when the routine, responsibility, lack of freedom and sleep get too much. Happy family life demands unparalleled levels of selflessness and maturity from parents, which is increasingly at odds with a society where, as individuals, we are expected to pursue our own personal dreams, ambitions and pleasures. While the media likes to focus on rising rates of family breakdown and single parenthood as symptomatic of the new selfishness, the majority of parents unquestioningly sacrifice a great deal of their own happiness for the sake of their children, and we should salute these unsung heroes. 'We'd make good soldiers,' says Ethan. They have three children. The eldest is ten, the youngest three. 'We just keep going, doing what has to be done, and in a way it's having faith in the process and in the other person. You have to trust that even though you are just padding round each other, you are both looking down the same track, knowing that it will come together again when everything is in position to do so.'

Juliet too has three children. She and her husband went through a particularly bad patch in their marriage after the birth of their second child, when Philip got too close to a woman at work. 'We both come from strong families, and have a vision that family is worth pursuing in the long term. It would have been so easy just to give up and say, "OK, let's each pursue our own happiness." Instead I said, "This is unacceptable and you are not leaving me," and we are so happy now. I do think marriages are amazing. I look at all the parents at our primary school and most of them are bringing up their children together. Obviously there are single parents, but it's not like they are falling down like ninepins. Even the couples who bicker a lot are still hanging in there, years later.'

Nancy's marriage ran into difficulty nearly a decade ago when her husband decided to give up work, forcing her to become the sole breadwinner, but she chose not to leave because of the children. 'You do have to give things up in order to have other things, but we live in a world where you are supposed to have everything – youth, money, sex, friendship. I haven't had a dream marriage, but I have had an awful lot of other things: a good job, really good friends, I live in a beautiful place and I have a lot of intellectual interests and two fantastic children who are doing very well. You can't have it all, and even if I found someone I absolutely adored, I can't imagine saying, "This is the love I have been looking for all my life," and having to face my tear-stained, angry children. I wouldn't be happy that way. When you've been with someone as long as I have, you realise that all marriage is a compromise, so why would you jump from one to another? There will only be a whole new set of problems. There just isn't a perfect relationship, and to go through all that getting to know someone again and then discovering that they are actually mean or rather unkind or secretly love reading science fiction – at least I respect the books my husband reads! I knew that I simply couldn't put my kids through the two homes thing, schlepping backwards and forwards. I preferred to put up with it rather than inflict that on them, and I am glad I did that, very, very glad.'

While it is true that few things put a marriage under more strain than having a baby, couples with small children tend to experience lower divorce rates than couples without children who have been married for the same length of time.[1, 2] The research evidence seems to suggest that the seeds of breakdown are sown long before the arrival of a child, and that the difficulties of family life simply add too much pressure to relationships which were unequal or fragile to begin with. Those marriages adversely affected by the sharp change of family life tend to involve young partners with less income, less education and fewer years of marriage before childbirth. They are also more likely to consider a relationship as an essential romance rather than a partnership or friendship. Children accentuate the changes that occur for all couples with the passage of time. When a couple enjoy a good relationship before childbirth, they are more likely to continue to find contentment as a family. Each couple has little choice but to fumble their way through unfamiliar territory as they argue and negotiate new rights and responsibilities, stretching their resources and energy levels to try to meet seemingly impossible demands. Marital satisfaction may decline more sharply during the first two years of parenthood than at any other time, but the presence of that child keeps more parents together, and the more children they have, the less likely they are to divorce.[3] Most navigate their way over the huge hurdles inherent to modern family life because they love their children and because they want above all to bring them up well. However, the pressures on parents can be immense at times, and approximately a fifth of all divorces occur within five years after the birth of the first child.[4]

Many couples reach a deeper sense of commitment, contentment and love for each other as a result of the hard graft of working through their difficulties together. They have a stronger bond because of that shared history, and their children become a source of great pleasure, which unites rather than divides them. What is remarkable is the fact that so many families show such resilience and adapt, given that modern life has thrown up many new difficulties. Family life is in transition, buffeted by a social revolution, which has made couples more dependent on each other. Families have become more vertical than horizontal, with a greater number of generations, often spread disparately across counties and countries rather than an extended family of the same age nearby to rely upon. The traditional assumptions about mothers and fathers are disappearing, and the roles of parents are becoming increasingly interchangeable. Rising numbers of men want a more emotionally involved life with their children than they had with their own fathers, and most working mothers express a keen desire for relief from domestic drudgery and the resentments their mothers experienced. Few can survive on the father's salary alone. Most women return to work at some point as mothers, yet workplace attitudes and practices have not shifted adequately to accommodate the new needs of families. It is parents who bear the brunt of this seismic change, with no route map to tell them how to be a 'happy' family any more as they grapple towards a new way of being which sort of works – on a good day.

Nobody can be completely prepared for the changes that a new baby brings. We imagine the cosy intimacy of cuddling a small baby that is ours and ours alone as the ultimate pinnacle of romance. But even in the most stable of partnerships, babies tend to throw our homes and lives into chaos, highlighting all of the crevices and hidden differences in a relationship. The Penn State Child and Family Development project conducted a large-scale study of early parenthood from pregnancy to the child's third birthday, and discovered that only 19 per cent of new parents felt that their relationship had improved as they adapted to the changes that a baby brings with comparative ease. The rest either embarked on a holding action in their relationship or found that it had deteriorated.[5] Some studies show that marital satisfaction increases for 18 per cent to 30 per cent of couples. But more than thirty longitudinal studies conducted between the late 1970s and 2000 in the US, England and Germany show that a majority of couples show a significant decline in their marital satisfaction after the birth of their first child.[6] Once partners become parents, the discoveries each makes about the other can have a lasting effect on their relationship. Every assumption about your identity and how you live your life gets thrown up into the air. You are now providers and protectors, there's a great deal to do, and 'No matter how much they love each other, no two people share the same values or feelings or have the same perspective on life,' write Jay Belsky and John Kelly in their classic study *The Transition to Parenthood*. 'Few things highlight these personal differences as pointedly as the birth of a child.'

Men and women may think of themselves as equals living similar, companionable, loving lives within the relationship when they are childless, but from pregnancy onwards the gender gulf between them is stark and often divisive. Pregnancy places the organs of a woman's body under immense strain, and it takes time and rest to recover from the extraordinary process of producing another human being, luxuries which few women in the modern world feel able to afford. Certain parts of a woman's body never regain their former shape. Nipples can become larger or darker and breasts either drop, change shape or disappear completely after breastfeeding. Stretch marks are marks of motherhood for life; there is often weight gain, which can be difficult to shed, and while the muscles of the abdomen do eventually come back into line with the rest of the body, they are unlikely to regain their previous concave form without rigorous exercise. As for the vagina, well, no one has ever put it better than a woman I interviewed for my book on new motherhood, *Life After Birth*, when she said, 'I feel so open now, very different, I get into the bath and half the water disappears.'

Many find their health is impaired by anaemia, backache, exhaustion, bladder or gynaecological problems as a result of the birth, which may have been such a shocking, even traumatic experience that it takes months for the memories to fade. Understandably, sex is not even on the agenda for most women in the months after giving birth. If a woman has given birth by Caesarean section there is also major surgery to recover from. In some cases, women find themselves close to the abyss. Ten days after she gave birth to their first child, Peggy haemorrhaged so badly she had to be rushed to hospital for a transfusion and in the emergency was given blood that didn't match her type, which meant that she felt under par for a long time afterwards. 'When we got to the hospital I had lost so much blood that my veins were flat and I remember watching Don turn as white as a sheet, in that calm way that you do when something this serious happens. I remember when it came to going home, I just wanted to go out to the park and breathe fresh air, to take a few moments to relish the fact that I was lucky to be alive. I expected him to understand that and share the moment with me, but he didn't appreciate it; he just wanted to get me home so that he could get on with other stuff.'

Men may live with anxiety about becoming a father, or the responsibilities of providing for a child. They may be short of sleep, they may feel real empathy for what their partner is living with during pregnancy, childbirth and those early days, but they do not change physically, strain their organs and their back reproducing or stand in front of the mirror and lament the loss of their pre-childbirth appearance. The physical process of reproduction highlights gender differences and alters the power balance between them. Women are often emotionally needy and vulnerable at this time. 'I found maternity leave really tough because it's a mixture of exhaustion and boredom,' says Katrina. 'Plus in those early days the baby is very needy and I didn't know what to do, so I found that responsibility quite stressful. We had decided to embark on IVF and have a baby together, but it hadn't occurred to me until David went back to work that at that point it would all be down to me.' Many feel an increased dependency upon men for physical protection, emotional support and often for financial help, which can be unsettling for a woman who has always taken pride in her independence or for a man who feels unable, or reluctant, to provide. Inevitably it is almost always the new mother who stays at home during the early weeks and months, while the new father gets up and goes to work as he has always done. While both have to adjust to their new roles as parents, it is usually women who face isolation at home, an encroaching sense of incompetence and inadequacy about their new responsibilities as mothers and the great highs and lows of new parenthood – love, hate, anger and anxiety about their baby. Very few men get post-natal depression, and those who do are usually the ones who are at home caring full-time for their child while the mother goes back to work as the breadwinner.

On top of the obvious new physical differences, there are a

whole host of modern constraints which separate couples once they become parents. There is never enough time. Working parents across all socio-economic classes in Britain work longer hours than anyone else in Europe, which affects family time and time with each other.[7] The number of those working more than forty-eight hours a week has more than doubled since 1998 from 10 per cent to 26 per cent, and one in six people now puts in more than sixty hours a week.[8] Approximately a third of working mothers across all social classes say they feel they are under time pressure in their everyday life, while 57 per cent of AB men and only 15 per cent of DE men feel the same way.[9] A large-scale study in the US comparing the quality of marriages in 2000 to 1980 found that substantially more men and women reported that long working hours had a negative effect on the quality of their marriage and family life in 2000, and that a sense of balance in their marriage was far harder to achieve when the demands of work exceeded forty-five hours a week with shift work, evening meetings or overnight trips. Unsurprisingly this study also found that there was a rise in the numbers of women in the same period who would, given the choice, opt for part-time work or full-time domestic responsibilities for a more contented marital and family life.[10]

Working parents communicate with each other by email or snatched diary sessions, split the working day either through shift work or with one taking charge of the morning drop-off or pre-work hours and the other assuming responsibility for the evenings (in the better, more equable arrangements). They spend their weekends on chores, and largely apart, with each taking charge of one child's needs. They make time to be together as a family but rarely find enough time to be together as a couple. 'I'm so looking forward to retiring and just being able to hang out with Frank,' says Dusty, who is in her late thirties, works full-time and has four children. The eldest is ten, the youngest, eighteen months. 'I definitely don't feel, "What will I do once the kids grow up?" I am counting the days on the calendar. We don't have enough space even for us. No one has any time, and there are all these pressures. You have to be a great family, with wonderful memories of quality time together; you have to make sure your children eat the right things and are well read and interesting, and then you also have to have a job. I feel there is all this stuff you have to do in the modern world to compete with other human beings, and yet there is no time just to chill and hang out.'

Frank works long hours in television, and is very ambitious. 'The tension in our lives centres around the fact that we are both completely stretched. I feel he works too hard and should spend more time with the family, and I suppose I typically pick up all the slack. I wish that I could just go to work and come home at 8.30 p.m. like he does and not feel terrible, but I can't do that because I am supposed to be a mother. Then there is also a certain amount of tension because it's just hard with four children. Our weekends are hell because you move from one thing to another and there is never time to sit down. Actually it's chaos, and you can never find an activity that suits everyone, which means we spend a lot of time watching *The X Factor*, which doesn't make anyone happy except the eight-year-old. Neither of us can really leave the other on the weekend without there being an inquisition about it because you are leaving the other one with such a lot of work. I am ambivalent about what we do together, so our family hobbies end up being Frank's hobbies. We go on mad sailing holidays where toddlers are dangling off into the sea and eight-year-olds are screaming and hiding, terrified as the waves crash, but he is out there having a great time while the rest of us hate it. I have nightmares about it, while he puts so much enthusiasm into it that he makes it work in the end, but it's not actually a choice. There is a tenacity to a relationship, and you go through all this because you believe in each other and you believe in the kids. I did hook up with the right guy, I respect him and admire him. But ten years down the line, if he has hooked up with some twentysomething from the IT department because we have had no time together I might tell you something completely different.'

Even the most equable, democratic and compromising of couples find that as the number of children grows, the time they have for anything luxurious like sleep, a meal out or half an hour to read a novel becomes an elusive dream. 'The change creeps up on you,' says Richard. 'The girls are obviously our priority, and a lot of time is devoted to them now. We used to have a lot more time to ourselves and saw our friends more but now the girls have to come first, whatever we do. You get to a stage where once you have got them to bed you just collapse, and although you might have a bit of time to yourself you're too exhausted to make the most of it. Having the first baby wasn't too bad in terms of the adjustment, but having the second really changed things in that we're both looking after one of them and there is no down time for either yourself or each other. I don't think we'll be having a third!' There is next to no time for the kind of conversation which builds intimacy. 'We all eat together, but that's not the same as sitting down to a meal with someone with no distractions, such as fish fingers flying around the place,' continues Richard. 'If they're both really tucking into something then we talk, but that's more like catch-up time, what's been going on in the day rather than having the opportunity to sit there and talk as a couple. We don't even have time for rows.'

The great paradox of modern relationships is that couples are thrust more than ever before on to each other for emotional and practical support, at a time when they are perhaps least able to give it, with almost no time to nurture that fundamental bond between them. With less extended family around for support and few spare hours in the working day to maintain those essential lifelong friendships which keep us rooted and sane, there often isn't anyone else other than one's partner to moan at or chew life's cud with. Megan's family lives too far away for day trips, she works full-time and finds it hard to nurture friendships at work, going out for drinks or work events because she feels she has to spend every spare minute of the day when she is not working with her son Hughie. She made friends with some other working mothers at her NCT classes and sees them about once a month. 'But it's always a little bit awkward because we don't see each other often enough, so we end up talking about what little Johnnie is doing or what it's like to look after them when you've been at work all week, that kind of thing. I don't feel like I know them on any deeper level. I am very much missing seeing and talking to my real friends, most of whom have either moved out of London or have kids themselves, so you can't see them at short notice or when you have a little spare time.'

New parents want the other to 'be there' for them, to comfort them when they're finding it tough and to share the highs and lows of family life, and when they are tired or overstressed it's hard not to lash out or blame each other. There is no one else. When Hughie was ill over the winter with a succession of colds, coughs and a serious vomiting bug with a high temperature, Charlie and Megan inevitably got ill too. Megan is the sole breadwinner, and she took as much time off as she could, but went back to work leaving Charlie in charge and still ill, trapped in that catch-22 most parents face when their children are small – never finding enough time to rest so that they can recover from illness themselves. 'We were very anxious about him because he was ill for such a long time, but I simply had to go back to work,' says Megan. 'I couldn't take any more time off, and that was when Charlie really exploded and threw everything back at me with "I am doing all of this because of you," and "You don't care about my health, all you want to do is go to work." After about an hour of this, with me thinking, This isn't going to work any more, we have to look for a childminder tomorrow, he calmed down, and was fine once he had got it all out of his system.'

Social attitudes about bringing up children have changed profoundly in recent decades, which has also had an impact on the nature of the couple relationship. A plethora of new research on child development has set unprecedented high standards for good parenting. It's no longer enough just to keep our young clothed and healthy until they are old enough to look after themselves. They need constant encouragement, conversation, intellectual stimulation, the right kind of play, school, social network, sports and foods as well as the most important ingredient of all – oceans of unconditional love. Parents spend more time with their children now than ever before, yet ask any working parent and they will probably tell you that it never feels like enough. When more mothers were at home than at work during the 1950s their children were out of their sight for much of the day, encouraged to play outside. Now parents worry, understandably, about the toxic social environment in which their children are growing up, and they feel less certain about how to raise them well in such a hazardous and materialistic world. We fuss over their schooling and their future. We drive them from after-school tutors to music lessons. We worry about teen depravity, peer pressure, drugs and how much they will blame us for failing them when they are adults, and forget that the most fundamental foundation for their future success and happiness is the relationship that we create between ourselves. A happy, constructive working partnership between two parents is the most positive and important gift that we can ever give to our children.

With each parent forging ahead on what feels like two separate tracks, it is easy to slide over into an emotional world where the love for and from a child compensates for the disappointments in a marriage. With no time for togetherness to consolidate their relationship, each is more likely to kiss and hug their children than each other. 'I am number four in the pecking order for everything,' says Kate. 'I remember saying that to him last year, that I come behind his job, the kids, the under-50s rugby team – I'm always at the back. He says I'm not, but there is always something else that he has to do and he says that I don't put him very high up the list either.' Florence and Grace have one child. 'It's been shattering for the relationship in some respects in that we fall out over our son all the time. It's a different kind of love, but for me it feels like *the* love and pushes the other relationship into second place. Grace is always saying, "If only you treated me like you treat our son," because I am unconditional with him, it is unmitigated devotion, whereas with Grace I am much more critical, I want her to be perfect.'

'It's like two people running a business where the business is the family,' says Amy, who has three children between the ages of three and ten. 'I assume and hope that we will find some more relaxed time together when the children are older but I wouldn't want to wish away their childhood either, so it almost feels as if our relationship is on hold. But then I worry that if we put it on hold for too long we might find that we have nothing in common when we look again. He puts 110 per cent into his work and always has done, while I put everything into the kids. As I am a night owl and he is an early bird, unless I go to bed early I don't see much of him. It's all about the children when he gets home from work, and then by the time the washing-up is done and they're in bed there's virtually no time to see each other.' Ethan, Amy's husband, says he works hard because he feels the responsibility of being the sole breadwinner profoundly. Like so many other working parents he is acutely aware that he cannot depend on his job always being there, and longs for the time when Amy can contribute to the family economy. Life with three small children in north London is expensive, and they started family life late. 'Sometimes I think, What have I done? We've created this expensive paradigm to live in, with a monster mortgage, and all of the school problems ahead of us, and I will be over sixty by the time the youngest goes to university, which is not particularly cheering. Because we married late we've created a hell of a box.' Like Amy, he feels that they have drifted apart due to lack of time. 'It's always the last thing because there are so many other things that you've got to do all the time. The kids keep it going. So much of what keeps partners together is that glue, that mental map you have in your mind of what you have created and want to maintain. You're just keeping the ship going because that's what you do. I am sure that if we went to a marriage guidance counsellor they would say that it's fine, but that's just another thing you have to do which we haven't got time for.'

Having a child throws up whole new areas of conflict which many couples have never had to address before, such as who does what on the domestic front and the value of their work outside the home. Someone has to stay at home or leave work early to pick up their tiny, precious person from a childminder or nursery, and that's usually the mother because she earns less, she wants to be there for her child or the father won't. Too often it is women who compromise their careers by working less while their children are small, or feel as if they have to choose between the two. Men go back to work and often work longer hours after the birth of a child, confident that they are fulfilling their family obligations; women continually have to justify why working does not make them bad mothers. If you disagree about sex, money or how often you go out – or not – you only face those issues occasionally. If you disagree about work issues, about who gets to stay late or who has to pick up a child or take them to the doctor, it's a daily issue, and if it's chores, you almost have to confront these things hour by hour. 'I changed the last four nappies; now it's your turn.' Arguments about work and domestic chores erode the common ground in a relationship more than any other factor because they challenge the common vision, shared values and the sense of obligation each has to the other in a committed, loving relationship. Conflict over the division of the workload is at its peak during the first two years of a child's life as couples adjust, and if those disagreements continue unresolved they act as continual reminders of 'you' and 'me' rather than 'us'. But they also have a particularly devastating effect on women who believed that they had an egalitarian partnership to begin with. They feel more let down, less supported, less valued and happy than those women in more traditional set-ups who always assumed there would be a less equal division of chores.[11]

With so little time for life as a couple, and so much to do when you've got young children, it's good to know that two fundamental principles help to keep both relationship and family life happy. Problems tend to snowball when men fail to get stuck into family life and help from the very beginning, or when women become so consumed with guilt about never being good enough mothers that they refuse to relinquish whole chunks of their child's welfare to the father. It takes a conscious effort, often repeated to avoid, or dig ourselves out of, these common holes. Women don't need helpers: they want partners who are actively involved, taking equal responsibility when they come home from work. It will come as no surprise to working mothers that recent research shows that it is the division of household tasks that causes more conflict within young families than anything else. Domestic chores zoom into orbit with a baby – there is always something to do, from sterilising bottles to the washing in between holding, feeding and loving your baby, and it's usually the woman who assumes these tasks, whether or not she is working. The notion of housework as solely women's work has diminished considerably, with women doing less and men assuming more since the 1960s. But research also shows that once there is a baby, men tend to do *less* housework than they used to do as they settle into a more traditional arrangement, with women taking more of the daily time-consuming chores such as the washing, shopping and cooking. When they buy in outside help in the form of a cleaner or childcare, it is usually women who organise and pay for it, and once those patterns are fixed they are hard to shift without considerable negotiation.[12, 13]

What might surprise men, though, is that just pulling their weight at home affects a woman's level of happiness within the relationship generally more than any other factor.[14] The more men adapt, help and support women after the birth of a child, the more likely they are as a couple to enjoy a happier, more emotionally satisfying relationship. It isn't easy to maintain a good relationship based on mutual respect while we are bringing up our children when the gendered assumptions of 'mothers' and 'fathers' are so embedded in our emotional hard-wiring. But the new ethos of equality and shared parenting offers more than a glimmer of hope – it is redefining relationship in radical ways.

'Sam can sense when I am down and picks me up,' says Diana, who works full-time, has two teenage children from a previous relationship and a ten-month-old baby. 'I can pick him up too, so there is a sense of us complementing each other. I had such a terrible row with my daughter a few days ago that I didn't even want to come home from work, look after the baby and then argue with my daughter some more about her homework. It just felt like give, give, give all the time and I was able to say that to Sam rather than pretend that everything was OK. So he just picked it all up, made me a cup of tea, packed me off to bed and gave me the TLC I needed at that moment. He makes me stronger.'

Wendy and Ian had a blissfully romantic time together until their first child arrived. 'We were both madly in love with her and it was a lovely time, but Ian was running his own business and didn't take any time off when he could have done, and I found it really difficult to cope. There were things that he could have done to help but he didn't. You've just had a baby, the baby's asleep, the health visitor tells you to sleep and you look at the pile of washing and think, There's no way I can fucking sleep. Everything was left to me, and I was also trying to keep my own business going.' Kate gave up a prestigious job in advertising when she had her first child. Her husband Rory travelled extensively for his work, and left her alone for long periods after the birth of their second child in particular. As a woman who once worked she found coping with two small children on her own exhausting, demoralising and developed quite severe post-natal depression. 'There were times when I got so fed up that he would say, "Go and stay with a friend for a few days," but then it would be even more depressing coming back to the mess and a pile of washing. He's got much better at it now that the girls are older. He goes to Sainsbury's and he cooks and he's a great dad, so he's not like a completely useless male, but he can be a complete slob. In his mind he doesn't do things on a Sunday. But if I didn't do things on a Sunday nothing would happen, so that pisses me off.'

Men have a tendency to compare what they do now with what their fathers did when they were young, and congratulate themselves on being so much more involved. Dusty and Frank both work full-time, but, 'On the domestic front he doesn't do much, he doesn't even put his clothes away,' says Dusty. 'He will put his clothes on top of the laundry basket but never inside the washing machine. It seems so trivial to argue about it that I have given up, so I spend all our money on more and more help. But if you were to ask him if he did his fair share he would say yes.' Philip works full-time and has nothing but admiration for the way Juliet juggles three children and a freelance job. 'She is a fantastic hands-on mum in that she's always there for them, taking them to and from school and making the packed lunches. But that is also why she is a very tired person, and that's what causes the most tension in our relationship, two working people trying to run a business and a home. How can anyone be expected to do the housework? I guess I do about 50 per cent of the housework, 20 per cent of the cooking and 70 per cent of the washing-up. We are pretty equal.' Juliet agrees that it is a source of tension in their lives but disagrees on the proportions, and feels that Philip has almost unreasonably high standards about how tidy and clean he expects their house to be. 'He is an obsessive tidier. He wants everything to be beautiful and worked-on. I do all the shopping, clothing and cooking, but he is very domestic in that he washes up every night and leaves the kitchen looking like an operating theatre. That's his thing, so he thinks he is domestic but he doesn't understand the millions of other things that need to be done, and I just get mad when he criticises me for not keeping the house tidier.'

There may be a great deal more argument as couples wrestle towards some sort of new equilibrium and fairness in family life, and there may be more resentment from women at having to coax and cajole men into being hands-on fathers. But that is better by far for our relationships and our children in the long term than the more traditional gender splits around mothering and fathering, where couples lead very different, divergent lives and women tend to feel a deeper animosity at male emotional and physical absence, privilege and economic advantages, and men tend to feel that their wives are solely absorbed by the children. A significant body of empirical research has established that when power is unequally distributed along traditional gender lines, it can be corrosive to family relations and marital satisfaction.[15] With a commitment to shared parenting, however, couples have to engage with each other from the very first days of their child's life. They have to communicate their needs and resentments and negotiate a rough but flexible fairness, so that each has time to rest or work. Children need a strong emotional connection to both their parents. When a man is deeply involved with his children it is harder for him to leave, and it is harder for a woman to let such a man go. By sharing so much more of the intimacy inherent to nurturing and protecting our children, more and more couples are finding a deeper common ground to their relationship, forging new and stronger bonds between them based on mutual respect. 'There is definitely a deeper understanding of each other which has developed because of the girls,' says Richard, who has two daughters under the age of five. Richard works full-time while his wife works part-time. 'Obviously it gets tiring, there is always something to do for them but our relationship is on an equal footing, and hopefully with the strength of that we can do as good a job as we can working together as parents. We both think it's vitally important to do as much as we can for the girls to make sure they are fed and watered, clean and happy at home, and that is partly an expression of our love, the care we give to them. We just want to build a loving family, which is obviously a different phase from the relationship we had before but I think it's part and parcel of that. If I could look into the future and see what I have become, I would like to think that people would say, "He's not done such a bad job with his kids, and he seems to be happy and is still married."'

A number of studies suggest that in families where both parents work there is far less tension when their assumptions about gender roles are not stereotypical.[16] The more flexible parents are about chores and childcare, the greater their sense of shared partnership. They are in this exhilarating and nerveracking adventure of raising a child together. Several studies indicate that a great many dual-earner families are adapting and coping well, and that there appear to be six key factors to their success: they make family time and well-being their priority; they emphasise equality and partnership through shared responsibility for childcare and household tasks and joint decision-making; they concentrate on work at work and find ways to increase a sense of play and fun at home; they live simply by limiting activities which interfere with family time together; they reduce their expectations about what it is possible to achieve domestically; and they take great pride in their family and how they manage to balance both parents' needs for work and home.[17] Well, that's a doddle, then! But it is important to know that it's possible to fashion a new equilibrium, provided each partner is prepared to put the needs of the family first.

'David looks after our life. He does the shopping and the cooking and he makes things work domestically,' says Katrina. They both work full-time, but Katrina earns more and has to work longer hours with a longer commute to the City, so David delivers and collects his son from the nursery on his way to and from work. 'I will rush home from work to be with the baby and then rush upstairs to log on and work, and he will deliver dinner to my desk and sterilise the bottles, while I might pack the nursery bag for the next day. He definitely does the lion's share most of the time, which makes it possible for me to do my job. What we don't have any more is time for David and me, or half an hour to read the newspapers on a Sunday morning. We're both completely preoccupied with Thomas, but we have this common bond and the baby must compensate for the fact that we never seem to be able to come together because it doesn't feel broken – that's a work term, meaning it feels fine.'

David has been surprised by how much his attitude to life and work has changed because he now bears so much shared responsibility for their son and their life together as a family. 'I feel much happier than I was before, and the highlight of my day is 5 p.m., when I run past everyone at the office and go to pick him up from nursery. That surprises me because when we talked through our childcare options, and how it would have to be me who left work at 5 p.m. instead of 6.30 p.m. twice a week, it really stressed me out because it was such a huge reduction of my working hours. But if anything I am more productive and efficient because I have more distance from work and am less obsessed by it. Thomas has put everything in perspective, and I feel less overwhelmed now by work pressures. Katrina has a very responsible, well-paid job and work is very important to her, whereas I can be more flexible, so I take on more of the chores. But we have both had to find more time by working less. There is so much to do now that it is hard to squeeze everything into one day: I want my life with Katrina, I want the life that is the three of us and I also want to have a little bit of my own life as well. But that's not a problem, rather it's a competition between good things because he has enriched our lives so much. There may be less down time in that we don't watch ridiculous television programmes any more – we bought a new TV six weeks ago and it occurred to us recently that we haven't even found the time to turn it on – but then we have absolutely no desire to. What we have instead is really fun quality time with Thomas, and that makes up for everything else. There are trade-offs, and I thought I was going to find some of that difficult but I really don't. Having a child is an event of such magnitude that you can't just sit there and think about what you might have lost because there is so much else that you have gained.'

Diana has two teenagers from a previous relationship with someone she remains on good terms with but who did little to help her with the children. Her second husband Sam is younger than her and much more involved with family life. He works part-time and consequently does more at home with their ten-month-old son, while she has returned to her higher-earning, full-time job. 'There are no gender stereotypes really, it's just muck in, and I learned that from my upbringing,' says Sam. 'As a woman, even if you don't want to be in a traditional role you find yourself pushed into it when you have children,' says Diana. 'You take on the emotional responsibility for the home and the children and you are always thinking ahead about things like, Do I need more milk, do the children need clothes or nappies, is there enough bread? I find all that wearing and really rather dull, and I resent always having to do it just because I am a girl. But with Sam there are moments when he can take on every-thing, and then there are moments when I can.' The assumptions made about women as mothers are still so pervasive that even within a more equable partnership it can be hard to resist the guilt of never being a good enough mother. 'It's not a complete bed of roses,' says Diana. 'The lows for me are when I come home and he's done all the washing, taken Zac to the park, decorated a room and cooked dinner, and it's like, "I am so amazing," and I just want to kill him. But that's because I feel like I ought to be doing those things as the mother, so he is always the good one and I am always the bad one. I can't even sit down and read the paper without feeling guilty.'

Countless working mothers try to appease this guilt by simply squeezing both jobs into the day. Molly has a two-year-old daugh-ter and works four days a week. 'I suffer from enormous guilt. We have a fantastic nanny but I rush back from work in the evenings and feel like I have to reclaim her, and it takes half an hour to make her mine again. I find the juggling just mentally exhausting. I take full responsibility for everything to do with Abigail – making sure there's food in the fridge and her clothes are sorted and the relationship with the nanny. I want to do all these things, and on a good day I am really happy about it but then sometimes I feel I am not a full-time mum and we ought to be sharing more. But then the other side of me thinks, I don't want to share because I spend so little time with my daughter anyway, and that actually this is my job, so I think I do struggle with my identity within the family mix.'

Others try to make do with no help at all. Juliet is self-employed and fits in her work while the children are at school, but can be up late into the night finishing off projects. 'I was never happy about being just a mother, and this way you do get to go out in the world and retain your sense of self-esteem. But that takes strength, and sadly I think the man does get pushed to the bottom of the pile because they are an adult and they've got to look after themselves, while you've got all this work to do and their uniforms and packed lunches to get ready, and by the end of the day you are so knack-ered, it's just, "Don't talk to me," and that has to be a real issue for relationships. Philip says he feels like he is at the bottom of the pile, and the other day I actually thought, Well, maybe he is, when I made freshly squeezed orange juice for the children and lined them up and there wasn't one for him. I realised that's the kind of thing I do, and it's not good.'

When it is the mother who goes back to work as the sole bread-winner, leaving the father as the full-time carer, such ingrained assumptions around 'women's work' are doubly difficult for women. Megan went back to work full-time because she loves her job and earns good money with health and pension benefits. Her partner Charlie felt it was important for one of them to be there while their son was still young, and he wanted to leave the job he had where he worked very long hours. But as soon as she went back to full-time work after her maternity leave, Charlie found the work and stress inherent to being home alone with their baby five days a week so wearing that he would regularly explode with rage at her. Megan finds it hard to get home in time to give Hughie a bath and put him to bed because of the constraints of her job. 'It's not as flexible an arrangement as I thought it might be, in that Charlie sees this as a job and he relies on me being home at a certain time so that he can sit back and relax a bit. But sometimes work runs on and I can't leave bang on 5 p.m. But he flips when that happens, so if I know I am going to have to work late one evening in advance I think very carefully about when might be the right time to tell him.' Megan understands that being at home alone all day with a baby is stressful, and she takes full responsibility for her son in the evenings and at weekends so that Charlie can relax and do other things such as DIY or gardening. She feels she has missed out on time with her son and loves being with him when she is not at work, but she also feels that Charlie still looks to her as the decision-maker over aspects of their son's life, such as whether they should take him to the doctor, because she is the mother. 'He'll do the general things, but anything out of the ordinary he expects me to do. I think he compartmentalises the job in a rather male way in order to deal with it.'

Many working women told me that their lives were so busy and stressful that their partner had to fall to the bottom of the heap, even coming after the cat! 'He can feed himself; she can't.' Motherhood feels like more than a full-time job now; earning a living as well feels at times like a bridge too far. But often it is a woman's reluctance to give up whole chunks of responsibility around their child's welfare, or their failure to insist on greater involvement from the father, which cranks up the pressure and forces the ever-widening divide between them as a couple. Women feel this reluctance in part because they want to do everything themselves, but also because to hand over responsibility would be tantamount to being a 'bad' mother. But the truth is that both sexes have to learn how to be a 'good enough' parent, and both have to adjust and learn new skills as their children grow and their needs change. The vast majority of mothers have always worked out of economic necessity. The big difference today is that a great many women can pursue their own ambitions and independent careers, as well as contribute to wider society, in ways which few would have dreamed possible little more than a hundred years ago. I know that working motherhood is tiring. I know that it takes unparalleled levels of cleverness when it comes to juggling the different demands of work and home in a twenty-four-hour day, and I know that for many women it is their own interests and needs which they put last, way behind the needs of their partner. But I also know that many women can be their own worst enemy, intent on having it all, reluctant to give up aspects of control over the way they bring up their children to their all-important father. Which is a shame because it's a win-win situation for everyone.

When a child's needs are paramount, there is no question that we have to put love for them first. 'The problem arises when we turn to them for what we no longer get from each other: a sense that we're special, that we matter, that we're not alone,' writes Esther Perel in *Mating in Captivity*. When intimacy with adults is perceived as complicated, tenuous and unreliable, when the quality of our own marriage or partnership changes so profoundly as we become parents, the reciprocity of love with a child feels that much more permanent and meaningful. But that's where the danger lies. 'Everything one vainly hoped to find in the relationship with one's partner is sought in or directed at the child,' write Ulrich Beck and Elisabeth Beck-Gernsheim in their landmark sociological text *The Normal Chaos of Love*. 'Doting on children, pushing them onto the centre of the stage – the poor, over-pampered creatures – and fighting for custody during and after divorce are all symptoms of this. The child becomes the final alternative to loneliness, a bastion against the vanishing chances of loving and being loved.'

Solutions lie in simply returning to the two most important fundamentals to a happier relationship and consequently to a happier family life: fathers need to do more, and women less. It takes a conscious effort to hand over aspects of your child's welfare to the father and allow him to do it his way. Katrina's high-powered job involves going to New York for a few days several times a year. She is rare in that most of her female colleagues return to part-time work or a step down after maternity leave, while she now has more responsibility for a department than ever before. Her son was just fifteen months old when I last met her yet she looked relaxed, healthy and happy in spite of the fact that they both have demanding and highly pressurised full-time jobs. 'Without David being the hands-on father that he is there is no way I could do all this, and I am really pleased that they have such a good relationship. It is really nice to be able to say, "No, it's you he wants," when Thomas wakes up crying in the night, and not to have to get out of bed! He can calm him down really quickly now, but when he was a baby it had to be me because I was with him all the time. The first time he soothed him back to sleep David looked so proud, and that was nice to see. It gave him such a lot of confidence, and now we share so much more. In the early days I did everything, but when I went to New York for the first time and he had complete responsibility he got very stressed about it and realised how it had been for me, which really bonded us. I think I do feel less guilt about working because everything is now shared between us. He is also a working dad. We have a nanny three days a week and he goes to nursery the other two days, and Thomas adores both. I need to know what's happening and I need to have some input, in that I agree with it or it makes sense, but I don't need to do it. I don't need to purée the carrots.'

As children grow older, working parents who share the load share more of a life together. Each has a mutual sense of investment and importance. Ruby's children are now nineteen and fourteen and she has always worked. 'I made a point of handing over aspects of domesticity and responsibility for the children from the very beginning. There was argument, but Lestor listened and took things on board because he cared. He does all the clearing-up, the rubbish and the washing-up and he does as much for the children as I do. I gave him complete responsibility from the beginning for the children's eyes and teeth. He took them to appointments with dentists and opticians. He makes sure they have everything they need, and I can't tell you how liberating that has been for me as a mother. It means I can forget about whole chunks of their welfare. It also makes him proud as a father; it was his thing with them, not mine, and he can look at their straight teeth and know that was solely because of his efforts.' Men gain in all sorts of unforeseen ways by having a more hands-on relationship with their children. They are not used only as the disciplinarians for children to be scared of, and they are allowed to express their own vulnerability through caring. Neither sex is seen as either the sole provider, or as the one having the status in the outside world. Alice works full-time and earns more than her husband, who is self-employed, and it is Theo who tends to spend those crucial after-school hours with their two sons. There was a time early on in their marriage after her father died when Alice felt very unsupported by Theo because he couldn't talk. 'He is not a good feelings man, but I think he has become more able to talk about those sorts of things because we have to discuss the children's feelings. Our kids are an emotional link between us, and inevitably we have to talk about them a lot so now there is a whole emotional landscape which we have to traverse together. I now see Theo very differently. He understands much more about how a child feels than I ever gave him credit for, and I think we are much closer because of that.'

When couples work together with a shared vested interest in the adventure of raising a family, they are better parents to their children. They have to talk to each other, even if that means argument. Research suggests that children spend much more time with their parents today than they did just twenty years ago, and that it is time with their fathers, not their mothers, that children miss most.[18] The majority of children with separated parents expressed a longing to see more of their fathers, according to one large-scale study of families in the west of England. This research also found that those with a relationship low on warmth and affection with their non-resident father scored higher on the depression scale, and that they were nearly three times as likely to exhibit their distress through problem behaviour than children who felt close to their fathers.[19] Reviews of the literature reveal that fathers who have a warm and responsive involvement with their children contribute greatly to their intellectual, social and emotional development, and that they are far less likely to grow up with gender stereotypes and expectations when it comes to forming their own relationships.[20] 'They talk to him and ask him for things in much the same way as they do with me. We are interchangeable in their eyes, which makes me feel really warm inside,' says Ruby. 'Their sense of security within family life is as complete as it could be.' Many women I met appreciated the way their partner invested so much more emotionally in their children than either of their own fathers had done. Kate had been scared of her father as a child, and as an adult she found him rude and difficult in company. 'Rory is the opposite. Even when he gets cross with the kids they aren't ever scared of him, and he gets on with anybody. I like the feeling that the kids can bring anybody round and he will be nice to them, which I couldn't do as a child at home, and still can't. The kids really miss him when he is away because he's so much better at cooking than I am, and he puts up with me. He's a good balance in that you can take him anywhere!'

'I want a different kind of marriage to my parents,' says Juliet. 'They were very bonded but it was like a united front against the children, whereas we have much more of a dynamic banter. One day I will be agreeing with Philip against the kids, and the next day I am agreeing with the kids against him, and I think that's much more healthy. I grew up with the idea that if ever I disagreed with something I was just argumentative or difficult, when actually I had a valid point of view.' Family life is more democratic and consequently closer because the children feel important and heard. Juliet also recognises ways in which Philip has forged a much healthier relationship with his children than he had with his own father. While Juliet and Philip both acknowledge that they row regularly about the domestic chaos with three children and two jobs, they each value their family times together more than anything else. 'We have had countless fantastic times with our children and we both relish and nurture them every day of their lives,' says Philip. He feels closer than ever to Juliet because of that shared family life. 'I think when you're in your twenties and then in your thirties struggling with small children, you are also to some extent trying to work out what you want from life. But then you get to a point where you realise what you are. I don't need to move on to something else, to go and live in another country or another place, and that's because of my work and the fact that every single day of my children's lives is precious to me. I can almost ring-fence them in that Noah is eight years and twenty-four days old and you see the timeline, how quickly life goes. For the first time in our marriage I can now see how life might be for us together when we're in our fifties and the kids have moved on. I want Juliet to be happy, independent, fit and able to do whatever she wants with her life. Our lives have been completely meshed together by the children.'

With such a rich life full of memories and shared experiences as parents, you build a more substantial life together based on a deeper, different kind of love. 'Children do not so much distract or subtract from the love of one mate for another as intensify the connection, mould it in the shape of the family, give us a reason outside of our own skins to be in this world,' writes Anne Roiphe in *Married: A Fine Predicament.* 'Our children gave us leaf-filled branches and roots growing down deeper into our lives. They did not come between us, they became a part of us.' Conventional advice from relationship counsellors and agony aunts to parents who find themselves travelling down separate, diverging tracks tends to take the form of 'Try to make some space for the two of you to be together,' which only makes new parents feel even more inadequate. Responsibility for the daunting task of consolidating that separate sense of adult culture is almost invariably dumped upon the woman, who is still presumed to be the emotional architect of any heterosexual relationship. Working mothers with small children are usually so stretched already that the rather patronising advice of 'Save a little bit of time for him if you want to save your marriage,' simply feels like a bridge too far. 'My mother constantly said to me, "You must make time for Nick as well, you can't not give him the time and attention he needs,"' says Molly. 'But I just had so much love for my tiny daughter, and I really needed him to support me in those early days, how could I?' When parents are also working they often simply haven't got the energy, time or money to go out for meals, and on those rare occasions when they do, they often lament, 'We only talk about the baby/children so we might as well do that at home.'

But that's a good sign. Once there is a baby, relationship and family life are not two entirely separate entities that have to be 'worked on' independently. Talking only about the baby or the children when you are alone shows that you are both focused on the most important responsibility, and one that only the two of you share. Inevitably there are fewer things to talk about other than the baby because there isn't time to do anything else. You have both moved on, and family life is now an integral part of your love life. Returning to the two basic principles, where women have to give up more of the responsibility for their child's welfare to a partner who takes on more of the daily work, means that you are building a shared life where you have to come together. By giving a child two hands-on, loving parents, the couple gets a better marriage. Each is then more easily able to accept the profound changes that children bring. Each finds new energy, a greater sense of balance to their life and is able to make new time together as a couple which is entirely different to the time they used to enjoy when they were childless. They have become united by a love which is far more significant than anything romance can offer. You're not damaging your relationship by making it secondary for a while; you are simply moving on to a stage where a small and vulnerable being has to take precedence. You don't have to carve out huge chunks of separate space for the two of you, just a thirty-second hug or a few loving words can be enough to nourish the bond of affection between you.

Once partners become parents, the only way forward to a deeper sense of shared love is together, as equals, subsumed for a while by a child's needs because they are so vulnerable. The happiest relationships with small children, and the ones least likely to break down, are those where the mother feels that her partner is right there beside her, enjoying and sharing every aspect of new parenthood, too. Men and women face a whole range of stresses and strains in their working lives that impact upon their relationship, but working mothers still confront particular issues because of their sex which need a special kind of understanding. Women need work for all the same reasons as men, but large numbers find that there are additional difficulties because they could become or are already mothers, difficulties such as unequal access to jobs and promotion, dismissal for being pregnant, lower pay. With enough support from their partner, women feel better about working and feel like better mothers, because the guilt and stress are less likely to spill over on to their children, who then grow up with healthier attitudes to women working and family life. It's a virtuous circle. Men are just as able as women to care for and love their children. Parenting skills are acquired through experience and are not particular to women just because they give birth. When fathers do their fair share, mothers enjoy better mental health, less exhaustion and might even fathom enough energy for a bit of nooky now and again.

As children grow older and become more independent, parents find that there is more time and emotional energy for themselves as a couple, time that has nothing whatsoever to do with the children. 'When the youngest of the three turned four, that felt like a big turning point in that you're no longer wiping someone else's bum, you're only wiping your own,' says Hilary. She and Robin have been married for twenty-one years and their children are now teenagers. 'From then on we could start doing more for ourselves. We spent so much time with the kids when they were young, and that was what we wanted to do, but now there is much more freedom and that has increased as they have got older.' Hilary told me how they had recently all gone on holiday to New York. She knew it was going to be difficult making it a successful family holiday with five different opinionated and strong-minded people, each wanting to do their own thing, but what she hadn't bargained for was how little she would want to spend time with her children at all. 'I told Robin that I might just throw a tantrum if we didn't spend some time on our own, I was that demented. So we hatched a plan. We told them to take a taxi to the Empire State Building and stand in the queue while we did some shopping nearby. They said, "We don't want to do that, we want to be with you." But we said, "Tough, we don't want to be with you, we need some time on our own." The children took one look at the queue and went on to Times Square to do some shopping, and then went back to the hotel and slobbed in front of seventeen channels. But they survived, and we got shot of them for a while and had tea together. That was the best cup of tea in the whole world, just moments together on holiday, that was really nice.'

When children are young, it is hard to imagine that there will ever come a time when you will have time for each other, for solitude, lie-ins and weekends with nothing much to do. But it comes sooner than you think, not suddenly but gradually, as children grow more independent and begin to pursue their own lives both inside and outside the home. Suddenly there is a Saturday afternoon with nobody under twenty around, or nights when the house is either empty with everybody sleeping elsewhere or full of teenagers intent on watching wall-to-wall horror movies, keen for you to go out and watch your own film. When Sureena and Spike had their second baby, he got quite ill. 'We never had any time to connect and we were both quite stressed. There was no money, and that was definitely the most difficult time in our relationship,' says Spike. They met in 1990 and their children are now twelve and sixteen. 'I was annoyed, and felt cut out and uninvolved because Sureena would breastfeed for ever, and anything I said was never the right thing. We could never go out because our son would just scream, but as the kids got older, that eased because I was able to do more for them and get involved, and now we do loads more together. We go out more and go away together, but you don't think that will ever happen when they are that small and demanding.'

As children fight to distinguish themselves as teenagers, they force you away. For many, the turmoil of the teenage years is the hardest stage of being a parent and another difficult milestone for marriages and relationships. Teenagers can be emotionally volatile and argumentative because growing up is not easy in today's world. But parents also face their own emotional vortex as they lament the loss of that precious child, loathe them at times – an emotion loving parents are not supposed to feel – and hit their own potentially angst-ridden midlife stage. Teenagers feign strength and a paper-thin autonomy. They still need their parents to provide that stable base as the rest of their earth moves, but they also need enough distance and privacy to be able to come to grips with their own emerging sense of independence. Reclaiming the right to your own relationship and leisure pursuits is an essential part of that process. Bringing up children is not easy, and parents face countless issues over the years that will divide them more than unite them, particularly once the children are teenagers and vulnerable to new dangers such as depression, drug and alcohol use and the experience of growing up and finding their place in a formidable adult world. When parents have learned how to listen to each other's opinions, mediate their own emotional responses and support each other through the first decade of a child's life, they are more skilled when it comes to dealing with the more difficult second decade. They will find it easier to reach common ground, that essential united front with teenagers because they have come back together as a couple in a more solid way.

Problems tend to come when parents cannot force enough space between them and their much-loved children as they grow older, by making sure they reach out to each other as adults with their own private and precious relationship. A great many of the relationships I have had the privilege to peek into seemed to veer dangerously towards fulfilling the emotional needs of their children at the expense of their own. If we want our children to grow up happy and secure with a healthy model for conducting their own adult love affairs, we have to make sure that we nourish our own relationship. The more a marriage satisfies an individual's needs and desires, the less likely that person is to try to meet those needs from the parent–child relationship inappropriately. When we are less emotionally embroiled with our children we are better parents, more alert to our children's signals and more able to let them set the pace.[21] When we invest a great deal of ourselves in our children, we have a tendency to expect a lot back, which isn't healthy. Ideally we should put enough love into them so that they grow up confident and self-assured, able to live their own lives without us. However much love we may get from our children when they are small, it's a one-way street as they grow older, as opposed to the dual carriageway of reciprocal adult love that we all need from our partners.

'What children do is complicate, implicate, give plot lines to the story, colour to the picture, darken everything, bring fear as never before, suggest the holy, explain the ferocity of the human mind, undo or redo some of the past while casting shadows into the future,' writes Anne Roiphe in *Married: A Fine Predicament*. 'There is no boredom with children in the home. The risks are high. The voltage crackling. I would not confuse this with joy. But it is as far from the silence of the grave as one can go.' Children forge an extraordinary bond between couples. They force us to extremes of great highs, where you feel a deeper sense of contentment and place than you ever imagined possible, and then plunge us to the depths of despondency as they drain every last remaining ounce of our energy, challenge every presumption about relationship and force us to face our own childhood demons once again. We need great powers of strength and self-restraint to be able to keep our children safe, and yet paradoxically separate out their interests from our own. We need courage to witness their growth and grief from their own mistakes as we allow them the luxury of living their own life. Once we have lived through the extraordinary adventure of raising our children together, we share an even richer union based on memories of family triumphs and disasters, pride at their achievements and a sense of contentment that much of our work is done. We've survived. They are fine. We are alone once again. 'I cried my eyes out the day my eldest turned eighteen,' says Ruby. 'It felt like such a landmark. Suddenly it was all over, my job was done and she was responsible for herself now. I remember thinking about how being released from that responsibility meant that I could turn back to Lestor and embrace him once again, that man I fell so deeply in love with all those years ago, and how much deeper and richer and unbreakable that love was because of what we had been through together with our children.'

Marital contentment is important because that stability fosters an environment where our children can flourish at the time in their lives when they are most vulnerable. Studies show that where there is warmth, satisfaction and cooperation between parents, there is more likely to be warmth and fewer authoritarian measures within the family. Happier marriages make for happier families. When both parents are prepared to tackle the huge differences of opinion and expectation that the presence of children brings, when they work together as a team and support each other adequately through an experience which can shift daily from being deeply demoralising to joyful and invigorating, they are stronger as a couple through the extraordinary journey of family life. Children help us to make discoveries about ourselves and about each other, and the skills we develop to resolve those deep conflicts can last a lifetime. 'When the children are around, it's different, you have to negotiate your relationship around them and they are very dominant and very loud,' says Imogen. 'When our children left for university a number of our contemporaries with kids the same age began to get divorced. But I think children value the stability of marriage, and that need persists even when they are adults themselves, and that's a good enough reason alone to stay married. In spite of everything we have been through, and perhaps because of it, we still enjoy each other's company. We have similar interests and are quite compatible in that we can do things together, and are also quite relaxed about allowing each other to have our own separate obsessions. You can't ever replace that shared knowledge of the other, or that history.'

Children link a couple for ever in irrefutable ways. They stretch the boundaries of love to the limit and boy, what a journey. Everything changes potentially for the better in the long run in relationships flexible enough to embrace the fruits of that love. Even sex, that most poignant emblem of romantic relationship, takes on a whole new significance, as Eric Bartels writes in *Over the Hill and Between the Sheets*, five years after the birth of his child: 'We make love a lot like we did at the very beginning: hungrily and messily and sometimes a bit impolitely. That makes me happy for obvious reasons, but it also makes another fantasy possible. In this one our children are grown, and as we watch them reach for whatever dreams they've imagined for themselves, we realise that we've weathered storms bravely enough to give them that chance. At that point, maybe we'll look at each other, wordlessly but with the same thought in mind: not bad for two people who were just in it for the sex.'

10

NEW NETWORKS

Family life is not collapsing; the structure of the nuclear model is changing. Some become first-time parents at an age when others become grandparents. Some start second families in midlife. Some live together, others maintain just as much commitment to each other living apart. Even the best relationship can end. People change. Things happen. Twenty per cent of children in Britain live with a single parent. One in eight children now lives through parental separation and forms a relationship with a new parent figure before the age of sixteen.[1] More than 10 per cent of all families with dependent children in the UK are now step-families.[2] Yet we are not comfortable with this new reality. The presumption is that the nuclear model is still the only right kind of family, and consequently there is huge pressure to pretend to be that perfect couple that somehow bucks the trend. The notion of privacy for that nuclear family to fester secretly becomes even more important as a means to preserve this façade of contentment. Given the odds on lifelong love these days, such pretence is unlikely to make a relationship more robust. We have to change with the times. There are numerous ways in which family life can be reinforced so that children grow up happy within a stable environment. The nuclear model is just one way. It can work well, but it can also fail children abysmally. Without honesty, transparency about the true nature of relationships or a template from the past to rely on, each family has to learn through trial and error how to reach an equilibrium which works for them. There are no quick and easy ways to establish a new relationship when there are also children to consider. Yet in spite of the obvious difficulties, many couples and their children are finding far greater support and happiness within the new extended family networks being formed today.

It is understandable that those who have lived through the collapse of a relationship they had always assumed would be for life should be even more nervous when it comes to making another commitment, particularly when they have children. Some renounce further commitments; others conduct love affairs well away from their family. Some decide to conduct two separate but 'linked' households with a new partner; others cohabit instead of marry. Yet almost half of all divorced men and just over a third of divorced women roll the dice on lasting happiness once more by remarrying, a testament to the power and importance of committed relationship in our lives.[3] Dean and Sue both married other people when they were very young and both were left by their respective spouses. Sue knew that what mattered most was her children. 'I liked being with Dean, but there was no way we could afford to live together at that point and my children were very young. I wanted to make absolutely sure it was the right thing to do, that I wasn't messing them up any more. I didn't want lots of men coming in and out of their lives, so I was very cagey.' They eventually lived together for thirteen years before they decided to get married. 'I turned fifty this year, so perhaps it was some sort of "midlifeism",' says Dean. 'But maybe too because it feels like a much bigger commitment the second time around. You're doing it with the experience of, well, having failed. Maybe that's too strong a word for it, but there is this sense of hanging back, a fear of failure, even though it has been the right thing to do for a long time. The big difference is that we have chosen this. It's a genuine relationship rather than just something we slipped into.' Sue says her biggest regret was that they haven't had more children together. 'But I have to admit there were times when I thought, I don't want to be left on my own scraping around in the gutter again with three or even four kids by two different men.'

Ursula's husband remarried, just two months after their prolonged and acrimonious divorce, in a lavish and ostentatious wedding ceremony. 'I was worried about the kids going to the wedding because I have been to second weddings where there are toasts congratulating the groom for getting over his divorce, and I didn't want them to hear that sort of thing. But they came back happy enough and there seemed to be no conflict.' However, just two years later, her children have got progressively angrier with their father and stepmother and go to stay with them less regularly. 'Their father gets cross when they say they're not coming for the weekend because they've got a rugby match. His move to Kent has been difficult for them because they are London teenagers on the cusp of independence, wanting to do things like take lessons in keyboard mixing, but he doesn't understand that. On the other hand he wants them to love him so he lets them do really dangerous things. What freaks my kids out is that their dad seems to have turned into a different person in this new marriage, and when bad things happen it's their fault. My ex-husband's new wife has children of her own who live with their father. When they had all been staying in Kent together they discovered that the children had been drinking alcohol but it was my kids who took the blame, and now they are considered by their stepmother to be so badly behaved that they are not allowed to be around hers.'

When Ursula ended up in bed with her new partner, she had intended to make him leave before her children got up for school, but they overslept. When the alarm went off, she told him quietly not to get out of bed and ushered her children downstairs, only to find the four of them less than half an hour later standing with their arms crossed in front of the sleeping man. 'The eldest even had the nerve to ask me if I had used protection!' Less than a week later Ursula got an email from her ex-husband berating her for exposing their children to strange men, 'When he was the first. I had never even had another man in the house before, so an even nastier period between us developed after that.' Now that Anthony has been a part of their lives for more than two years, as a benign presence and an adult friend, her children have more than accepted him, but they have yet to accept their stepmother. 'They can't understand why their dad and his wife can't be more like me and Anthony because we make enough space between us for them, while they never see their father on their own. Anthony is gentle with them. He doesn't make them feel as if he is trying to come in and take things over. They sit and watch the cricket together and he comes to watch them play football, which their father doesn't do any more, and he says helpful things like, "You need to work on your left foot a bit more."'

Age-old gendered assumptions about roles can complicate second relationships, and the new extended family can make a difficult situation worse. Women can feel they have to adopt the role of peacemaker, or try to be a better mother to his children. 'My kids don't like their stepmother much,' says Ursula. 'They complain that she tries to be like a mother to them when, as one of them put it, they've already got one. They don't need two.' Some men can feel as if they have to step into the role of disciplinarian; others can be too keen to jump in with their own views on parenting. 'There were issues that arose when we moved into this house,' says Dean. 'Suddenly you have an instant family. Discipline is too strong a word for it perhaps; it's more a case of different views on how they should be parented, and what the step-parent's role is.' Others simply lack experience in the subtle ways parents devise over time to get their children to behave. The lines of influence from parent to child are less clear, and research suggests that it can be that much harder to forge new relationships with adolescents than it is with younger children. 'My new partner complains that when I ask the kids to do something they do it, but they won't do what he asks them. I tell him that it's because of the *way* that he asks them,' says Sarah. 'He goes in and says, "Why haven't you picked up your bowl and taken it back to the kitchen?" in a cross way, and then walks out of the room, rather than, "Could you pick up your bowl please," and then standing over them until they do it. You just have to say it in the right way and not get into an argument. We talk about it, but I am very conscious that I don't want to be put in a position where I have to take sides or undermine him in front of them. That has been difficult, learning how to be a bit of a diplomat.'

A stepfather who has never had children climbs a steep learning curve as a new parent, chucked in at the deep end, unused to the daily exhaustion of putting a child first and consequently being put last. Sam felt the responsibilities of suddenly having a ready-made family particularly keenly because his working hours meant that he could take on a great deal of the childcare while Diana worked full-time. 'I was the primary carer, going from knowing nothing about looking after children to taking them to school. I tried not to be like their dad but rather the big brother/uncle/matey person in their lives. I was very aware that if these were my kids, I would hate the fact that someone else was teaching them to ride their bike or tie their shoelaces. I joke sometimes about how I feel like the caretaker in that you do all this for them, and you build this loving relationship with them but then finally, when there are decisions to be made about them or only two tickets for the Christmas play, you're not there.' Diana says she had to make it clear from the very beginning that her children had to come first. 'Sam did complain about it occasionally, and said things like "I am second best," and I said, "Yes, you are," and he found that offensive at times. But he needed to understand that I am the centre of their world. If I wasn't here they would have nothing, but he could rebuild his life, so they have to come first. There is no way that I am going to have them feeling left out. I explained that it didn't mean I loved him any less, just that they needed me more. But I only think he really understood that when we had our own baby.' Sam agrees. 'Zac is now number one for me, and that's interesting given all that we have been through with the other two. Now I understand how Di felt, and that's plugged a few gaps in the jigsaw puzzle.'

We are in uncharted territory when it comes to the formation of new families and the extended family networks which inevitably follow. A major study in America comparing the state of marriage in 1980 to 2000 has found that we are adjusting slowly socially and culturally to the concept. The survey, published in a book called *Alone Together*, showed that second marriages with stepchildren tend to be happier with less conflict and are slightly less prone to divorce than they were just over twenty years ago. 'In other words, the presence of stepchildren appeared to lower marital quality in 1980, but to improve marital quality in 2000,' the authors conclude.[4] In spite of the obvious complexities, all the signs are that when a second relationship is handled sensitively, when both sets of parents shape their relationship flexibly around the needs of the children, and where relations with the non-resident parent are free from animosity, the experience can be beneficial for all concerned.

Easier said than done, of course. The early months of a second relationship are rarely simple. There are more than just two people to consider, and what would otherwise have been a loving, private honeymoon period in a first partnership can become as stressful as life was during a previous divorce with children, who in all likelihood are still struggling with their own feelings of loss and rage. They can see how much happier their mother or father is with their new friend, and the whole family often reaps the benefits of a better standard of living. But a new step-parent also means the final dashing of any secret hope that their own parents might get back together. They may be jealous, missing the time they used to be able to spend alone with their own mum or dad. For ex-partners, watching their old lover enter a new relationship can reopen old wounds, with the same intense feelings of loss, betrayal and anger they felt during the separation. Sometimes people find that their ex wants to re-engage with them at this point by trying to renegotiate custody, maintenance or access arrangements. With so many moving parts to consider and keep happy in a new relationship, it is hardly surprising that the divorce rate among second marriages is still 50 per cent higher in those with stepchildren, than in those without.[5]

However, experience from those who have been through it show that there are some things which help the transition. Accept that a stepfamily can never operate in the same way as a nuclear family. Expect problems, and don't bail out too easily. It does require a great deal more patience, tolerance and flexibility to establish a second relationship when there are children. A new partner can never compensate for the failings of a former spouse, and past marriages and relationships tend to reverberate through new partnerships unless that person is able to learn from their mistakes. 'It's there in the old habits of heart and mind, in old loyalties and legacies, in fears and vulnerabilities, in the "ghosts" of past lives,' writes the psychologist Edith Mavis Hetherington in *For Better or For Worse*, 'and these ghosts can erode the stability of a new marriage unless laid to rest.' Rates of separation and divorce are higher among second and third relationships often because people continue to bolt at the first sign of difficulty rather than learn how to change the dynamic between them. But people also tend to be less tolerant of bad behaviour in a second committed relationship. Having lived through the ructions of separation or divorce once, they no longer fear the unknown quite so much.

When there is ongoing resentment and animosity between their parents, children are bound to find it harder to settle in and accept new step-parents and siblings, and it can be that these unresolved issues damage children more than either parent remarrying. Often the young are forced to take sides, buttoning their lip about what goes on in either home, or what one parent has said about the other. The blame for ongoing difficulties between adults easily gets dumped on to the children. Some find they become scape-goats for the new step-parent, blamed for the absent parent's crimes and misdemeanours, for being the cuckoo in the nest. As the new step-parent, don't expect instant love, gratitude and affection from stepchildren, for it is a child's acceptance of the new status quo which holds the key to a happier future more than anything else. Successful stepfamilies eventually create new family routines, traditions and celebrations which include a whole new network of extended family and friends. Many grandparents, par-ticularly paternal ones, lose contact with their grandchildren after a separation – a source of great loss and sadness for both – but they can be key players in the new family life. Research shows that a significant factor in building resilience in children, so that they can triumph over painful experiences, is the support of a range of significant 'others' in their lives, such as grandparents, older sib-lings, wider family, friends and teachers.[6]

Diana has made a conscious effort to keep in close contact with her ex-partner's parents, who now treat her new baby as if it were a new grandchild of their own, and she invites everybody, including her former partner's new wife and her parents, to special occasions such as her daughter's eighteenth birthday. 'They have all been involved in my daughter's life and it's about my beautiful firstborn child, not about me,' she says. 'We have this lovely extended family now, but my ex's new wife is far more complicated about it. She sort of hangs back from the conversation, and she has made the odd scene, which is a shame because as the kids say, she ought to move on. He did leave me for her, after all!'

The new extended families of today can provide children with new role models as well as emotional support through the normal difficulties inherent in growing up. The more people there are around for young people to consult, the better. 'I never pretended to be their father,' says Ralph of Madeline's teenage sons. 'But we sit around the kitchen table and talk stuff through for hours, and they do ask me for advice, or lifts someplace when it's a knife-edge situation sort of thing and they don't want to ask their mum!

When I was in America I started getting these texts in the middle of the night because they were having a row with her about something. "Come back now! Mum's gone mental! You are the only one who can sort her out!"'

The relationships that are being formed between step-parents and half-siblings can be just as meaningful and important as if they were full blood relations. Marcus's second wife died five years ago, but his relationship with his stepchildren is still so solid that he is prepared to donate one of his kidneys to help the eldest, who has suffered from serious ill health all her life and will soon need an operation. Deborah's stepson is twenty-five, severely autistic and still lives with them. While she acknowledges that it can be difficult at times, it is Deborah who lavishes time and affection on him and makes sure he gets to appointments with doctors. Ann still sees her aged parents occasionally, even though they have behaved in a divisive and unloving way in the past, siding with their son-in-law over custody of her children during an acrimonious divorce because they disapproved of the fact that she is a lesbian. Her children are grown up now with children of their own, and Ann and her new partner Julia have the grand-children to stay one weekend a month. 'We've created a more extended, much more affectionate and supportive family of our own,' says Ann. 'We also have some wonderful friends, two of whom were witnesses at our civil partnership ceremony, so we have kind of created two families – our respective children and grandchildren, but also the coming together of friends.'

More and more people, including those not in stepfamilies, find that breaking through the paradigm of the nuclear family and building a wider network of support is the only way to cope under the weight of new pressures and expectations of a lasting relationship today. Many working parents depend upon grandparents, other family members, close friends and neighbours for help with looking after their children. Others consciously break up the nuclear model with au pairs or lodgers. 'Some people think we are

weird but we have always had lodgers who poo in the same loo
and drink out of the same cups, so that kind of mixes things up
a bit in that there is always someone else around,' says Robin.
Many of those who have experienced the break-up of a substantial relationship choose to build a more complex web of intimate
connections to others based on deep friendships. Sasha Roseneil's
study of fifty-three people who were not living with a partner
in the Leeds area found that most 'were enmeshed in complex
networks of friends, partners, biological kin and sometimes ex-
partners and their kin'.[7]

Many have come to question the need to be shoehorned into
some prescribed notion of how marriage or a relationship should
be when we now have the opportunity to create more individual
arrangements. 'I have this friend who is divorced with children,
who has met an older man, and she wants to go the whole way
and live together because she feels it won't be real unless they do,'
says Peggy, who is in her fifties and content to live alone after two
failed marriages. 'But why do that when you also have a teenage
daughter who isn't likely to relish the idea of having a strange man
who isn't her father in the house? Why do that when he has a
lovely house that you can go and stay in while her daughter is off
with her dad? Why squeeze yourself into this classic family pro-
file when you can each get to go home for some space and privacy
when you need it? I remember looking at my parents, who lived
in this tiny three-bedroom house, and wondering why they were
still forcing each other to sleep in this tiny bed when they could
actually be enjoying separate rooms. It wasn't that great a marriage, but maybe it would have been better if they had! There was
always something about that level of intense togetherness in relationships that I could never quite understand. I like my solitude.'

More and more people talk of their closest friends as family,
share their deepest concerns about their children with them and
encourage those children to think of these adults as adopted aunts
and uncles, surrogate godparents without the religion. 'My parents were pleased when my husband left me with two children

because they had never liked him and they didn't think he looked after me properly,' says Diana. 'But they didn't support me either, after he left. They thought that I was all right simply because I wasn't living on benefits in a council flat. They never phoned or visited, so I had to develop my own network. I found this amazing au pair who became my eldest child's godmother and I have got great friends who saw me through.'

In some ways, perhaps, we are returning to the models of relationship and family life which existed for centuries before the ideal of the nuclear family took hold during the middle of the twentieth century. Stepfamilies, cohabitation and children born out of wedlock have always been common. Twenty-five to 30 per cent of all marriages were remarriages until the eighteenth century in England. Common-law unions continued to rise during the late eighteenth and early nineteenth centuries, in spite of the State's attempts to control marriage, absconding fathers and seducers of aristocratic young women for their inheritance with Hardwicke's Marriage Act of 1753.[8, 9] A wide range of adults from paid help to neighbours and extended family have always been involved in the care of children before it was presumed that only Mother would do. While we are led to believe that we are living with unprecedented rates of family breakdown, the truth is that for centuries 'family' always meant a much looser collection of people living together before the ideal of complete isolation and privacy within your own individual home was a possibility. Few couples would expect to spend more than a year or two together after their children had left home, for after just seventeen years of marriage there was a 50 per cent chance that one of the pair would have died.[10] Marriage lasted longest during the Victorian period, when declining mortality rates had not yet been offset by rising divorce rates, but with the exception of that blip, which lasted until the 1950s, the average length of a marriage hasn't changed much for centuries – it remains eleven years.[11]

However much State or Church has tried to legislate for how we live in love during the past, the fact is that it is the two protagonists who determine the nature of their relationship. Most try to do the right thing by each other. The statistics may be turning full circle with legally sanctioned marriage as an institution declining – it is estimated that some 30 per cent of couples will choose cohabitation in the UK by the year 2021[12] – but all relationships, whatever their status, suffer in this shifting climate from the taboos which surround them. We can only make them work if we relinquish the notion that couples need complete privacy in order to flourish, for it is incredibly hard for people to develop the insight or the requisite skills to ride out their personal difficulties when they lack a window on to the domestic lives of others. It is harder still to admit defeat or seek solace and support through the profound disruption of a separation when the nuclear family model still has such a tenacious hold as the only right way to be. The pressure to be that perfect couple is still so great that often people feel unable to talk about their problems outside the relationship, without it being seen as disloyal or a betrayal rather than a means to seek advice, support or a greater perspective on their difficulties.

The modern marriage is rather like a castle with a very wide moat. Couples pull up the drawbridge and hunker down behind a high wall of privacy, which is considered crucial for the preservation of the nuclear family. No one can see in. We lack transparency at precisely the point in history when we need it most. Consequently there is no outside measure against which we can judge how well or how badly we are doing inside our own castle. As the nature of the nuclear family changes, with so many couples and their children living through the turmoil of separation followed by the establishment of a new, extended family, we need a new honesty about the true nature of how relationship ebbs and flows through life in order minimise the impact of such a trauma. With enough support from that wider network earlier on, perhaps more could be saved from having to live through it at all.

'You get this idea from the telly and newspapers of what you are supposed to be like as a couple,' says Adanna, 'but nobody really knows what other people's relationships are like. It's only since I have been living on this estate that I have realised that a lot of other women hate housework as much as I do.' They moved recently to a new block of flats where the walls are so thin you can hear rows ringing round the hollows between the balconies. 'You don't want to tell everyone your business, so sometimes we will stop and shut the windows if we are about to have row because it doesn't sound very good, does it? You don't want other people to think, They're not like us, are they? when of course everybody rows. I know that now. It's normal but it's something that we plug into, like we're supposed to have this man who is always loving towards you, and fantastic children who are slightly cheeky but never argue or hate you, and a wonderful tidy home, but that just doesn't exist.'

'I would have liked to have been able to talk about it to some-one,' says Elizabeth, who went through a difficult period in her marriage when she discovered that her husband had been having an affair. 'But I felt I couldn't tell my mother because she didn't much like my husband anyway, and really that would have meant admitting she was right. She would have said, "Get out, leave him," when I didn't want to do that. I am very close to my brother and his wife, but if I had told him he would have gone round and punched him on the nose. He wouldn't have forgiven him, either. I have very good friends, but I just felt it wasn't something I wanted to share, for his sake, so I just did a lot of thinking.' For others, the supposed sanctuary of the nuclear-family castle allows a pernicious loneliness to flourish when the balance of power is so out of kilter that it borders on abusive. Like many other men, Deborah's husband didn't like the idea that she might talk about their marriage difficulties to outsiders. 'He felt it wasn't right, so I felt trapped because I couldn't possibly talk to him and I would have had to be very careful talking to anyone in case it got back to him, it was such a small community. I would have gone mad if I hadn't been able to talk to my sister on the phone.'

Rajani decided not to tell her parents that her husband was being violent towards her because they lived in Indonesia, too far away to be able to support her, and they hadn't wanted her to marry him in the first place. 'I remember going home once and my father noticing the marks on my face and my telling him it was nothing. My mother-in-law noticed them, but she never said anything to their son. She would make a point of saying things like, "Your marriage is your marriage and we don't want to interfere," but she did interfere when it suited her. I didn't talk to my friends, either. I made up stories about falling over because I was ashamed. I had helped women through tribunals, women who faced violent men, but my own private life was shit. I was a high-flyer at Cambridge, I had married this amazing man and it had failed. I had failed, and that was a huge thing to have to admit. My friends were shocked when I told them we were separating and why, because we gave this picture of a happy couple who threw parties where everything was just fine.'

Wendy didn't tell anyone for years that her husband could be abusive both emotionally and on occasions physically. 'There are two things: one is that if I share this with someone I have to acknowledge that it is actually happening. The second is that when I was brought up, whatever happened inside our house was nothing to do with the neighbours. I grew up with this in-built belief that you don't hang out your dirty washing, and that you worried about what other people might think. There's an element of shame, in that here I am, a powerful working woman in my own right. But there is also collusion from the woman's point of view by not telling, because the perpetrator isn't going to tell anyone, is he?' Wendy's closest friends had no idea how difficult her marriage had become. She was only able to talk about what had happened when she decided that she wanted a separation. 'That's when you discover that you are not, as you previously thought, alone and a total failure. I had no idea that a quite good friend had been to hospital twice because her husband had been hitting her, and that he had also been visiting prostitutes. You *have* to tell people because if you don't, you fool yourself into thinking that you can change this man and that he really loves you, which no doubt he does.' By talking to a friend she realised that she no longer felt safe in her own home, and that she had to register their details with the domestic violence unit at the police station. They took her seriously, and by listening to her story were able to reassure her that she was justified in standing up to the abuse. 'When the police officer asked me for some examples of when he had been violent, and I told her, her response was, "Oh, pretty violent then," and that made me think, OK, it is violent. I had an objective measure. She didn't know anything about me, but in her view Ian's behaviour was pretty violent. That's why people must go to the police because it's only then that your own standards and your own ability to put up with shit are put in the cold light of day. That's when you stop kidding yourself and think, Come on, this is really not on, and do something about it.'

'Today, when family life is so much more private, a great deal more is left to the couple to work out for themselves. Conjugal love is now the excuse to leave family alone and isolate its members, particularly women and children, from the world of work and the real sources of power,' writes the historian John Gillis in his history of marriage, *For Better, For Worse*. 'Today's conjugal myth perpetuates the illusion that each family is essentially on its own and that love between two people is sufficient to produce just and amicable relationships.' But it wasn't always like that. Courtship and marriage were far more integrated and supported by a rich social fabric of family, friends and the local community until the late nineteenth and early twentieth centuries, when the concept that the nuclear family had to be afforded total privacy took hold. Banns had to be published for three consecutive Sundays if a couple were to marry in church, just so that those who knew each as an individual could pass comment on their background and report any impediment. Whether or not they were legally married, couples lived close to their kin and were regularly in and out of others' lives. For both rich and poor, there was little idea of privacy for 'conjugal bliss' within the home. Houses were densely populated with boarders or servants, and not designed to allow couples much space to be alone. Corridors went straight through bedrooms, and often whole families lived in one room. The rich were expected to spend more time apart than they did together, and for the poor, 'Few couples could carve out private spaces where they might take meals, or even conduct their sex lives, discrete from other household members,' writes historian Stephanie Coontz in *Marriage, A History*.

In the past, before the nuclear family idyll, when there were marital difficulties everybody knew about them. 'Every union was a potential burden on the parish and therefore could not be considered a purely private matter,' writes Gillis. 'As a consequence, what began as a public event remained a focus of communal concern until dissolved by death or other misfortune.' Every aspect of each other's lives was open to public scrutiny and neighbours kept a close eye on warring couples. Often they were sent before the courts. Scolding wives were publicly punished with ducking stools, and 'cuckolds', or wife-beaters, were fined by church courts or publicly humiliated. In some European countries the collective rules of the community were enforced by noisy public shame punishments called 'rough music' or 'charivari', a noisy demonstration which humiliated offenders either by circling their house at night and screaming or banging on pans, or by seizing them and parading them backwards on donkeys. The main purpose of these collective controls was preserving social and patriarchal order. Wife-beaters were punished, but husbands who succumbed too much to their wives were subject to even more humiliation. Cuckolded husbands in parts of France on Mardi Gras were paraded about on a chair which was then added to the bonfire, with the poor man replaced by a straw mannequin. The consequence of such scrutiny was that the private life of a couple could never be completely hidden from view. As those social checks and balances began to diminish, it was all too easy for patriarchy and abuses of power to flourish. 'In the twentieth century the family occupies a basically different relationship to the community than it did in the eighteenth,' writes Edward Shorter in his book *The Making of the Modern Family.* 'Nowadays the dividing line between private and public spheres is clearly drawn, and efforts to blur it are seen as offences against civil liberty.'

While it's clear that some privacy is desirable – nobody wants a parade of neighbours and family through their living room – we have perhaps marooned ourselves by cutting off too many sources of support. The American authors of *Alone Together* found that couples in 2000 had fewer close friends than those surveyed in 1980. They also shared fewer friends, and spent less time with them socially, probably due to a number of factors such as longer working hours and devoting most of their free time when they weren't working to their children. However, a number of recent studies in the US have shown that social integration is crucial for the health of a relationship. A supportive network can lower the likelihood of divorce, particularly during the first six years of marriage.[13] When a couple share close friends they are more able to offer support, with greater perspective on the dynamics within the partnership. 'I could engage with my friends and expect them to rescue me from my predicament,' says Beatrice, who went through a particularly difficult time in her marriage when her husband became unemployed and depressed. 'I could get lots of loving from my girlfriends by moaning to them about how awful he was. But none of them could say, "What's your part in it?" When people enjoy an extensive and overlapping network of friends and relatives, they tend to have better mental and physical health than those who lack these resources, which in turn contributes to relationship health. It also means they are more likely to have support should that relationship end.[14] It isn't a symptom of disloyalty if you share your problems outside the couple bond. It is a sign that you value your relationship enough to seek solutions, rather than just solace, from those you trust.

If separation, divorce and the establishment of new partnerships is an inevitability for many in today's world, then we need greater transparency to minimise the conflict and difficulties during such a transition. Yet often, the first close friends hear about another couple's problems is when they announce they are separating. It is during relationship difficulties which could lead to separation and family breakdown that this modern emphasis on privacy, perfection and individual self-sufficiency does the most damage, for couples and their children need the support of a wider community at such times of adversity more than ever. How much easier would it be for children and their families to adjust to the end of a relationship if they had been cushioned by support free of blame or harsh judgement throughout? Separation and conflict between parents are powerful formative experiences for children, and can influence the nature of their own adult relationships as they trust love less and bolt at the first sign of trouble. But when those children are supported enough through the profound change of parental separation, studies show that there are measurable benefits in terms of their mental health, reduced alcohol and drug use in adolescence, as well as fewer sexual partners.[15] There is little yet in the way of long-term research, but common sense would suggest that without that support they are less likely to be able to break the negative cycle in which the children of divorce seem to be more prone to divorce themselves.

We are living through nothing less than the tail end of a social revolution in our love lives, described by Lawrence Stone in *Road to Divorce* as 'Perhaps the most profound and far-reaching social change to have occurred in the past five hundred years.' 'A gigantic moral, religious and legal revolution has accompanied and made possible the shift from a system of marriage prematurely terminated by death to a system of marriage prematurely terminated by choice. It is an open question whether individuals and societies can adapt more easily to conditions caused by a free exercise of the will than to conditions caused by the inexorable accident of fate.'

Marriage as an institution may well be dying, but there is no evidence to suggest that our need for relationship has diminished or that the commitments we make to one another are any weaker. If anything, our desire for love, for a contented, stable partnership is more intense than ever before now that so many other aspects of life feel uncertain. 'Marriage' can mean different things to different cultures. Beyond the universal biological imperative to love, make love and reproduce, there is one other common factor to every couple throughout the world: 'marriage' in all its forms fosters community by uniting not just two people but also two families and their networks of friends. With more stepfamilies, that network gets wider and the myth of isolated perfection within the nuclear model is gradually being broken down, but not fast enough for it to be of real use to those living through such a transition today. We have consciously to push down those castle walls. Relationship is about connection. It is about the resources we pool and share together and the truths we learn about ourselves through each other. We need to feel the deep link that comes from strong social bonds to a wide range of other people for a sense of place, purpose and value, for as Marie Stopes writes in *Married Love*, 'It is through the community of human beings and not in our individual lives that we reach an ultimate permanence upon this globe.'

There has been considerable political unease at the speed with which people have embraced the new freedoms afforded by the social revolution in our relationships, and drifted away from the institution of marriage into alternative family forms. Successive British governments have been slow to meet this change with adequate social policies and adjustments to legislation designed to support relationships. There is no reason why heterosexual cohabitants should not now enjoy similar rights as homosexuals in civil partnerships. Working parents are desperate for more family-friendly policies at work, high-quality, affordable childcare and better protection for working mothers. Instead of more progressive policies which support all relationships, whatever their status and their fundamental importance to society as the glue of care for each other, successive governments have tried to straddle the new with the old with schemes which attempt to reinforce the idea of the nuclear family. Statistics are bandied about to 'prove' that those who are married stay together longer, but these figures do not and cannot compare like with like. It is possible that if the cohabiting couples surveyed had been married, their break-up rate would have been just the same. 'Cohabiters and non-cohabiters do not appear to differ in their rates of divorce or level of dissatisfaction when relationship duration is measured from the very beginning of the relationship instead of the date of legal union,' conclude the researchers of a major longitudinal study.[16]

Rates of cohabitation, lone parenthood, divorce and remarriage have risen in the past thirty years. The full-time employment rate of mothers has trebled, while the part-time rate has doubled.[17] But to see this as some sort of moral decline in the emotional fabric of our family lives is misleading. When you look at the research and talk to people, a very different picture of relationships emerges. All of the evidence suggests that couples want to find ways to maintain relationships, commitment and to 'do the right thing' by each other through a maze of new difficulties. Most young people still hope to marry at some point in their lives, and believe in the values of loving commitment. Many test relationships by cohabiting; others couldn't be more committed to each other if they were married, being linked by history, children and a deep affectionate respect for each other. Most people still live as couples with or without children. Most children still grow up with their own parents. Most births after the age of twenty-five are within marriage.[18] The vast majority of mothers, even when they are working, continue to put their children first, often compromising their own careers and welfare to do so. We can now have love without marriage and sex without love, but more than 90 per cent of people still prefer to have sex within a steady relationship.[19]

Our culture may be highly sexualised, promiscuous and pornographic, but men and women still go to extraordinary lengths to hide their sexual activity. They value honour and monogamy: very few men are prepared to leave their wife for a mistress, and there is some evidence to suggest that people value sexual fidelity more than ever before now that so many other aspects of life cannot be relied upon. We pledge allegiance because of our feelings for each other, and not because of some proscribed respect for the institution of marriage.

We are not living through an age of moral decay in family life, merely one of transition. The vast majority of men and women want to do what's best for their children. There is little concrete evidence to suggest that people switch partners easily – at the drop of a hat – for purely selfish reasons, and more evidence indicates that external factors such as social deprivation, stress from work or unemployment, less education and low income affect the quality of people's relationships and precipitate separations.[20] Instead of devising policies which support the fundamental building blocks of a good relationship – communication and parenting skills, conflict resolution and emotional intelligence, to name just a few – we pathologise families as dysfunctional whenever they break down, overlooking the clear research which shows that children can grow up healthy and happy to become balanced, constructive, law-abiding, economically creative citizens from a wide variety of family arrangements. A growing body of research evidence finds that the core values of a healthy childhood full of love, guidance, support and safety, matter more than the structure of their family. Single parents and step-parents can be just as capable, loving and successful as married parents.

We now have the freedom to form the bespoke relationships of our choosing, and raise our children on the sound and age-old moral values of honesty, fairness, respect, flexibility and democracy regardless of how many caring adults they have in their lives, and frankly the more the better for all concerned. We can forge more companionable loving relationships as equal partners where we endeavour to work together towards the common goals of bringing up children and enjoying family life. Core values are stronger than ever as parents endeavour to do the best for their children. Yet we are in unfamiliar territory, lacking enlightened policies which support us, and we need a new extended family network of friends and neighbours to help us cope with today's pressures – job insecurity and longer working hours, gendered assumptions about mothers working, increased costs and expectations of parenting, unrealistic presumptions about the need for happiness and romance at every stage of a relationship, and all this set against a wider cultural backdrop where divorce is more prevalent. 'I feel hopeful for my children. I have a feeling that by the time they have children of their own there will be real parity for the sexes, not only at work but at home,' writes Sabrina Broadbent about her life as a single mother.[21] While it has been tough, her children show every sign of being rounded, happy, capable young people. 'The other day I saw a man, laptop over one shoulder, nappy bag over the other, struggling on to the rush-hour tube with a baby in a buggy. Perhaps my daughters and their partners really will have it all – love, work and children. Now that would be something worth signing up to.'

We need greater transparency, semi-porous membranes between the family and the wider world. We need greater honesty about the challenges we all face, as well as a greater acceptance of the way that relationship changes through the course of life and why partnerships can end. In this brave new world, with greater openness within a new extended network of family and friends, perhaps our children and their children will find even greater riches within the intimate partnerships of their choosing. Peggy has spent much of her life as a single mother. 'My daughter got married recently to the most gorgeous man. When he stood up to make his speech he said such beautiful things about her. I would have loved it if someone could have said those things about me, but that hasn't happened. The wedding was so lovely, full of her friends who were children when I first met them and they are now having babies of their own. They've all been in this house – I have fed them, stepped over them – and they all beat a path to Wales to be there for her wedding. I'm glad that there hasn't been so much damage done by our divorce that she couldn't find happiness in her own relationship. I hope with all my heart that it works.'

11

SEPTEMBER DAYS

In *Metamorphoses*, Ovid tells the tale of Baucis and Philemon. The gods Zeus and Hermes, disguised as wanderers, search for food and shelter but have been denied by every single household in the village. When Baucis and Philemon welcome them in, the gods offer them any favour in return. They ask not for riches but to be able to die at the same time. 'Since we have lived all our lives peacefully together, let me not live to bury Baucis, nor Baucis live to bury me.' Many years later, without warning, 'talking of old times', Philemon turns into an oak and Baucis into a linden tree with just enough time to kiss each other goodbye before their limbs and branches become entwined. It's a powerful and heart-warming image. They had been married for more than sixty years, 'Content in each other's company. In that household there were no servants, no employers; each of the two old people gave orders, and each obeyed,' – the substance of a nourishing lifelong companionship. It's a deeply romantic idea, two people as united in death as they are in life until, as Jonathan Swift's more humorous eighteenth-century version *Baucis and Philemon* points out, some pastor chops down both trees for firewood or to mend his barn. Yet there is profound truth contained in the essence of that myth, for the need for companionship and support from a partner becomes that much more vital as we grow older and frailer and as other props fall away. For those who have spent the best part of a contented lifetime together, the prospect of living without that constant presence in their life is unimaginable.

The nourishment of a good relationship matters hugely throughout our lives, as I hope this book has shown. But as we age and retire, as our physical and mental horizons grow more limited, as our parents die and our children move away to form families of their own, a healthy interdependence with a person who really knows and cares for us becomes more important than at any other life stage. 'I felt that I was melting into this man with whom I had travelled a long, steep road, tripping, falling, getting up again, through fights and reconciliations, but never betraying each other. The sum of the day, our shared pain and joys, was now our destiny,' writes Isabel Allende in her memoir *The Sum of Our Days*. When you share a past, it is that much easier to share a future. 'If I were just divorced and younger, then maybe it would be different,' says Marjorie, whose husband left her for a woman nearly half his age. 'But I am fifty-seven, and I don't want to be on my own. I do need someone, but anyone I meet from now on will be older too, and you think, Oh my God, in six years' time they could be really ill and need looking after! Old age with someone you have just met feels a bit challenging and frightening. If you haven't got that whole life together before, and kids in common, it's very different, and I can't help thinking that he has thrown the best bit away.'

Every long-term relationship is made up of different phases. We experience a series of marriages, each with their own potential difficulties. We grow older and wiser individually, and as a couple, through the normal, common relationship trials of juggling careers with home and the needs of children, our own independent desires with the selflessness and kindness required to foster companionship. 'Together they had overcome the daily incomprehension, the instantaneous hatred, the reciprocal nastiness and fabulous flashes of glory in the conjugal conspiracy,' writes Gabriel García Márquez in *Love in the Time of Cholera*. 'It was the time when they loved each other the best, without hurry or excess, when both were most conscious of and grateful for their incredible victories over adversity. Life would still present them with other mortal trials, of course, but that no longer mattered: they were on the other shore.'

From midlife onwards, people begin to take stock as they adjust slowly to the concept that time is running out and shouldn't be wasted. There is a tendency to look outside the relationship to friends, to new interests, to other sources of intimacy or to challenges at work in a fresh flurry of busyness before the more sedentary years ensue. Accepting that we are growing older isn't easy for any of us, and watching the person you have known intimately for decades gradually deteriorate both physically and mentally in front of your eyes heightens the inevitability of your own demise. There's a growing sense of fewer good times to come. You can literally count the number of Christmases and summers ahead on your fingers and toes. There is loss of dreams and ambitions, loss of what might have been for you together as the future is forfeited to caring for each other and quieter pleasures. Some of the difficulties earlier on in the relationship may rear their head once more: love is redefined when one gets ill and the other assumes the more maternal role of carer; earlier childhood betrayals can resurface when the more vulnerable person feels an unavoidable dependence on the other. The balance of power within the partnership can be thrown out of kilter, raising questions once more about how one manages one's own independent needs with those of the other and of the relationship. With greater ill health and a growing sense of redundancy within the world, people can become grumpier, more frustrated and bitter as they age, conflict levels rise and sexual performance diminishes. Some find adjusting to this phase so difficult that they seek counselling or even divorce. Eva and her husband had been married for nearly thirty years, but after he retired he became a chronic alcoholic. He is deteriorating physically, killing himself with drink and won't seek help, so as a final act of despair and self-preservation she has divorced him at the age of sixty-five. 'I feel very sad, resigned to the fact that there is nothing I can do to help him. That's why I divorced him, either to help him or to help myself. If he stopped drinking I would go back to him tomorrow but he can't help himself, and in a way I can see how he feels. He is seventy-three, you go through all that rehab, you don't know how you will come out of it, and how much longer are you going to live anyway?'

Old age is a bugger, the most difficult period for people individually and as a couple, yet these are the years when we most need that life partner beside us to see us through to the end. Good communication is more important than ever. Often people avoid anything negative in conversation such as the grim prognosis of a chronic illness. But people in later life need the comfort that comes from being able to discuss the really difficult things – their deepest fears about growing older, about becoming more dependent and about dying – with those they trust with such intimacies. Research shows that those with a close relationship and good communication have lower levels of anxiety and depression over the disabilities of ageing and higher levels of self-esteem.[1]

Many find these September days to be their golden years, with a deepening sense of intimacy and commitment. With people living longer and having fewer children, relationships have a whole new blast of life to travel and explore new interests either separately or together after the children have left home. One in five couples now celebrate their fiftieth anniversary together. Many of the issues that cause conflict between younger couples such as sex, how you bring up children and how money is spent become far less important in later life. Jack and Rachel have been married for forty-three years and are in their late sixties. They had a difficult period when Rachel was suffering from a thyroid disorder and was depressed and aggressive for several years. At one point things got so bad that Jack seriously thought about separating.

'But I have got much more out of life through this long-term partnership than I would have alone, and it has just got better and better. Not a day goes by that we don't have a good laugh,' says Jack. 'We used to argue about all sorts of things, trivia really, if we didn't see things the same way but now we just laugh about those things, turn them into a jokey comment. If you can see the funny side and stand back and look at these two elderly people bickering, it seems so silly. We've found a greater peace. It's not a boring peace, in that we're still two different people, even though we share a lot of interests. It's the companionship that matters. We both like to read, and sometimes we do the crossword together and challenge each other with comments like, "Fancy you not getting that!"'

Rose and Tim have been married for more than forty years and have had more than their fair share of difficulties. They married young and were sexually inexperienced. Each has had the occasional sexual dalliance outside the marriage, which never threatened their relationship until Tim became emotionally involved with another woman in midlife and left Rose not just once but twice. Each time Rose took him back, against the advice of many friends. 'I knew the story wasn't over yet, and a lot of what keeps us grounded, stable and calm is all that shared history, all those memories of the lovely things we have done together. I think we're both less bothered now with the minutiae of life, like whether or not the ironing's done. We'd rather sit down and talk over a gin and tonic. We don't eat in front of the telly any more, either. We look at each other and talk to each other as we eat, and that's been a huge change since he's been back. I wouldn't dream of leaving the house now without kissing him goodbye, and I wouldn't have done that in the past. You take each other for granted when you are younger. Now I think, Well, we might not see each other again, so you have to make each goodbye a nice one.' Rose found an inner strength that she never knew she had while they were apart, which she feels has made her more able to approach their relationship in later life with greater independence and resilience. 'I know I can live on my own, and his leaving taught me that because I used to be so scared of just being alone. That's a huge lesson – the likelihood is that will happen again because he is older than me, and men tend to die first.'

Those in more contented partnerships have learned through trial and error how to treat each other with greater kindness and respect. But most importantly, they have learned how to allow enough flexibility within their picture of the relationship to give their partner space. The intense jealousies of the past are no longer pressing. Charles met Jilly when he was in his early sixties and she was in her mid-fifties. 'I suppose I must have fancied her like mad, but you reach an age when it's not quite so overt. We just got on really well and spent some lovely days together. There is a stability there because we are older; there's less urgency. I can remember when I was younger feeling quite jealous about girl-friends just looking at someone else, which is ridiculous, I know, but I don't feel jealous now. She has other admirers who ring her up and take her out but I don't stop and contemplate her having energetic sex with them in a car because this is different. It's more profound, more long-term, structured with trust.' After decades of living a bachelor life, Charles has moved in with Jilly. He is retired and able to help her with research, for she works long hours in a full-time job. He also loves being home, able to cook for her and their friends. 'That is quite a pivot in our life together, the caring for each other and the catering, the kindness that comes with food.'

However, some couples who were unhappy together earlier in life are in danger of being even unhappier with the frustrations and anxieties of growing older, for that is when inhibitions fade and disillusionment and hostilities become entrenched, with embittered bickering. Resentments at each other's presence and dependency flourish, for there is nowhere to hide. 'How deep back the stubborn gnarled roots of the quarrel reach, no one can say,' writes Tillie Olsen in her novel *Tell Me a Riddle*. 'But only now, when tending to the needs of others no longer shackled them together, the roots swelled up visible, split the earth between them, and the tearing shook even to the children, long since grown.' Couples who haven't resolved their differences, confronted their demons, forgiven misdemeanours, accepted that their partner has limitations and that some of their dreams and expectations will never be fulfilled, or alternatively, found the strength to separate from a misery-filled relationship, are in for a much harder time as they get older. You need a loving past, an image of your partner as someone kind and companionable, active and physically attractive to be able to cope with the onus of caregiving, the personal sacrifice and the pain of watching them suffer. There can be less privacy, less time for personal pursuits, and older couples are often poorer too, lacking the financial means to escape each other even if they could do so. There is no better argument for divorce than the horrors of being trapped in a miserable marriage in old age, with that unhappiness exacerbated by the knowledge that it is now too late to confront it with separation. 'If only people knew how painful it is –,' writes Sofia Tolstoy in her *Diaries*. 'Even more painful is the realisation in the *last* days of our life together, that there are no mutual feelings between us, that for the whole of my life I have single-mindedly and unwaveringly loved a man who was utterly selfish.'

Iris and Gerry are in their early sixties, in an embittered marriage which is still dominated by the affair that Gerry had after the birth of their child more than twenty years ago. 'It lasted eight or nine months,' Gerry told me. 'Ha,' spat Iris, 'it gets shorter every time you mention it.' Iris finds it hard to forgive her husband, and wishes that she had left him all those years ago. She feels a fool. He lied to her, and tried to minimise the damage by pretending the affair had been platonic. She felt doubly emotionally betrayed, for this wasn't mere sex – he confided in his lover and consoled her. Iris feels socially humiliated, for he never told his family how serious it was, and to this day she feels that she has 'lost all my forties and my fifties'. 'I've lost twenty years, being in a half-life,' she told me in front of Gerry. 'I wanted the relationship I had with someone I revered as a soul mate back, but that couldn't happen because I didn't feel the same way about him any more. I couldn't leave because of the shame. You can't have two failed marriages, and because I had small children and no money and he wouldn't leave, I couldn't get on with making a new plan for my life. I was forty, and at the time you think that's old, but it isn't. I could have had twenty years of building up some sort of career and a new life, but I never had a great deal of confidence and that betrayal took the last of it away.'

Their relationship is punctuated by an underlying bickering as Iris lashes out, wounding him verbally with sarcasm and put-downs, punishing him for the deep hurt she has lived with for so long. When I suggested that since she hadn't left, she had no choice now but to put the whole thing behind them, she agreed, and said that was why they had spent two months in Australia. 'I wish with hindsight that we had sat down and talked about the whole thing when it happened,' says Gerry, 'and I'm pleased that we've started talking about it now because at least that means we can get something better out of our last few years together. I'm still living in cloud cuckoo land, thinking that one day she'll wake up and say that she loves me,' he adds, throwing out a lifeline which he hopes Iris will catch. But she sits in her chair hidden in an alcove so that she cannot even make eye contact with him and refuses to extend the slightest hint of an olive branch. 'Yes, but if I say that, he's going to think it's all OK, isn't he?'

There is a paucity of research into the relationships of older couples. However, Fran Dickson's study of couples who had been married for more than fifty years found a sharp distinction between the happy and the unhappy.[2] For many of those who have been happier, the sudden freedom of retirement brings a period of intense togetherness in which they can relish the joys of travel and other leisure pursuits with a sense of sharpened delight because they have accepted that their time is now limited. After nearly forty years of teaching and married life, Jack and Rachel sold their house in Norfolk and moved back to London so that they could use the city while they were still physically able to. They are happy to do things apart, but like to go for walks along the river, to exhibitions and films together. They travel and they own a timeshare in a house in Spain, which they now use outside the school holidays. 'Apart from growing older and not having as much energy, now is the best time because of the companionship,' says Jack. 'We have so much freedom, and we're not financially restricted in the way that we were when we first got married, having to borrow fifty pounds from a loan shark. We're not well off, teachers aren't, but we've got this house and a regular income and we have a lot of fun together. But I also saw how difficult it was for my mother when my father died. I don't think people realise how hard that is for people when a relationship comes to an abrupt end just when they need it most. In the back of my mind there was also the thought that this would be a nice place for Rachel to be should I die first, because then she will have friends around the corner and only a small house to maintain.'

The more miserable couples in Fran Dickson's research bickered and contradicted each other constantly. They were cold and unaffectionate towards each other, they lived separate lives because that was easier than doing things together, and displayed the sort of anger and sadness when talking about their relationships that I witnessed in the sitting room of Gerry and Iris. In less happy marriages couples often hold quite different versions of the key events of their life together, and as discussion so often leads to argument rather than compromise, one partner tends to make many decisions unilaterally. It's easier that way. It is external constraints that seem to hold them together – religious or personal belief that marriage is for life means that divorce has never been an option. 'My mother used to say, "We worked through to happiness," which sounds like it was a bit of a struggle,' says Louise, who is in her eighties and has been married for fifty-five years. 'I think the same has been true for us in some ways, in that there have been various tensions, but I believe in staying together through thick and thin as my parents did. But it is hard through the thin, and there were quite a lot of bad times, although I would hate him to hear that now. But all that thinking, Why did I ever get married? It's such a loss of freedom, isn't it? I gave up something of myself to be a wife without it being appreciated by my husband. He never really knew how much it cost me. We never talked about it, and of course I can't now that he is so old and ill.'

For many others the constraints are financial, in that divorce is too costly to contemplate or, in the case of many women, the financial security of being a dependent wife means swapping an unhappy marriage for greater poverty with no certainty of any more happiness alone. Libby's forty-year marriage was fairly traditional – her husband was a successful businessman while Libby ran the home and went back to work part-time once her children were at secondary school. Fifteen years ago their marriage fell apart when her mother became seriously ill and her husband refused to change his business travel plans so that he could be with her. Her mother died while he was away. She was grief-stricken, and found it hard to forgive him, for she had begged him to cancel his trip to be with her. They separated temporarily for six months before she allowed him back, but their marriage has never recovered. Her husband is diabetic and depressed, and they spend a great deal of time apart. He stays three nights a week at a flat in London, which she is not allowed to visit. She isn't even allowed to know where it is. Libby goes out with her own friends, travels alone and is now 'Much happier on my own. I've got lots of friends and he is not as significant in my life any more, which is good for me but not so good for the marriage. I'd sum it up by saying that he has been a very good provider but a lousy husband. He's generous but not very kind to me now. He's hostile, a bully and all his anger seems to be directed at me. He has always said he isn't having an affair, but if I found out that was untrue then I would have to go because I would have been a fool for fifteen years, the disloyalty would be overwhelming. I thought about moving out years ago but then I thought, I can't be bothered, it's too much effort and it's got to be the last resort. Fifteen years ago, if I had known that this was how we were going to end up, I would never have allowed him back, but you always think, Oh, it will be all right next week.'

We may look forward to the escape of retirement when the hurly-burly of life gets too much, but work and status in the outside world gives us an essential, external structure to rely on and without it, many are thrust suddenly back on to their relationship for support, identity and stimulation. The foundations of the relationship have to be firm and flexible enough to take the load. For women who have enjoyed aspects of their home life alone, they find that their partner is always around now to fill the space, and have expectations, and that 'Does make considerable emotional and psychological demands,' says Andrew Balfour, a consultant clinical psychologist who specialises in the needs of older people at the Tavistock Centre in London. 'You can't use work and the structures of younger adulthood in the same way. There's nothing there now to mediate or buffer all of the other strains in a relationship, and then if you add to that the fact that you are now on a downward trajectory and this is the first socially imposed aspect of that, the anxieties can be profound.'

Roy met Juan twenty years ago on holiday in Spain, and their relationship flourished, with each travelling as much as possible to be with the other. Roy was in his early forties and the plan had always been that he would take early retirement so that he could move out to live with Juan permanently. But when the time came eight years ago, 'I fell apart. I got really ill, and I guess that was because I was facing such huge changes. I'm quite a constant person, I have worked all my life and suddenly I was faced with the prospect of leaving the people I knew and loved and going to another country where I didn't speak the language, and I think maybe it was too much all in one go.' Roy also needed a minor operation and was in great pain. Then he got flu. Meanwhile they were buying a house together in Spain, and for more than six months Roy found he was unable to make such a radical change to his life and leave the country that had been his home for over fifty years. When Juan had to cancel his visit to the UK over Christmas because he too was ill, Roy took the next flight out to Spain to be with him. 'I booked for two weeks, stayed for four and then three weeks after that I was living there. From the moment I got there I never looked back.' Roy has now adapted to his retirement, but has found that living together and being home all the time while Juan is at work has radically altered the power balance in their relationship and the nature of their squabbles. He is happy to do all the housework and the cooking, but often feels that Juan is less civil, even rude to him simply because he is there all the time to take the hit. 'Juan comes home for lunch, so I will say at breakfast, "What time suits you to eat, half past two?" and he'll say something like, "No, I think two-thirty-two and twenty-seven seconds would be better." Honestly, I could smack him! But he is also having a stressful time at work, his health isn't great either and I am trying to get him to look into the possibility of early retirement, which he is resisting. He recently had two months off work sick, so it isn't always easy to know how to help him.'

When there is so much loss in growing older – loss of purpose with retirement, loss of sexual prowess and energy with ill health, and fewer friends and family members around as they too succumb to the inevitabilities of later life – depression is common. Rates of depression are twice as high among older people than in the general population, even higher among those in nursing or residential homes and there is a striking rise in the suicide rate among men over sixty.[3] Ill health causes depression, which in turn creates even more ill health and can exacerbate existing conditions such as diabetes, cancer and heart disease.[4] It may well be too that as the brain ages, people find it harder to cope with stress, illness and painful life events and are consequently more vulnerable to depression. From the psychoanalytic perspective, depression can be a symptom of an inability to cope or to engage with the reality of those substantial losses of later life, and that can sometimes manifest as a stasis, a way of holding back time.[5] Whatever the cause, the quality of daily life for both partners will be affected,

for the equilibrium between them is upset with profound consequences. Libby's husband is in his sixties, has long-term
depression and cannot acknowledge that he needs help. 'It feels
like such an entrenched situation because you change with the
years, and he cannot accept that I am no longer the little girl he
married. I have grown stronger as I have got older, while he has
got weaker, and ill. The place would fall apart without me, but it
feels like such a heavy burden having to carry everything. He
doesn't do anything around the house or in the garden any more.
I know an awful lot of people my husband's age who are similarly
hostile. One friend's husband has been depressed and on tablets
for ten years years and shows no sign of getting any better. The
only way she can cope with it is to go on holiday as much as possible because he's not like that when they are away. It's just that
when two people are stuck in the house for long periods together
it gets quite suffocating.'

The power balance in what was previously a far more egalitarian partnership has been irrevocably altered. Nancy's husband
made the unilateral decision to give up work without a proper
pension ten years ago when he was fifty-eight. 'By disempower-
ing himself voluntarily, by boxing himself into a corner he has
made me more powerful, which isn't what I wanted at all, while
his role just gets more and more negative. I try to be kind, but I
am often very snappy with him because I still feel so angry about
being pushed into this position,' says Nancy. 'But it is also dread-
ful to see someone you care about so diminished. He used to dress
wonderfully and be very dapper, and he is still a good-looking
man, but he dresses like a tramp and that is not a good sign of
how you feel. I know lots of house-husbands his age living with
far more powerful, sorted women. Perhaps it's the way men burn
out at work.'

Studies indicate that when people are in greater need of care
because of depression or an illness which involves cognitive
impairment, such as a stroke or dementia, their partners suffer
more isolation and marital unhappiness than they would do as

carers of someone with a physical ailment.[6] The onus on the carer is constant, with the heartbreaking sight of living with someone who is now less of the person they once were and unable to offer support and intimacy in return. There is still such stigma associated with depression and mental illness that carers are often reluctant to seek support outside the relationship or expose their partner to humiliation in the wider world. With dementia there is progressive physical and intellectual deterioration, memory loss and confusion, which frustrates both the patient and the carer. The carer becomes their partner's memory, feeding back stories of the past and reminders of day-to-day needs in much the same way as a mother does for a small child. As with a child, it is the emotional attachment which keeps them there, tied to the tending of their partner's needs because of their shared and largely happy past. Research seems to suggest that carers of partners with dementia resist residential care longer than any other kind of carer because to do so means giving up their partner completely, abandoning them to even greater confusion and anxiety at those occasional moments of intellectual clarity. True love is perhaps allowing someone you care about to feel valued and as dignified as it is possible to feel as their life draws nearer to its close. But often there is uncertainty as to how best to help their loved one, as well as a great sense of inadequacy because they cannot.

Gareth had a stroke in his mid-fifties, which wiped out much of his speech and meant that he could no longer work. 'It has changed his whole demeanour, his whole persona,' says Imogen. 'At the time it was very upsetting, and you go into emergency mode. It was like a tornado going through our lives, not knowing what was going to happen and whether he was going to recover. He is much better now, but he is different to how he was before. The core of the person he was, which revolved around reading and writing, has been taken away from him even though his intelligence and his personality are still there. But the ability to express oneself is central to one's personality, and it is very upsetting for all of us to see him so reduced and so changed. He also relies on me much more now than he used to, and that's difficult too, but it's a new kind of love, perhaps, that makes me want to help him.' Even so, 'This bit is tougher than I ever imagined it would be. There's an underlying anxiety all the time: will he be OK, will it happen again, and a sense of aloneness in the marriage because I miss the person he used to be. His hinterland is shrinking. I have never lived with someone much older but it feels like that, like accelerated ageing. He has become a crabby old person, his nature less sunny, and that throws your own mortality into perspective.'

As the healthier of the two, Imogen does all the compromising. They live in a quiet suburb because Gareth can't cope with a lot of noise around him, and Imogen commutes into London to a highly pressurised full-time job that she loves. 'My life at work is fast, snappy, relentless, it's talk, talk, talk, and then when I come home I have to slow my language and my frames of reference right down. It can be really awkward, as if I am living life in two places.' Their social life has been compromised because Gareth finds anything with too much conversation going on hard, so dinner parties, parties and plays are difficult. 'But there are other things we can do together, like going to exhibitions, gardening, visual stuff.' Even simple tasks such as making a dental appointment or coping with a telephone call with a voice-activated automated system can prove too much to manage. Imogen came home from a work trip abroad to find that the house had been flooded and Gareth hadn't been able to cope with the bureaucracy involved in contacting insurance companies and putting dehumidifiers around the house. 'He won't ask others for help. He finds that demeaning, so he relies on me totally.'

The spouse acts as the first line of defence when their partner is ill, and there are practical issues, too, on top of the financial worries over loss of income and anxieties about their future together and how they will cope. The ill have immediate needs as patients. They have to be tended to, taken to hospital appointments, and all these new demands have an impact on the work and leisure time of the well partner as they slide almost without notice from being a husband or wife into being primarily a 'carer'. When a person is ill or frail and dependent, they are also likely to be more impatient, irritable and in pain, and cannot offer their partner the mutual support they once enjoyed when they were healthy. Even the most angelic spouse is likely to feel anger and resentment at some point with their new, exhausting role in the relationship, and then guilt that they should feel this way when their partner is suffering so much more. Lynn Barber writes eloquently about how she felt she was the 'bad' wife when her husband was terminally ill in hospital in her memoir *An Education*. 'I just hated being in hospital, hated being the "patient's wife", hated the fact that I didn't know what to talk to David about – that when he tried to talk seriously about dying, for instance, I brushed him off and that when I tried to tell him about everyday things, or friends who had called, I sounded like the silliest sort of airhead.' She visited him once or twice a day but felt that she was always making excuses to leave. 'Proper wives sat like pylons at their husband's bedside, only occasionally moving to get a cup of tea. They stayed there all day, maybe even all night. Going down in the lift one day, one of them said to me, "All we can do is give them our love," and I bared my teeth in a snarl. I just couldn't do this caring lark – it made me feel inadequate and cross. I felt cross with David too, for deserting me.'

Talking about all of this, either to each other or to someone outside the relationship, may be difficult and if the 'carer' cannot find ways to express all that pent-up frustration somewhere else, it is likely to be offloaded on to their partner, exacerbating relationship difficulties. Help is given grudgingly or aggressively, accompanied by criticism, or with the veiled punishment of overprotection – humiliating and belittling a person by doing things for them they could do for themselves. There is considerable evidence that ill health is more damaging to the marital satisfaction of the well spouse than it is to the patient, who is either less aware of the emotional dynamic between them because of their own pain and suffering, or needs to reinterpret their relationship as being closer because they need their well partner more.[7] Gareth can now look back on his stroke five years ago with perspective and acknowledges that in many ways it was tougher on Imogen. 'It was difficult, emotionally, for me in that I was damaged goods, but now I think I am much better and my kids tell me I am a nicer person because it used to be all work, work, work. I didn't realise at the time how significant the damage was. I was a holy fool, while Imogen did all the worrying for me because she could see how bad it was.'

A new ambivalence enters the relationship when the illness is terminal; the little time left needs to be relished, so what on earth is the point of squabbling over money or petty details like how the toothpaste tube is squeezed? 'When my husband left hospital after the operation, we entered a land where time is liquid, rich and thick like honey,' writes Joan Gould in her memoir *My Ghost*. Yet there is also a guilty sense of selfishness for the well partner that they should even consider their own needs, or how they might manage without the other. 'Did I delude myself then, because there were moments of heroism and devotion, that we were heroic?' continues Gould. 'Did I forget the fundamental enmity of the sick and the well, at 4 a.m., when the sick one needs to be heard and the well one needs to sleep, when the sick one knows this is it, and the well one knows this is not it, there are years ahead and someone has to fight with the plumber in the morning?'

Imogen dislikes the fact she is now in a new position of power, with the sense of sharing problems and having someone to offer solutions no longer there. 'We used to be far more collaborative, we discussed things and came to decisions together. He was always quite an argumentative sort of person, whereas now I hear him reflecting what I say rather than coming up with his own ideas, so the whole scope of our marriage has been diminished. One of the things I have enjoyed most is that imaginative exchange of ideas, and he is no longer that person, and while he is not an invalid he is quite fragile. I know that the best thing for him is to continue with normality but is that the best thing for me? There's a myth around the devoted spouse to the partner who becomes ill, and that makes me feel guilty because I don't really feel that way. I am happy to do it because it is the best compromise for the future. But do I really want to spend my whole life devoting myself to making things better for him? No! I want to live *my* life!'

She has thoughts sometimes that her life has been overly compromised when she still has so much health and energy as a woman in her mid-fifties. Sometimes she feels so lonely that she wonders whether she might be better off alone. 'But then I think of the companionship and the sense that I would rather keep him near because all that history together does mean a lot. It may not be the great passionate affair that it once was, but that sense of partnership and a shared past, and children having a place to come to and the feeling that we belong together as a family, not just as a couple, have great value. There is a sense of mutual support; I know he is on my side and that he will do whatever he can for me, and I feel the same for him. Underneath it all we are compatible, with an affectionate respect for each other, and the bad things that have happened don't outweigh that. There's more that keeps us together than drives us apart.'

The fact that she cannot confide her ambivalent feelings with her close friend and partner of more than thirty-four years imposes a distance between them which wasn't there before. 'It would be really damaging and would hurt him hugely to go to the edge by saying these things, and unimaginably cruel to leave him now. I don't think he has the resilience to pull himself out of it because he has already lost so much confidence in himself through the stroke. Instead, I want to make it possible for us to do things together that we still enjoy, cutting out the things he can't do but also steering it so that I can still do things on my own. I really love my work. I am fairly honest with myself about why I am doing this; I am not painting a rosy picture of the devoted wife, where everything is fabulous. I am trying to find a way to live with the knowledge of how fragile everything is. It's like living in a constant state of uncertainty.'

These new issues of dependency in later life throw people back to their childhood, the last time they would have felt a similar level of lack of control over their lives. There are some remarkable similarities in the intensity of emotions integral to the early and the later years of life – a fragility which makes both the young and the old fuss, overly anxious about small dangers, intensely focused on their own needs and ailments as the world seems to shrink once again to a life largely within the four walls of their home. 'I haven't been analysed myself for a couple of years now, but I would love some help coping with a body that has started to behave as if it were a psychotic infant,' says the octogenarian psychoanalyst Hannah Segal in an interview with the *Guardian* newspaper.[8] 'It's like some narcissistic baby. Nothing is good enough for it. Nothing is ever quite right.' Both the very young and the old lack status, and control over their lives, their needs sidelined as secondary to the all-important, wage-earning, productive economy. Both move at roughly the same slow pace, they fall over frequently and need others to pick them up and put them back on their feet again. Both rely heavily on having someone caring close by to give their lives shape and meaning, both fear being abandoned because they know they are so dependent emotionally, practically and sometimes financially on family members. Andrew Balfour tells me that often people with dementia like to hold dolls, and that it is not uncommon for those in residential homes to believe that their mothers and fathers are coming to get them, 'Which conveys the link better than anything, although we have to remember these are not children, these people are adults. But I think it helps us to understand the quality of their anxiety. The ways in which your earliest dependency relationships have been experienced will be the template you take into old age. People for whom that has been frightening or who haven't been able to rely on their caretakers will find that threatening, and are not likely to make very good patients. There can be all kinds of responses to the threat: people don't just exhibit fear at their vulnerability, they can go mad, like King Lear trying to project that vulnerability on to those around him through an imperious control.'

Once again we are reminded of the cyclical nature of our closest intimate relationships. Often we choose partners who feel familiar, who resemble our social background, tastes and aspirations in order to maximise the possibility of stability over time in what has to be one of the biggest gambles of our lives. But we cannot know how deepening intimacy and dependency within that relationship, or events such as having a child, infidelity, bereavement, becoming older or ill will affect the dynamic between us. Major life events can dredge up difficult emotions from the past for both of us. The more we love, the more we offer up the tender centre of our deepest selves to another, the more exposed we are to the same betrayals, failings and disappointments that we experienced in the past. Some can go through decades of stable and contented life together, building businesses, homes and families successfully, without the emotional difficulties of depression, breakdown, or unemployment to throw them back to this abyss until they hit the wall of truth about their limitations in midlife. The impact of ageing and encroaching retirement, the recognition that one might never achieve all one's ambitions, the first signs of lack of energy and ill health can then hit them full square, with devastating consequences for both partners in the relationship. For a carer who has never felt loved or looked after enough as a child, these new responsibilities can heighten their own emotional neediness.

Imogen has been thrust once again into the role of being the more responsible one, highlighting how she has consistently put her own desires last throughout her life. Her mother lost a baby when Imogen was small and 'I think she just lost interest in me; I became quite detached and self-contained. There was always this assumption that I was OK, and I have carried that with me, really. There were a number of times when I could have left the marriage, with the affair, over having always to be the one here for the children, but I didn't. I do think that perhaps I should have stood up for myself more as an independent person, to have had the confidence that I would be fine and he would make it through, but of course it's so hard even to talk about those things now that he is ill. It's been a hard slog, a bit like watching a child grow up. You have to let him find his own way and make his own choices, yet in many ways he can't.'

The more marked gender distinctions tend to blur a little with age: women become more independent, feisty, assertive, outspoken and less constrained by conventional notions of femininity, while the machismo of men tends to soften. For women the gendered aspects of caring for a more fragile spouse are all too apparent. When you have spent the best part of two decades as a mother, and then more than likely lavished a great deal of attention on both sets of elderly parents, it is much harder then to set limits on what you do when it comes to caring for a more fragile partner. The 'mother' is the one who holds everything together in a crisis, and is likely to want to protect her children from the worst of it. For older women who have grown up with more traditional gender stereotyping and been married to a man who has supported them financially, there is a presumption that this is just part of their job description as wives, and their needs as carers are hidden or downplayed. But younger women are not necessarily so self-deprecating. They have been influenced by a different historical time, so men who divorce and remarry much younger women in midlife perhaps risk their health and happiness in later life. These women do not necessarily want to spend decades compromising their own lives in order to look after an older, frailer man when they are likely to have the financial means to escape it.

Couples of a similar age understand where the boundaries and limitations of their generation lie. Tim feels that the fact Rose was able to forgive him unreservedly after his infidelities has played a huge part in their reconciliation and current happiness. 'Rose was amazing. How many people's partners would take them back after that? She never judged me or criticised me publicly, which made it easier for me to come back, and she never rubbed my nose in what I had done, which I still feel terrible about. I left her for someone thirteen years younger, and even though we got on I would sit round the table with her friends and think, I have nothing in common with these people, they don't seem to know anything or have the same range of experiences and that's very isolating. I wanted to go back to a world which I know had more breadth and interest in it. Perhaps the most important thing in a long-term partnership is to be tolerant because you are never going to build another relationship with roots like these. I realised then that nobody could ever understand me as Rose did. What matters now far more than anything is caring for each other.'

With those shared roots couples are able to temper the losses of later life with nostalgia. They can look back to better times, or to moments when they were needy and helped by their partner in the past. 'I think of all the times when he has supported me. I am the supporter now, and glad to be around to be able to do it for him,' says Louise. Her husband of more than fifty years is in his late eighties and very frail with cancer. They have twin beds and he gets up several times in the night to go to the loo. He can get back into bed but 'He gets all tangled up with the bedding so we do what we call the "duvet drop" – I lift it up and drop it down on him – and he's always terribly grateful. It is interesting that the marriage has come full circle. He was always so kind and patient with me when I had post-natal depression and he never held it against me, although I remember holding it against him quite a lot. I remember him saying once, "When you are depressed the Church gets quite a bashing, doesn't it," because it was quite a thing being a minister's wife, never being able to let your hair down. I also get a carer's allowance for him now, so I feel that's one of my jobs, to put the duvet back on.'

Older couples have to adjust their expectations, focusing on what they can do together, in spite of the pain and immobility, rather than on what they cannot. 'We used to enjoy walking, and took a flask of tea with us, which he can't do any more so that's sad. But it has been so good watching Wimbledon together recently and talking about all the players we have watched and enjoyed in the past, like Jimmy Connors. He dropped off to sleep even more than I did, but he was there sharing it and that was lovely,' says Louise. When couples reach their final years after close on a lifetime together, they understand that relationship can never be a balanced tally of quid pro quo. There is no obligation to give back exactly what you get. Each offers something personal and particular to the other. They cope by focusing on every tiny positive spark in their partner, and attributing all of their negative behaviours to the disease or affliction. They fashion a new intimacy between them based on kindness, physical affection and attention paid to the smallest needs, which bears a striking resemblance to the intensity of intimacy between parents and children now that sex is rarer or redundant as the primary building block for togetherness. 'We've both had operations, and that has altered our sex lives,' says Rose. 'But we touch and cuddle each other more than we've ever done in our lives together.'

Rose is aware that her illness – bowel cancer – has shocked Tim but, 'He has been fantastic, I have had accidents since the operation and that's been so embarrassing and demoralising, but he has been there for me all the time, cleaning up after me, and has never once made me feel bad about it.' For Tim, this caring is part of love after a lifetime together. 'You get more fragile physically, but in my case our relationship has been strengthened by that fragility. I just want to make sure she is as content and as happy as it is possible to be without my being overbearing or demanding, and I want her to carry on with as normal a life as possible. I don't talk about the problem unless she raises it, and the next few years are going to be quite tough. She will need another operation, and sometimes it does upset me. You have jobs in marriage and they change through time, and it is love that makes it easier to do the less pleasant things for our relationship as we get older, not duty. I want to do these things. She was the same when I had my heart bypass – she literally saved my life by forcing me to have the operation when I was reluctant. Then after the operation I hadn't eaten because the food was so diabolical, and she brought me a poached salmon sandwich. She knew exactly what I would like and I thought, "Thank God, I am going to live!" That tiny act comes from knowing someone well and caring enough, and I try to do the same for her.'

Time feels so finite now that they manage to talk occasionally about death in terms of how the other might live if they should be the one to die first, but not the other way around. 'Seeing Rose unwell brings me up short, and I start to think, How much longer have we got together? I worry about the cancer coming back and get upset . . . I couldn't stay in this house without her. We've brought up our children here, had friends here, had rows here and made big decisions here over the past thirty-five years. I have thought about it a bit, but I haven't said anything to Rose.' But by addressing the subject at all they are helping each other to face the inevitable, when one of them will be alone. Rose wants Tim to retire completely, and they have plans to sell their home at some point and move into central London so that they can go out easily with shops and cafés close by. But 'He is determined that he won't get physically frail and has gone back to the gym. Almost every day he says, "I am not going to get old, I am not going to let myself fall apart, so there is perhaps a little reluctance to accept how things are because of course he will get old and frail,' says Rose.

Louise knows that her husband, who is ten years older than her and terminally ill with cancer, will go first but that doesn't make things any easier. 'It's going to be very sad when the end comes. I do think about it; things like, If it's a heart attack what will I do, ring 999? I think about the funeral quite a lot too because he won't talk about what he wants. I haven't asked him about it but I must try, I don't want to upset him, but perhaps I ought to say, "Have you written down what you would like?" I am avoiding the subject, but maybe he is too. We sit here and read the paper together, and I wonder sometimes what it will be like when it is just me sitting here by myself reading the paper, and what the nights will be like alone. It's important to think about it, but actually it is unimaginable because we've lived a lifetime together and this is bound to be the biggest shock of all.'

There are plenty of moments earlier on in the lifespan of a long marriage when both partners feel such intense loathing for the other that they have fantasies of widowhood. But when it actually happens the effects can be devastating, so profound that it comes top of the list of stressful life events on the Holmes and Rahe scale. The shock and loss can trigger serious illness and depression, and it is not uncommon for people to die of grief. One study following 4,486 widowers aged over fifty-five found that 213 – 40 per cent more than the rate for those still married – died within six months of their wife's death.[9] It's a form of grief entirely different to any other previously experienced, save perhaps the agonising experience of losing a child, which most parents are thankfully spared. We expect our parents to die one day. We imagine what that might be like, even as children, and when it happens, there is great sadness, the loneliness of being an orphan and next in line; regret over past differences, time wasted and things left unsaid, but we continue to live our independent lives. When your spouse dies, a large part of you dies too; your history has been so interconnected emotionally, mentally and physically that their absence provokes a temporary madness, a sense of meaninglessness because every aspect of your daily life has previously been so entwined. 'Grief turns out to be a place none of us know until we reach it,' writes Joan Didion in her memoir *The Year of Magical Thinking*. 'We might expect that we will be prostrate, inconsolable, crazy with loss. We do not expect to be literally crazy, cool customers who believe that their husband is about to return and need his shoes.'

Marcus's wife was diagnosed with terminal cancer in her late fifties. They had seventeen more months together before she died three years ago. During those months they eased up on work commitments and travelled together to places she had always wanted to visit with their three children. Their relationship worked, Marcus tells me, because they were always honest and open with each other, and with that fundamental basis of trust they could talk frankly about her death. She wrote the guest list for her funeral, and even visited venues for the wake afterwards. 'We've always shared the blackest humour,' says Marcus. 'My wife was brought up a Roman Catholic and believed in life after death whereas I don't, so I said to her, "If you give me a sign from the other side – and it's got to be a really good one like a hole in one – then I might convert." It hasn't happened yet, but you never know.' Marcus, like many bereaved partners, found himself consumed by the administration of wrapping up his wife's estate in the days and weeks after her death. 'You think, Christ, I'm two death certificates short, I didn't realise Barclaycard would need one. When they ask you how many death certificates you want say twelve. But then at night . . . crikey . . . when you find yourself really missing that person, the grief is overwhelming and so private. Or you're driving along and it could be a piece of music or just a thought that triggers it and you have to stop because you're just sobbing.'

Friends and family rally round in the days and weeks surrounding the funeral, but once that ritual period of mourning has passed, the bereaved spouse gets down to the real process of grieving their loss every minute of the day, alone. The final 'glass shade', that protective bubble of privacy, which cuts off a marriage and its difficulties from the rest of the world, is never greater than around bereavement. Death is something which we all now fear to the point of phobia. The bereaved are pitied but avoided, few know what to say and may even cross the street to avoid having to say anything at all. There is a sense that bad luck may be catching, for the ultimate fear is that it could happen to you, and widows often find themselves excluded from other couple activities. We're shielded from death by a prolonged life expectancy and the hospitalisation of the terminally ill. We escape from the discomfort of having to talk about it, and therefore face our own mortality, by assuming that the bereaved need to be left alone to grieve, or soothed with platitudes such as 'time heals'. But for the widowed, and most are women – 70 per cent of bereaved over sixty-fives are female compared to 22 per cent of men, with women living longer alone, on average fifteen years as opposed to six years for men[10] – the grief is beyond anything imaginable as the truth slowly sinks in that this is, indeed, for ever. 'How often – will it be for always? – how often will the vast emptiness astonish me like a complete novelty and make me say, "I never realised my loss until this moment?" The same leg is cut off time after time. The first plunge of the knife into the flesh is felt again and again,' writes C. S. Lewis in his classic essay on the death of his wife, *A Grief Observed*. 'You tell me, "She goes on." But my heart and body are crying out, come back, come back. I know that the thing I want is exactly the thing I can never get. The old life, the jokes, the drinks, the arguments, the lovemaking, the tiny, heartbreaking commonplace.'

Marcus too misses his wife of twenty years because of the day-to-day way their lives became so entwined in what Joan Didion describes as 'the unending absence which follows, the void, the very opposite of meaning'. It is a void, which no amount of consolation from others can fill. 'People say time is a healer, but time doesn't heal the pain. The scars and hurt are still there, and will remain until the day I die,' says Marcus. 'Everywhere I look, everywhere I go there are reminders of the life we had together, and the passage of time makes things different but the reminders are still there. It's just that I don't think about her 100 per cent of the time any more; it drops after a while to about 80 per cent and now, perhaps, three years later, I only think of her 30 per cent of the time. It was a fantastic marriage, she was a remarkable woman and nothing will ever change that fact. We counselled each other a lot, and I miss that like mad. It's not just doing all of the donkey work, but it suddenly occurred to me the other day that everything that comes through the door, every phone call, I now have to deal with entirely alone without that counsellor to share it with. My friends were fantastic and I would wish everyone the same support, but the grief is so private that you can't really share that properly with anyone else. Whatever else happens in my life, the loss of that relationship will always be the same.'

Once again our partner throws up an invaluable mirror to our fragility, only this time through their absence. 'You keep on missing that person and realising this is concrete, and that makes you think about your own mortality,' says Marcus. He avoids any overt self-pity by focusing on the fact that by dying at the age of fifty-eight, it was far worse for his wife in that she has missed out on twenty years of her life. He has found a new girlfriend. For those who are older the sudden isolation can be much more alarming. There is no one else to focus on now but themselves, which brings home the fact that they are older too, and that much closer to death. There is no one there now to help them when they need it. 'There's no one to fasten your bra if you've broken a wrist, drive you back from your cataract operation or bring you soup and newspapers if you're laid up,' writes Katharine Whitehorn in her autobiography *Selective Memory*. 'Lucky if you have a friend or a sister, awkward to the point of tears if you're quite on your own.'

The greatest evidence perhaps of the importance of marriage and lifelong relationship for our physical, emotional and mental well-being is the great void that it leaves in its wake when one partner dies. The triumph of love lies in the small daily kindnesses and considerations, which make one feel valued, seen and understood, not in the great romantic, gushing gestures. We need that gentle kindness of intimacy most in our later years when we are fragile and vulnerable, and with the deep knowledge that comes from a shared past we help each other to cope with the inevitabilities of our own demise. The presence of a committed partner gives our lives meaning because they were there too. They witnessed the highs and lows of bringing up children, the challenges we faced at work and in our careers; they helped us through illnesses and personal turmoil, and they shared the most intimate moments of delight and laughter. That witness makes those experiences tangible, real and meaningful. These are the triumphs of true love. You cannot ever return to the person you were before that partnership began because you will have been so profoundly changed by it. That is the big difference between the end of an affair and the end of a marriage in all its senses. You never stop missing that person's presence in your life. 'Losing your husband has two separate aspects: there's missing the actual man, your lover, his quirks, his kindness, his thinking,' writes Katharine Whitehorn in *Selective Memory*. 'But marriage is also the water in which you swim, the land you live in: the habits, the assumptions you share about the future, about what's funny or deplorable, about the way the house is run – or should be; what Anthony Burgess called a whole civilisation, a culture, "a shared language of grunt and touch". You don't "get over" the man, though you do after a year or two get over the death; but you have to learn to live in another country in which you're an unwilling refugee.'

12

THE MARRIAGE OF TRUE MINDS

In 1838, Charles Darwin divided a piece of paper into two columns with the words 'Marry' on one side and 'Not marry' on the other – 'This is the question'. Under 'Marry' he listed children, home and 'Charms of music and female chit-chat', as positive gains; under 'Not marry' he listed 'Freedom to go where one liked' and 'Not forced to visit relatives' as two of the main advantages to life as a single man. Then, on the other side of the paper, he concluded that should he marry, 'I never should know French, or see the continent, or go to America, or go up in a balloon, or take solitary trips in Wales – poor slave, you will be worse than a Negro – and then horrid poverty . . . Never mind, my boy – cheer up – one cannot live this solitary life, with groggy old age, friendless and cold and childless, staring one in one's face, already beginning to wrinkle. Never mind, trust to chance – keep a sharp look out. There is many a happy slave.'

Committing to a relationship doesn't have to be this stark a choice any more. With enough of a sense of self and respect for the autonomy of our partner, we can continue to pursue our own interests *and* relish the rewards of intimacy. Age-old notions of self-sacrifice and conformity to presumed assumptions of how couples should be together are less pronounced. Nowadays we can tailor partnerships to suit us better as two individuals sharing a life together. The best relationships allow each partner to relish their sense of individuality within that union and not feel compromised, as Darwin found when he married his cousin Emma Wedgwood in 1839. They had ten children and were married for forty-three years. Near the end of his life he wrote in his autobiography: 'I marvel at my good fortune that she, so infinitely my superior in every single moral quality, consented to be my wife. She has been my wise adviser and cheerful comforter throughout life, which without her would have been during a very long period a miserable one from ill health. She has earned the love and admiration of every soul near her.'[1]

The tussle between individuality and commitment feels greater now perhaps because we have complete freedom of choice. 'I've come across couples who won't buy a house together unless there's a room for him, a room for her and a room that can be theirs together, which would have been unheard of when I first started practising,' says relationship counsellor Pam Fawcett. 'Plus people are marrying later and have established themselves. They don't want to give things up, and why should they? But that does mean that it is harder to establish balance and boundaries.' It means that everything is up for negotiation. It means that we have to take complete responsibility for making our relationships more robust from the inside with greater understanding of the psychological processes which affect intimacy, rather than trusting everything to luck or love. It means that should the relationship end, both have to accept their part in its demise with good grace. Stereotypical assumptions of relationship, with the polar extremes of romanticised bliss or the mind-numbing boredom of being trapped within the 'trouble and strife' of a miserable marriage lead us to believe that all relationships are similar and consequently out of our control. 'Practically every poem, every bit of art, every film is about romance,' says Florence, who has been living with her female partner for more than ten years. 'But then all the novels about marriage that I have ever read are very negative. It's all about how awful it is, when it isn't awful. You have to have elements of romantic love but that is impossible to sustain, and we have no cultural model or template for that much more important part of loving other than our own parents.'

As the external forces, such as religion or the difficulties and stigma surrounding divorce which kept marriages together in the past, have grown weaker, the omnipotent force of romance seems to have invaded our hearts and minds as the only way to be together. 'It's a lovely marriage in many respects, but I think it is lacking in all the tick-boxes that one would expect from a love affair such as passion, and that merged life, sharing decisions and an intellectual balance. We have such a different way of looking at things. I know it works but that's only possible when you realise that you don't have to get everything from one person and that infinitely more important is that sense of ease, which seems like such a low-key demand,' says Alice, who has been married for more than twenty years. In spite of fifteen years of marriage and three children, Juliet still wonders whether she is Philip's *grand amour*, such is the power of the notion of One True Love. 'I know that sounds mad but when we were younger, every summer he would go off with one of his sisters – he never wanted to go somewhere with me, so early on I think I felt a sense of rejection, even though in the end he did choose me. He used to criticise me whenever I had any romantic notion about finding the right partner through fate, and we ended up getting married because he felt it was time. There is always this nagging question in my mind of whether he would have found "The One" had he met someone else, and I will never know the answer to that. I know I was a good logical choice. I used to have fairy-tale ideas of how there was only one man destined for you, and I believed that love was this mystical union where two people became one. Now I am much more realistic, and I know it's not like that. You're two separate people who share a life, and it's amazing how much is left unsaid when you say so much over the years. Maybe that's what keeps you together, the space between you.'

Our expectations of love and marriage are unprecedented. Never before have couples lived in such exclusive isolation, held together by a romantic ideal rather than more pragmatic social and economic realities. We expect a great deal from love – that it should be enough to produce just and amicable relationships when, as Erich Fromm writes in *The Art of Loving*, 'Love is an art, just as living is an art; if we want to learn how to love we must proceed in the same way we have to proceed if we want to learn any other art, say music, painting, carpentry or the art of medicine or engineering.' We expect a great deal of each other – that our partner should be sexually appealing as well as a stable companion; an intellectual equal who will also be a good parent; someone with whom we are completely compatible, sharing a similar outlook, attitudes, values and pursuits who will remain solvent and never be boring – the perfect complement to how we imagine ourselves, or, more usually, would like to. It is very easy then to feel disappointed, as if we are somehow missing out on the 'real thing'. These unrealistic expectations of love and of each other are recent developments. There was little expectation prior to 1960 that love could or should last a lifetime, and it was not until the late twentieth century that the majority of women told pollsters that love outweighed all other considerations when it came to choosing a partner.[2] Now, ever more extravagant and seemingly 'traditional' wedding ceremonies try to pin down the unreliability of love with ritual. True love is perceived as something transforming, sexually electric and lasting – the main incentive for marriage when all of the research suggests that the first chemical fix fades within two to three years. 'Passion depends upon uncertainty and brevity in regard to time,' writes Eugène Marcel Prévost in *The Chastity of Married Life*, 'while the hours of a married couple are inordinately long and regular.'

There is no soul mate who fits every dimension of our personality hand in glove, so that we never have to argue. There are hundreds of thousands of people out there with whom we could create something unique, for it is their individuality, their very difference, that highlights who we are and opens the door into an exhilarating new world, which is their world. The risks of commitment are now perceived as being so high and the pool to choose from so great that dating agencies computing the likelihood of compatibility are highly lucrative enterprises. But it is how we deal with the inevitable incompatibilities between us that matter in a relationship. The idea that we will one day fall in love with 'The One' obviates the need to assess the family background, the ambitions, the emotional insecurities and expectations of that person with the same sort of scrutiny we would conduct without hesitation over other important aspects of adult life such as a business deal or buying a house. The truth of good loving, as I hope this book has shown, is that it grows with time, with experience, through adversity, negotiation, confrontation, compromise and forgiveness. The modern companionate 'marriage', whether that be a couple who are cohabiting, gay, straight, living together or apart, can only be held together by its two most important protagonists. That requires particular skills: greater self-awareness about the way we bring our own emotional insecurities and disappointments with life into the relationship; greater honesty about who we are and what we want from life as well as from each other; greater trust in the other as an autonomous being with their own separate needs and interests; conscious efforts to bridge the distances between us when they get too wide, particularly physically during sex; as well as greater tolerance of each other's weaknesses and mistakes. These are skills which we can only learn and fashion ourselves over time, through experience, when there is commitment.

A good relationship is something that we achieve rather than the natural consequence of love or mythical notions of compatibility, which lure us into a sense of complacency. The myths of romantic love allow us to make excuses for our lack of moral behaviour, with 'I couldn't help myself' regarding sexual infidelity, or 'I love him but am not in love with him any more' about divorce. These myths allow us to sit back while our most precious partnership is buffeted by seismic new pressures and expectations – that one person has to provide you with everything that you want from life, or that a relationship has to be always happy, perfect, sexually and emotionally fulfilling.

The belief that relationship needs to be protected by an opaque bubble of privacy at all times also creates misleading assumptions and feelings of inadequacy as we compare our own experiences to idealised and romanticised notions of how a relationship should be. Abuse and violence get hidden, the prospect of divorce a terrifying spectre which we would rather not think about, instead of a reality which has to be addressed at the earliest opportunity in order to limit its likelihood. When few divulge what really goes on behind the walls of their lifelong relationship, the myth endures that most people manage them with ease, when most hover close to the abyss at one time or another, and only manage to find a stable, lasting peace by working through those immense difficulties together.

Perhaps the most misleading romantic myth of all inculcates the importance of merging, the blurring of boundaries, the loss of a sense of yourself as an individual as you give up things that matter to you for the sake of relationship, when the most successful couples retain a profound sense of their own autonomy. The concept of merged souls may make for electrifying sex at the beginning of a relationship but it can also inspire dread, leading many a 'commitment-phobe' to flee, fearing being engulfed. It's a recipe for dishonesty if that love is to become a lifelong partnership, for you can only maintain fantasies of merging if you do not talk about the things which highlight the differences between you, and that creates a separateness rather than a true bond as you manage the transition from that first passionate enmeshing to a relationship with the potential to stand the test of time. That couple who seem so in love, so compatible and content because they are never apart, will only manage to maintain that stability if neither partner places difficult demands on the relationship and if their own personal problems within the relationship are avoided rather than confronted. We embrace the notion that we have one true soul mate somewhere in order to avoid the truth that we are essentially alone in this world. 'The real fierceness of desire, the real heat of a passion long continued and withering up the soul of a man is the craving for identity with the woman that he loves,' writes Ford Madox Ford in *The Good Soldier*. 'We are all so afraid, we are all so alone, we all so need from the outside world the assurance of our own worthiness to exist.'

We are born alone and we die alone, but committed relationship can offer unparalleled opportunities for a rich sense of significance throughout life. When trust grows, each can look into the mirror that their partner holds up to their behaviour, their attitudes and their personality. With the deepening intimacy that comes with trust, uncomfortable truths and emotional insecurities often resurface. With the help of that mirror we can begin to understand how we erect barriers to protect our deepest vulnerabilities, and how we heave blame and anxiety on to the other person as if they were an extension of ourselves. Love with commitment gives us an essential springboard to aim for something higher, as our partner encourages us to reach for a dream, to achieve because they believe in us. They can also bring us up short, challenge our arrogant presumptions or prejudices and provide an essential ballast for debate, strategies for dealing with dilemmas at work, or difficulties with friends and family.

At its best a relationship has the power to make us more self-aware and mature. At its worst, it can devastate a person's sense of self-worth. It is only when you know who you are and can maintain that sense of integrity and autonomy within a lifelong relationship that you are able to love freely and therefore equally. Your partner should never be more important to you than your relationship with yourself, and it is only with that firm sense of identity that you can build a loving relationship based on mutual respect where your needs and your voice are not diminished. Research seems to indicate that the more emotionally mature and confident you are as an independent person, the more able you are to respect the spaces between you in a relationship. You are also more likely to settle with someone who is quite different to yourself and therefore be open to greater reflection and change when conflict highlights your weaknesses as well as your strengths.[3] 'Love that lasts, ultimately, is love that mutually maximises self-esteem,' writes Robert Solomon in his book *About Love*. 'Love that fails, love that falls apart, is passion or companionship that leaves the self untouched, or worse, that degrades the self and renders the shared self something less than it was before love came along.'

It's an upward spiral. With greater self-assurance you are less likely to erect emotional defences because you trust that exposing your bad bits will not drive your lover away. Good loving teaches us how to be better people. 'I never really understood the importance of manners until I met Lestor. My mother never says "please" or "thank you", but his manners are impeccable and he regularly ticks me off for mine,' says Ruby. 'They matter even more in a marriage because they show respect and courtesy.' Gerry and Iris met in their mid-thirties after each had been through a failed first marriage. 'When I got married the first time I was a bit naive. Nobody tells you how to be married,' says Gerry. 'But over the years Iris has taught me a lot about empathy and thinking about other people's feelings so I think I am a lot more caring and supportive as a person.' Sue feels that 'Dean brings out the better qualities in me. That's not to say my personality is dependent upon somebody else, but certainly the person you are with will affect how you are. If you feel loved you are naturally more confident, and if I disagree with him about something I can say so and not feel like I must be wrong or can't speak up.' There is nothing new in the notion that we can become better people because of our partners. 'You shall polish and refine my sentiments of life and manners, banish all the unsocial and ill-natured particles in my composition,' wrote John Adams, vice-president to George Washington and the second president of the United

States, in a letter to his wife Abigail in 1764, 'and form me to that happy temper, that can reconcile a quick discernment with a perfect candour.'[4] Their marriage lasted fifty-four years.

'Marriage helps a person integrate all the opposite values of life one might otherwise manage to avoid or remain ignorant of,' write the psychologists Arthur and Elaine Aron in their book *Love and the Expansion of Self*. Many of the happier couples I met talked about how their personalities seemed to complement each other and create a more rounded sense of wholeness because of the differences between them. 'Tom reins me in and I give him a kick,' says Carol. They met in 1984. 'If it had been down to me I would have spent all our money, but if it had been all down to him we would still be in the one-bedroomed flat we bought twenty years ago. I've pushed all the time – let's have more children, up the mortgage and go on more holidays. If he'd been like me we would probably be living broke in a caravan, whereas if I'd been more like him we'd have just had the one child instead of three.' Katrina feels that David has opened up her worldview. 'He is much more intellectual than I am, he reads newspapers and knows more about European history and politics. I've come from a very conventional middle-class family with no problems, and because of David I have learned that most people do have some issues and to be more understanding of that, rather than simply assume that everyone is fine and what's all the fuss about.' Molly is quite clear about the fact that she is 'The motivator. I bought a car because I thought it was a nice colour, and he went visibly pale but walked away with a smile on his face. It's when he tries to make me think like him that I lose that spontaneity, and I can't do that because if I were more like him it would be so boring. I think I have made him more spontaneous, though, to just do things for the hell of it, and he has made me concentrate a little more, to listen to what people have to say rather than talking over them.' Oliver says that Jerome 'Complements me hugely by calming me down. I can be quite volatile, my work is quite stressful and I have to be quite strong there, which sometimes leads me to overcompensate and get into conflict situations quite easily. But he is much more serene, and I feel I have become more stable emotionally since we have been together.'

Character strengths and weaknesses are highlighted and compensated for by opposite traits in our partner. Amy has come to understand how messy and unpunctual she can be because her husband likes to be on time and will plan things beforehand. 'Our personalities are so opposite in some ways, but I need him because I have no concept of how time passes or how to be organised.' Megan feels similarly about her marriage. 'I am much more outgoing and comfortable talking to strangers, whereas Charlie is more reticent, so in that way we do balance each other out. But I am a procrastinator and he is far more organised. If something difficult needs doing I will push it to one side, whereas he will say, "We have to sort this now," and will make me sit down and address it. He's tenacious: if something is broken and needs fixing he will just do it, whereas I will look at it for weeks.'

Jaya and Charu have been together for more than twenty-five years. 'We're both strong in different ways,' says Jaya. 'I'm the extrovert and the more social one, and she is much more grounded in the relationship, very fair and thoughtful about things, whereas I am more compulsive. She has taught me a lot about listening, really listening to other people. I have definitely become a nicer person, more sensitive to other people. I have a quieter kind of confidence, which means I don't have to be so much of an extrovert, I don't feel I have to be out there to prove myself. After twenty-five years together we have watched each other grow. She was with me when my father died, and helped me through that, and I have supported her through difficulties with her parents. Her mother has undermined her so much over the years, and I am forever trying to make her feel good about who she is. She has loosened her ties with her family in the last few years in ways that I would never have thought possible. I have seen her grow in terms of her confidence as a woman, and as a woman in the world, which is wonderful. We have been through life changes, job changes, illnesses and all the ups and downs, and she is someone I feel completely at one with. She only has to smile in a certain way and I feel blessed.'

Love means wanting to improve ourselves in our partner's eyes. Love allows us to feel better about ourselves because we need to give, and to consider the needs of another as much as our own to feel connected to the wider world. Love allows us to accept our own imperfections, our flawed or ageing physiques, our short tempers and failings because we have no choice but to accept those of our partner. Love allows us to hate at times, to expose our deepest, darkest demons. But that doesn't mean that each has to be swallowed whole by the other for their relationship to thrive. In happier relationships each feels that their sense of individuality is enhanced by the differences between them. Each feels able to pursue independent interests within a framework of trust, mutuality and respect. A rather cheesy metaphor would be that the relationship is stronger because each has their own boat to sail in. Currents might take them to different places as circumstances change through life, but they keep both boats moving in the same direction. A fitting personal anecdote springs to mind. For some insane reason we decided to hire a canoe to travel down the River Wye to Hay one summer. My husband quickly assumed the role of captain, with instructions on how to paddle, and then when I tried to do things my way he declared that it was easier if I didn't do anything at all, so I sat back huffing away in self-righteous indignation and admired the view. He lost control of the boat in a strong current, crashing into the bank, and we capsized beneath a weeping willow tree. Luckily the youngest child could swim and we didn't have the dog with us, for he would surely have been swept away by the current and never seen again. We finally managed to right the canoe and haul ourselves back into the boat and sat shivering, soaked to the skin, as we continued downriver. Had we hired two different boats we would probably have remained dry, each in control of our own destiny and able to set our own pace.

A sense of self as an autonomous being is essential to the health and stability of a relationship if it is to stand the test of time. With a strong, mature sense of our own individuality we are more able to negotiate and argue as equals, more able to provide stability and role models for our children, more able to withstand the stress of family life and to maintain dignity and honour through a divorce or separation, should that partnership fail. Two heads are better than one when it comes to dealing with life's adversities. Parents of severely disabled children who are happily married report less depression and more positive family relations than their maritally distressed counterparts.[5] Differences in the way that we communicate, in our attitude to argument and in our temperaments seem to help rather than hinder when coping with extreme stress. In studies of couples with a seriously ill child, similar problem-solving skills in both parents did not necessarily lead to greater marital satisfaction. It sometimes helped when one could compensate for the other. When fathers managed the crisis by withdrawing into work, they put pressure on their partners to behave less emotionally and focus more on simply caring for the child on a day-to-day basis. Mothers were then allowed to vent their rage and distress with their partners and force them to become more emotional and involved with the routines of their child's daily care. It may be that when both partners like to approach stress pragmatically by tackling the smaller problems, they get competitive about controlling those aspects of their lives together and neither takes responsibility for addressing the equally important emotional burdens provoked by family illness.[6]

When Ella was made redundant, her girlfriend Philippa pressed her to fight for compensation. 'Ella would have just walked away from it, but I wouldn't have put up with it so I certainly won't let her put up with it. I am much more Machiavellian, so I am helping her to put a case together,' says Philippa. Not long after her redundancy, Ella was taken seriously ill with secondary cancer, a brain tumour needing surgery and radiotherapy. 'We had a lot of things going on but we had to cope with it, and that has definitely made us stronger because we have an honesty now between us,' says Ella. 'Philippa was there for me through all the darkest hours. There were times when I felt I might not make it. When you're faced with something like that it is easy to surrender and to forget how strong you can be, and Philippa stopped me doing that. I think I got to understand then that if you love someone for their faults, that's what real love is.' The love that comes with accepting a person for their weaknesses as well as their strengths means that even divorced couples can come together to support each other at times of deep stress. Julia was married to Robert for twenty-four years. Shortly after they divorced, amicably, their son died in an accident on a gap year and they mourned together as his parents, supporting each other through a gruelling inquest. 'I felt responsible for Robert, and I took care of everything because that was what I did when we were married. Robert collapsed with grief; it aged him literally overnight so I was very protective of him. He has always been so fragile.'

Feminism has had a profoundly beneficial effect on the nature of a woman's sense of self, and our understanding of the way that issues of control can affect the balance of power within a relationship. The most hardy and nourishing partnerships are based on good friendship, a respect for each other's differences and a sense of equity where neither feels humiliated, diminished or compromised to the point of self-sacrifice for the sake of the other. Total equality is never possible. There are times in every relationship when one of the pair is weaker and more dependent on the other, with the arrival of children, or as a result of ill health or unemployment. When a partnership is based on principles of fairness it is more likely to be strong enough to take that load. Long-term commitment allows each their turn, to dare to compromise without feeling exploited. 'If I made my husband a cup of tea I would feel resentful about it because he had let me down in so many other ways,' says Madeline. 'But with Ralph I don't feel that way at all. I will gladly do it, or the cooking, and never resent it because he fulfils his part of the bargain. We share a life together, every aspect of it. We laugh a lot and it feels balanced.'

Equality in relationship never means being the same; it means respecting and relishing the substantial differences between you. It means continually talking to each other so that problems and decision-making are shared, for neither wants the other to feel unappreciated, resentful or unloved. It means there is less room for abuse or issues over who controls the relationship or how you live, for each feels an equal ability to influence the other. It means each wanting to empower the other to ensure you get your needs met both inside and outside the relationship because you care for each other. In more equal partnerships couples presume less and negotiate more. They also have more to talk to each other about. Their roles become so similar that they are almost interchangeable, with each able to take on any task. Consequently you are more likely to show empathy and understanding for each other's difficulties because you experience the world in much the same way. And there is rarely a dull moment. 'Even though we fantasise about Juliet being able to give up work because she feels so torn about it and so tired, and I would love our house to be a little cleaner, I'll admit that,' says Philip, 'I admire her hugely for sticking with her profession. That's partly what makes our relationship successful, that I am never disappointed in her. I am astonished that I have spent twenty-five years with her and have never got bored. I admire her, need her, respect her and I like the fact that I can never predict what she will think or say.'

Much of what we used to take for granted about how to make a committed relationship work is in a state of flux, and it is easy at times of uncertainty to long nostalgically for a time when everything must have been much more stable, when 'men were men and women were women' and everyone knew their place. We forget the chronic hardships, the invisibility and the ill health of women. 'Records of the early seventeenth-century physician Robert Napier concerning more than a 1,000 female patients treated for mental illness conclude that they were especially troubled by the oppression they experienced as wives and daughters,' writes Marilyn Yalom in her book *A History of the Wife*. Some marriages with kind husbands bore the hallmarks of a happy partnership, but with such deep inequities embedded within the institution, many more were limited by the constraints of a patriarchal set-up. As Charlotte Perkins Gilman writes in *Women and Economics*, published in 1898, 'The woman is narrowed by the home and the man is narrowed by the woman.' Even the 1950s seem to hold a rosy glow for the overstretched working mother doing a double shift at work and then at home. When we feel overwhelmed by cramming thirty-six hours of responsibility into each day, it's easy to imagine that it must somehow have been easier when marriages had to last until 'death do us part', and women could just stay home all day long dusting and making cakes. We forget that there was little in the way of contraception, divorce was difficult, abortion against the law and that these were years of a more pernicious kind of drudgery, where men were considered henpecked if they did any housework or were seen pushing a pram, where women could only be wives and mothers and that consequently rates of depression soared.

An integral part of that social revolution has been the changing role of women, and consequently there's a strong tendency still to blame feminism and working women for every failed marriage. However, all the academic and anecdotal evidence suggests unequivocally that relationships are strengthened by more equal partnerships, not weakened by them.[7] The stress on working couples, which can indeed lead to divorce or separation, comes from the conflicts between work and family that earning a living so often provokes, in *both* genders. When either men or women work long hours, do shift work or have no choice but to spend time apart it is harder to maintain the relationship. Family breakdown is more common among couples living with routine work-related separations.[8] It is our external culture which compromises families, piling on the pressure by refusing to adapt enough to the new needs of working people with a more family-friendly culture. Too many highly educated women still feel that they have to choose between pursuing their careers and being good mothers. Others, lower down the social scale, feel they have no choice but to work because their families can no longer survive by relying on the male breadwinner alone. There are still huge differences between 'his' marriage and 'hers', but less so than there used to be as individual couples, across all social classes, thrash out a fairer balance between themselves without a template to rely on, hammering out a more bespoke arrangement which often flies in the face of the more stereotypical assumptions of masculinity and femininity or motherhood and fatherhood. 'When it comes to any particular marital practice or behaviour there may be nothing new under the sun,' writes Stephanie Coontz in *Marriage, A History*, 'but when it comes to the overall place of marriage in society and the relationship between husbands and wives, nothing in the past is anything like what we have today, even if it may look similar at first glance.'

We are pioneers, and equitable relationships have to be worked at. All of the evidence suggests that we are succeeding. 'The most successful marriages combine greater equality, two incomes, shared social ties and a strong commitment to marital permanence,' write the authors, sociologists at the University of Pennsylvania in their book *Alone Together*, which compares survey evidence of marriages in 1980 to those in 2000. 'After being in a state of flux for half a century, contemporary marriage may be moving towards a new synthesis of institutional, companionate and individualistic features with generally positive consequences for men, women and children.' When we achieve that partnership, that marriage of true minds, we have more support when it comes to bringing up children or during times of stress or adversity. It is entirely positive to have to reassess and renegotiate our relationship at regular intervals. It means that we are less likely to slip into complacency or travel down separate tracks. It means there is always the possibility of change and renewal, for greater closeness and understanding when both now have such a vested interest in that relationship continuing. With a sense of shared commitment, support and history, couples who surmount the inevitable hurdles in their relationship and find a deeper peace also find their time together to be happier in later life. 'There are actually many females in the world, and some among them are beautiful,' Karl Marx wrote to his beloved wife Jenny in 1856 after thirteen years of marriage. 'But where could I find again a face, whose every feature, even every wrinkle, is a reminder of the greatest and sweetest memories of my life?'[9]

Lasting intimacy is good for our health and sense of well-being and investing in that relationship could be the best insurance policy of our lives. A lengthy, committed relationship provides us with a central defining narrative now that so many other identifying aspects of life seem transient and less reliable. Few jobs are secure, local community structures such as the Church and extended family have dwindled as couples move more frequently following work, housing and better schools for their children. Many feel they barely know their neighbours. The numbers of people living in the average household have declined in the past two decades and there is an increase in the numbers of people who live alone, which often means there are fewer people in the immediate vicinity to confide in or rely upon.[10, 11]

We are living at a time of fast-paced change and instability. Global warming and financial meltdown have created great anxiety about our future. Trust in state provision of health care or local services has been undermined, so it is important to know that those who find themselves content in a committed partnership tend to live longer, healthier lives, and that the longer two people are together, the more cumulative the protective factors of that partnership.[12] Our partner is the first line of defence when it comes to ill health or disability. They provide care when we are sick, encourage healthier behaviour and can reduce stress or stress-related illness, provided the relationship is sound. With demographic change and rising numbers of people over sixty, as well as diminished savings and pension arrangements to buy in the help that the frail and aged need, the care and support that comes with the commitment of a lifelong partnership could be the key to a healthier and happier time from midlife onwards. Rising costs of living mean that the pooled resources of the family become even more important. Bringing up children is now so expensive that even seemingly well-off middle-class families find themselves stretched. The TUC's Commission on Vulnerable Employment published in May 2008 found that half of all children living in poverty in the UK have a parent in work.[13] Couples and their growing children are forced upon each other more for support and the extended social networks which surround them. Fewer warring marriages can afford a separation; fewer young people can afford to leave home. There is little now to rely on other than each other; we need to get better at looking after each other.

Relationship is a basic human need, and it is good for us. The fact that a child needs as much love as possible to grow up well is now accepted, but that need for attachment continues throughout life. We all need to feel secure, validated, accepted for who we are, and to feel that we can have an impact on someone else, to love. But there is one big difference. Love for a child has to be unconditional; love between two consenting adults has to be symmetrical and is always conditional on our behaviour. We are responsible for our actions, and we have responsibilities towards each other. Longitudinal research into the life course of a marriage or relationship lasting longer then ten years is thin on the ground. A landmark review conducted by Thomas Bradbury and Benjamin Karney of over a hundred studies found several key elements to marital quality and stability over time.[14] Each spouse brings individual strengths and weaknesses to the relationship and these are fundamental to the way they cope as a couple with changing circumstances through life. We cannot predict or control the chance nature of life, but we can do a great deal to help improve the life skills and the emotional literacy of all of our young people so that more have the necessary strengths to resolve the inevitable conflicts between them and can support each other through the adversities that life inevitably deals.

Francine Klagsbrun interviewed eighty-seven middle-class couples, who had been married for at least fifteen years in the 1980s. She found that long-married couples managed to maintain a positive attitude in the face of change and were pragmatic, in that they were able to accept those things that would in all probability never change. They believed in commitment, acknowledged their emotional dependence on one another, enjoyed each other's company and cherished their shared history.[15] Other research highlights the value of friendship, a growing interest in each other as well as a deep desire for their relationship to succeed. Mutuality of decision-making, trust and equity have also been found to be important, as has psychological as well as physical intimacy.[16] My own research, based on interviews with 120 people, supports these findings. Every tiny sign of affection or appreciation is like one small stitch in the intricate tapestry of a happy relationship. Tolerance and honesty may be crucial, but if that honesty is a veiled insult then it is often better not to say anything at all. A reporter on a local newspaper for many years who was often sent to interview couples celebrating their golden wedding anniversary about the secrets of their success, told me that 'They always say the same old clichés, "Never go to bed on an argument," or "It's about give and take." Then one day I met a couple who had been married for sixty years. When I asked them how they had managed it, he said, "I never apologise to her," and she said, "I never listen to a word he says!" I remember thinking that with that sort of sense of humour they must have had a great marriage.'

I hope that the experiences and advice coming from the couples I have had the privilege to meet, who have been so honest and incisive about what makes their relationships tick – or tock – at times of difficulty, have helped when it comes to understanding the tortuously complicated fabric of your own particular and unique partnership. If there is just one lesson to learn it is that we are all doing much better than we ever give ourselves credit for. There is every reason to feel entirely optimistic about the state of modern love. Rather than looking for some idyllic notion of a happy marriage, ask yourself how you would rate it on a percentage scale. If it's 80 per cent happy, then you have a gift in the palm of your hand that needs to be cherished. If it's 50 per cent happy, then you have some weeding and watering to do in the garden of your relationship to stop it becoming so overgrown that you cannot see the beauty of the plants within it. Sometimes all that means is one of you changing things in small ways – taking hold of their hand as you walk down the street, offering help or thanks when it isn't asked for, consciously stepping into their world for a few moments when the distance between you feels that it is widening – for the whole dynamic between you to shift in bigger ways. If it is 30 per cent happy then maybe you should see a counsellor before that percentage dwindles even further. Or perhaps you really should make that break, to be better off alone or with someone else.

To make love last we need to redefine it, for it is stronger, broader and deeper than the ubiquitous portrait of passionate, romantic love our culture worships. We need greater honesty about real sex. We may make love in a highly sexualised climate, but most people are not swinging naked from the chandeliers – you could injure yourself badly that way! We need a greater appreciation of the ways in which two people heave unrealistic expectations and their own insecurities on to a fragile partnership, expecting it to be strong enough to take the whole load. We need to recognise how important equality is to a healthy partnership and how we sow the seeds of destructive combat and unhappiness years before we even get to separation or divorce. We need to understand that while having children can and does put many relationships under strain, many others do not experience any more of a marked decline in marital quality than childless couples would have experienced over the same period. The most successful partnerships welcomed the challenging way that becoming a family changed their relationship as both the hardest and the best part.

Knowledge strengthens us, as does the honesty that comes from shared experience. Moments of intense frustration, hatred, loneliness and irritation exist in every long-term relationship, but when the whole is sound, when there is enough love and respect to keep things moving forward together, committed relationship offers us the best crucible there is for psychological growth, contentment and a sense of self and place.

NOTES

CHAPTER 1: OTHER PEOPLE'S MARRIAGES

1 Jonathan Gardner and Andrew Oswald, 'How is Mortality Affected by Money, Marriage and Stress?', *Journal of Health Economics*, vol. 23, no. 4, 2004

2 John Gottman and Nan Silver, *The Seven Principles for Making Marriage Work*, Orion, 2000

3 Gardner and Oswald, 'How is Mortality Affected by Money, Marriage and Stress?'

4 John Simons (ed.), *High Divorce Rates: The State of the Evidence on Reasons and Remedies*, One Plus One Marriage and Partnership Research, 1999

5 W. Kim Halford and Howard J. Markman (eds), *Clinical Handbook of Marriage and Couples Intervention*, Wiley, 1997

6 Paul R. Amato and Alan Booth, *A Generation at Risk: Growing Up in an Era of Family Upheaval*, Harvard University Press, 1997

7 Francesca M. Cancian, *Love in America: Gender and Self-development*, Cambridge University Press, 1990

8 Frank D. Fincham and Thomas N. Bradbury (eds), *The Psychology of Marriage*, Guilford Press, 1990

9 Gottman and Silver, *The Seven Principles for Making Marriage Work*

10 Halford and Markman (eds), *Clinical Handbook of Marriage and Couples Intervention*

11 Stephen Wesley and Edward Waring, 'A Critical Review of Marital Therapy Outcome Research', *Canadian Journal of Psychiatry*, vol. 41, 1996

12 Claire Rabin, *Equal Partners, Good Friends*, Routledge, 1996

CHAPTER 2: FROM ROMANCE TO REALITY

1 Susan Sprecher, F. Scott Christopher and Rodney Cate, 'Sexuality in Close Relationship' in Anita L. Vangelisti and Daniel Perlman (eds), *The Cambridge Handbook of Personal Relationships*, Cambridge University Press, 2006

2 Semir Zeki, *Splendors and Miseries of the Brain: Love, Creativity and the Quest for Human Happiness*, Wiley, 2009

3 Robert C. Solomon, *About Love: Reinventing Romance for our Times*, Hackett Publishing Company, 2006

4 Helen Fisher, *Anatomy of Love*, Ballantine Books, 1994

5 Lawrence Stone, *The Family, Sex and Marriage in England 1500–1800*, Penguin, 1979

6 John R. Gillis, *For Better, For Worse: British Marriages 1600 to the Present*, Oxford University Press, 1985

7 *Daily Mail*, 4 February 2008

8 Rebecca Mead, *One Perfect Day: The Selling of the American Wedding*, Penguin, 2007

9 Gillis, *For Better, For Worse*

10 Robyn Parker, 'Why Marriages Last: A Discussion of the Literature', Australian Institute of Family Studies, Research Paper no. 28, 2002

11 Richard Bulcroft, Kris Bulcroft, Karen Bradley and Carl Simpson, 'The Management and Production of Risk in Romantic Relationships: A Post-modern Paradox', *Journal of Family History*, vol. 25, 2000

12 Stone, *The Family, Sex and Marriage in England 1500–1800*

13 Carolyn E. Cutrona, *Social Support in Couples*, Sage, 1996

14 Jacqueline Sarsby, *Romantic Love and Society: Its Place in the Modern World*, Pelican, 1983

15 Andrew J. Cherlin, 'The Deinstitutionalization of American Marriage', *Journal of Marriage and the Family*, vol. 66, no. 4, 2004

16 Kathleen Kiernan, 'Redrawing the Boundaries of Marriage', *Journal of Marriage and the Family*, vol. 66, no. 4, 2004

17 Cherlin, 'The Deinstitutionalization of American Marriage'

18 Sara McLanahan and Irwin Garfinkel, 'Fragile Families and Child Wellbeing', Edith Dominion Memorial Lecture, One Plus One, 2006

19 Penny Mansfield, Jenny Reynolds and Lisa Arai, 'What Policy

Developments Would be Most Likely to Secure an Improvement in Marital Stability' in Simons (ed.), *High Divorce Rates: The State of the Evidence on Reasons and Remedies*

20   Solomon, *About Love: Reinventing Romance for our Times*
21   Guy Bodenmann, Sandrine Pihet, Shachi D. Shantinath, Annette Cina and Kathrin Widmer, 'Improving Dyadic Coping among Couples with a Stress-Oriented Approach: A Two-Year Longitudinal Study', University of Fribourg, Switzerland, 2004
22   Amato and Booth, *A Generation at Risk: Growing up in an Era of Family Upheaval*
23   Osmo Kontula, 'Sustaining Successful Marriages and Relationships: Dream or Reality? The Role of Sexuality in Couple Relationships', International Commission on Couple and Family Relations, Helsinki Conference, 10–13 June 2008
24   Ayala Malach Pines, *Falling in Love*, Routledge, 2005

CHAPTER 3: FIGHTING FOR YOUR LIFE

1   Janice Driver, Amber Tabares, Alyson Shapiro, Eun Young Nahm and John Gottman, 'International Patterns in Marital Success or Failure' in Walsh (ed.), *Normal Family Processes*, Guilford Press, 2003
2   Howard Markman, Scott Stanley and Susan L. Blumberg, *Fighting for Your Marriage*, Josey Bass Publishers, 1994
3   Edith Mavis Hetherington and John Kelly, *For Better or For Worse*, Norton, 2002
4   Danielle Julien, Charleanea Arellano and Lyse Turgeon, 'Gender Issues in Heterosexual, Gay and Lesbian Couples' in Halford and Markman (eds), *Clinical Handbook of Marriage and Couples Intervention*
5   Linda K. Acitelli, 'Gender Differences in Relationship Awareness and Marital Satisfaction among Young Married Couples', *Personality and Social Psychology Bulletin*, no. 18, 1992
6   Gottman and Silver, *The Seven Principles for Making Marriage Work*
7   J. K. Kiecol-Glaser, T. Newton, J. T. Cacioppo, R. C. MacCallum, R. Glaser and W. B. Malarkey, 'Marital Conflict and Endocrine Functions: Are Men Really More Physiologically Affected than Women?', *Journal of Consulting and Clinical Psychology*, no. 64, 1996
8   Hetherington and Kelly, *For Better or For Worse*

9   Amy Holtzworth-Munroe, Natie Smutzler, Leonard Bates and Elizabeth Sandin, 'Husband Violence: Basic Facts and Clinical Implications' in Halford and Markman (eds), *Clinical Handbook of Marriage and Couples Intervention*

10 Vangelisti and Perlman (eds), *The Cambridge Handbook of Personal Relationships*

11 Lyn Shipway, *Domestic Violence: A Handbook for Health Professionals*, Routledge, 2004

12 Ibid.

13 Ibid.

14 Holtzworth-Munroe, Smutzler, Bates and Sandin, 'Husband Violence: Basic Facts and Clinical Implications'

15 J. H. Grych, G. T. Harold and C. J. Miles, 'A Prospective Investigation of Appraisals as Mediators of the Link between Interparental Conflict and Child Adjustment', *Child Development*, vol. 74, no. 4, 2003

16 Patricia K. Kerig, 'Moderators and Mediators of the Effects of Interparental Conflict on Children's Adjustment', *Journal of Abnormal Child Psychology*, vol. 26, no. 3, 1998

17 Jenny Reynolds (ed.), 'Not in Front of the Children – How Conflict between Parents Affects Children', One Plus One, 2007

18 'Teenagers' Attitudes to Parenting: A Survey of Young People's Experiences of being Parented, and Their Views on How to Bring Up Children', National Family and Parenting Institute, 2000

19 Hetherington and Kelly, *For Better or For Worse*

20 Jay Belsky and John Kelly, *The Transition to Parenthood*, Vermillion, 1994

21 Simons (ed.), *High Divorce Rates: The State of the Evidence on Reasons and Remedies*

22 David Schnarch, *Passionate Marriage: Sex, Love and Intimacy in Emotionally Committed Relationships*, Norton, 1997

23 Wesley and Waring, 'A Critical Review of Marital Therapy Outcome Research'

24 Neil S. Jacobson and Michael Addis, 'Research on Couples and Couple Therapy. What Do We Know? Where Are We Going?', *Journal of Consulting and Clinical Psychology*, vol. 61, 1993

25 Simons (ed.), *High Divorce Rates: The State of the Evidence on Reasons and Remedies*

26 Jacobson and Addis, 'Research on Couples and Couple Therapy. What Do We Know? Where Are We Going?'

27 Driver, Tabares, Shapiro, Nahm and Gottman, 'Interactional Patterns in Marital Success or Failure'

CHAPTER 4: BETTER THE DEVIL YOU KNOW

1 Cindy Hazan and Phillip Shaver, 'Romantic Love Conceptualised as an Attachment Process', *Journal of Personality and Social Psychology*, vol. 52, no. 3, 1987
2 Wyndol Furman and Anna Smalley Flanagan, 'The Influence of Earlier Relationships on Marriage: An Attachment Perspective', in Halford and Markman (eds), *Clinical Handbook of Marriage and Couples Intervention*
3 Ibid.
4 Ibid.
5 Pines, *Falling in Love*
6 Ibid.
7 Arthur Aron, Greg Strong and Helen Fisher, 'Romantic Love' in Vangelisti and Perlman (eds), *The Cambridge Handbook of Personal Relationships*
8 Hazan and Shaver, 'Romantic Love Conceptualised as an Attachment Process'
9 Christopher Clulow (ed.), *Adult Attachment and Couple Psychotherapy*, Brunner-Routledge, 2003
10 Pines, *Falling in Love*
11 Ibid.
12 Ulrich Beck and Elisabeth Beck-Gernsheim, *The Normal Chaos of Love*, Polity Press, 1995
13 Walker Toman, *Family Constellation: Its Effects on Personality and Social Behaviour*, Springer, 1961
14 Clulow (ed.), *Adult Attachment and Couple Psychotherapy*
15 Ibid.
16 Ibid.

CHAPTER 5: BALANCE OF POWER

1 Maureen Waller, *The English Marriage*, John Murray, 2009
2 Gillis, *For Better, For Worse*
3 Jan Pahl, 'Individualisation and Patterns of Money Management

Within Families', paper presented at the ESPAnet Conference, University of Oxford, 9–11 September 2004

4 Ibid.

5 Cancian, *Love in America: Gender and Self-development*

6 Paul R. Amato, 'Tension Between Institutional and Individual Views of Marriage', *Journal of Marriage and the Family*, vol. 66, no. 4, 2004

7 Oriel Sullivan, 'The Division of Domestic Labour: Twenty Years of Change?', *Sociology*, vol. 34, no. 3, 2000

8 Gottman and Silver, *The Seven Principles for Making Marriage Work*

9 Sarsby, *Romantic Love and Society*

10 Ibid.

11 Coontz, *New York Times*, 7 November 2006

12 Rainer Maria Rilke, *Letters to a Young Poet/The Possibility of Being: The Complete Works*, MJF Books, 2002

13 Rubinstein (ed.), *The Oxford Book of Marriage*, Oxford University Press, 1990

CHAPTER 6: THE DOUBLE BED

1 John H. Harvey, Amy Wenzel and Susan Sprecher (eds), *The Handbook of Sexuality in Close Relationships*, Lawrence Erlbaum Associates, 2004

2 Linda J. Waite and Maggie Gallagher, *The Case for Marriage*, Broadway, 2001

3 Edward O. Laumann, John H. Gagnon, Robert T. Michael and Stuart Michaels, *The Social Organization of Sexuality: Sexual Practices in the United States*, Chicago Press, 2000

4 Kaye Wellings, Julia Field, Anne M. Johnson and Jane Wadsworth, *Sexual Behaviour in Britain: The National Survey of Sexual Attitudes and Lifestyles*, Penguin, 1994

5 Laumann, Gagnon, Michael and Michaels, *The Social Organization of Sexuality: Sexual Practices in the United States*

6 Geoffrey Gorer, *Sex and Marriage in England Today*, Panther, 1973

7 Martin P. Richards and B. Jane Elliott, 'Sex and Marriage in the 1960s and 1970s', in David Clark (ed.), *Marriage, Domestic Life and Social Change: Writings for Jacqueline Burgoyne (1944–1988)*, Routledge, 1991

8   Maureen Sutton, *We Didn't Know Aught: A Study of Sexuality,
     Superstition and Death in Women's Lives in Lincolnshire During the
     1930s, 1940s and 1950s*, Stamford, 1992
9   Roy Porter, *The Facts of Life: The Creation of Sexual Knowledge in
     Britain 1650–1950*, Yale University Press, 1995
10   Ibid.
11   Richards and Elliott, 'Sex and Marriage in the 1960s and 1970s'
     in Clark (ed.), *Marriage, Domestic Life and Social Change*
12   Catherine Mercer, Kevin Fenton, Anne Johnson, Kaye Wellings,
     Wendy Macdowall, Sally McManus, Kiran Nanchahal and Bob
     Evans, 'Sexual Function Problems and Help-Seeking Behaviour
     in Britain', *British Medical Journal*, vol. 327, 2003
13   E. O. Laumann, A. Paik and R. Rosen, 'Sexual Dysfunction
     in the United States', *Journal of American Medical Association*,
     vol. 281, 1999
14   Harvey, Wenzel and Sprecher, *The Handbook of Sexuality in
     Close Relationships*
15   Ibid.
16   F. Scott Christopher and Susan Sprecher, 'Sexuality in Marriage,
     Dating and Other Relationships: A Decade Review', *Journal of
     Marriage and the Family*, vol. 62, 2000
17   Mary Roach, *Bonk*, Canongate, 2008
18   Ibid.
19   Laumann, Gagnon, Michael and Michaels, *The Social
     Organization of Sexuality: Sexual Practices in the United States*
20   Wellings, Field, Johnson and Wadsworth, *Sexual Behaviour
     in Britain: The National Survey of Sexual Attitudes and
     Lifestyles*

CHAPTER 7: THE DOUBLE BED PART II: INFIDELITY

1   Christopher and Sprecher, 'Sexuality in Marriage, Dating and
     Other Relationships'
2   Annette Lawson, *Adultery*, Oxford University Press, 1990
3   Dr Shirley Glass, *Not Just Friends*, Free Press, 2004
4   Wellings, Field, Johnson and Wadsworth, *Sexual Behaviour
     in Britain: The National Survey of Sexual Attitudes and Lifestyles*
5   Lana Staheli, *Affair-Proof Your Marriage: Understanding, Preventing
     and Surviving an Affair*, HarperCollins, 1998

CHAPTER 8: THE LONG GOODBYE

1   Reynolds (ed.), 'Not in Front of the Children', One Plus One
2   Fiona McAllister (ed.), *Marital Breakdown and the Health of the Nation*, second edition, One Plus One, 1995
3   Ibid.
4   Ibid.
5   Paul R. Amato, 'The Consequences of Divorce for Adults and Children', *Journal of Marriage and the Family*, vol. 62, no. 4, 2000
6   Ben Wilson and Steve Smallwood, 'The Proportion of Marriages Ending in Divorce', *Population Trends*, vol. 131, 2008
7   *Guardian*, 30 August 2008
8   Thomas N. Bradbury, *The Developmental Course of Marital Dysfunction*, Cambridge University Press, 1998
9   Duncan J. Dormer, *The Relationship Revolution*, One Plus One, 1992
10 Wilson and Smallwood, 'The Proportion of Marriages Ending in Divorce'
11 Fisher, *Anatomy of Love*
12 Centre for Research on Families and Relationships, Research Briefing no. 6, University of Edinburgh, October 2002
13 Amato, 'The Consequences of Divorce for Adults and Children'
14 McAllister, *Marital Breakdown and the Health of the Nation*
15 London School of Economics and Political Science/Seddons, seddons.co.uk, 2007
16 Amato, 'The Consequences of Divorce for Adults and Children'
17 Hetherington and Kelly, *For Better or For Worse*
18 Judy Dunn, 'Family Relationships, Children's Perspectives', Edith Dominion Memorial Lecture, One Plus One, 2008
19 Hetherington and Kelly, *For Better or For Worse*
20 Mansfield, Reynolds and Arai, 'What Policy Developments Would be Most Likely to Secure an Improvement'
21 Amato, 'The Consequences of Divorce for Adults and Children'
22 Family Resources Survey 2006–7
23 Julie Lynn Evans, *What About the Children?*, Transworld, 2009
24 Dunn, 'Family Relationships, Children's Perspectives'
25 Ann Mooney, Chris Oliver and Marjorie Smith, 'Impact of Family Breakdown on Children's Well-being', Thomas Coram Research Unit, evidence review, 2009

26 Susie Burke, Jennifer McIntosh, Heather Gridley, 'Parenting After Separation', The Australian Psychological Society, 2007

27 Hetherington and Kelly, *For Better or For Worse*

28 Fran Wasoff, 'Private Arrangements for Parent–Child Contact', ESRC and Scottish Executive Public Policy seminar, Edinburgh, 3 May 2006

29 'New Childhoods: Children and Co-Parenting After Divorce', ESRC Research Briefing no. 7, March 2000

30 Burke, McIntosh and Gridley, 'Parenting After Separation'

31 Wasoff, 'Private Arrangements for Parent–Child Contact'

32 L. Trinder, M. Beck and J. Connolly, *Making Contact: How Parents and Children Negotiate and Experience Contact After Divorce*, York Publishing Services, 2002

33 Hetherington and Kelly, *For Better or For Worse*

34 Anne Marie Ambert, *Divorce: Facts, Causes and Consequences*, York University, 2005

35 Stephanie Coontz, *Marriage, A History*, Penguin, 2006

36 Ambert, *Divorce: Facts, Causes and Consequences*

37 Katie Roiphe, *Observer*, 1 July 2007

38 Lawrence Stone, *Road to Divorce*, Oxford University Press, 1990

39 Ibid.

40 Centre for Research on Families and Relationships, Research Briefing no. 6

41 Hetherington and Kelly, *For Better or For Worse*

42 *Guardian*, 27 August 2008

43 Fiona McAllister, 'Effects of Changing Material Circumstances on the Incidence of Marital Breakdown' in Simons (ed.), *High Divorce Rates: The State of the Evidence on Reasons and Remedies*

44 Ibid.

45 Froma Walsh, 'Changing Families in a Changing World' in Walsh (ed.), *Normal Family Processes*

46 Simons (ed.), *High Divorce Rates: The State of the Evidence on Reasons and Remedies*

47 Marika Jalovaara, 'Socioeconomic Differentials in Divorce Risk', *Demographic Research*, vol. 7, 2002

48 Torkild Hovde Lyngstad, 'The Impact of Parents' and Spouses' Education on Divorce Rates in Norway', *Demographic Research*, vol. 10, 2004

49 Ted L. Huston and Heidi Melz, 'The Case for (Promoting)

Marriage: The Devil is in the Details', *Journal of Marriage and the Family*, vol. 66, no. 4, 2004

50   McLanahan and Garfinkel, 'Fragile Families and Child Wellbeing'

51   Ibid.

CHAPTER 9: HAPPY FAMILIES

1   Matthew R. Sanders, Jan M. Nicholson and Frank J. Floyd, 'Couples' Relationships and Children', in Halford and Markman (eds.), *Clinical Handbook of Marriage and Couples Intervention*

2   Philip A. Cowan and Carolyn Pape Cowan, 'Normative Family Transitions, Normal Family Processes and Healthy Child Development' in Walsh (ed.), *Normal Family Processes*

3   Fisher, *Anatomy of Love*

4   Cowan and Cowan, 'Normative Family Transitions, Normal Family Processes and Healthy Child Development'

5   Belsky and Kelly, *The Transition to Parenthood*

6   Cowan and Cowan, 'Normative Family Transitions, Normal Family Processes and Healthy Child Development'

7   Peter Fraenkel, 'Contemporary Two-Parent Families' in Walsh (ed.), *Normal Family Processes*

8   Madeleine Bunting, *Willing Slaves*, HarperCollins, 2005

9   'Networked Family', Future Foundation /nVision research, 2006

10   Paul R. Amato, Alan Booth, David R. Johnson and Stacey J. Rogers, *Alone Together: How Marriage in America is Changing*, Harvard University Press, 2007

11   Kristin D. Mickelson, 'The Moderating Role of Gender and Gender Role Attitudes on the Link Between Spousal Support and Marital Quality', *Sex Roles: A Journal of Research*, vol. 55, 2006

12   Scott Coltrane, 'Research on Household Labour', *Journal of Marriage and the Family*, vol. 64, 2000

13   Pahl, 'Individualisation and Patterns of Money Management Within Families'

14   W. Bradford Wilcox and Steven L. Nock, 'What's Love Got to Do With It?', *Social Forces*, vol. 84, no. 3, 2006

15   Shelley A. Haddock, Toni Schindler Zimmerman and Kevin P. Lyness, 'Changing Gender Norms' in Walsh (ed.), *Normal Family Processes*
16   Fraenkel, 'Contemporary Two-Parent Families'
17   Haddock et al., 'Ten Adaptive Strategies from Successful Families', *Journal of Marital and Family Therapy*, vol. 27, 2001
18   Haddock, Zimmerman and Lyness, 'Changing Gender Norms'
19   Dunn, 'Family Relationships, Children's Perspectives'
20   Haddock, Zimmerman and Lyness, 'Changing Gender Norms'
21   Belsky and Kelly, *The Transition to Parenthood*

CHAPTER 10: NEW NETWORKS

1   Dunn, 'Family Relationships, Children's Perspectives'
2   National Statistics, 2007
3   Williams, *Rethinking Families*
4   Amato, Booth, Johnson and Rogers, *Alone Together*
5   Hetherington and Kelly, *For Better or For Worse*
6   Walsh, 'Family Resilience: Strengths Forged through Adversity' in Walsh (ed.), *Normal Family Processes*
7   Sasha Roseneil, 'Towards a More Friendly Society: Work, Care and Play in the 21st Century', paper presented to the Centre for Policy Studies in Education, University of Leeds, 2004
8   Gillis, *For Better, For Worse*
9   Stone, *The Family, Sex and Marriage in England 1500–1800*
10   Ibid.
11   Waller, *The English Marriage*
12   Williams, *Rethinking Marriage*
13   Alan Booth, John Edwards and David Johnson, 'Social Integration and Divorce', *Social Forces*, no. 70, 1991
14   John Mirowsky and Catherine E. Ross, *Social Causes of Psychological Distress*, Aldine de Gruyter, 2003
15   S. A. Wolchik, I. N. Sandler, R. E. Millsap, B. A. Plummer, S. M. Greene, E. R. Anderson, S. R. Dawson-McClue, K. Hipke and R. A. Haine, 'Six-year Follow-up of Preventative Interventions for Children of Divorce: A Randomized Controlled Trial', *Journal of the American Medical Association*, no. 288, 2002

16   K. M. Lindahl, N. M. Malik and T. N. Bradbury, 'The Developmental Course of Couples' Relationships' in Halford and Markman (eds), *Clinical Handbook of Marriage and Couples Intervention*

17   Williams, *Rethinking Families*

18   Ibid.

19   Christopher Clulow (ed.), *Sex, Attachment and Couple Psychotherapy*, Karnac Books, 2009

20   J. D. Teachman and K. A. Polonko, 'Cohabitation and Marital Stability in the United States', *Social Forces*, no. 69, 1990

21   *Guardian*, 13 June 2009

CHAPTER 11: SEPTEMBER DAYS

1   Anthony Mancini and George Bonanno, 'Marital Closeness, Functional Disability and Adjustment in Late Life', *Psychology and Aging*, no. 21, 2006

2   Fran Dickson, 'Ageing and Marriage: Understanding the Long-term in Later-life Marriage' in Halford and Markman (eds), *Clinical Handbook of Marriage and Couples Intervention*

3   Rachel Davenhill (ed.), *Looking into Later Life: A Psychoanalytic Approach to Depression and Dementia in Old Age*, Karnac Books, 2007

4   Ibid.

5   Steven P. Roose and Harold A. Sackeim, *Late-Life Depression*, Oxford University Press, 2004

6   Ibid.

7   Cutrona, *Social Support in Couples*

8   *Guardian*, 8 September 2008

9   Cancian, *Love in America*

10   Victoria Hikeutch Bedford and Rosemary Bleszner, 'Personal Relationships in Later-life Families' in Duck (ed.), *Handbook of Personal Relationships*, Wiley, 1997

CHAPTER 12: THE MARRIAGE OF TRUE MINDS

1   Rubinstein (ed.), *The Oxford Book of Marriage*
2   Coontz, *Marriage, A History*
3   Arthur and Elaine Aron, *Love and the Expansion of Self*, Hemisphere Publishing Corporation, 1986
4   Bel Mooney (ed.), *The Penguin Book of Marriage*, Penguin, 1989
5   F. J. Floyd and D. E. Zmich, 'Marriage and the Parenting Partnership: Perceptions and Interactions of Parents with Mentally Retarded and Typically Developing Families', *Child Development*, no. 62, 1991
6   Ibid.
7   Williams, *Rethinking Families*
8   J. K. Vormbrock, 'Attachment Theory as Applied to Wartime and Job-Related Separations', *Psychological Bulletin*, no. 114, 1993
9   Rubinstein (ed.), *The Oxford Book of Marriage*
10 John T. Cacioppo and William Patrick, *Loneliness*, Norton, 2009
11 Williams, *Rethinking Families*
12 Gardner and Oswald, 'How is Mortality Affected by Money, Marriage and Stress?'
13 *Guardian*, 5 May 2008
14 Thomas N. Bradbury and Benjamin R. Karney, 'Understanding and Altering the Longitudinal Course of Marriage', *Journal of Marriage and the Family*, vol. 66, no. 4, 2004
15 Francine Klagsbrun, *Married People: Staying Together in the Age of Divorce*, Bantam, 1985
16 Parker, 'Why Marriages Last: A Discussion of the Literature'

AFTERWORD

A number of books have been so helpful throughout the years of research that I would like to mention them here to pay particular thanks to their authors. For the history of relationships I have found *Marriage, A History* by Stephanie Coontz, *Road to Divorce* by Lawrence Stone and *For Better, For Worse* by John Gillis to be invaluable. There is a relationship bible, *Clinical Handbook of Marriage and Couples Intervention*, edited by W. Kim Halford and Howard J. Markman that contains numerous reviews of the state of play on the latest research. Helge Rubinstein's *The Oxford Book of Marriage* and Bel Mooney's *The Penguin Book of Marriage* have been very useful pointers on the literature, reminding me of the richness of the writing on this subject.

BIBLIOGRAPHY

Linda K. Acitelli, 'Gender Differences in Relationship Awareness and Marital Satisfaction Among Young Married Couples', *Personality and Social Psychology Bulletin*, no. 18, 1992

Isabel Allende, *The Sum of Our Days*, HarperCollins, 2008

Al Alvarez, *Life After Marriage*, Macmillan, 1982

Paul R. Amato and Alan Booth, 'Changes in Gender Role Attitudes and Perceived Marital Quality', *American Sociological Review*, vol. 60, no. 1, 1995

Paul R. Amato, 'Explaining the Intergenerational Transmission of Divorce', *Journal of Marriage and the Family*, vol. 58, no. 3, 1996

Paul R. Amato and Alan Booth, *A Generation at Risk: Growing Up in an Era of Family Upheaval*, Harvard University Press, 1997

Paul R. Amato, David R. Johnson, Alan Booth and Stacy J. Rogers, 'Continuity and Change in Marital Equality between 1980 and 2000', *Journal of Marriage and the Family*, vol. 65, 2003

Paul R. Amato, 'Tension Between Institutional and Individual Views of Marriage', *Journal of Marriage and the Family*, vol. 66, no. 4, 2004

Paul R. Amato, Alan Booth, David R. Johnson, Stacy J. Rogers, *Alone Together: How Marriage in America is Changing*, Harvard University Press, 2007

Paul R. Amato, 'The Consequences of Divorce for Adults and Children', *Journal of Marriage and the Family*, vol. 62, no. 4, 2000

Dr Anne Marie Ambert, *Divorce: Facts, Causes and Consequences*, York University, 2005

American Academy of Matrimonial Lawyers Foundation Keynote Address to the ILLFR 55th International Conference, Helsinki, 10–13 June 2008

Arthur Aron and Elaine Aron, *Love and the Expansion of Self*, Hemisphere Publishing Corporation, 1986

Arthur Aron, Greg Strong and Helen Fisher, 'Romantic Love' in Anita L. Vangelisti and Daniel Perlman (eds), *The Cambridge Handbook of Personal Relationships*, Cambridge University Press, 2006

Jane Austen, *Mansfield Park*, Penguin, 2003

Dr Michael Bader, *Arousal: The Secret Logic of Sexual Fantasies*, Virgin, 2003

Andrew Balfour, 'Intimacy and Sexuality in Later Life', in Christopher Clulow (ed.), *Sex, Attachment and Couple Psychotherapy*, Karnac Books, 2009

Lynn Barber, *An Education*, Penguin, 2009

David P. Barish and Judith Eve Lipton, *The Myth of Monogamy*, Owl Books, 2001

Anne Barlow, *New Labour's Communitarianism, Supporting Families and the Rationality Mistake*, University of Bradford, 2002

Rosemary Basson, 'Report of the International Consensus Development Conference on Female Sexual Dysfunction: Definitions and Classifications', *The Journal of Urology*, vol. 163, 2000

Ulrich Beck and Elisabeth Beck-Gernsheim, *The Normal Chaos of Love*, Polity Press, 1995

Victoria Hikeutch Bedford and Rosemary Bleszner, 'Personal Relationships in Later-life Families' in Steve Duck (ed.), *Handbook of Personal Relationships*, Wiley, 1997

Gail Belsky (ed.), *Over the Hill and Between the Sheets*, Springboard, 2007

Jay Belsky and John Kelly, *The Transition to Parenthood*, Vermillion, 1994

Ingmar Bergman, *Scenes from a Marriage*, Bantam Books, 1974

Jessie Bernard, *The Future of Marriage*, Yale University Press, 1982

Guy Bodenmann, Sandrine Pihet, Shahi D. Shantinath, Annette Cina and Kathrin Widmer, 'Improving Dyadic Coping Among Couples with a Stress-Oriented Approach: A Two-Year Longitudinal Study', University of Fribourg, Switzerland, 2004

Bruce Bower, *Past Impressions*, www.sciencenews.org

Thomas N. Bradbury (ed.), *The Developmental Course of Marital Dysfunction*, Cambridge University Press, 1998

Thomas N. Bradbury and Benjamin R. Karney, 'Understanding and Altering the Longitudinal Course of Marriage', *Journal of Marriage and the Family*, vol. 66, no. 4, 2004

Nathaniel Branden, *The Psychology of Romantic Love*, Tarcher Penguin, 1980

Julia Brannen and Jean Collard, *Marriages in Trouble*, Tavistock Publications, 1982

Louann Brizendine, *The Female Brain*, Transworld, 2007

Stephen Brook (ed.) *The Penguin Book of Infidelities*, Penguin, 1994

Timothy H. Brubaker, 'Families in Later Life', *Journal of Marriage and the Family*, vol. 52, no. 4, 1990

Malcolm Brynin and John Ermisch (eds), *Changing Relationships*, Routledge, 2009

Richard Bulcroft, Kris Bulcroft, Karen Bradley and Carl Simpson, 'The Management and Production of Risk in Romantic Relationships: A Post-modern Paradox', *Journal of Family History*, no. 25, 2000

Madeleine Bunting, *Willing Slaves*, Penguin, 2005

Susie Burke, Jennifer McIntosh and Heather Gridley, 'Parenting After Separation', The Australian Psychological Society, 2007

John T. Cacioppo and William Patrick, *Loneliness*, Norton, 2009

Francesca M. Cancian, *Love in America: Gender and Self-development*, Cambridge University Press, 1998

Alan Carling, Simon Duncan and Rosalind Edwards (eds), *Analysing Families*, Routledge, 2002

Edward Carpenter, *Love's Coming of Age*, 1906

Laura L. Carstensen, John Gottman and Robert Levenson, 'Emotional Behaviour in Long-Term Marriage', *Psychology and Aging*, vol. 10, no. 1, 1995

Betty Carter and Monica McGoldrick, 'The Family Life Cycle' in Froma Walsh (ed.), *Normal Family Processes*, Guilford Press, 2003

Centre for Research on Families and Relationships, Research Briefing no. 6, University of Edinburgh, October 2002

Centre for Research on Family, Kinship and Childhood, 'Post-Divorce Childhoods: Perspectives From Children', University of Leeds

Andrea Chapin and Sally Woffard-Girand (eds), *The Honeymoon's Over*, Warner Books, 2007

Andrew J. Cherlin, 'The Deinstitutionalization of American Marriage', *Journal of Marriage and the Family*, vol. 66, no. 4, 2004

Ying-Ching Lin and Priya Raghubir, 'Gender Differences in Unrealistic Optimism about Marriage and Divorce: Are Men More Optimistic and Women More Realistic?', *Personality and Social Psychology Bulletin*, vol. 31, no. 2, 2005

Andrew Christensen and Neil S. Jacobson *Reconcilable Differences*, Guilford Press, 2000

F. Scott Christopher and Susan Sprecher, 'Sexuality in Marriage, Dating and Other Relationships', *Journal of Marriage and the Family*, vol. 62, 2000

David Clark (ed.), *Marriage, Domestic Life and Social Change: Writings for Jacqueline Burgoyne (1944–88)*, Routledge, 1991

Christopher Clulow, *To Have and to Hold*, Aberdeen University Press, 1982

Christopher Clulow (ed.), *Rethinking Marriage: Public and Private Perspectives*, Karnac Books, 1993

Christopher Clulow (ed.), *Partners Becoming Parents*, Sheldon Press, 1996

Christopher Clulow (ed.), *Adult Attachment and Couple Psychotherapy*, Brunner-Routledge, 2003

Christopher Clulow (ed.), *Sex, Attachment and Couple Psychotherapy*, Karnac Books, 2009

Catherine Cohen and Stacey Kleinbaum, 'Toward a Greater Understanding of the Cohabitation Effect: Premarital Cohabitation and Marital Communication', *Journal of Marriage and the Family*, vol. 64, no. 1, 2002

Lester Coleman and Fiona Glenn, 'When Couples Part: Understanding the Consequences for Adults and Children', One Plus One, 2009

Marcus Collins, *Modern Love*, Atlantic Books, 2003

Warren Colman, 'Understanding Affairs', paper presented to One Plus One Annual Conference, May 1995

Scott Coltrane, 'Research on Household Labour', *Journal of Marriage and the Family*, vol. 62, 2000

Scott Coltrane, *Gender and Families*, AltaMira Press, 2000

Rand D. Conger and Glen H. Elder, *Families in Troubled Times*, Aldine De Gruyter, 1996

Stephanie Coontz, 'The World Historical Transformation of Marriage', *Journal of Marriage and the Family*, vol. 66, no. 4, 2004

Stephanie Coontz, *Marriage, A History*, Penguin, 2006

Carolyn Pape Cowan and Philip A. Cowan, *When Partners Become Parents*, Basic Books, 1992

Philip A. Cowan and Carolyn Pape Cowan, 'Normative Family Transitions, Normal Family Processes and Healthy Child Development' in Froma Walsh (ed.), *Normal Family Processes*, Guilford Press, 2003

Jill Curtis, *Making and Breaking Families*, Free Association Books, 1998

Carolyn E. Cutrona, *Social Support in Couples*, Sage, 1996

Carolyn E. Cutrona, 'A Psychological Perspective: Marriage and the Social Provisions of Relationship', *Journal of Marriage and the Family*, vol. 66, no. 4, 2004

Rachel Davenhill (ed.), *Looking into Later Life: A Psychoanalytic Approach to Depression and Dementia in Old Age*, Karnac Books, 2007

Kevin M. David and Bridget C. Murphy, 'Interparental Conflict and Late Adolescents' Sensitization to Conflict: The Moderating Effects of Emotional Functioning and Gender', *Journal of Youth and Adolescence*, vol. 33, 2004

Daniel Defoe, *Roxana: The Fortunate Mistress*, Oxford University Press, 1996

Henry V. Dicks, *Marital Tensions*, Karnac Books, 1967

Fran Dickson, 'Ageing and Marriage: Understanding the Long-term in Later-life Marriage', in W. Kim Halford and Howard J. Markman (eds), *Clinical Handbook of Marriage and Couples Intervention*, Wiley, 1997

Joan Didion, *The Year of Magical Thinking*, Fourth Estate, 2005

Duncan J. Dormer, *The Relationship Revolution*, One Plus One, 1992

Janice Driver, Amber Tabares, Alyson Shapiro, Eun Young Nahm and John Gottman, 'Interaction Pattern in Marital Success or Failure' in Froma Walsh (ed.), *Normal Family Processes*, Guilford Press, 2003

Stephen Driver and Luke Martell, 'New Labour, Work and the Family', *Social Policy and Administration*, vol. 36, no. 1, 2002

Simon Duncan, 'Mothers, Care and Employment: Values and Theories', CAVA Working Paper, University of Leeds, 2003

Judy Dunn, 'Family Relationships, Children's Perspectives', Edith Dominion Memorial Lecture, One Plus One, 2008

William Dutton, Eileen J. Helsper and Monica Whitty, 'Me, My Spouse and the Internet', Oxford Internet Institute/One Plus One Seminar, 2008

Nora Ephron, *Heartburn*, Virago, 1996

Amy Louise Erickson, *Women and Property in Early Modern England*, Routledge, 1993

John F. Ermisch, 'Personal Relationships and Marriage Expectations – Evidence from the 1998 British Household Panel Study', University of Essex, 2000

John F. Ermisch, 'Trying Again: Repartnering After Dissolution of a Union', ISER, 2002

ESRC Research Briefing No. 7, 'Children and Co-parenting After Divorce', 2000

ESRC Research Briefing No. 21, 'Children's Perspectives and Experiences of Divorce', 2000

Mary Evans, *Love: An Unromantic Discussion*, Polity Press, 2003

Family Policy Studies Centre Briefing Paper 1, 'Family Law Act 1996'

Elsa Ferri, John Bynner and Michael Wadsworth (eds), *Changing Britain, Changing Lives: Three Generations at the Turn of the Century*, Institute of Education, 2003

Frank D. Fincham and Thomas N. Bradbury, *The Psychology of Marriage*, Guilford Press, 1990

Helen Fisher, *Anatomy of Love*, Ballantine Books, 1994

Kathryn Flett, *The Heart-Shaped Bullet*, Picador, 1999

F. J. Floyd and D. E. Zmich, 'Marriage and Parenting Partnership: Perceptions and Interactions of Parents with Mentally Retarded and Typically Developing Families', *Child Development*, no. 62, 1991

Ford Madox Ford, *The Good Soldier*, Penguin, 1946

Peter Fraenkel, *Dual Career Couples: Balancing Work and Family Life*, Smart Marriages, 1999

Peter Fraenkel, 'Contemporary Two-Parent Families' in Froma Walsh (ed.), *Normal Family Processes*, Guilford Press, 2003

Erich Fromm, *The Art of Loving*, Allen & Unwin, 1980

Future Foundation /nVision, 'Networked Family', 2006

Jonathan Gardner and Andrew Oswald, 'How is Mortality Affected by Money, Marriage and Stress?', *Journal of Health Economics*, vol. 23, no. 6, 2004

Jonathan Gardner and Andrew Oswald, 'Do Divorcing Couples Become Happier by Breaking Up?', *Journal of Royal Statistical Society*, vol. 169, no. 2, 2006

Anthony Giardina, *The Country of Marriage*, Flamingo, 1997

Anthony Giddens, *The Transformation of Intimacy*, Polity Press, 1993

Val Gillies, 'Family and Intimate Relationships: A Review of the Sociological Research', ESRC Research Group, June 2003

John R. Gillis, *For Better, For Worse*, Oxford University Press, 1985

John R. Gillis, 'Marriages of the Mind', *Journal of Marriage and the Family*, vol. 66, no. 4, 2004

Stephen Goldbart and David Wallin, *Mapping the Terrain of the Heart*, Aronson, 2001

Giles Gordon, *About a Marriage*, Penguin, 1972

Gill Gorell Barnes, Paul Thompson, Gwyn Daniel and Natasha Burchardt, *Growing Up in Stepfamilies*, Oxford University Press, 1998

Gill Gorell Barnes, *Family Therapy in Changing Times*, Palgrave Macmillan, 2004

Geoffrey Gorer, *Sex and Marriage in England Today*, Panther, 1973

John Gottman and Nan Silver, *The Seven Principles for Making Marriage Work*, Orion, 2000

Francis Grier (ed.), *Oedipus and the Couple*, Karnac Books, 2005

J. H. Grych, G. T. Harold and C. J. Miles, 'A Prospective Investigation of Appraisals as Mediators of the Link between Interparental Conflict and Child Adjustment', *Child Development*, vol. 74, no. 4, 2003

J. H. Grych, 'Marital Relationships and Parenting' in M. H. Bornstein (ed.), *Handbook of Parenting*, vol. 4, Lawrence Erlbaum Associates, 2002

Shelley Haddock, Toni Schindler Zimmerman and Kevin P. Lyness, 'Changing Gender Norms' in Froma Walsh (ed.), *Normal Family Processes*, Guilford Press, 2003

Shelley Haddock et al., 'Ten Adaptive Strategies from Successful Families', *Journal of Marital and Family Therapy*, vol. 27, 2001

W. Kim Halford and Howard J. Markman (eds), *Clinical Handbook of Marriage and Couples Intervention*, Wiley, 1997

John H. Harvey, Amy Wenzel and Susan Sprecher (eds), *The Handbook of Sexuality in Close Relationships*, Lawrence Erlbaum Associates, 2004

J. Haskey, 'Social Class and Socio-economic Differentials in Divorce in England and Wales', *Population Studies*, vol. 38, no. 3, 1984

Cindy Hazan and Phillip Shaver, 'Romantic Love Conceptualised as an Attachment Process', *Journal of Personality and Social Psychology*, vol. 52, no. 3, 1987

Susan S. Hendrick and Clyde Hendrick, *Romantic Love*, Sage, 1992

Edith Mavis Hetherington and John Kelly, *For Better or For Worse*, Norton, 2002

Mahzad Hojjat, 'Sex Differences and Perceptions of Conflict in Romantic Relationships', *Journal of Social and Personal Relationships*, vol. 17, 2000

Elizabeth Jane Howard (ed.), *Marriage: An Anthology*, Orion, 1997

Olwen Hufton, *The Prospect Before Her – A History of Women in Western Europe vol. 1: 1500–1800*, HarperCollins, 1995

Steve Humphries, *A Secret World of Sex*, Sidgwick and Jackson, 1988

Ted L. Huston and Heidi Melz, 'The Case for (Promoting) Marriage: The Devil is in the Details', *Journal of Marriage and the Family*, vol. 66, no. 4, 2004

Eva Ilouz, *Consuming The Romantic Utopia*, University of California Press, 2007

John W. Jacobs, *All You Need is Love and Other Lies About Marriage*, HarperCollins, 2004

Neil S. Jacobson and Michael E. Addis, 'Research on Couples and Couple Therapy. What Do We Know? Where Are We Going?', *Journal of Consulting and Clinical Psychology*, vol. 61, no. 1, 1993

Marika Jalovaara, 'Socioeconomic Differentials in Divorce Risk', *Demographic Research*, vol. 7, 2002

Lynn Jamieson, 'Intimacy, Negotiated Non-Monogamy and the Limits of the Couple' in Jean Duncombe et al., (eds), *The State of Affairs*, Lawrence Erlbaum Associates, 2004

Brett Kahr, *Sex and the Psyche*, Allen Lane, 2007

Debra Kalmuss, Andrew Davidson, Linda Cushman, 'Parenting Expectations, Experiences and Adjustments to Parenthood', *Journal of Marriage and the Family*, vol. 54, no. 3, 1992

Patricia K. Kerig, 'Moderators and Mediators of the Effects of Interparental Conflict on Children's Adjustment', *Journal of Abnormal Child Psychology*, vol. 26, no. 3, 1998

P. M. Keith and R. B. Schafer, 'Marital Types and Quality of Life', *Marriage and Family Review*, vol. 27, no. 1–2, 1998

Kathleen Kiernan, 'Redrawing the Boundaries of Marriage', *Journal of Marriage and the Family*, vol. 66, no. 4, 2004

Hyoun K. Kim, Deborah M. Capaldi and Lynn Crosby, 'Generalizability of Gottman and Colleagues', *Journal of Marriage and the Family*, vol. 69, no. 1, 2007

Francine Klagsbrun, *Married People: Staying Together in the Age of Divorce*, Bantam, 1985

Carmen Knudson-Martin and Anne Rankin Mahoney, 'Moving Beyond Gender Processes That Create Equality', *Journal of Marital and Family Therapy*, vol. 31, no. 2, 2005

Osmo Kontula, 'Sustaining Successful Marriages and Relationships: Dream or Reality?', International Commission on Couple and Family Relations, Helsinki Conference, 10–13 June 2008

Wendy Langford, *Revolutions of the Heart*, Routledge, 1999

E. O. Laumann, A. Paik and R. Rosen , 'Sexual Dysfunction in the United States', *Journal of the American Medical Association*, vol. 281, 1999

Edward O. Laumann, John H. Gagnon, Robert T. Michael and Stuart Michaels, *The Social Organization of Sexuality: Sexual Practices in the United States*, Chicago Press, 2000

Annette Lawson, *Adultery: An Analysis of Love and Betrayal*, Oxford University Press, 1990

C. S. Lewis, *A Grief Observed*, Faber, 1961

Jane Lewis, David Clark and David Morgan, *'Whom God Hath Joined Together': The Work of Marriage Guidance*, Routledge, 1992

Jane Lewis with Jessica Datta and Sophie Sarre, 'Individualism and Commitment in Marriage and Cohabitation', Lord Chancellor's Department, September 1999

K. M. Lindahl, N. M. Malik and T. N. Bradbury, 'The Developmental Course of Couples' Relationships' in W. Kim Halford and Howard J. Markman (eds), *Clinical Handbook of Marriage and Couples Intervention*, Wiley, 1997

Guiping Liu and Andres Vikat, 'Does Divorce Risk Depend on Spouses' Relative Income? A Register-based Study of First Marriages in Sweden in 1981–1998', MDIDR Working Paper, February 2004

T. Loving, K. Hefner, J. Kiecolt-Glaser, K. Glaser and W. Malarkey, 'Stress Hormone Changes and Marital Conflict: Spouses' Relative Power Makes a Difference', *Journal of Marriage and the Family*, vol. 66, 2004

Torkild Hovde Lyngstad, 'The Impact of Parents' and Spouses' Education on Divorce Rates in Norway', *Demographic Research*, vol. 10, 2004

Fiona McAllister, 'Effects of Changing Material Circumstances on the Incidence of Marital Breakdown' in John Simons (ed.), *High Divorce Rates: The State of the Evidence on Reasons and Remedies*, One Plus One, 1999

Fiona McAllister (ed.), *Marital Breakdown and the Health of the Nation*, One Plus One, 1995

Mary McCarthy, *The Company She Keeps*, Penguin, 1967

Sara McLanahan and Irwin Garfinkel, 'Fragile Families and Child Wellbeing', Edith Dominion Memorial Lecture, One Plus One, 2006

Anthony Mancini and George Bonanno, 'Marital Closeness, Functional Disability and Adjustment in Late Life', *Psychology and Aging*, vol. 21, 2006

Penny Mansfield, Jenny Reynolds and Lisa Arai, 'What Policy Developments Would be Most Likely to Secure an Improvement in Marital Stability', in John Simons (ed.), *High Divorce Rates: The State of the Evidence on Reasons and Remedies*, One Plus One, 1999

Howard Markman, Scott Stanley and Susan L. Blumberg, *Fighting for Your Marriage*, Jossey-Bass Publishers, 1994

Carol Martin-Sperry, *Couples and Sex*, Radcliffe Medical Press, 2004

Janet Mattinson and Ian Sinclair, *Mate and Stalemate*, Institute of Marital Studies, 1979

Rebecca Mead, *One Perfect Day: The Selling of the American Wedding*, Penguin, 2007

Catherine Mercer, Kevin Fenton, Anne Johnson, Kaye Wellings, Wendy Macdowall, Sally McManus, Kiran Nanchahal and Bob Evans, 'Sexual Function Problems and Help-seeking Behaviour in Britain', *British Medical Journal*, vol. 327, 2003

Kristin D. Mickelson, 'The Moderating Role of Gender and Gender Role Attitudes on the Link Between Spousal Support and Marital Quality', *Sex Roles: A Journal of Research*, vol. 55, 2006

Mary Midgley, *Beast and Man: The Roots of Human Nature*, Routledge, 1979

Mario Mikulincer, Phillip R. Shaver and Dana Pereg, 'Attachment Theory and Affect Regulation: The Dynamics, Development and Cognitive Consequences of Attachment-Related Strategies', *Motivation and Emotion*, vol. 27, no. 2, 2003

Ann Mooney, Chris Oliver and Marjorie Smith, 'Impact of Family Breakdown on Children's Well-being, Thomas Coram Research Unit, evidence review, 2009

Bel Mooney (ed.), *The Penguin Book of Marriage*, Penguin, 1989

Alice Munro, *The Bear Came Over the Mountain*, Vintage, 1999

National Family and Parenting Institute, *Teenagers' Attitudes to Parenting: A Survey of Young People's Experiences of Being Parented and Their Views on How to Bring Up Children*, 2000

A. S. Neill, *Summerhill – A Radical Approach to Education*, Penguin, 1970

Nigel Nicolson and Joanne Trautmann (eds), *The Letters of Virginia Woolf*, Harvest Books, 1982

Virginia Nicholson, *Singled Out*, Penguin, 2007

Mark O'Connell, *The Marriage Benefit: The Surprising Rewards of Staying Together*, Springboard Press, 2008

Tillie Olsen, *Tell Me a Riddle*, Virago, 1990

Cele C. Otnes and Elizabeth H. Pleck, *Cinderella Dreams: The Allure of the Lavish Wedding*, University of California Press, 2003

R. B. Outhwaite, *Clandestine Marriage in England 1500–1850*, Hambledon Press, 1995

Jan Pahl, 'Individualisation and Patterns of Money Management Within Families', paper presented at the 2004 ESPAnet Conference, University of Oxford, 9–11 September

Robyn Parker, 'Why Marriages Last: A Discussion of the Literature', Australian Institute of Family Studies, Research Paper no. 28, 2002

Esther Perel, *Mating in Captivity*, Hodder & Stoughton, 2007

Ethel S. Person, *Dreams of Love and Fateful Encounters*, Penguin, 1988

Adam Phillips, *Monogamy*, Faber, 1996

Ayala Malach Pines, *Falling in Love*, Routledge, 2005

Ralph de Pomerai, *Marriage: Past, Present and Future*, Constable, 1930

Roy Porter, *The Facts of Life*, Yale University Press, 1995

Claire Rabin, *Equal Partners, Good Friends*, Routledge, 1996

Janet Reibstein and Martin Edwards, *Sexual Arrangements*, Heinemann, 1992

Jenny Reynolds (ed.), *Not in Front of the Children: How Conflict Between Parents Affects Children*, One Plus One, 2007

Barbara J. Risman and Danette Johnson-Sumerford, 'Doing It Fairly: A Study of Post-gender Marriages', *Journal of Marriage and the Family*, vol. 60, 1998

Mary Roach, *Bonk*, Canongate, 2008

Stacy J. Rogers and Paul R. Amato, 'Is Marital Quality Declining?', *Social Forces*, vol. 75, no. 3, 1997

Anne Roiphe, *Married: A Fine Predicament*, Bloomsbury, 2003

Steven P. Roose and Harold A. Sackeim, *Late-Life Depression*, Oxford University Press, 2004

Phyllis Rose, *Parallel Lives*, Vintage, 1994

Sasha Roseneil, 'Towards a More Friendly Society: Work, Care and Play in the 21st Century', paper presented to the Centre for Policy Studies in Education, University of Leeds, 2004

Catherine Ross, John Mirowsky and Karen Goldsteen, 'The Impact of the Family on Health', *Journal of Marriage and the Family*, vol. 52, 1990

Catherine Ross, 'Reconceptualising Marital Status as a Continuum of Social Attachment', *Journal of Marriage and the Family*, vol. 57, 1995

Helge Rubinstein (ed.), *The Oxford Book of Marriage*, Oxford University Press, 1990

Stanley Ruszczynski (ed.), *Psychotherapy with Couples*, Karnac Books, 1993

James Salter, *Light Years*, Penguin, 1975

Jacqueline Sarsby, *Romantic Love and Society*, Pelican, 1983

Maggie Scarf, *Intimate Partners*, Ballantine Books, 1987

David E. Scharff, *The Sexual Relationship*, Tavistock Publications, 1982

Karen B. Schmaling and Tamara G. Sher, 'Physical Health and Relationships', in W. Kim Halford and Howard J. Markman (eds), *Clinical Handbook of Marriage and Couples Intervention*, Wiley, 1997

Gunter Schmidt, 'Sexuality and Late Modernity', *Annual Review of Sex Research*, 1998

David Schnarch, *Passionate Marriage*, Norton, 1997

Julie A. Schumacher and Kenneth E. Leonard, 'Husbands and Wives: Marital Adjustment, Verbal Aggression and Physical Aggression as Longitudinal Predictors of Physical Aggression in Early Marriage', *Journal of Consulting and Clinical Psychology*, vol. 73, no. 1, 2005

Pepper Schwartz, *Love Between Equals*, Free Press, 1994

A. Shapiro, J. Gottman and S. Carrere, 'The Baby and the Marriage', *Journal of Family Psychology*, vol. 14, 2000

George Bernard Shaw, *Getting Married*, First World Library, 2007

George Bernard Shaw, *Man and Superman*, Penguin Classics, 2004

Lyn Shipway, *Domestic Violence: A Handbook for Health Professionals*, Routledge, 2004

Edward Shorter, *The Making of the Modern Family*, Fontana, 1975

John Simons (ed.), *High Divorce Rates: The State of the Evidence on Reasons and Remedies*, vols 1 and 2, One Plus One, 1999

Carol Smart and Bren Neale, *Family Fragments*, Polity Press, 1999

Carol Smart, 'Divorce in England 1950–2000: A Moral Tale', CAVA Workshop Paper 2, 1999

Pamela J. Smock, 'The Wax and Wane of Marriage', *Journal of Marriage and the Family*, vol. 66, no. 4, 2004

Marion F. Solomon, *Narcissism and Intimacy: Love and Marriage in an Age of Confusion*, Norton, 1989

Robert C. Solomon, *About Love*, Hackett Publishing Company, 2006

Lana Staheli, *Affair-Proof Your Marriage: Understanding, Preventing and Surviving an Affair*, HarperCollins, 1998

Robert J. Sternberg, *The Psychology of Love*, Yale University Press, 1988

Lawrence Stone, *The Family, Sex and Marriage in England 1500–1800*, Penguin, 1979

Lawrence Stone, *Road to Divorce*, Oxford University Press, 1990

Lawrence Stone, *Uncertain Unions and Broken Lives*, Oxford University Press, 1992

Marie Stopes, *Married Love*, Oxford University Press, 2004

Oriel Sullivan, 'The Division of Domestic Labour: Twenty Years of Change', *Sociology*, vol. 34, no. 3, 2000

Maureen Sutton, *We Didn't Know Aught: A Study of Sexuality, Superstition and Death in Women's Lives in Lincolnshire During the 1930s, 1940s and 1950s*, Stamford, 1992

Maurice Taylor and Seana McGee, *The New Couple*, HarperSanFrancisco, 2000

Sofia Tolstoy, *Diaries*, Alma Books, 2009

J. D. Teachman and K. A. Polonko, 'Cohabitation and Marital Stability in the United States', *Social Forces*, no. 69, 1990

Judith Treas and Deirdre Giesen, 'Sexual Infidelity Among Married and Cohabiting Americans', *Journal of Marriage and the Family*, vol. 62, 2000

L. Trinder, M Beck and J. Connolly, *Making Contact: How Parents and Children Negotiate and Experience Contact After Divorce*, York Publishing Services, 2002

Anita L. Vangelisti and Daniel Perlman (eds), *The Cambridge Handbook of Personal Relationships*, Cambridge University Press, 2006

J. K. Vormbrock, 'Attachment Theory as Applied to Wartime and Job-Related Separations', *Psychological Bulletin*, no. 114, 1993

Linda J. Waite and Maggie Gallagher, *The Case for Marriage*, Broadway, 2001

Maureen Waller, *The English Marriage*, John Murray, 2009

Judith S. Wallerstein and Sandra Blakeslee, *The Good Marriage*, Bantam, 1996

Judith S. Wallerstein, Julia M. Lewis and Sandra Blakeslee, *The Unexpected Legacy of Divorce*, Hyperion, 2000

Annette Walling, *Families and Work*, Office for National Statistics, July 2005

Froma Walsh, *Strengthening Family Resistance*, Guilford Press, 1998

Froma Walsh (ed.), *Normal Family Processes*, Guilford Press, 2003

Fran Wasoff, 'Private Arrangements for Parent-Child Contact', ESRC and Scottish Executive Public Policy Seminar, Edinburgh, 3 May 2006

Kaye Wellings, Julia Field, Anne M. Johnson and Jane Wadsworth, *Sexual Behaviour in Britain: The National Survey of Sexual Attitudes and Lifestyles*, Penguin, 1994

Stephen Wesley and Edward Waring, 'A Critical Review of Marital Therapy Outcome Research', *Canadian Journal of Psychiatry*, vol. 41, September 1996

Edith Wharton, *Tales of Men and Ghosts*, Borgo Press, 2005

Katharine Whitehorn, *Selective Memory*, Virago, 2007

W. Bradford Wilcox and Steven L. Nock, 'What's Love Got to Do With It? Equality, Equity, Commitment and Women's Marital Quality', *Social Forces*, vol. 84, no. 3, 2006

Fiona Williams, *Rethinking Families*, Calouste Gulbenkian Foundation, 2004

Ben Wilson and Steve Smallwood, 'The Proportion of Marriages Ending in Divorce', *Population Trends*, vol. 131, 2008

Robert F. Winch, *The Modern Family*, Holt Rinehart Winston, 1971

Marilyn Yalom, *A History of the Wife*, HarperCollins, 2001

Victoria Zakheim (ed.), *The Other Woman*, Warner Books, 2007

Semir Zeki, *Splendours and Miseries of the Brain*, Wiley, 2009